Copyright Law in the Digital World

Manoj Kumar Sinha · Vandana Mahalwar
Editors

Copyright Law in the Digital World

Challenges and Opportunities

Springer

Editors
Manoj Kumar Sinha
The Indian Law Institute
New Delhi
India

Vandana Mahalwar
The Indian Law Institute
New Delhi
India

ISBN 978-981-10-3983-6 ISBN 978-981-10-3984-3 (eBook)
DOI 10.1007/978-981-10-3984-3

Library of Congress Control Number: 2017931569

Printed on acid-free paper

This Springer imprint is published by Springer Nature
The registered company is Springer Nature Singapore Pte Ltd.
The registered company address is: 152 Beach Road, #21-01/04 Gateway East, Singapore 189721, Singapore

Preface

The intriguing relationship between freedom of expression and copyright law has deepened in the 21st century. Freedom of expression and copyright are seen as two harmonizing concepts, but there exists two opposing views also against this backdrop. Some characterise copyright as "engine of free expression". Copyright incentivises the creations and promotes the freedom of expression. The obverse of this reasons the copyright law to operate as a fetter on what others do express and hence, results in a tension between copyright law and freedom of expression. The potential coexistence and conflict between the freedom of expression and copyright law has brought into being much of academic reviews and interpretations. Copyright law, more because of advent of the internet; open-source software initiatives; peer-to-peer exchanges and changes to copyright rules, is under the scholarly debates. The debates about copyright law unfold the questions relating to substantive law, right to education, freedom of expression and the concept of ownership. These debates question our existing legal system on how do they work and how should they work in the internet age. There are scholars who argue that over emphasis on commercialising the literary and artistic creations is epistemically unfavourable to the overall advancement as it inhibits the stream of information. The philosophical or theoretical justification behind the copyright law is utilitarian i.e. best situations are those in which people are in total as happy or fulfilled as possible. The internet has landed as one of the most revolutionary social development which has exploded more prospects to access the information. The emergence of digital media and network connections has enabled the dissemination of information which was previously unimaginable. The intellectuals set up dichotomous justifications for copyright protection, as a few view copyright owners having control over their creations and extracting some commercial value, while others perceive it as a mechanism which promotes the mass interests. Technological advancements upsetting the link between copyright and freedom of expression, have radically impacted the scope of protection under the copyright law.

This volume is set of papers reflecting the diverse perspectives on copyright law. A good number of papers canvass almost the entire breadth of copyright law which will appeal the professionals in the copyright world.

The editors would like to express sincere thanks to all the contributors for their significant contributions and insights without which this book may not have been possible.

New Delhi, India

Manoj Kumar Sinha
Vandana Mahalwar

Contents

Editors and Contributors

About the Editors

Manoj Kumar Sinha is the director at the Indian Law Institute, New Delhi. He obtained his Ph.D. in international law from Jawaharlal Nehru University, New Delhi, after attaining his LL.B. from the University of Delhi, India, and his LL.M. from the University of Nottingham, UK. His areas of specializations include human rights, international humanitarian and refugee law, international criminal law, international law, international institutions, and constitutional law. He has published extensively in these areas in prominent Indian and international law journals. He currently serves on the editorial boards of various reputed national and international journals, as well as research bodies of many universities in India and abroad.

Vandana Mahalwar is an assistant professor at the Indian Law Institute, New Delhi, India. Prior to this, she was an assistant professor at the Faculty of Law, University of Delhi, India. She holds a B.A.L., LL.B. (Gold Medal), and LL.M. (Gold Medal) from Maharshi Dayanand University, Rohtak, India, and obtained her Ph.D. in law from the National Law University, Delhi, India. With various publications in reputed journals to her credit, her current focus is on issues pertaining to the right of publicity, character merchandising, and intellectual property laws.

Contributors

T.G. Agitha Inter University Centre for Intellectual Property Rights Studies, Cochin University of Science & Technology, Cochin, India

V.K. Ahuja Faculty of Law, University of Delhi, Delhi, India

R. Rajesh Babu IIM Calcutta, Kolkata, India

Poonam Dass Faculty of Law, University of Delhi, Delhi, India

Yashomati Ghosh National Law School of India University, Bangalore, India

Amit Jyoti S. Gomber Centre for Intellectual Property and Technology Law, Jindal Global Law School, O.P. Jindal Global University, Sonipat, India

Vandana Mahalwar Assistant Professor, The Indian Law Institute, New Delhi, India

Anirban Mazumder National University of Juridical Sciences, Kolkata, India

C.P. Dayananda Murthy Damodaram Sanjivayya National Law University, Visakhapatnam, India

C.P. Nandini Damodaram Sanjivayya National Law University, Visakhapatnam, India

K.D. Raju Rajiv Gandhi Institute of Intellectual Property Law, IIT Kharagpur, India

Rodney D. Ryder Advocate Supreme Court of India, New Delhi, India

Cheng Peng Sik Faculty of Law, University of Malaya, Kuala Lumpur, Malaysia

N.S. Sreenivasulu National University of Juridical Sciences, Kolkata, India

Pek San Tay Faculty of Law, University of Malaya, Kuala Lumpur, Malaysia

V.K. Unni IIM Calcutta, Kolkata, India

Idea-Expression Dichotomy and Originality Requirements for Copyright Protection: An Analysis of the Jurisprudential Underpinnings of the Judicial Pronouncements in India

T.G. Agitha

Abstract This chapter intends to examine the significance of idea/expression dichotomy and the requirement of originality in the copyright law both in the traditional and modern context; that is, in the context of the emergence of new technologies. It also aims at examining the Indian case law in these areas and the problems created by the judicial pronouncements in this area. The basic requirements of protection differ considerably for different forms of IP depending upon the nature, scope and extent of protection extended by each forms of IP. Such basic requirements are with a view to retain a robust public domain facilitating further creativity. In the copyright context the major requirements are that of originality in expression of the copyright content and the mandatory exclusion of idea, facts, themes and plots from copyright coverage. The originality requirement, which is very minimal in nature, is with a view to exclude further propertisation of already available information/creations. Ideas, facts, themes, plots etc., on the other hand aim at exclusion of building blocks from protection. The Indian jurisprudence which could be deduced from the judicial pronouncements in India in this respect is in need of urgent scrutiny. The strength and weaknesses of Indian decisions and the implications of it on the dissemination of information which is an equally important concern of copyright protection is the major objective of this chapter.

T.G. Agitha (✉)
Inter University Centre for Intellectual Property Rights Studies, Cochin University of Science & Technology, Cochin, India
e-mail: tgagitha@gmail.com

M.K. Sinha and V. Mahalwar (eds.), *Copyright Law in the Digital World*,
DOI 10.1007/978-981-10-3984-3_1

1 Introduction

Lord Macaulay depicts copyright as "a tax on readers for the purpose of giving a bounty to writers."[1] He believed that property, being the creature of the law, can only be defended on the ground that it is a law beneficial to mankind.[2] Others, like Justice Brandies joins him by stating that the noblest of human production such as knowledge, truths ascertained and conceptions and ideas become free as the air to common use after voluntary communication to others, and the attribute of property upon such incorporeal productions could be continued after such communication only in certain classes of cases where public policy demands it.[3] For him, such situations in which there is conferment of property right over information—for example when there is a creation or invention or a discovery—are exceptions to the general rule.[4] Information is a public good. It is non-exclusive and non-rivalrous. Propertization of information creates artificial scarcity. Still there may be situations when it is justified for better public good. For example, copyright protection is justified in economic terms by Landes and Posner on the ground that it trades off the cost of limiting access to a work against the benefits arising out of providing incentives to create more works.[5]

Conceptually, the unassailable objective of copyright law is to encourage further creativity by rewarding creators for their works. But this objective is fulfilled only when such creation, thus secured, is properly disseminated among the general public. Since every author builds on existing creations and available information, hence the copyright, which confers on the author exclusive property rights over his

---

[1] A Speech delivered by Thomas Babington Macaulay in the House of Commons on the 5th of February, 1841 Opposing Proposed Life + 60 Year Copyright Term available at http://homepages.law.asu.edu/~dkarjala/OpposingCopyrightExtension/commentary/MacaulaySpeeches.html. He says: "The tax is an exceedingly bad one; it is a tax on one of the most innocent and most salutary of human pleasures; and never let us forget, that a tax on innocent pleasures is a premium on vicious pleasures. I admit, however, the necessity of giving a bounty to genius and learning. In order to give such a bounty, I willingly submit even to this severe and burdensome tax. Nay, I am ready to increase the tax, if it can be shown that by so doing I should proportionally increase the bounty. My complaint is, that my honourable and learned friend doubles, triples, quadruples, the tax, and makes scarcely any perceptible addition to the bounty.".

[2] A Speech Delivered in a Committee of the Houses of Commons on the 6th of April, 1842, by Thomas Babington Macaulay on the third of March, 1842, Lord Mahon obtained permission to bring in a bill to amend the Law of Copyright. This bill extended the term of Copyright in a book to twenty-five years, reckoned from the death of the author available at http://homepages.law.asu.edu/~dkarjala/OpposingCopyrightExtension/commentary/MacaulaySpeeches.html.

[3] Dissenting note in *International News Service* v. *Associated Press* 248 US 215 (1918).

[4] 248 US 215, 250 (1918). Also read Yochai Benkler, who, in agreement with Justice Brandies, argued that privatization of information should be allowed only to the extent and limited to those instances when the Govt. has good reasons that would justify regulation of information production and exchange Benkler 1999.

[5] Landes and Posner 1989. Since the cost of copying is often insignificant when compared to the cost of creation, the only way to discourage others from making copies will be to price it at or close to the marginal cost. But then the creator's total revenue may not be sufficient to cover the cost of creating the work. Thus copyright protection becomes relevant.

works, becomes a difficult tool in furthering creativity unless effectively handled. Even in the economic perspective it is understood that copyright protection promotes economic efficiency only when its principal legal doctrine is to maximize the benefits from creating additional works so that they outweigh the losses from limiting access and cost of administering copyright protection.[6] Or else, copyright protection will become counterproductive.[7] Therefore, striking the correct balance between facilitating access to copyrighted works and providing incentives to creator is the central idea of copyright law.[8] This could be ensured only when the welfare losses from the monopoly pricing and reduction in competition are balanced with reduced scope of copyright protection. Since copyright is a monopoly its burdens should not outweigh its benefits.[9]

The mandatory minimum requirements for copyright protection and the exclusions of the building blocks of creativity from copyright coverage are the most significant methods used to strike the correct balance. In the case of copyright law, the requirement of originality of expression, and the exclusion of ideas, facts, themes, systems etc., from copyright protection, are aimed at promoting economic efficiency by balancing the effect of copyright protection with the social costs due to limiting access. The originality and expression requirements serve different objectives. The originality requirement ensures that as a *quid pro quo* to copyright protection consumers get something more than just copies of existing works whereas the expression requirement ensures that the building blocks of creativity remain free for use by all.[10]

2 Idea v. Expression

Landes and Posner explain the economic rationale of not protecting ideas in terms of its impact on creativity. If an idea can be expressed in ‘n’ number of ways and the idea of the first author alone is protected, the cost of expression of remaining ‘n − 1’ authors would increase because each one would have to invest time and effort in coming with an original idea for his work or to substitute additional expression for the part of his idea that overlapped the first author’s. The number of works created would be reduced and social welfare would fall.[11] They explain why

[6] *Ibid*. They say that “The less extensive copyright protection is, the more an author, composer or other creator can borrow from previous works without infringing copyright and the lower therefore, the cost of creating a new work”.

[7] *Id*., p. 332.

[8] *Id*., 326; Also read Abrams 1992.

[9] Chafee 1945.

[10] Goldstein (1996) *Copyright*, second edition § 2.2.1.4 (2:9).

[11] Landes and Posner 1989. Instead of stressing on the welfare loss arising out of monopoly of the idea and the higher price per copy that is normally associated with monopoly, the authors emphasized on the increase in the cost of creating more works and the reduction in the number of works.

the rule that excludes ideas from copyright protection and protects only expression of ideas is Pareto optimal in this way. Every author is also a user of ideas developed by others. The comparatively less cost in coming up with an idea rather than attempting to express it—which is a costlier process—and the chances of enticing rewards from licensing the idea to others would encourage rent seeking if ideas themselves become subject matter of copyright protection.[12] Though this may encourage people to come up with more and more ideas, this may also have the negative impact of discouraging dissemination of ideas, resulting in welfare loss. Landes and Posner expect that since every originator of an idea gets a normal return during the lead time even in the absence of copyright protection, the authors, who have no clue as to who would be the first to come up with an idea, will unanimously agree to a rule that protects expression and not ideas.[13]

Application of idea-expression distinction will vary with the type of work in issue.[14] The boundary between idea and expression in a particular field is decided on the basis of policy judgment about the extent to which monopoly should be allowed in that field to the original contributions of creators and the requirement as to what should be left to public domain for free use by others working in the same field.[15] As a consequence, the line between idea and expression in a particular type of work will depend upon many factors.[16]

Expression encompasses not only a work's precise words, sounds, or visual depictions but also elements that lie beneath the work's surface, occupying the stratum between literal expressions and underlying ideas.[17] Since copyright protection extends beyond the literal aspects, where a work's idea leaves off and its expression begins becomes a troublesome question and depends, to a great extent, upon specific instances. Goldstein is of the view that the two guiding principles for the courts in defining protectable expression are (i) neither draw the line too narrow to leave the author without incentive nor draw it too broadly to block further creations, and (ii) the courts should in close cases err on the side of finding protectable expression.[18]

---

[12] Landes and Posner 1989.

[13] Landes and Posner 1989.

[14] Goldstein.

[15] *Ibid.*

[16] This will be evident from studies on the extent of copyright protection for computer programs and other utilitarian works, which is beyond the scope of this study.

[17] Goldstein.

[18] *Ibid.*

2.1 Distinguishing Ideas from Expression

Since ideas are not protected, any work, if differently told or expressed, will not violate an earlier work. However, as already discussed, copyright protection cannot be limited to cases of literal or word by word copying. If the protection is limited literally to the text, a second comer would escape copyright violation by making immaterial variations to the first author's work.[19] For example, if a second comer copies the detailed plot sequences of a drama, but uses different dialogues it constitutes non-literal infringement.[20] *Nichols* v. *Universal Pictures Corp.*,[21] was the first decision to expressly recognize copyright protection against non-literal copying. Judge Learned Hand, in that case, categorically stated that copyright protection has never been limited literally to the text while adverting to the complexities involved in doing so. Protection against non-literal copying makes it extremely difficult to find when expression stops and idea begins.

The issue in *Nichols* was whether Universal had infringed Ms. Nichols's copyright in her play, 'Abie's Irish Rose', by making a motion picture, 'The Cohens and The Kellys'. Reviewing the similarities and differences in incident, character, and overall plot of the play and the film, Judge Hand concluded that "the defendant took no more—assuming that it took anything at all—than the law allowed."[22] This case is important since it introduced the abstractions test in order to differentiate between ideas and expression in the following words:

> Upon any work, and especially upon a play, a great number of patterns of increasing generality will fit equally well, as more and more of the incident is left out. The last may perhaps be no more than the most general statement of what the play is about, and at times might consist only of its title; but there is a point in this series of abstractions where they are no longer protected, since otherwise the playwright could prevent the use of his "ideas," to which, apart from their expression, his property is never extended.[23]

The Indian copyright law does not expressly exclude ideas from copyright protection. However, in *R.G. Anand* v. *Deluxe Films*[24] after referring to various judicial decisions, from both Indian and western jurisdictions, the Supreme Court of India stated that "an idea, principle, theme, or subject matter or historical or

---

[19] *Nichols* v. *Universal Pictures Corp.* 45 F.2d 119 (2nd Cir. 1930).

[20] Samuelson 2013.

[21] 45 F.2d 119 (2nd Cir. 1930). He said: "It is of course essential to any protection of literary property, whether at common law or under the statute, that the right cannot be limited literally to the text, else a plagiarist would escape by immaterial variations. That has never been the law, but, as soon as literal appropriation ceases to be the test, the whole matter is necessarily at large, so that, as was recently well said by a distinguished judge, the decisions cannot help much in a new case."

[22] 45 F.2d 119 (2nd Cir. 1930).

[23] 45 F.2d 119 (2nd Cir. 1930).

[24] AIR 1978 SC 1613: (1978) 4 SCC 118: PTC (Suppl.) (1) 802 (SC).

legendary facts being common property cannot be the subject matter of copyright of a particular person."[25]

Unfortunately, the Supreme Court decision has not given sufficient guidance on the manner of distinguishing unprotectable ideas from protectable expression while deciding copyright infringement cases. Though the Supreme Court did not make any reference to the Nichols case, it introduced a method similar to that of abstraction test indicated in that case in the following words:

> (T)he fundamental fact which has to be determined where a charge of violation of the copyright is made by the plaintiff against the defendant is to determine whether or not the defendant not only adopted the idea of the copyrighted work but has also adopted the manner, arrangement, situation to situation, scene to scene with minor changes or super additions or embellishment here and there. Indeed, if on a perusal of the copyrighted work the defendant's work appears to be a transparent rephrasing or a copy of a substantial and material part of the original, the charge of plagiarism must stand proved. Care however must be taken to see whether the defendant has merely disguised piracy or has actually reproduced the original in a different form, different tone, and different tenor so as to infuse a new life into the idea of the copyrighted work adapted by him. In the latter case there is no violation of the copyright.[26]

The major propositions laid down by the Court in this case are that: (i) there can be no copyright in an idea, subject matter, themes, plots or historical or legendary facts and violation of the copyright in such cases is confined to the form, manner and arrangement and expression of the idea by the author of the copyright work; (ii) where the same idea is being developed in a different manner, though there may be similarities due to the source being common, the courts should determine whether or not the similarities are on fundamental or substantial aspects of the mode of expression adopted in the copyrighted work; and (iii) where the same theme is presented and treated differently so that the subsequent work becomes a completely new work, no question of violation of copyright arises.

In other words, the expressive elements are reflected in the manner and arrangement of the idea, plot or theme and only if a substantial copying of the manner and arrangement of an idea is copied situation to situation or scene to scene copyright violation occurs. If the same idea is reproduced in a different form, different tone and different tenor so that the outcome has a new and independent existence, or it becomes a completely new work, there is no violation of copyright. The problem with *R.G. Anand* is that it left us with lots of ambiguity. It is clear from the decision that it recognizes non-literal infringement. However, it simply left some imprecise ideas as to the scope of protection from non-literal copying. Still the idea expression dichotomy is not clear and the court has not clarified how to eliminate ideas and scenes a faire even from the manner and arrangement.

---

[25] PTC (Suppl.) (1) 802 SC, at p. 823.

[26] *Ibid.*

To worsen the situation, the Supreme Court was repeatedly mentioning an additional viewer test[27] for addressing the issue of copyright infringement. This test adds more ambiguity to the already obscure ruling, since a reader, spectator or viewer, is quiet incompetent to separate protectable expressions from unprotectable ideas and to see if the substantial copying made is that of protectable expression. This test also contradicts with the earlier finding of the Court—which is an accurate one—that the similarities between the two works to be compared in infringement cases should be with respect to the substantial aspects of the mode of expression. The only rational interpretation of the ruling is that the viewer test needs to be applied, if at all, at a later stage of the analysis, after identifying the similarities with respect to the mode of expression, in the comparison stage.[28] But that does not appear to be the natural consequence of the ruling of the Court and moreover, the viability of this methodology is dubious. Therefore, though prima facie it appears that the Court is laying down a method similar to abstraction test, the viewer or lay observer test, in fact, obscures the ruling of the Court.

Unsurprisingly, the Indian judiciary had a tough time in properly appreciating and applying the principles enunciated in R.G Anand.[29] Many of the Courts failed to understand even the minimum guidelines set forth by *R.G. Anand.* In *Raja Pocket Books* v. *Radha Pocket Books*[30] the plaintiff claimed copyright in the comic character "NAGRAJ" and the name Nagraj. The defendant came up with another comic character Nagesh having some similarity in get up. The Delhi High Court reiterated the finding of the Supreme Court in *R.G. Anand* and admitted that there

---

[27] See propositions 3 and 7 in *R.G. Anand.* "whether or not the similarities are on fundamental or substantial aspects of the mode of expression adopted in the copyrighted work one of the surest and the safest test to determine whether or not there has been a violation of copyright is to seeing the reader, spectator or the viewer after having read or seen both the works is clearly of the opinion and gets an unmistakable impression that the subsequent work appears to be a copy of the original". *R. Madhavan* v. *S.K. Nayar* (2002) 25 PTC 1 (Del.) is a case in which while discussing the copyright infringement of a novel by the script/film the Kerala High Court, along with many other grounds, relied also on the viewer/spectator test.

[28] In *Computer Associates International Inc.* v. *Altai Inc.* 982 F.2d 693, The U.S. Court enunciated the abstraction, filtration comparison test (AFC test) which works, as per the Court, in the following way:

> In ascertaining substantial similarity under this approach, a court would first break down the allegedly infringed program into its constituent structural parts. Then, by examining each of these parts for such things as incorporated ideas, expression that is necessarily incidental to those ideas, and elements that are taken from the public domain, a court would then be able to sift out all nonprotectable material. Left with a kernel, or possibly kernels, of creative expression after following this process of elimination, the court's last step would be to compare this material with the structure of an allegedly infringing program. The result of this comparison will determine whether the protectable elements of the programs at issue are substantially similar so as to warrant a finding of infringement.

[29] It is disturbing that after some steadiness in the recent judgments the most recent judgment has gone back to the era of lack of clarity relying on the wrong precedents.

[30] 1997(17)PTC84(Del).

can be no copyright in an idea, subject matter, themes, plots or historical or legendary facts and violation of the copyright in such cases is confined to the form, manner and arrangement and expression of the idea by the author of the copyrighted work. However it failed to properly appreciate the spirit of *R.G. Anand* and mistook the higher levels of abstractions—which actually formed part of ideas—to be expressions. Thus the Court, applying "the surest and safest test" held that the central idea of the two characters being the same, any reader going through both the works will clearly get an unmistakable impression that comic Nagesh is a copy of NAGRAJ. The court accepted the fact that though the theme and the central idea were the same, it was "presented slightly and somewhat differently". However, on the basis of the visual and phonetic similarities and the overall impression of the two works[31] the Court reached at the conclusion that the plaintiff has a prima facie case and granted injunction. Though the Court was thinking that the rules of comparison adopted by it in judging the resemblance in both the works were those laid in down in *R.G. Anand*, it actually muddled up the concepts of trade mark and copyright.[32]

In this case the Court failed to take note of the fact that 'Nagraj' is a legendary theme and since the underlying concept remained the same, there is likelihood of resemblance in the broad features of the comic characters when a comic series is made. The court also failed to address the issue whether certain features alleged to have been copied, such as scaling the walls and the roofs alike, hurling snakes, etc., were public domain matter as per the scenes a faire doctrine.[33] In deciding the question of copyright infringement what the court should have actually considered was whether the manner and arrangement of the stories developed by the plaintiff were substantially copied by the defendant. Unfortunately the court failed in understanding the spirit of R.G. Anand and moreover, mixed up copyright concepts with that of trademark.

This is a clear case where applying the "surest and safest test" the Court failed to take into account the idea expression dichotomy. The Court also gave prima facie recognition to the plaintiff's copyright in his comic character Nagraj.[34] Since Nagaraj is a legendary concept no single author can monopolize it using copyright

[31] Nagraj and Nagesh having same meaning, namely, King snakes; Colour of comics is also green, gauntlets are ripped in both cases, functionally, both are capable of doing same and similar work, namely, scaling the walls and the roofs alike, hurling snakes, causing the objects to melt and the snakes capable of returning back and merging in the body of the character. For the purpose of climbing, both use the same material, namely, rope in the form of snake.

[32] This is evident from the fact that what it identified as similarities included visual and phonetical similarity and that it took into account the likelihood of the overall impression of the two works deceiving consumers or causing confusion among them so that they may make mistake in the goods of defendant for that of the plaintiff.

[33] *Scenes a faire* have been defined as "incidents, characters or settings which are as a practical matter indispensable, or at least standard, in the treatment of a given topic." See Alexander v. Haley, 460 F. Supp. 40 (S.D.N.Y. 1978). See also Kurtz 1989 generally and Murray 2006 and M. Nimmer.

[34] 1997(17)PTC84(Del) at p. 90.

law. Even otherwise, copyright over characters is a disputed issue.[35] While addressing the complex question of copyright in characters the Court does not appear to have paid proper attention to the idea expression distinction or the scenes a faire doctrine. Even if one agrees, at least for argument sake, that characters per se are protected under the copyright law, the general requirements under copyright law such as originality and idea expression dichotomy are applicable even in such situation. The court never asked the question if a legendary character and its character related mannerisms and behavioural patterns were outside the scope of copyright protections as per the scenes a faire doctrine.

Another worse instance of misreading of R.G. Anand is *Mr. Anil Gupta* v. *Mr. Kunal Dasgupta*[36] in which the Delhi High Court held that a television reality show 'shubh Vivah', if launched, would infringe the copyright in a detailed concept note of another television reality show 'Swayamvar' and granted injunction against it. The court accepted the claim of the plaintiff that he, being the first person to conceive a reality show with the idea of a woman selecting a groom in public forum before a TV audience, has copyright over it and held that 'Subh Vivah', a TV reality show by the respondent, based on the concept of spouse selection, cannot be permitted. The interesting part of the case was that both the shows were not launched when the case was initiated in the trial court and therefore the details of them were not known. Even after detailed discussions on *R.G. Anand*, the court concluded that though an idea is not copyrightable, "if the idea is developed into a concept fledged with adequate details, then the same is capable of registration under the Copyright Act". This is in stark contrast with the ruling in *R.G. Anand*, since a concept note, however detailed it might be, of a serial proposed to run into several hundreds of episodes, can be nothing but an idea or theme or a plot which, as per *R. G. Anand*, and the well established concept of the copyright world over, falls beyond copyright coverage.

This decision is a perfect example of a total mess up in the analysis of the fundamental principles of copyright law. The discussion of the court reveals an absolute lack of understanding of the concepts of originality and idea expression dichotomy. By equating the 'novelty and innovation' in the plaintiff's concept of combining a reality TV show with a subject like match making for the purpose of marriage, with originality in the copyright context, the Court revealed its ignorance on the concept of originality. It is clear that the Court here confuses "originality" in the copyright law with the "novelty" requirement under the patent law, which is an altogether different standard for an altogether different purpose. By acceding to the claim of copyright over detailed concept note of a yet to be staged reality show, the

---

[35] Nimmer and Nimmer 2010. Also read Karjala 2006 The author says that the most important problem in protecting character under copyright law is the idea expression dichotomy and character, isolated from all the detailed events occurring in a particular story is very close to an idea. Popular characters may have high economic value. But the copyright law is not designed to maximize the economic returns to the creator.

[36] (2002) 25 PTC 1 (Del.).

Court deranged the entire jurisprudence of idea expression dichotomy and the harm done is not rectified till date.[37]

The Bombay High Court followed the same path in *Zee Telefilms Ltd.* v. *Sundial Communications Pvt. Ltd.*,[38] which was decided in the same year. It reiterated the finding of the Delhi High Court that if an idea is developed into a concept fledged with adequate details it is capable of registration under the Copyright Act. In this case also both the plaintiff and the defendant had not developed their works into adequate details since both have not launched their respective TV serials which were the subject matter of the controversy.[39] The court compared the theme of the story and the character sketches of the plaintiff and defendant and relied on Anil Gupta case to decide the case at hand. It felt that since the plaintiffs have developed the idea or the theme of the story into various concept notes including a pilot, character sketches, detailed plot of first episode and ten episodic plots it is not a case of a mere idea but a protectable expression. Though it referred to the principles enunciated in *R.G. Anand* v. *Deluxe* Films, they were wrongly construed by the Court.

Fortunately, the entire judiciary is not lost in the idea expression dichotomy quagmire. In the next year, the Calcutta High Court came up with the correct interpretation of *R.G. Anand* in *Barbara Taylor Bradford* v. *Sahara Media Entertainment Ltd.* [40] In this case the plaintiff alleged that a TV serial ready to be produced and televised by the respondent is an infringement of her book "A Woman of Substance". Only eighty episodes of the serial, which was expected to run into more than two hundred episodes, had been completed and was ready to be televised. Of them, only the first episode had been broadcasted by then. The claim for infringement was not based on that episode and the substantial material on the basis of which the claim of infringement had been supported was an interview taken

---

[37] Another amusing aspect of the judgment is that it restricted televising of the programme 'Subh Vivah' merely for four months after which the defendants were given the freedom to transmit it if the plaintiff is not transmitting its programme 'Swayamvar'. This decision leaves one to wonder how the plaintiff who, if at all, enjoys copyright protection, be denied of his rights after four months, too less a duration than they are statutorily entitled to.

[38] 2003 (27) PTC 457 (Bom.).

[39] The plaintiff was planning to launch a TV serial "Krish Kanhaiya" in which he was planning to narrate the story of a dysfunctional family in which the god comes in the form of a boy and solves all the problems. He prepared and got registered with Film and Writers' Association a detailed concept note. He got his idea developed into various concept notes including a pilot, character sketches, detailed plot of first episode and ten episodic plots. The defendants, with whom he shared these details with a view to launch his serial came up with another serial which was alleged to have substantially copied from his concept notes.

[40] 2004 (28) PTC 474 Cal.

by a freelance journalist from one of the respondents in which he had mentioned that the serial was an Indianized adaptation of the book by the plaintiff.[41]

The Court was convinced that at this stage of event, what were copied, if at all, were ideas rather than expression, and referring to R.G. Anand, the court stated:

> If plots and ordinary prototype characters were to be protected by the copyright law, then soon would come a time in the literary world, when no author would be able to write anything at all without infringing copyright. Fathers, mothers, revenge, lust, sudden coming into fortune, Count of Monte Cristo themes, beggar girl marrying rich boy, rich girl marrying poor boy, and one thousand such themes, characters and plots would become the subject-matter of copyright and an intending author, instead of concentrating upon the literary merit of his expression, would be spending his life first determining whether he is infringing the copyright of the other authors who have written on this topic or that. The law of copyright was intended at granting protection and not intended for stopping all literary works altogether by its application.

The Court felt that even if it was accepted that the serial was based on the book, the final result, which was yet to be seen, might prove all claims of infringement of copyright as practically frivolous and false once the serial is released. The court considered this as a strong prima facie ground against accepting that the plaintiffs had a case to go to trial. It added that in a situation like this grant of injunction would be an interference with free trade.

The court, therefore, concluded that the plaintiff's act of approaching the Court with a plaint on the "sketchy, basic and sparse similarities" was wholly wrong and it was even more wrongful to obtain an injunction on such scanty and hopelessly insufficient material. The court wanted the plaintiffs to suffer for the consequences of filing a case without any prima facie strength or merit and for obtaining wrongfully an injunction, causing serious damage to the defendants. It, therefore, required the appellants to pay the respondents costs of Rs. 10,000 per day of hearing before the first Court and Rs. 15,000 per day of hearing in the case before it. Damages were also required to be paid for injunction wrongfully obtained. This decision is an appropriate one correctly appreciating the significance of copyrightability standards. It also tends to discourage frivolous litigation which may have an adverse impact on creativity and access.

In *HT Media Limited* v. *UTV News Limited* [42] the Calcutta High Court had to address the issue as to whether someone who develops an idea and expresses it in a peculiar way, is entitled to copyright protection for that peculiar mode of expression

---

[41] With respect to the case in hand the Court described the situation thus:

> We do not know what the serials are going to be like. We do not know the situations which will be shown. We do not know that scenes which will be displayed. We do not know how the characters will be portrayed. We do not even know the details of the storyline. All that we know is that one of the team of persons engaged in production, which is quite a large team, has said to a certain fishing journalist that there are some characters which are as per the book of the plaintiff No. 1 and that the serials have been based on the book and Indianised and adapted.

[42] 31 August, 2010 Calcutta HC available at http://indiankanoon.org/doc/89585664/.

and if that mode of expression is original. In this case, the plaintiff, a leading publishing house which had launched a business daily by the name of Mint in collaboration with a reputed international business alleged that its advertisements were infringed by the defendant. Plaintiff released a series of advertisements where there was an announcement in the form of a sentence with only some of the words in English and the other words were made up of Greek letters that may or may not constitute words in that language. The main thrust of the advertisement was to bring home to the readers the idea that business news is generally so incomprehensible that they may be beyond the audience. The plaintiff stated that the concept of the notion that ordinary business news as it is presented may be Greek to the audience not versed in traditional business language was expressed by it by the use of English words interspersed with Greek alphabets. By this, it wanted to convey the message that the plaintiff's publication was different and that its communications were more undemanding for the readers when compared to their rivals'.

The plaintiff insisted that since it had conceptualised the idea for the first time and expressed it in a tangible form, it was entitled to the exclusive use of that manner of expression of that idea and any variant of such expression would amount to infringement of its copyright. The defendant published similar series of advertisements allegedly copying the plaintiff's pattern of advertising depicting Greek words between English expressions. The plaintiff gave a strange version to "expression" in copyright law by stating that by juxtaposing English words against Greek letters or words he has expressed his idea and was only claiming protection for expression rather than idea.

The Court rejected the plaintiff's contention that its mode of expressing "it's all Greek" by using English words along with Greek letters and words was expression and not idea. It stated that no copyright could be claimed unless the defendant's advertisement was an imitation of the same English words with identical words or letters from an unintelligible script. It held that both the idea to convey the sense of "it's all Greek", and the idea to use English and Greek alphabets to convey such sense, collectively forms the idea or the theme of the plaintiff's advertisement campaign and therefore outside the coverage of copyright protection. Certainly mode of expression is an idea and only the form of expression is eligible for copyright protection. This is a sensible judgement and it appeared that courts in India are slowly catching up with the philosophy of idea expression dichotomy.

Unfortunately the clock is set back by the Bombay High Court in its recent decisions in *Urmi Juvekar Chiang* v. *Global Broadcast News Limited*[43] and *Beyond Dreams Entertainment Pvt. Ltd.* v. *Zee Entertainment Enterprises Ltd.*[44] In

[43]2008 (36) PTC 377 Bom.

[44] 2015 (62) PTC 241 (Bom.). The Court held that "having regard to the particular character sketches in the concept notes, the detailed setting of the dramatic material, the overall tracks, plots, family tree, etc., the material is sufficiently developed into a concrete literary work capable of having its own life as a copyrighted materials.

both the cases, again, relying on *Mr. Anil Gupta* v. *Mr. Kunal Dasgupta*[45] and *Zee Telefilms Ltd.* v. *Sundal Communications Pvt. Ltd.*,[46] the court held that the copyright in the 'detailed concept note' of the plaintiffs for TV reality show/serial were infringed by the similar TV programmes by the defendants.

In *Krishika Lulla* v. *Shyam Vithalrao Devkatta*,[47] which was a Criminal Appeal, the Supreme Court had an occasion to look into the issue of copyright in the Title of a literary work. The complainant in that case claimed copyright in the title of the synopsis of a story "Desi-Boys". The Supreme Court held that a title of a work has been considered not fit to be the subject of copyright law as there is nothing original in the combination of two words "Desi" and "Boys". Title, short phrases and combinations of words, however fanciful they are, are not eligible for copyright protection since they lack originality, and constitute idea rather than expression.[48] They may have commercial value but that has no significance in the copyright context.

The above discussion signifies that the Indian judiciary is yet to develop a robust jurisprudence in the area of idea expression dichotomy. It also reveals that still there is lack of clarity among the Indian judiciary regarding separating ideas from expression, especially in complicated situations. Though a considerable improvement can be seen in the approach of court as many high courts are slowly picking up the copyright concepts correctly, unfortunately, as seen in the recent Bombay High Court decision, fluctuations are still visible in the approach of judges in this area. Since idea expression dichotomy is a complex area, aberrations are likely, but some of the decisions cross the boundaries of rationality.

2.2 Functional/Utilitarian Works

In certain situations the protection of expression may extend to protection of the use of the expression. Copyright protection in such cases may result in conferring monopoly on the functional aspect of the work much against the spirit of copyright law and it adds to the already available rights under copyright law, an exclusive right to use. Ordinarily the rights covered under copyright law do not affect the right to use the work. However, there may be occasions where the right to reproduction or right to public performance overlap with right to use. *Baker* v. *Selden*, in which protection was sought for original book keeping forms, is a good example to it. Still, use of a work may constitute infringement when it affects the enjoyment of a right in situations like public performance of a sound record or a play. Nimmer rightly says that the mere fact that the rights granted by the copyright law affects the

---

[45] (2002) 25 PTC 1 (Del.).

[46] 2003 (27) PTC 457 Bom.

[47] 2015 (10) SCALE 718.

[48] Goldstein.

use of a copyrighted work does not, ipso facto, preclude an infringement suit.[49] But when the rights granted under the copyright law results in monopoly of use not only of the work itself but also of the system or function, it ends up with monopoly over idea which is prescribed under the copyright law.[50] However, even functional or utilitarian works may be extended copyright protection on many occasions if they contain artistic expression. But then the protection is limited to such artistic expression and not to the functional element. On the basis of the U.S. Supreme Court decision in *Mazer* v. Stein[51] Denicola has stated that utility and art are not mutually exclusive and in a useful art the latter alone is protected under copyright law.[52] The U.S. Copyright Office responded to *Mazer* v. *Stein* specifying that if the sole intrinsic function of an article is its utility the fact that the article is unique and attractively shaped will not qualify it as a work of art.[53]

There are situations in which Indian judiciary appears to have failed in understanding the problem in conferring copyright protection to functional works, especially in cases involving artistic works where there are copyright-design overlap. In certain cases, when a two dimensional artistic work is converted into three dimensional form it becomes an object having some utility. Copyrightability of such works is a complex issue since, as we have seen, every artistic work, having some utility when depicted in three dimensional form, does not, ipso facto, become uncopyrightable. Goldstein states that the pictorial, graphic or sculptural feature incorporated in the design of a useful article is conceptually separable if it can stand on its own as a work of art traditionally conceived and if the useful article in which it is embodied can be equally useful without it.[54] When conceptual separation of artistic and functional elements is possible, artistic element alone should be recognized for copyright protection. But unfortunately the Indian judiciary has failed to evolve a proper conceptual foundation on the issue of copyrightability of utilitarian works.

Escorts Const. Equipment Ltd. v. *Action Const. Equipment P. Ltd.*[55] is such a case in which the Plaintiff sought an ad interim injunction to restrain the defendants from manufacturing, marketing or otherwise dealing in Pick N-Carry Hydraulic Self Mobile Cranes, the three dimensional form of an industrial drawing of the plaintiffs. The plaintiffs alleged that by virtue of the provisions of the Copyright Act, they are the exclusive owners of the artistic work consisting of the industrial drawings, and they have the exclusive right to reproduce or depict in three dimensions the drawings of the said crane. In addition to the industrial drawing of the entire crane plaintiffs also claimed copyright in the following key components: (i) the boom and slider assembly, (ii) the lower structure assembly, (iii) main frame axle assembly,

[49] Nimmer and Nimmer 2010.

[50] *Ibid.*

[51] 347 U.S. 201 (1954).

[52] Denicola 1983.

[53] C.F.R § 202.10 (b) (Supp 1956). Also read Nimmer, Supra n. 48, § 2.08[B][3].

[54] Goldstein.

[55] AIR 1999 Del. 73.

(iv) the different housing, (v) the pump coupling, (vi) the pulley block assembly, (vii) gear box housing, (viii) wheel reduction gear, (ix) the differential, (x) clutch assembly. The Delhi High Court correctly identified that the aforesaid parts of the crane are made in a particular shape so as to interrelate with other parts mechanically, and that those parts are not made to appeal to the eye but solely to make the crane work or function. They would be judged by performance and not by appearance. Consequently, the aforesaid key components or parts are incapable of being registered as designs under the Designs Act, 1911. Nonetheless, the Court held that the crane manufactured by the defendants, being a substantial reproduction in three dimensional forms of the drawings of the plaintiffs' crane, infringed the copyright in their original artistic work. The court never bothered to ask the question if the three dimensional depiction resulted in a machine rather than an artistic work, could the three dimensional depiction be considered an artistic work. Despite the clear conviction to the effect that the overall claim and the claim over the independent components of the industrial drawing actually covered pure utilitarian elements and not artistic elements, the court went to decide in this way. The court failed to take note of the fact that the decision extended copyright protection to functional elements, which fell beyond the purview of copyright protection and it was quite unconcerned about the consequences of such a decision on competition.[56] There cannot be a better example to establish an absolute insensitivity of a court to the objectives and nature of copyright protection.

However, it is heartening to see that the same High Court, on a later occasion, responded in a different manner to a claim of copyright protection over medicinal formulations. The Court, in *Dr. Reckeweg and Co. Gmbh.* v. *Adven Biotech Co.*, rightly denied copyright protection to medicinal formulations.[57] It was a case in which the plaintiffs claimed, inter alia, copyright in the medicinal formulation of their products though they admitted that their medicinal preparations were as per the directions in the German Homeopathic Pharmacopeia. The Court held that chemical formulation of a medicine is mere information and no person can claim copyright in mere information or an idea. It also adverted to the fact that such a claim over the medicinal formulation indirectly amounted to a claim over the medicine itself, which is precluded even under the patent law in the absence of novelty and inventive step. As stated in *Baker* v. *Seldon*,[58] allowing such claims would be a fraud upon the public and would be tantamount to allowing a longer protection (copyright) to a functional subject matter, which is eligible only for patent protection, without examining the complex issues like that of its inventive step.

---

[56] Anyways, the recent amendment to the copyright act under Section 52 (w) which states that "the making of three-dimensional object from a two-dimensional artistic work, such as a technical drawing, for the purpose of industrial application of any purely functional part of a useful device" shall not constitute an infringement of copyright has put to rest such controversies. But it is doubtful if such an amendment was necessary to exclude such subject matter from copyright protection.

[57] 2008(38)PTC308(Del).

[58] 101 US 99 (1879).

Another interesting case in which the Delhi High Court dealt with the issue of public performance of functional work was *Institute for Inner Studies* v. *Charlotte Anderson*.[59] One major issue in this case was whether claims of copyright raised by plaintiffs on Pranic Healing Techniques contained in books explaining them were legally sustainable. The plaintiffs were seeking permanent restraint on the defendants' activities of spreading Pranic Healing teachings, techniques, practices and courses, or any other techniques, practices, courses and other teachings invented by the Master Choa Kok Sui ("Master") and organizing and continuing to organize workshops, training programmes, and seminars in relation to Pranic Healing without authorization from the plaintiffs.

The Delhi High Court discussed the concept of idea and expression dichotomy in detail in this case as it sought to prevent the implementation of facts and narrations stated in the book of Pranic Healing authored by the Master on the ground that the performance of the said works would result in the copyright infringement. The court held that in relation to books and literature describing useful art, principle, historical fact or events or mode of performing ancient exercise or any other process, the copyright protection shall vest in the language employed to describe the art in the book, the selection and arrangement of the facts or Asanas and their presence in the sequential manner in the book. However, the protection shall not be extended to the right to performance of the said Asanas of Yoga or Pranic Healing as it would give monopoly right to the art or technique itself. Thus it was held that the descriptions of different Asanas and the expression of Asanas in different postures merges with the idea of performing physical exercises and are, therefore, beyond the scope of copyright protection. The Court, therefore, stated that the plaintiff could not be allowed copyright protection to performance of Pranic Healing techniques on the basis of the copyright claim in the book describing illustrating and compiling the exercises or Asanas of Pranic Healing. The Court is correct in its analysis since performance of a utilitarian function cannot be equated with public performance of a literary work and an interpretation to the contrary would muddle up the concepts of copyright law and patent law.

Though copyright in functional work is a complex issue, the courts can overcome the difficulty if they mull over the objectives of copyright law and the obligation to limit the private rights on products of creativity for ensuring access to them.

2.3 Doctrine of Merger

Another interesting concept evolved in the context of idea expression dichotomy is the doctrine of merger which acts as an exception to the general rule that an idea, if expressed in a particular way is protectable under copyright law. In cases where the

[59] 2014(57)PTC228(Del).

work's underlying idea can be effectively expressed only in one or a limited number of ways courts consider that there is merger of expression with idea and therefore, withhold copyright protection even from a work's original expression because protecting such expression would confer monopoly over the idea upon the copyright owner without fulfilling the requirements of patentability.[60] The merger doctrine concentrates on if a work is capable of alternative expression.[61] This doctrine is applicable only in the case of functional works. Generally courts are inclined to uphold merger where the idea in issue represents a building block for creating an expression.[62] The merger theory has been criticized by Professor Nimmer, who has stated that "it is factually erroneous to conclude that there is any system or method which can be performed by the use of only one particular form of written expression.[63]

In *Baker* v. *Seldon*,[64] a case often cited to explain the concept of merger, protection was sought for original bookkeeping forms as contained in a book explaining a new method of bookkeeping. The defendant's book used a similar plan so far as results were concerned, but made a different arrangement of the columns, and used different headings. The plaintiff contended that the ruled lines and headings, used for illustrating the system are a part of the book and as such are secured by the copyright. He objected to the use of them by the defendant stating that no one can make or use similar ruled lines and headings, or ruled lines and headings made and arranged on substantially the same system, without violating his copyright. Thus, the copyright claim in that case extended to the system of bookkeeping itself.

The court held that the truths of a science or the methods of an art are the common property of the whole world and any author has the right to express or explain and use them in his own way. Therefore, it rejected Selden's claim stating that copyright in Selden's book does not confer exclusive right to the use of the system or method of bookkeeping as it only secures the exclusive right to the expression as part of a book. If such a claim is allowed, it would result in the monopoly of the system of bookkeeping.

Blank forms of bookkeeping are primarily utilitarian or functional in nature and therefore, it would have been easily excludable on that ground alone. But the court also brought in the merger doctrine in this case stating that in the case of a book on science or the useful arts, "if the art it teaches cannot be used without employing the methods and diagrams used to illustrate the book, or methods and diagrams similar to them, such methods and diagrams are to be considered as necessary incidents to

---

[60] Goldstein. Goldstein states that generally the courts may end up with a finding of merger if the idea in issue is a building block, essentially required to create an expression.

[61] "Idea Expression Dichotomy in Copyright Law" at p. 26.

[62] Goldstein.

[63] Nimmer 2010.

[64] 101 US 99 (1879).

the art, and given therewith to the public."[65] In other words, if the expression of some work, if protected would block the use of such work, the expression merges with the idea and becomes unprotectable. However, this case was criticised by Nimmer by saying that there are hardly any cases in which an idea can be expressed only in one way and in this case itself the defendant had used somewhat different expression.[66]

Escorts Const. Equipment Ltd. v. *Action Const. Equipment P. Ltd.*[67] is a case which could also explain the merger doctrine as the idea of a Pick N-Carry Hydraulic Self Mobile Cranes that could be expressed in two dimensional way only in one or a very limited number of ways. Unfortunately, the Delhi High Court, in that case, wrongly upheld copyright infringement.

Another Indian case, in which the merger doctrine was invoked, was *Mattel, Inc.* v. *Mr. Jayant Agarwalla.*[68] In this case the Delhi High Court, however, took the correct decision. The plaintiff in this case alleged that it's copyright in the game Scrabble and the game rules were violated by the defendant's online game Scrabulous. The defendant, a firm engaged in IT solutions has launched an online word game under the mark Scrabulous as an application available through the popular networking web site www.facebook.com, www.scrabulous.info, and www.scrabulous.org. The plaintiff claimed that every version of its game since 1932 is an artistic work under Section 2(c) of the Copyright Act 1957. Apart from claiming the ownership in the artistic layout of the game board they also claimed to be the owners of copyright in the rules of the game, which according to them, is a literary work. After referring to *Nichols* v. *Universal Pictures Corp*,[69] *Baker* v. *Selden*[70] and *R.G. Anand*,[71] the court stated that only the creative expression of ideas and facts is rewarded by law, and it does not protect every expression. When the idea and expression are inextricably connected, there is a merger of the two and it would not be possible to distinguish between them. The Court, in this case, held that this doctrine of merger is applicable with respect to games as they consist of abstract rules and play ideas. The arrangement of colours, values on the board, the collocation of lines, value for individual alphabetical tiles, etc., have no intrinsic meaning, but for the rules. If these rules, which form the only method of expressing the underlying idea, are to be subject of copyright, the idea in the game would be given monopoly; a result that is not intended by the lawmakers. The court correctly concluded that the copyright claim of the plaintiff cannot be granted. If the rules of the game are protected it will go much beyond protection of original expression,

---

[65] 101 US 99 (1879).

[66] Nimmer.

[67] AIR 1999 Del. 73.

[68] 2008 (38) PTC 416 (Del.).

[69] 45 F.2d (2d Cir. 1930).

[70] 101 US 99 [1879].

[71] (1978) 4 SCC 118.

since here the expression merges with the idea or the functional aspects of the game.

In *The Chancellor Masters and Scholars of the University of Oxford* v. *Narendera Publishing House*, the same High Court wrongly upheld merger doctrine.[72] In this case the plaintiff, a well-known publisher of academic books, who was publishing in India since 1912, alleged that the defendant violated the copyright in their text books for school children, *Oxford Mathematics Part A and Part B*, by a word-to-word copying of the questions. The plaintiff also alleged infringement of copyright in the arrangement of the exercises in each chapter and the internal arrangement of questions in them. The court was of the impression that such a claim, if allowed, would extend copyright protection to ideas since mathematical questions and their answers constituted "expressions of laws of nature". It felt that since language is a limited medium which enables description of such laws of nature only in a few ways, it is a case of merger of idea and expression and recognition of copyright in the questions themselves would deny access to ideas, thus robbing one of the primary objectives of copyright law, viz., promotion of creativity.

It is felt that this logic of finding merger of idea and expression in questions set on the subject of Mathematics on the ground that such questions are expressions of Laws of nature is not correct. The objective of copyright law is much different from that of patent law; one aims at protecting the expression whereas the other protects the use or function. Since the scope of copyright law is much limited to the expression, even scientific principles or laws of nature, if expressed in an original way, becomes the copyright of the author (to the extent of that specific expression) unless such expression is possible only in one way or a limited number of ways so as to extends it to the use or function of it. In this case though the Court has stated that in mathematical context questions can be put only in a limited number of ways, it does not appear to be correct since unless the questions are fill in the blank type it could be explained in many ways even in a subject like mathematics. As we are aware, almost all the practical questions addressing a specific way of calculation in the area of mathematics could be framed in that specific context and are possible of being expressed in many ways without encompassing the functional aspect of the subject. Therefore the idea/expression analogy based on which the Court denied copyright to question papers appears to be incorrect.

Emergent Genetics India Pvt. Ltd. v. *Shailendra Shivam*[73] is an interesting case in which the plaintiff claimed copyright in the sequencing formula of the hybrid seeds. The Plaintiff alleged that on examination of Random Polymorphic DNA Test (hereafter "RAPD" test), the most common methods of DNA Fingerprinting test, the plant varieties of the Defendants i.e. VIDHATA, KESHAV and AMOGH are verified to be genetically or genotypically identical with its own products, i.e. BRAHMA, KRISHNA and ATAL. The Plaintiff relies on a chart, summarizing the

[72] 2008 (38) PTC 385 (Del.).

[73] 2011(47)PTC494(Del).

results of the RAPD test in its case, on a comparison of the two rival samples. It was contended by the plaintiff that since the Defendant's products and those of the Plaintiffs are genotypically identical, the former have misappropriated the seeds of the Plaintiff and are selling them as their own. Moreover, the Defendants have also reproduced the unique sequencing formula of the hybrid seeds, thereby resulting in copyright infringement of the literary work of the Plaintiff.

The court held that so long as a researcher constructs a DNA sequence based on a sequence discovered in nature, there is no independent creation, no minimum creativity and thus no originality. The Court also relied on the idea-expression merger doctrine to reject the copyright claim of the plaintiff. The idea of combining various gene components or constituents, is expressible only in limited ways. Granting copyright protection would mean that others are precluded from practising the method of DNA sequencing. Here, a specific sequence expressed in a manner is the only way to express the underlining idea of the gene; therefore, there is a merger of the idea with the expression, which precludes the copyrighting of DNA sequences that are codes for proteins.

Instead of relying on the merger doctrine, which is comparatively difficult to establish, the court could have relied on the functional aspect of the claim. The sole significance of the plaintiff's so called literary work is its functional output. However, it is heartening to see that the recent cases are in the correct direction.

2.4 *Doctrine of Scenes a Faire*

Doctrine of scenes a faire applies generally to fictional works and withholds protection from those elements which are commonly attributable to incidents or character.[74] This doctrine establishes the necessity to exclude from copyright protection, certain elements that conventionally flow from the situation being portrayed however expressive they may be, since similarity in such situations are natural consequences of such portrayal.[75] The logic generally used in this doctrine is similar to the one in the merger doctrine: similarity of expression results from the fact that the common idea is only capable of expression in more or less stereotyped forms and therefore needs to be excluded from copyright protection.[76]

---

[74] Goldstein. The Scenes a faire doctrine was first applied in *Cain* v. *Universal Pictures Co.*, 47 F. Supp. 1013, 1017 (S.D. Cal. 1942) in which some church sequences such as playing of the piano, the prayer, the hunger motive etc., in a novel were allegedly infringed in a motion picture. The court held that such scenes are inherent in the situation itself and therefore, not copyrightable.

[75] Murray 2006. The author states that certain subject matter—stock images, tried and true storylines, fables and folklore, scenes of nature, common visual and cultural references, all of which fall under the title of "scenes that must be done"—are not able to be copyrighted because they are part of the public domain and no one can obtain a monopoly on such images by putting them into a fixed and tangible medium of expression. Also read Nimmer.

[76] Goldstein.

In *NRI Film Production Associates (P) Ltd.* v. *Twentieth Century Fox Film Corporation*[77] the plaintiffs filed a suit for a declaration that the Movie 'Independence Day' (I.D.) produced by the defendants infringes the copyright of their film script 'Extra Terrestrial Mission' (E.T.M.). The main theme of both is a war between aliens and the U.S. Force. The appellant mostly relied on some unique style of expressions in his script, to establish infringement.[78] The court, after analysing them, rightly held that treatment and presentation of the concept in the film I.D. is totally different from the script E.T.M., and that the picturisation of blasting of nuclear missiles, disruption of communications, traffic jams etc., are nothing but "scene a faire" commonly found in scientific fictions and therefore excluded from copyright protection. Scenes a faire doctrine affords immunity from liability for similar incidents or plot which necessarily follow from a common theme or setting.[79]

It is interesting to note that the Indian judiciary had opportunity to look into different aspects of idea expression dichotomy. Though there are stray instances of disappointing decisions, it appears that the judiciary is gaining more conceptual clarity over the years.

3 Originality

Copyright law always tends to strike an appropriate legal balance between the rights of authors and publishers on the one hand and the rights of users and consumers on the other.[80] Eligibility for copyright protection, or copyrightability, is one of the major components of the balance drawn by copyright law between the competing claims of copyright owners and copyright users. The major factor in determining copyrightability is originality in expression, which ensures that the copyrighted work should supplement to the available cultural assets and thus contribute to the welfare of the society. However, unlike the patent law, the additional input/creativity needed is very minimal.

One of the major decisions which explained the meaning of originality is *University of London Press Limited* v. *University Tutorial Press Limited.*[81]

---

[77] ILR 2004 Karnataka 4530.

[78] The plaintiff relied on the presence of common elements such as such as the President's direct involvement in the war; the President's presence in the last scene at the time of departure of the aliens; the concept of energy shield and the vivid description of it; the vivid and detailed expression of nuclear missiles fizzling out like broken balloons in E.T.M.; the descriptive concept of spaceship and its movement from outer space passing through moon with cloud covers, the descriptive effects of spaceship with dazzling lights descending on the earth focussing the beaming light from the bottom on the Whitehouse etc.

[79] Nimmer, Supra n. 48, § 13.03[B][4] 13-88.6.

[80] Abrams 1992.

[81] [1916] 2 Ch 601.

J. Peterson, in this case, observed that the word original did not mean that the work must be the expression of original or innovative thought since Copyright Law is not concerned with the originality of ideas, but with the expression of thought. In the copyright context the word 'original' simply indicates the requirement of independent creation by the author, rather than copying from any earlier work.[82] As different from the Civil Law, which looks for imprints of author's personality, the Common Law tradition was to equate originality with independent creation.[83] But this does not mean novelty, i.e., not in existence before. There can be two identical protected works so long as they are independently created.[84] Courts were not supposed to enquire into the aesthetic merit, but were simply bound to judge on the author's contribution in determining originality. Goldstein and Hugenholtz, while analysing the history of copyright law in the U.S., have stated that in the early period the courts required some showing of aesthetic merit as a condition to copyright. But later it rejected such a qualitative threshold on the ground that "it would be dangerous undertaking for persons trained only to the law to constitute themselves final judges of the worth of pictorial illustrations".[85] 'Originality', in effect, means little more than prohibition of actual copying. No matter how poor the author's addition, it is sufficient to constitute originality.[86]

In the case of compilation of facts the question of originality becomes more troublesome because facts, themselves not copyrightable, become copyrightable once they form part of compilations. The main hurdle in examining the copyrightability of compilations of facts is the question of originality threshold in them. Is mere industrious selection and compilation of factual data by itself sufficient to qualify a work as original, or whether some additional element of authorship or judgment in the selection and arrangement of the individual units in the compilation is necessary?[87]

Initially two approaches were available in determining originality: "the sweat of the brow doctrine"[88] and the requirement for "selection, creativity and judgement in choosing"[89] the compiled materials.[90] The originality requirement under the "the sweat of the brow" approach could simply be reduced to this: that a work needs to originate from the author. In other words, lack of actual copying is the touchstone of originality under this approach. This approach, thus, reduces originality to

[82] Paul Goldstein.

[83] Goldstein and Huganholtz 2010.

[84] Ginsburg 1989.

[85] Goldstein and Huganholtz 2010, quoting from Bleistein v. Donaldson Lithographing Company 188 U.S. 239, 251 (1903).

[86] Nimmer, quoting from Alfred Bell & Co. v. Fine Arts Inc. 191 F.2d 99 (1951).

[87] Abrams 1992.

[88] Introduced in *Jeweler's Circular Publishing Co.* v. *Keystone Publishing Co* 281 F 83, 88 (2d Cir 1922).

[89] *Eckes* v. *Card Prices Update* 736 F2d 859 (2d Cir 1984).

[90] Abrams 1992.

nothing more than absence of plagiarism. The underlying notion of the "sweat of the brow" or "industrious collection," approach was that copyright was a reward for the hard work that went into compiling facts. The classic formulation of the doctrine appeared in *Jeweler's Circular Publishing Co.* v. *Keystone Publishing Co.*[91] The decision conferred private property rights on a person who collects materials using his labour irrespective of whether there is literary skill or originality or whether the materials collected are in public domain or not. The main problem with the "sweat of the brow" doctrine is that it extends copyright protection in a compilation beyond selection and arrangement to the facts themselves, much against the fundamental principles of copyright law. Under the doctrine, the only defence to infringement was independent creation. A subsequent compiler was "not entitled to take one word of information previously published," but rather had to "independently work out the matter for himself, so as to arrive at the same result from the same common sources of information."[92] The second approach, which originated in the mid to late nineteenth century, insisted that a minimum amount of creativity existed in the selection and arrangement of facts for compilations to be copyright eligible.[93] As opposed to the independent labour standard, this approach insisted an additional infusion of the author's personality into the subject matter for making it eligible for copyright protection.[94] Finally, in *Feist Publications, Inc.* v. *Rural Telephone Service Co*,[95] the U.S. Supreme Court resolved this controversy rejecting the sweat of the brow doctrine, and stated:

> Original, as the term is used in copyright, means only that the work was independently created by the author (as opposed to copied from other works), and that it possesses at least some minimal degree of creativity.

There are many jurists, who hold the view that the *Fiest* decision is "unprecedented",[96] or that it lays down an extremely high standard for originality[97] or that it has interjected a distinct inquiry concerning creativity into the originality equation[98]

---

[91] 281 F. 83, (CA2 1922). The Court at p. 88 stated the originality requirement in the following words: "The right to copyright a book upon which one has expended labour in its preparation does not depend upon whether the materials which he has collected consist or not of matters which are *publici juris*, or whether such materials show literary skill or originality, either in thought or in language, or anything more than industrious collection. The man who goes through the streets of a town and puts down the names of each of the inhabitants, with their occupations and their street number, acquires material of which he is the author."

[92] *Feist Publications, Inc.* v. *Rural Telephone Service Co* 499 U.S. 340 (1991).

[93] Yen 1991. For a list of such cases see footnote 3 of the article. Also read 1992, http://lawdigitalcommons.bc.edu/bclr/vol34/iss1/4.

[94] Dowd 1992.

[95] 499 U.S. 340 (1991).

[96] Goldstein.

[97] CCH Canadian, EBC v. Modak.

[98] Abrams 1992.

or that it is a "significant departure from precedents".[99] However, a close analysis of the decision reveals that the "modicum of creativity" requirement for copyright protection of compilations is no way different from the nineteenth century requirement of selection, judgment and creativity. Therefore, there is no logic in arguing that the creativity requirement in the context of literary work cannot be allowed in the context of compilation of factual data. Similarly, it is quite illogical to suggest that no additional input is required in the case of compilation of materials from the public domain whereas it is mandatory in the case of fictional and artistic works.

It is evident from judgment itself that the minimal level of creativity required in Feist is not literary or artistic creativity, but only an additional input required to render a compilation of uncopyrightable content copyrightable.[100] The following statement of the U.S. Supreme Court in Feist reveals it:

> Original, as the term is used in copyright, means only that the work was independently created by the author (as opposed to copied from other works), and that it possesses at least some minimal degree of creativity. To be sure, the requisite level of creativity is extremely low; even a slight amount will suffice. The vast majority of works make the grade quite easily, as they possess some creative spark, "no matter how crude, humble or obvious" it might be. *Originality does not signify novelty; a work may be original even though it closely resembles other works so long as the similarity is fortuitous, not the result of copying*. (Emphasis added)

The Court stated that, originality is not a stringent standard and it does not require that facts have to be presented in an innovative or surprising way. However, the selection and arrangement of facts cannot be so mechanical or routine, as to reject the requirement of creativity whatsoever. The standard of originality is low, but it does exist.[101] Thus it becomes evident that the Fiest requirement is not in any way different from the selection, creativity and judgement in choosing test that existed from the mid nineteenth century. Moreover, this test is perfectly in tune with the originality concept in copyright law since, as rightly said by the Court, the mere fact that a work is copyrighted does not mean that every element of the work may be protected. Copyright protection can extend only to those components of a work that are original to the author. If the compilation author adds his own creativity to

---

[99] Paul Goldstein.

[100] The Court expressed the problem in identifying originality in compilations thus: "Many compilations consist of nothing but raw data—i.e., wholly factual information not accompanied by any original written expression. On what basis may one claim a copyright in such a work? Common sense tells us that 100 uncopyrightable facts do not magically change their status when gathered together in one place. Yet copyright law seems to contemplate that compilations that consist exclusively of facts are potentially within its scope."

[101] The Court rejected copyright in Rural's data because it simply published the most basic information—name, town, and telephone number—about each person who applies to it for telephone service and arranged them in the alphabetical order. Both the "selection" and "arrangement" of the data lacked the modicum of creativity necessary to transform uncopyrightable factual data into copyrightable expression. Though the white pages directory of Rural is useful, it is not original in the copyright sense.

the facts by expressing them in his or her own way, he or she will be able to claim a copyright only in this specific written expression. Others may copy the underlying facts from the publication, but not the precise words used to present them, or not the expression given to it by the compiler. In other words, originality in factual compilations has to be identified as the author's inputs in expressing them. This definitely being the case with all other works, it must be true for compilations as well.

In CCH Canadian, the Canadian Supreme Court, while considering the correct approach to originality, appears to have rejected both the 'sweat of the brow' or "industriousness" standard of originality (as the court felt that the originality standard is too low) and the Fiest requirement of 'modicum of creativity' which it considered to be the other extreme, and tried to evolve a 'middle path'. The court felt that the exact standard of originality fell between these extremes. However, while rejecting the creativity requirement, the Court required the expression of an idea to be the result of exercise of skill and judgment, and such exercise of skill and judgment was required to be something more than trivial so that it could not be characterized as a purely mechanical exercise.[102] This, in effect, blurs the borders of Fiest and CCH Canadian decisions—as it is difficult to differentiate between 'modicum of creativity' and the requirement of non-triviality of skill and judgement —and renders the 'middle path', suggested by CCH Canadian, indiscernible.

In brief, it becomes evident that if one follows the real objective of copyright law in maintaining a balance between owners and users of copyright, he cannot but opt for the non-trivial skill and judgement standard of originality.

3.1 Judicial Trend in India

Though originality has the same meaning for all forms of works, it may pose different types of complexities with respect to different forms of works. Therefore, it may be pertinent to explore the meaning of originality in the context of different forms of works.

3.1.1 Originality in Literary Works

(1) **Originality in Books**

In India, Originality standard can be found to be fluctuating. *Macmillan and Company Ltd.* v. *K. & J. Cooper*[103] decided by the Privy Council, rejected the 'sweat of the brow' standard of 'originality'. In deciding the issue of infringement

---

[102] By skill, the Court meant the use of one's knowledge, developed aptitude or practised ability in producing the work and by judgment, the use of one's capacity for discernment or ability to form an opinion or evaluation by comparing different possible options in producing the work.

[103] 1923 (1924) 26 BOMLR 292: AIR 1924 PC 175.

of an abridgement of Sir Robert North's Translation of the book *Plutarch's life of Alaxander the Great*, the Court held that the abridgement, which simply consisted of detached passages selected from the book and knit together using some words, is outside the purview of copyright. The Court stated that the precise amount of knowledge, labour, judgment or literary skill or taste which the author of any book or other compilation must bestow upon its composition in order to acquire copyright in it can only be defined in the context of every independent case. However, it rejected originality of expression in the case before it as there was no evidence to establish any amount of knowledge, labour, judgment or literary skill or taste applied to the composition of the text of the appellants' book to entitle them to the copyright of it.

On the basis of the facts of the case the Court stated that by selecting and combining passages without losing the logic and continuity is not sufficient to constitute the required level of knowledge, skill and labour. It laid down the standard of originality in the following words:

> (I)t is the product of the labour, skill and capital of one man which must not be appropriated by another, not the elements, the raw material, if one may use the expression, upon which the labour and skill and capital of the first have been expended. *To secure copyright for this product it is necessary that the labour, skill and capital expended should be sufficient to impart to the product some quality or character which the raw material did not possess, and which differentiates the product from the raw material.* (Emphasis added)

Thus, the court held that by simply copying several passages from the original and pasting it without losing the continuity is not sufficient to constitute originality for the purpose of conferring copyright protection for an abridgement. In other words, the skill in the selection of crucial portions from the book without any additional input from the person who creates abridgement is not the adequate level of originality. In order to 'originate from the author' the labour skill and capital extended by the subsequent author should result in a product different from the existing one.

But with respect to marginal notes appended to the appellants' book the court had a different opinion. It felt that the notes were altogether different since they made the book more attractive, the study of it more interesting and informing, enhanced its efficiency, and consequently increased its value as an educational manual. The Privy Council was of the view that though one could trace everything in those notes to some classical dictionary or other work, those "notes were well chosen, were neatly condensed, were sufficiently copious, were accurate and must have required for the framing of them classical knowledge, literary skill and taste, labour and sound judgment as to what was fitting and useful to be brought to the notice of schoolboys and students about to enter the University". Therefore, the notes were held original and copying them constituted infringement.

It is evident from the conclusions of the Privy Council in the context of the abridgement and the marginal notes that it went in favour of the second approach followed from the nineteenth century that the selection and arrangement should have a minimum amount of creativity to meet the requirement of originality.

In *S.K. Dutt* v. *Law Book Co.*[104] the plaintiff, the author of the book "The Indian Partnership Act by Mukerji and Dutt", came up with the proposition that he enjoyed copyright in those passages which he had quoted either from other text book writers or from decided cases and the defendants, by quoting the same passages from those texts and cases, infringed his copyright in the selection. The crux of the plaintiff's argument was that by quoting a passage from a decision or from another work he was in effect "selecting" the passage and since the copyright law protects selection he was protected and nobody else could thereafter make the same selection. The court rejected this claim and held that so far it related to the selection made by the plaintiff from other sources such as texts and cases, the plaintiff can claim originality in them only to the extent of the skill and judgement extended by him in such selection and arrangement and that the plaintiff had thoroughly failed in establishing it. The court also rejected the allegation of infringement since the defendant had followed an arrangement different from that of the plaintiff and what had been allegedly copied from the plaintiff by the defendant were actually taken by both from a common source. This decision reiterates the view expressed by the Privy Council in *Macmillan and Company Ltd.* v. *K. & J. Cooper*[105] that every expression of ideas is not protected by copyright law and unless the copied element is original to the author the copying will not constitute infringement. In this case also the court, rejecting the "sweat of the brow doctrine", held that since the plaintiff failed to establish any special skill or judgment in the incorporation of the selected materials in his book, there was no infringement.

However, in *V. Govindan* v. *Gopalakrishna Kone*,[106] the Madras High Court took a different approach following the 'sweat of the brow' doctrine. In that case the plaintiff alleged infringement of copyright in his English—English—Tamil dictionary, the court responded to the defendant's plea of common source by stating that those who put forward the plea of common source will have to prove that they have gone to the common source and borrowed from there using his skill, labour and brains and not merely copied from the plaintiff's dictionary.[107] The end result of this logic is that it permits appropriation of even public domain materials.

---

[104] AIR 1954 All. 570. The court expressed the view that "only those selections are protected which the plaintiff makes for purposes of incorporating them in a "book of selections". It does not protect a selection which the plaintiff makes for purposes of explaining a legal or a scientific proposition that he has to explain while writing a commentary for the other man who after the plaintiff writes a commentary on that subject must, 'per necessity' have to make the same selection.

[105] 1923 (1924) 26 BOMLR 292: AIR 1924 PC 175.

[106] AIR 1955 Mad 391. In *ShamLal Paharia* v. *Gaya Prasad* AIR 1971 All. 182 the Allahabad High Court also took the same stand.

[107] On Law reports also the Court took the same view: "Even in law reports, containing only approved reports of cases decided by Courts, there is copy-right. In modern complex society, provisions have to be made for protecting everyman's copyright, whether big or small, whether involving a high degree of originality, as in a new poem or picture, or only originality at the vanishing point, as in a law report."

The decision of the Andhra Pradesh High Court in *V. Errabhadra Rao* v. *B.N. Sharma*,[108] reveals that the courts in India were not sharing a uniform view on the issue of the standard of originality required under the copyright law. The issue before the court in this case was if the book of the respondents "Hyderabad Pai Police Charya' was an original work or a translation of the appellant's book "Police Action Against Hyderabad", pamphlet "Real face of Hyderabad" and other articles. In that case the Court stated that an original contribution does not require that it is confined to a field which has never been carried hitherto by any other person, either in respect of ideas or material comprised therein. On the other hand, originality only meant that the work should not be copied from another work, but should originate from the author. Thus, the issue of originality "depended", as per the court, "much on the skill, labour, knowledge, and the capacity to digest and utilise the raw materials contributed by others in imparting to the product the quality and the character which those materials did not possess and which differentiates the product from the materials used".[109] The court identified that in spite of the fact that the materials in the respondent's book were partly drawn from appellant's books, and partly drawn from his own writings and historical facts the book was an original composition wherein the author has exercised his skill, labour, knowledge, and judgement in producing the book, as it cannot be identified with any of the materials utilized by him therein.

In short, the court, while appreciating the fact that no work can exist quite independently of existing works and historical facts stated that such reliance need not negate originality in such works. It followed the same standard laid down in the Macmillan case by insisting that in order to be copyrightable, the new work needed to be different from the earlier work as a result of the labour, skill and judgement extended by the author.

In 1978, while examining the issue of infringement of copyright in a film in *R.G. Anand*,[110] the Supreme Court had an occasion to look into the question of originality. The court, at the outset, laid down the principle that violation of copyright was determined on the basis of substantial copying of the form, manner and arrangement and expression of the idea of an author of the copyright work by another. It went on to add that if the same idea is developed in a different manner, the source being common, similarities are bound to occur, and in such cases it has to be determined whether the similarities are on the fundamental or substantial aspects of the mode of expression adopted in the copyrighted work. If the defendant has actually reproduced the original in a different form, different tone and different tenor so as to infuse a new life into the idea of the copyrighted work adapted by him, there is no violation of the copyright. On the other hand, if the defendants work is nothing but a literal imitation of the copyrighted work with some variations here and there it would amount to violation of the copyright. In the case at hand it

---

[108] AIR 1960 AP 415.

[109] *Ibid.*

[110] AIR 1978 SC 1613: (1978) 4 SCC 118.

felt that but for the central idea of provincialism which is not protected by copyright, from scene to scene, situation to situation, in climax to anticlimax, pathos, bathos, in texture and treatment and purport and presentation, the picture was materially different from the play. This made the film original and infringement was ruled out.[111] In other words, if the subsequent work is transformed into a new work due the difference in treatment or manner of presentation it gets an originality of its own and falls beyond the copyright coverage of the first author.

Unfortunately, the lower judiciary, in their subsequent decisions in relation to different types of works, many often failed to properly appreciate the Privy Council decision in *Macmillan and Company Ltd.* v. *K. & J. Cooper*[112] and the Supreme Court decision in R.G. Anand.[113] For example, the following statement of the Court in *The Chancellor Masters and Scholars of the University of Oxford* v. *Narendera Publishing House*[114] is laying down a standard of originality which is much beyond the legal requirement.

The Delhi High Court, in that case, stated in the context of mathematical questions and answers in a text book, that since the sequencing and schematic arrangement of the questions in the various chapters of the book conforms to the specifications and requirements of the J & K Board, negated originality. The Court insisted that, for claiming copyright protection the plaintiffs had to show original effort, unique to their schematic arrangement or sequencing. Unless the plaintiff showed how it evolved an arrangement so unique that the scheme is entitled to copyright protection, independent of the dictates of the Board it is not eligible to copyright protection. Though there can be creativity in such schematic arrangement, the court infers that prima facie there is no material in support of it and reaches the opinion that the plaintiffs' claim of copyright in questions, answers, and their requiring or arrangement, is insubstantial. This, it appears, is a wrong understanding of originality, since originality simply means independent creation and a mere

[111] After analysing the story of the film the Court found that of the three main themes portrayed in it and which formed an integral part of it, the last two aspects had not been figured at all in the play written by the plaintiff/appellant. Moreover, the Court found it very difficult to divorce one theme of the film from the others without affecting the beauty and the continuity of the script of the film. It also felt that the treatment of the story of the film was different in many respects from the story contained in the play. The trial Judge and the High Court were of the opinion that the similarities were on trivial points and did not have the effect of making the film a substantial and material imitation of the play. After consideration of the essential features of the film and the play the Court opined that the plaintiff has not proved by clear and cogent evidence that the defendants committed colourable imitation of the play and have thus violated the copyright of the plaintiff. After listing out the similarities and the dissimilarities in the expression of the themes the court concluded the effect of the dissimilarities far outweigh the effect of the similarities. Thus, on a close and careful comparison of the play and the picture the court was unable to identify substantial copying of expressions in the play by the film.

[112] 1923 (1924) 26 BOMLR 292: AIR 1924 PC 175.

[113] AIR 1978 SC 1613: (1978) 4 SCC 118.

[114] 2008(38)PTC385(Del).

involvement of the J & K Board in the creation of the syllabus based on which the text book is created is quite insufficient to deny originality.

(2) **Originality in Compilations**

As already seen, originality in compilations further complicates the issue of copyright balance. For example, in the case of compilation of non-copyrightable materials, what constitutes the original expression/contribution of the compiler is a complex problem. Going by the original principles or objectives of copyright law it is not difficult to conclude that in the case of compilations, and especially in the case of compilation of non-copyrightable compilations, social welfare insists for an independent input from the compiler to render her eligible for copyright protection. The principle laid down by *Macmillan* v. *Cooper* is relevant even in the case of compilations.

However, the decision in *Burligton Home Shopping (P) Ltd.* v. *Rajnish Chibber*[115] the Delhi High Court stands apart. It failed to take into account the objectives of copyright law. In that case the plaintiff, a mail order service company, alleged that its clientele database has been copied by the defendant, a former employee of the company, who has put up a competing mail order shopping business. The court by holding that "a compilation of addresses developed by anyone, by devoting time, money, labour and skill, though the resources are commonly situated, amounts to a "literary work" wherein the author has a copyright" followed the "sweat of the brow" doctrine. The court, in this case, was unconcerned about the issue whether what was copied was original to the author or whether it fell within copyrightable subject matter. The result of this decision was to extend copyright protection to facts which are in the public domain. It failed to follow the precedent set by Indian Courts since the Privy Council decision to the effect that copyright protection insisted on a minimal contribution from the part of the author and that the protection is limited simply to the contribution of the author was not followed by the court.

(3) **Originality in Case Reports**

Though case reports also can be termed as compilations, they are slightly different from factual compilations in that the case reports are not strictly in public domain, at least under the Indian law.[116] Section 52 (1) (q) (iv) of the Copyright Act 1957

[115] (1995) 15 PTC 278 (Del.).

[116] They constitute "Government works" under Section 2(k) (iii) of the Copyright Act, 1957. Though the Kerala High Court *in Infoseek Solutions* v. *Kerala Law Times* 2006 (4) KLT 311 has stated that such judgements are not Govt. Work since their reproduction and publication are exempted from infringement of copyright and the judgment or order is "of" a Court, Tribunal or other judicial authority and is not "a work which is made or published by or under the direction or control of the Court, Tribunal or other judicial authority" to bring it within the term "Government work" as defined in Secttion 2(k), I respectfully disagree with that view. It is felt that a provision for an exception to copyright infringement for the reproduction of a type of work necessarily implies the existence of copyright in that type of work and unless the court etc., permits it cannot be published, and therefore, it is perfectly within the ambit of Section 2(k).

states that the reproduction or publication of any judgement or order of a court, tribunal or other judicial authority, shall not constitute infringement of copyright.[117] In other words, though the judicial decisions are not in public domain in the strictest sense of the word, the legal provision imparts an equivalent status to them, allowing anyone interested to reproduce and publish them. Now the crucial question is if anyone interested to publish them should go to the original source of them or are they permitted to copy them from an already published case reports. Thus, the main issue in this respect is almost the same as the issue in copyrightability of compilation of facts. Therefore the same legal principles are applicable here also.

While the Single Bench decision of the Delhi High Court explained the correct position of law,[118] the Division bench of the Delhi High Court[119] differentiated between the text of the judgement and the head notes and agreed with the single bench on the issue of the text of the judgement. However, the Kerala High Court[120] has taken the position that "a law report is a composite document and its head-notes, editorial comments, foot-notes, setting, layout, presentation, etc. and even the skill and labour involved in choosing as to whether a judgment should be reported, lead to the reporter and publisher acquiring copyright over such report, as a composite document including the text of the judgment as to published by the reporter." The Kerala High Court found no justification in distinguishing between head-notes etc. on the one hand and the main text on the other, while considering the question of originality in case reports.[121] This decision is faulty in that it grants copyright protection to the subject matter which was allowed by the law to be freely reproduced by anyone and thus tilts copyright balance against public welfare. It also

---

[117] Unless the reproduction or publication of such judgment or order is prohibited by the court, the tribunal or other judicial authority, as the case may be.

[118] *EBC* v. *Navin J Desai* 2001 PTC 57. The Court held that simply because the manuscripts of the judgments are obtained from the raw source, they are carefully reviewed, corrections made, cross references and cross citations added, lay out and pagination is done, arranged in a specific sequences and after giving a uniform style of dates, and printed and published in the journal by the plaintiff, *none of these activities/elements render it a creativity original to the plaintiff*. It also said that the judgments of the Court are available to every person and just because another person instead of obtaining the judgments from the raw source has copied them from the publication of the plaintiff will not mean that the work has become the original literary work of the publisher who published it for the first time. Relying on Nimmer, the court held that corrections of typographical mistakes, insertion of commas and full stops wherever necessary and giving paragraph numbers to judgments are trivial and not copyrightable. The court also denied their claim that they have a style of writing and therefore they have a copyright. Another interesting view taken by the Court was that the Supreme Court decisions, being materials in public domain there cannot be any monopoly in them and others are at liberty to use the same material of the plaintiff. Every man can take what is useful from them, improve, add and give it to the public to whole comprising of the original work with his additions and improvements. Under the guise of copyright the plaintiff cannot ask the court to restrain the defendants from making his material available to the public.

[119] 2002 (25) PTC 641 (Del.) (DB).

[120] *Infoseek Solutions* v. *Kerala Law Times* 2006 (4) KLT 311: 2007(34) PTC 231 (Ker): AIR 2007 Ker 1.

[121] 2007(34) PTC 231 (Ker) at p. 245.

forgets the spirit of Section 52 (1) (q) (iv) of the Copyright Act 1957. The approach could be identified as one favouring the "sweat of the brow" doctrine which allows public domain materials to be appropriated and privatised.

The Supreme Court of India, when it had an occasion to look into the matter of copyright in Law Reports in *Eastern Book Company Pvt. Ltd* v. *D.B. Modak*,[122] took a complex position. The appellant alleged that its law reports SCC were substantially copied by the defendants who had brought out software called 'Grand Jurix' and a software package called 'The Laws', both published on CD-ROMs. As per the appellants, all the modules in the defendants' software packages have been lifted verbatim from the appellants' work; the respondents have copied the appellants' sequencing, selection and arrangement of the cases coupled with the entire text of copy-edited judgments as published in the plaintiff-appellants' law report SCC, along with and including the style and formatting, the copy-editing paragraph numbers, footnote numbers, cross-references, etc.; and such acts of the defendant/respondents constitute infringement of the plaintiff- appellants' exclusive right to the same. The appellants claimed that their copy-edited version of the text of judgments as published in SCC is a creation of their skill, labour and capital and their contributions/inputs/additions[123] contributed originality to the case reports and entitling them for copyright protection.

The Supreme Court, while considering the issue of copyrightability of the inputs by the EBC, discussed the issue of originality in compilations. It rejected both the 'sweat of the brow' approach and the *Feist* approach requiring 'a modicum of creativity' and chose the 'middle path' taken by the Canadian Supreme Court in *CCH Canadian* v. *Law Society of Upper Canada*[124] as the correct approach.[125] The ratio of the Supreme Court can be identified as the following:

> To claim copyright in a compilation, the author must produce the material with exercise of his skill and judgment which may not be creativity in the sense that it is novel or non-obvious, but at the same time it is not a product of merely labour and capital. The derivative work produced by the author must have some distinguishable features and flavour to raw text of the judgments delivered by the court. The trivial variation or inputs put in the judgment would not satisfy the test of copyright of an author.

On this "touchstone", the Court considered the inputs by the appellants in their journal 'SCC' and reached at a convoluted decision. However, its findings are really

---

[122] AIR 2008 SC 809: 2008 (1) SCC 1.

[123] The Appellants identified some 27 categories of inputs like adding cross citations, adding margin headings, adding concurring, partly concurring, dissenting, partly dissenting etc., breaking existing paragraphs and adding new paragraph numbers, changing text as per corrigenda issued etc.

[124] [2004] 1 S.C.R. 339.

[125] However, the Court made it clear that the decision of the court "would be confined to the judgments of the courts which are in the public domain as by virtue of Section 52 of the Act there is no copyright in the original text of the judgments. To claim copyright in a compilation, the author must produce the material with exercise of his skill and judgment which may not be creativity in the sense that it is novel or non-obvious, but at the same time it is not a product of merely labour and capital.

confusing. With respect to certain inputs[126] it stated that though they had improved the readability of the judgment that "does not give the flavour of minimum requirement of creativity". Interestingly, here the court brings in the originality threshold of *Feist*. However, it went on to add that "(t)he exercise of the skill and judgment required to produce the work is trivial and is on account of the labour and the capital invested and could be characterized as purely a work which has been brought about by putting some amount of labour by the appellants". Here though the Court appears to have correctly understood the spirit of CCH Canadian, since it mixes up the two principles—since it proceeded with the view that they are different—creates confusion as to the originality threshold and also as regards the ratio of the case.

Interestingly, with respect to some other inputs[127] the Court states that they are the result of skill and judgment in great measure[128] and therefore copyrightable.

---

[126] Such as adding cross-citations to the citation(s) already given in the original text; adding names of cases and cross-citations where only the citation of the case is given; adding citation and cross-citations where only name of the case is given; inserting citation in case history where only the title and year of the impugned/earlier order is given; presenting in their own style the cases when they are cited repeated in the judgment; providing precise references to the quoted matter in the judgment by giving exact page and paragraph number as in the original case source/treatise/reference material; adding margin headings to quoted extracts from statutes/rules, etc.

[127] (i) segregating the existing paragraphs in the original text by breaking them into separate paragraphs; (ii) adding internal paragraph numbering within a judgment after providing uniform paragraph numbering to the multiple judgments; and (iii) indicating in the judgment the Judges who have dissented or concurred by introducing the phrases like 'concurring', 'partly concurring', 'partly dissenting', 'dissenting', 'supplementing', 'majority expressing no opinion', etc.

[128] The Court stated: "The editor who inserts para numbering must know how legal argumentation and legal discourse is conducted and how a judgment of a court of law must read. Often legal arguments or conclusions are either clubbed into one paragraph in the original judgment or parts of the same argument are given in separate paragraphs. It requires judgment and the capacity for discernment for determining whether to carve out a separate paragraph from an existing paragraph in the original judgment or to club together separate paragraphs in the original judgment of the court. Setting of paragraphs by the appellants of their own in the judgment entailed the exercise of the brain work, reading and understanding of subject of disputes, different issues involved, statutory provisions applicable and interpretation of the same and then dividing them in different paragraphs so that chain of thoughts and process of statement of facts and the application of law relevant to the topic discussed is not disturbed, would require full understanding of the entire subject of the judgment. Making paragraphs in a judgment could not be called a mechanical process.

It requires careful consideration, discernment and choice and thus it can be called as a work of an author. Creation of paragraphs would obviously require extensive reading, careful study of subject and the exercise of judgment to make paragraph which has dealt with particular aspect of the case, and separating intermixing of a different subject. Creation of paragraphs by separating them from the passage would require knowledge, sound judgment and legal skill. In our opinion, this exercise and creation thereof has a flavour of minimum amount of creativity. The said principle would also apply when the editor has put an input whereby different Judges_ opinion has been shown to have been dissenting or partly dissenting or concurring, etc. It also requires reading of the whole judgment and understanding the questions involved and thereafter finding out whether the Judges have disagreed or have the dissenting opinion or they are partially disagreeing and partially agreeing to the view on a particular law point or even on facts. In these inputs put in

The court concluded by proscribing the defendants from copying the head notes and the footnotes and editorial notes appearing in the journal of the plaintiff-appellants. The defendants were also required not to use "the paragraphs made by the appellants in their copy-edited version for internal references and their editor's judgment regarding the opinions expressed by the Judges by using phrases like 'concurring', 'partly dissenting', etc. on the basis of reported judgments in SCC", the effect of which is better known to the court alone.

Whatsoever, it is quite disheartening to see that even after expressly rejecting the "sweat of the brow" doctrine it followed the same doctrine in an implied manner by protecting feeble, unconvincing, contributions from the Plaintiff in the text of the case report. It is beyond one's imagination to attribute originality to paragraphing and phrases like 'concurring', 'partly dissenting', etc., since paragraphing is just a formatting process and the phrases mentioned are just explaining some factual situations in the shortest possible manner. The most ironic part of the decision is that the plaintiffs virtually did not get the protection sought by them. It had no significant impact on the defendants.[129] The decision was also conspicuous for its contradictory statements.[130] Though the Supreme Court identified the objective of copyright law as "balancing of the interests and rights of the author and the user and in protecting the public domain", it is strongly felt that the decision was not in that direction.[131]

(Footnote 128 continued)

by the appellants in the judgments reported in SCC, the appellants have a copyright and nobody is permitted to utilize the same.".

[129] The following observation from *Mathew Bender* v. *West Law* 158 F.3d 674 (2nd Cir. 1998): "One useful way to appreciate how little creativity inheres in West's citation decisions is to consider what West's competitors would have to do to avoid an infringement claim were we to find West's citation decisions copyrightable." The defendants still enjoyed their right to copy from SCC with impunity provided they do it with some care and caution.

[130] 2008 (36) PTC 1, at p. 49. Various statements of the court were even self-contradictory. For example see:

> The judicial pronouncements of the Apex Court would be in the public domain and its reproduction or publication would not infringe the copyright. *That being the position, the copy-edited judgments would not satisfy the copyright merely by establishing amount of skill, labour and capital put in the inputs of the copy-edited judgments and the original or innovative thoughts for the creativity are completely excluded.* Accordingly, *original or innovative thoughts are necessary to establish copyright in the author's work* (here the court even went beyond the Feist requirement). The principle where there is common source the person relying on it must prove that he actually went to the common source from where he borrowed the material, employing his own skill, labour and brain and he did not copy, would not apply to the judgments of the courts because there is no copyright in the judgments of the court, unless so made by the court itself. *To secure a copyright for the judgments delivered by the court, it is necessary that the labour, skill and capital invested should be sufficient to communicate or impart to the judgment printed in SCC some quality or character which the original judgment does not possess and which differentiates the original judgment from the printed one.*

[131] *Ibid.*

Another disturbing aspect of this decision is the exact ratio of it with respect to originality of case reports. Due to its knotty analysis of originality threshold and the perplexing conclusion, the Court has rendered the practical implementation of its ratio yet another head ache. However, it is heartening that some of the subsequent High Court decisions have effectively made use of the confusions created by the Supreme Court judgment in a very positive way, by striking the perfect balance.[132]

For example, in *Dr. Reckeweg* v. *Adven Biotech Pvt.* Ltd.,[133] the Delhi High Court was quite strategic in applying the precedent laid down by EBC. In this case, the plaintiff manufacturing Homeopathic specialities known as R series in Germany for 60 years alleged that their copyright in literature or catalogue was violated by the defendants by reproducing the unique composition of their homeopathic medicines A1 to A75 since they hold proprietary rights in such formulations by virtue of copyright in their literature. They sought for an order restraining the defendants from infringing their copyright in their literature.

The court considered three issues: (i) copyright in relation to nomenclature of drugs; (ii) copyright in the listing of medicines in a particular fashion; (iii) the descriptive and cumulative effect of compilation.

The court identified the standard of originality laid down in EBC thus:

> The Court in the context of evaluating the copyrightability in the reporting of the judicial judgments and orders, held that mere skill, labour and time expended will not qualify a work for copyright protection. It held that work must be original "in the sense that by virtue of selection, coordination or arrangement of pre-existing data contained in the work, a work somewhat different in character is produced by the author".[134]

---

[132] Notwithstanding the decision of the case that this case is a precedent only with respect to materials within "public domain" such as case reports, many High Courts followed it on different respects.

[133] 2008 (38) PTC 308 (Del.).

[134] It is interesting to see the way it reaches the ratio in EBC:

> Our Supreme Court had the benefit of the two judgments of the United States Supreme Court and the Supreme Court of Canada. It noticed the original "sweat of the brow" doctrine and the low threshold of originality required for copyright protection. The Fiest Publication standard of "modicum of creativity" too was noticed, as well as the impracticality of continuing with the sweat of the brow test. The court then noted the Canadian solution, i.e. "exercise of skill and judgment in the production of a work". It is enlightening to note that our Supreme Court noted that the two positions i.e. the "sweat of the brow" on the one hand, and "modicum of creativity" were extreme positions; it preferred a higher threshold than the doctrine of "sweat of the brow" but not as high as "modicum of creativity". Significantly the court then emphasized that the product, or the expression, in compilations, etc. should be a "work somewhat different in character… produced by the author" to qualify for copyright protection. Thus, our law too has recognized this shift, and mandates that not every effort or industry, or expending of skill, results in copyrightable work, but only those which create works that are somewhat different in character, involve some intellectual effort, and involve a certain degree of creativity.

There cannot be a better way to deduce the ratio of EBC than this.

After laying down the principle, the court applied it to the case in hand in the following manner. First, it addressed the claim of copyright in relation to the nomenclature of the drugs in the series R1, R2 etc. and concluded that since "R" is a part of the English Alphabet and the other part of the nomenclature is in the ascending order of the Hindu-Arabic numerals, the use of alphanumeric series does not reveal any amount of creativity or exercise of skill and judgment, as laid down in CCH Canadian. As per the established proposition of law names and titles, in the normal course, cannot be afforded copyright protection until it has qualities and characteristics of original creative work. Therefore, it was held that, no copyright can be granted on the nomenclature of the drugs as the R1 series.

Next, the Court addressed the claim of copyright on the curative element compilation. The plaintiffs alleged that the exhibition of the curative element compilation on the products and in their brochure by the defendants violated their copyright in their brochure and literature. These curative element compilations employ certain medical and common terminology to convey what problems the medicines would cure. The Court held that the plaintiffs have failed to demonstrate how they have employed any skill, judgment and labour in describing the curative elements, let alone any creativity. The Court adverted to the fact that there are certain ways in which such curative elements can be described and the description in the case before it was fairly common, employing standard terminology. Thereafter it held that in the absence of any additional averment as to the uniqueness of such description or intellectual creativity, no copyright subsisted in the curative element compilation.

The Court also addressed the plaintiffs' claim of copyright on the description of the medicines. The plaintiff simply used technical terms to describe the medicines or only added phrases, commonly employed to further explain the nature of the medicines to such technical terms. For example, the plaintiffs contended that their "cough drops" description cannot be copied by the defendants and instead they can use alternatives such as "expectorant drops". The Court held that since common conditions can be described or expressed only in a few well known ways, to say that the plaintiffs can claim protection of such common words would be to allow them to appropriate stretches of the language. Hence, it rejected any intellectual creativity or skill expended by the plaintiff in their claimed expression so as to satisfy the test indicated by the Supreme Court.

Another set of claims addressed by the Court the related to copyright over the sequencing of the medicines in a particular order. Since the plaintiffs manufacture their products as per the directions in the German Homeopathic Pharmacopeia their sequencing was considered a derivative work by the Court. It felt that the plaintiffs' sequencing, being a collection or sequencing of already existing information, the standard of creativity required to qualify as a work in which copyright subsists is higher than the standard required in cases of primary works. The plaintiffs have not specifically averred as to the manner in which the sequencing was done and the technique or criteria employed to place the medicines in that particular sequence. Instead, from their averments it becomes evident that the list expands numerically as and when they discover or market a new medicine. The Court held that in the absence of any specific pleading in relation to the originality of the sequence, their claim to copyright in this regard too has to fail.

Lastly, the Court considered the claim of copyright in relation to the literature of the plaintiff. The literature of the plaintiff is in fact a compilation of the names, the series of the medicines, its curative elements etc., which, as has been held above are not individually capable of being protected under copyright law. The brochure of the defendants, which the plaintiffs allege has infringed their copyright, only enlists the series, the names of the medicines and the curative effects—all three components on which no copyright can be claimed. The defendants have not copied the plaintiffs' literature in its entirety. It is true, that the defendants have copied some of the mistakes and omissions of the plaintiff committed in its literature. But law does not remedy every act of copying. Therefore, even if it were assumed that the literature of the plaintiffs, considered as a whole and not in parts, were capable of copyright protection, as has been held in Dr. Recekeweg and Ors v. SM Sharma,[135] copying of individual factors, themselves not capable of copyright protection because of lack of creativity, cannot result in the grant of an injunction.

In *Mattel Inc.* v. *Mr. Jayant Agarwalla*[136] the plaintiffs claimed copyright in respect of the three game-boards, with the diagonal criss-cross design with placement of the double word, triple word, double and triple letter values, as well as rules of the game. Every literary or artistic work, to be afforded protection, should be original under the Act. The Court traced the meaning of originality through various case laws and finally relies on the decision in *Eastern Book Company* v. *DB Modak,*[137] which, following the approach of the *Canadian Supreme Court in CCH Canadian Ltd.* v. *Law Society of Upper Canada,*[138] rejected the 'sweat of the brow' doctrine, (which conferred copyright on works merely because time, energy, skill and labour was expended, that is, originality of skill and labour), and held that the work must be original in the sense that by virtue of selection, co- ordination or arrangement of pre-existing data contained in the work, a work somewhat different in character is produced by the author. Thus, the Copyright law in India mandates that not every effort or industry, or expending of skill, results in copyrightable work, but only those which create works that are somewhat different in character, involve some intellectual effort, and involve a certain degree of creativity. Court applies this standard of originality, in respect of the plaintiffs' claim to copyright in various aspects of the game. Interestingly, it traces the post Eastern Book Company

---

[135] 130 (2006) DLT 16.

[136] 2008(38)PTC416(Del).

[137] 2008 (1) SCC 1.

[138] [2004] 1 S.C.R. 339.

copyright standard to "modicum of creativity" and concludes by stating that so far as the collocation of lines on the game board are concerned, the diagonal colour scheme with values for words, and the combination thereof, the element of modicum of creativity has not been shown and the creative expression, if any, is minimalistic not to warrant copyright protection.

The judicial trend in evolving the standard of originality in literary works in India appears to be satisfactory, apart from the confusing conclusions from some quarters, including the Supreme Court.

3.1.2 Artistic Work

An artistic work, like any other work, to become eligible for copyright protection, should have both originality and creativity.[139] Any distinguishable variation created by an author to an unoriginal work, however modest it might be, is sufficient to constitute originality. For example, any artistic work modelled on an original object or person is copyrightable since it originates from the author. However, others are free to copy the original; but not the creation of another person. Still there are confusing decisions with respect to the effect of a mere technical modification introduced into a subsequent artistic work on originality.

In *C. Cunniah and Co.* v. *Balraj and Co.*[140] it was alleged that the respondent's painting "Bala Murugan" was a colourable imitation of the appellant's painting "Mayura Priya" and thus violated his copyright. There were two issues to be settled in this case. First was whether the appellant's painting of Balasubrahmania, the childhood representation of a Hindu deity, was original as "the subject dealt with in that picture was a common subject in which no copyright could be acquired by anyone". Second was whether the respondent's painting was an original drawing entitled to copyright or a mere copy of the appellant's painting violating his copyright.

The Madras High Court answered the first question in the affirmative. It reiterated the legal principle that the essential requirement of originality is expenditure of original skill or labour in execution and not originality of thought. Though pictorial representation of Lord Balasubrahmanya in a human form is a conventional subject, a picture of Lord Balasubrahmanya drawn by an artist made up of conventional ideas as to his posture, his form, the ornaments he wears, the vahanam he uses and other matters are still entitled to copyright protection if the picture produced is the result of skill and labour of the artist. The court held that the appellant's painting was the result of his independent skill and labour and thus eligible for copyright protection.

---

[139] Nimmer. Nimmer states that if a highly creative public domain painting is reproduced by a person without contributing anything to it it is ineligible for copyright protection. Similarly, even when a work is entirely the product of an author it may be denied copyright protection if it lacks in a modicum of creativity.

[140] AIR 1961 Mad. 111.

To the second question whether the respondents' picture was an independent production of the artist, employing his own skill and labour, rejecting the trial court's view that there were differences in the features on the face of the God on both the paintings and in other details of the paintings the Court held that the respondent's painting is a substantial copy of the appellant's. It felt that the differences, if any, were the result of a technical process viz., inversion.[141] In the opinion of the court, had the respondent independently created his work there would not have been such striking similarities in the facial lineaments of the boy-God, in the ornaments worn by him, in the features of the peacock and in the particular manner in which a bunch of hair is curled on the forehead of the face. As "Bala Murugan" reproduced in substantial part the special features of the pictures of the God in "Mayura Priya", including his vahanam, the background and the jewels he wears and the features on the face of the figure, the claim of independent creativity by the respondent was rejected by the court and infringement of appellant's copyright upheld. This appears to be the correct approach since mere technical difference, if accepted as sufficient to render a subsequent work copyrightable, contradicts with the copyright objective of maintaining the public domain while rewarding creativity.

In this context it is interesting to examine the decision in a similar case by the same court in *Associated Publishers (Madras), Ltd.* v. *K. Bashyam alias 'Arya'*.[142] The plaintiff in this case created a painting of Mahathma Gandhi by combining two photographs—taking the head from one and the body from the other and then after reversing/inverting it combining it—the court held that "the result is something different and that something was the product of the labours and efforts of the plaintiff".[143] Relying on the Privy Council decision in *Macmillan and Company Ltd.* v. *K. & J. Cooper*[144] (though it related to originality in a literary work) the Court held that the same principles would govern artistic work.

> The true question is whether the same plan, arrangement and combination of materials have been used before for the same purpose or for any other purpose. If they have not been so used, the plaintiff is entitled to a copyright, although he may have gathered hints for his plan and arrangement or parts of his plan and arrangement from existing and known sources. He may have borrowed much of his materials from others, but if they are combined in a different manner from what was in use before, he is entitled to a copyright. It is true that he does not thereby acquire the right to appropriate to himself the materials which were common to all persons before, so as to exclude those persons from a future use of such materials; but then they have no right to use such materials with his improvements

[141] Inversion is a technical process, by which the picture is taken without the head, and then the body is reversed and then the head is fixed to the reversed trunk of "Mayura Priya."

[142] (1962)1MLJ258. Also read The *Daily Calendar Supplying Bureau, Sivakasi* v. *The United Concern* AIR 1967 Mad 381.

[143] The interesting point is that this decision was by the same High Court and it deviated from the earlier position of the Division Bench decision and the judge in the current case was also a member of the Division Bench in the earlier decision.

[144] 1923 (1924) 26 BOMLR 292: AIR 1924 PC 175.

superadded, whether they consist in plan, arrangement, or illustrations, or combinations, for these are strictly his own.

The court held that though it is difficult to state any principle upon which the standard is based, and to specify the precise amount of the knowledge, labour, judgment or skill or taste which the artist must bestow upon his composition in order to acquire a copyright, the plaintiff definitely expended skill and labour in making such a combination, and that is sufficient for copyright protection.

It is felt that the court went wrong in accepting differences introduced exclusively based on technical changes as originality. The plaintiff simply copied the head from one photograph and the body from another and just laterally reversed the body and then combined both. Similarities even in minute details that existed between the plaintiff's painting and the two photographs were established before the court. Still it held that the difference resulting from technical act is sufficient to constitute originality. It is clear that the Privy Council decision was wrongly interpreted by the Court since we have already seen that it insisted on an additional input from the part of the author, apart from mere selection and combination to attract originality.

Interestingly, the court answered the second question, if the defendant's painting was an independent creation or a copyright violation, in favour of the plaintiff since it felt that the minor differences that appear in both is a result of deliberate attempt from the part of the defendant and therefore it is a copy of the plaintiff's painting.

In *Daily Calendar Supplying Bureau, Sivakasi* v. *The United Concern*[145] the Court found that the reproduction of the substantial parts of the painting of the plaintiff by the defendant in his picture was to such an extent that both the pictures were mathematically exact.[146] The only differences found were in the colour scheme, shape of the face, nature of the curly hair, and the nose, better proportioned lips and fingers, ornaments in the ears, dreamier eyes, ornamented vel, younger and more beautiful looks etc. The Court felt that these variations should have been made by the defendants only after they had incorporated in their picture the substantial features of the plaintiff's painting, already referred to, most probably by using a photographic process. The Court held that there was substantial copying of the plaintiff's painting by the defendant since it was satisfied, upon a careful perusal of

---

[145] AIR1967Mad381.

[146] The plaintiff established this by a well-known photographic process by reducing both his painting and the defendant's painting to exactly similar dimensions and then measuring certain dimensions with the help of a pair of dividers. It was thus proved that the measurements of the two pictures tallied. The court found that the measurements of the mouth, the nose, the ear and the palm are equal in both the figures and the distance between the tip of the forehead to the second mark between the forehead where the hair begins and up to the eve-brow where there us a rectangular mark is the same. From the one ear joint to the other ear joint, the jaw measures exactly the same.

the two pictures and the surrounding circumstances, that the defendant's picture reproduced substantial parts of the plaintiff's picture, its plan, its design, its arrangement of all the important component parts, which help an artist to obtain a representation of the idea of a deity on plastic material. Though the reproducer, after incorporating these elements in his painting added a deeper colour to the lips or gave a darker shade to the hair or made it more curly, added to the vel a few ornaments or even lengthen the Vel by a few inches, the essential reproduction of the substantial features of the plaintiff's picture had already been effected and that constitutes the infringement of the copyright. The facts of this case, especially the measurements effected after the photographic reduction of the two pictures to the same size, show that the defendant, who brought out his picture for the first time in 1958 should have utilised one of the several copies of the plaintiff's original from which he made a reproduction, and therefore, satisfied that the defendants have been guilty of infringement of the plaintiff's copyright.

3.1.3 Musical Work

Originality requirement in musical works is an interesting issue. As in the case of any other work, here also, striking a balance between protecting original creativity and promoting further creativity is the major issue.[147] In the context of musical works, originality is most often found in melody and it only requires independent effort and not novelty.[148] However, Nimmer is of the view that the creativity creative requirement with respect to musical work is the "overall impression… of a new work."[149] In other words, unlike in the case of literary work, where the lay observer test is the least welcome, here the listener test has some significance. It is the expression that attracts the listener. In music, distinguishing between idea and expression is an impossible task.[150]

Ram Sampath v Rajesh Roshan[151] is a case in which the issue was infringement of a musical work in the plaintiff's musical composition/theme tune titled "The THUMP". Plaintiff alleged that the music contained in the soundtrack of the film the Krazzy 4 was a copy of his musical composition/theme tune 'THE THUMP". In particular, it was alleged, that the music of two songs viz. "KRAZZY 4" and "Break Free" contained copies of the theme tune "The THUMP". The musical work "The THUMP" was of a duration of 1 min whereas the entire film "KRAZZY 4" was

---

[147] Keyt 1988. Available at: http://scholarship.law.berkeley.edu/californialawreview/vol76/iss2/5.

[148] Nimmer.

[149] *Ibid.*

[150] Supra n. 145, at pp. 442, 443. Also read Castanaro 2008, Also read Michael Keyes 2004 and Smith 1983.

[151] 2009 (40) PTC 78.

about 2.15 h. The two songs "KRAZZY 4" and "Break Free" with two remixes thereof were of 4 1/2 and 2 1/2 min respectively. The music in those songs which was allegedly similar to the plaintiff's work "The THUMP" was not of more than a few seconds. The defendant has admitted that four bars of total duration of 6 s (which are the same as or similar to the bars of the plaintiffs musical work) are played 4–5 times in the song "Break Free" and in the title at the end of the film.

The Court held that the true test in deciding whether the latter musical work is a copy or plagiarism of the former is by way of examination as to whether a person ignorant about music, on listening the latter musical work, would be reminded of the former which he might have listened several days before, the latter is a copy of the former.

The court felt that though a musical work may have a length of several minutes, the listener often remembers a "catch part" to which he is immediately hooked on. It is necessary to look for such "catch part" or the "hook part". If the "catch part" or "hook part", howsoever small, is copied infringement can be presumed In the present case, though the part which is copied is small and is only of 6 s, it is repeated at least four to five times in the defendants' work even as per their own admission. From this the Court reached the conclusion that "what is worth copying 4–5 times over in the same work is most certainly worth protecting". In this case originality in musical work is identified with "catch part" or "hook part" of the music.

The Court has relied on the following statement of Copinger on copyright law to see what constitutes infringement of musical work:

> As to whether a substantial part of a musical work has been copied, the question remains whether the alleged infringement has made use of a substantial part of the skill, labour and taste of the original composer… It is clear that a relatively short part of a work can amount to a substantial part, particularly if what has been taken is the vital or essential part of the work, as opposed to being musical commonplace. A relevant question may be whether the amount taken is so small that it is impossible to recognise the original work, or whether it can still be recognised, but where the part taken has been added to other material." Where the claimant's work contains material that was not original to him, then in the usual way these parts should be left out of the comparison exercise and attention centred on those parts which were original. Particularly in the field of popular music, the vital or essential part of the work may be a short refrain or hook line. The problem becomes even more acute with the modern practice of "sampling", whereby a short piece of music is taken and often repeated many times in the making of a new recording. The same point arises in relation to 'ringtones'. The piece taken is often a distinctive part of the original work and thus immediately recognisable, which is of course the reason why it was taken. In cases of this kind, although it will be relevant to ask whether the piece which was copied was the result of any particular inventiveness on the part of the original author or was, for example, merely a hackneyed phrase, it is suggested that it will often be appropriate in these cases to apply the rule of thumb that "what is worth copying is worth protecting.

It appears that the 'catch part' or 'hook part' of every song is something peculiar to it or something exclusive to it and therefore constitute its original expression. Therefore this judgement is correct in the context of musical work.

4 Conclusion

An overview of the judicial pronouncements on copyrightability and copyright subject matter reveals an intricate situation: on the one hand, a gradually evolving sincere effort to strike the correct balance between private rights and public domain, and on the other, a brazenly callous attitude of handling copyright issues. One cannot assure that the situation is gradually improving since some of the recent judgements reveal the uncanny attitude of the judiciary in India. The country has evolved a pretty good jurisprudence in areas relating to idea expression dichotomy, merger doctrine and originality threshold. Though there were moments of wavering, the Indian judiciary has regained the balance on other occasions. Had the judiciary bothered to appreciate the objectives of copyright law viz., to incentivize further creativity and to facilitate dissemination of such creative output, it would have strived to reach at more balanced conclusions.

References

Abrams HB (1992) Originality and creativity in copyright law. Law Contemp Probl 55:1

Benkler Y (1999) Free as the air to common use: first amendment constraints on enclosure of the public domain, 74 N.Y.U. L. Rev. 354, 357

Castanaro VM (2008) It's the same old song: the failure of the originality requirement in musical copyright. Fordham Intell Prop Media Ent LJ 18:1271

Chafee Z (1945) Reflections on copyright law: I. Columbia Law Rev 45: 503, at p 506

Denicola R (1983) Applied art and industrial designs: a suggested approach to copyright in useful articles. Minnesota Law Rev 67:707, at p 712

Dowd JR (1992) A selective view of history: Feist publications, Inc. v. Rural telephone service C. B.C.L Rev 34:137, at 146

Ginsburg JC (1989) French copyright law: a comparative overview. J Copr Soc'y 36:269–285

Goldstein P, Huganholtz B (2010) International Copyright. Oxford University Press

Goldstein (1996) Copyright, second edition § 2.2.1.4 (2:9)

Karjala DS (2006) Harry potter, Tanya grotter, and the copyright derivative work. Ariz State Law J 38:17, at p 24

Kurtz LA (1989) Copyright: the scenes a faire doctrine. Fla L Rev 41:79

Keyes JM (2004) Musical musings: the case for rethinking music copyright protection. Mich Telecomm Tech L Rev 10:407, 421, 424

Keyt A (1988) An improved framework for music plagiarism litigation. 76 Cal L Rev 421

Landes WM, Posner RA (1989) An economic analysis of copyright law. J Legal Stud 325–363, at p. 326

Murray MD (2006) Copyright, originality, and the end of the *scènes à faire* and merger doctrines for visual works. Baylor Law Rev 58:779, at 782

Nimmer MB, Nimmer D (2010) Nimmer on Copyright, § 2–12

Samuelson P (2013) A fresh look at tests for non-literal copyright infringement. Northwest Univ Law Rev 1821 107

Smith R (1983) Arrangements and editions of public domain music: originality in a finite system. Case W Res L Rev 34:104, 104

Yen AC (1991) The legacy of feist: the consequences of a weak connection between copyright and the economics of public goods. Ohio State Law J 52: 1343–1378, at 1344

The Economics of Intellectual Property and Economic Entrepreneurship of Copyrights

Rodney D. Ryder and N.S. Sreenivasulu

Abstract Intellectual property rights have been recognized on the foundation of economic viability and entrepreneurship. Concernment of copyright also provides for economic entrepreneurship in certain industries in particular in the creative industries including the media. Perhaps, law of copyright developed in the lines of development of creative industry and the media. Copyright which was once considered not as a commercially viable right, has become significant contributor to the commercial entrepreneurship in the creative industry and the media. The growth of various winds of media such as print media, electronic media film media and the digital media have contributed vehemently in realizing the commercial entrepreneurship in copyright. In the contemporary world, when we analyze the fabric of creative industry and observe the nuts and bolts of activities of the media, one can understand the significance of copyright and the important role that it plays in these sectors. It is argued that more than scientific, technological or creative contribution; it is the commercial viability and the economic entrepreneurship that drives the intellectual property rights regime. Infact, the basic justification for the conferment of intellectual property rights including copyright is largely dependent on the entrepreneurship flavor of these rights. In this background, the current chapter examines the economic justifications of intellectual property rights and the commercial entrepreneurship of copyrights.

1 Introduction

Creation of knowledge and access to knowledge have transformed the economy. Intellectual property rights are the modes and means of knowledge economy. Perhaps it is a term which has been named after the world of knowledge. In 1969

R.D. Ryder
Advocate, Supreme Court of India, New Delhi, India
e-mail: rodney@scriboard.com

N.S. Sreenivasulu (✉)
National University of Juridical Sciences, Kolkata, India
e-mail: seenukushi@yahoo.co.in

M.K. Sinha and V. Mahalwar (eds.), *Copyright Law in the Digital World*,
DOI 10.1007/978-981-10-3984-3_2

'Peter Ducker' coined the term 'knowledge economy.[1] It is all about value and value addition to the knowledge when such knowledge is extremely useful in the growth of the economy. In the second half of the twentieth century, the knowledge economy transformed capitalism to the point where knowledge replaced plants, equipment, and labor as the means of creating value.[2] Today if knowledge is the means for creating value, then intellectual property is the means for extracting that value.[3] Similarly, being a branch of intellectual property, copyright has been the basis of economic entrepreneurship for certain industries in the contemporary world. The current chapter dwells on the economic background and basis for intellectual property rights. At the same time, it analyses the economic entrepreneurship of copyrights in select industries.

2 Economics of Intellectual Property Rights

Economic factors largely determine the law and policy with reference to protection and promotion of intellectual property. Perhaps, it is more so in case of intellectual property in the modern context. It is very much felt that economic reasons have influenced in the promotion of intellectual property rights all over the world.[4] At this juncture an inquiry into the economic dimensions and justifications for intellectual property is an interesting business. There are various types of intellectual property rights recognized by the law where the creator of knowledge would enjoy certain privileges and rights. The driving force behind all these different types of intellectual property rights is their economic significance. In general, intellectual property rights are conferred upon those innovations and creations which are useful or have commercial value. Industrial demand or commercial viability is one among the different requirements of conferment of intellectual property rights. It is not just creativity or innovativeness but the economic significance of the same is required to be honored with intellectual property rights. In the market driven world, economics is of greater significance. The intellectual property regime perceives that research and development should not be just of academic interest, but rather it should have some economic and industrial significance in the market to entail protection and reward through conferment of intellectual property rights. Although intellectual property is intangible in character, it consists of bundle of property rights. For instance, patent gives right to make, use, sell, transfer the patented invention. The objective of the intellectual property regime is to promote and protect innovation and creation and reward innovative and creative activity.[5] For the functioning of the

[1] Ducker 1969.

[2] Florida and Kenny 1991.

[3] Arena and Carreras 2008.

[4] Sreenivasulu 2013.

[5] US Council for International Business 1985.

economy in an effective way, innovation and creation are essential. Especially in the competitive free market economy, innovations and creations keep the upsurge of the economy guaranteed.

In this context, innovation and creation are very much required for economic growth and prosperity. The perspective that individuals are able to acquire property right over the result of their investment is encouraging individuals and enterprises to invest in research and development.[6] These property rights would be granted to one who can economically maximize profits.[7] Intellectual property rights enhance economic development of the nation. Therefore, it is more because of its economic dimensions that intellectual property rights are protected than the scientific or technological reasons. There is always an element of scientific or technological progress and importance that every protected intellectual property brings forth. But the reality is that the scientific or technological elements or features however meritorious, they may be not sufficient to grant intellectual property rights without the presence of economic dimensions of such scientific or technological progress. Hence, you don't get protection under the intellectual property regime for scientific or technological progress without economic value being attached to it. Any justifications for the protection of intellectual property rights have been influenced by the economic significances of these rights.

3 Economic Justifications for Intellectual Property Rights

In general proprietary right resulted out of labor is known as property. Property is nothing but proprietary right resulted out of labor. One who labors, deserves certain reward in the form of proprietary rights. Here, there is no difference between physical or mental labor as such. But when it comes to intellectual property, it is always the result of mental labor. Since intellectual property is a form of property in the legal sense, it is always measured in terms of economic value attached to it in the market. In a market driven economy, goods and products having potential economic value would have huge demand and commercial viability. Jurisprudentially speaking, one deserves rights over his labor, irrespective of whether it is physical labor or mental labor. In this context, few theories on the jurisprudential meaning and connotations of property are very much relevant.[8] While searching for economics of intellectual property, generally jurists fall back on the original theories of property and proprietary rights.

---

[6] Lunn 1985.

[7] Lehmann 1989.

[8] Sreenivasulu 2011.

4 Economics of Labour Value

Intellectual property rewards the efforts involved in the production of some work. Efforts are always measured in terms of labor and labour, either physical or mental attached with some material or commercial value. The classical labor theory of jurisprudence is of great relevance in the context of property and proprietary rights. Famous English jurist John Locke propounded the labor theory. John Locke states that human labor deserves certain proprietary rights. According to him, whoever labors deserves reward in the form of proprietary rights.[9] Originally, labor theory does not specifically talk about physical or mental labor. Perhaps when locke propounded the theory since labour was understood merely as the physical labour, the justifications for property and proprietary rights were all around physical labour only. The opponents of intellectual property contend that at the time when Locke propounded this theory he may not have thought of mental labor. The proponents of intellectual property protection however contend that his theory seems to have no reservations in its application and it needs not be restricted only to physical labor. According to the pro intellectual property thinkers; it is felt that conceiving and executing ideas involve mental work, which could be considered as mental labor. Since there are no restrictions or reservations with respect to the concept of labour which could be either physical or mental, there shall be equal application of jurisprudential theories. Therefore, the labor theory, which rewards the one who labors, could also justify reward for the one who does mental labor. On these lines, protection of intellectual property rights which are result of mental labor, could be justified under the Locke's Labor theory.

5 Economics of Utility

Further, the Utilitarian theory[10] propounded by the English jurist Jeremy Bentham states that maximum benefit of the maximum members of the society should be guaranteed by the law in force and in the regulation there under. In terms of economics, intellectual property should provide benefits both at micro level and at macro level as well. At micro level, intellectual property should reward those who endeavored in creating the intellectual property while attaching value to it. At macro level, creation and use of intellectual property should provide overall benefit to the mass or the society in terms of providing the addition to the existing knowledge in the society which is commercially sought after. Intellectual property rights serve the purpose of being an initiative or encouragement for innovative or creative work, which does ultimately benefit the society. The owner of the intellectual property is supposed to work on the subject of intellectual property and

[9] Chisum 1998.

[10] Ibid, pp. 45–47.

make it and its proceeds available to the public. Hence, the proceeds of mental labor or intellectual property rights ultimately reach the public. Besides, intellectual property rights are granted to the owner for a particular period of time after which the intellectual work falls into the public domain and there could be no restrictions on public usage of such work thereafter. Further, intellectual property rights are protected only when they are capable of industrial application. The purpose of industrial application of any innovative work is to exploit the work commercially, market it and make it available to the public. Considerably, the maximum benefit of any subject of intellectual property protection would be reaped by the public at large. In this way, intellectual property rights serve the purpose of maximum benefit of the maximum members of the society. Therefore, it is argued that the utilitarian theory also justifies the reward for intellectual efforts in the form of conferment of intellectual property rights and their protection.

6 Economics of Personality

The third theory which is being considered for justifying the intellectual property rights would be personality theory propounded by Hegel. The personality theory also has got to say something with respect to protection of property rights in intellectual efforts. The theory states that property is extension of one's personality and it is personality which blooms through the protection of one's proprietary rights. Here, one can assume that individual personality has got some economic importance in terms of bestowing the outcome with individual or personal identification and status which is nothing but personal extension or extension of personality of the creator or the owner. Intellectual property values the economics of personal extension. Though, people might argue that Hegel's personality theory does not say anything specifically about intellectual property. However, the theory was general in nature and non-specific with respect to neither physical property rights nor non-physical property rights. Besides, there is nothing according to Hegel's theory which would prohibit protecting and possessing non-physical property rights. Therefore, there is nothing wrong if one say that Hegel's personality theory is in support of protecting and possessing property rights. There may not be anything specific and particular about protection of intellectual property rights under the theory, but there is nothing against intellectual property rights. Nevertheless, the jurisprudential notions and philosophical foundations of the theory justify possessing property rights in general. Logically, intellectual property is also a form of property; it might be a peculiar type of property but still a property which is logically justified and having rationale under the theory. Besides, any theory, policy and practice for that matter would not have contingency arrangement or would not be wholly comprehensive to meet the various needs. Moreover, when the logic and rationality is firm and viable, specificity is irrelevant. The advocates of intellectual property and people in support of protection of intellectual property do take account of John Locke's Labor theory, Jeremy

Bentham's Utilitarian theory and Hegel's Personality theory[11] for justifying the protection offered to non-physical property rights such as intellectual property rights. Infact, in the market driven world of contemporary times, it is economic factors which play vital role in the policy making than the other reasons. No doubt intellectual property rights are having enormous economic value and viability and therefore there should not be any problem for offering protection and promotion to intellectual property rights.

7 Economics of Copyright

Having discussed the economics of intellectual property and the justifications for protecting intellectual property which are majorly based on economics involved there in, let us have an idea on economics of copyright in detail. Works in literary, scientific and artistic domain are evidently both the creation and the expression of the culture of a society. They are the reflections of the norms and values a society lives by and of the activities, aspirations and achievements of its people in various fields. These works influence the people in a very fundamental way. Who has not been molded by books of history, religion or literature? Who has not been swayed by music coming to him via radio, television, a CD, a film or a live concert? The cultural significance of creative works is self evident from the way they enrich the lives of the people, entertain them, uplift their mood, become a vehicle of emotional catharsis and give a meaning and substance to life. The cultural significance of copyright and related rights lies in the extent to which they spur creation of such works and bring them to the public. Their economic significance lies in their ability to contribute to the national economy, through the industries, which are essentially based on products/activities in which copyright subsists, e.g. publishing, music, films, and computer software. In recent years, scholars and researchers have undertaken studies which reflect and provide substantial evidence for the tremendous contribution of copyright and related rights, to the national economies. It should be understood that intellectual property in general and its link with economic development is a complex issue and is a subject matter of intense debates in academic realm. The focus of this chapter is basically to analyze the economic characteristics of copyright and related rights, which till date have been studied basically from a legal perspective. However, it is increasingly becoming clearer that copyright plays an important part in our everyday lives in all fields which may be production or distribution or consumption. The discussion will be initiated with a listing of industries where the economic character of copyright can be easily visible and thereafter a brief survey of some of these main industries or economic activities.

[11] Sreenivasulu 2013.

8 Industries Based on Copyright and Related Rights

WIPO in its Guide on Surveying the Economic Contribution of the Copyright based Industries, on the basis of the comparison between the various studies and approaches, has listed nine groups of core copyright industries and they are as follows:

1. press and literature;
2. music, theatrical productions, operas;
3. motion picture and video;
4. radio and television;
5. photography;
6. software and databases;
7. visual and graphic arts;
8. advertising services; and
9. Copyright collective management societies.

Apart from the above core industries which have been explained as industries that are wholly engaged in creation, production and manufacturing, performance, broadcast, communication and exhibition, or distribution and sales of works and other protected subject matter, there are other categories of industries where copyright plays an important role though not dominant. These categories are:

Interdependent Copyright Industries: Industries that are engaged in production, manufacture and sale of equipment whose function is wholly or primarily to facilitate the creation, production or use of works and other protected subject matter. Though not an exhaustive list, some of the industries included in this category are TV sets, Radios, VCRs, CD Players, DVD Players, Cassette Players, Electronic Game equipment, and other similar equipment; computers and equipment; and musical instruments. Photographic and cinematographic instruments; photocopiers; blank recording material; and paper.

Partial Copyright Industries: Industries in which a portion of the activities is related to works and other protected subject matter and may involve creation, production and manufacturing, performance, broadcast, communication and exhibition or distribution and sales. Some of the industries included in this category include apparel, textiles and footwear; jewellery and coins; other crafts; furniture; household goods, china and glass; wall coverings and carpets; toys and games; architecture, engineering, surveying; interior design; and museums.

Non-dedicated Support Industries: Industries in which a portion of the activities is related to facilitating broadcast, communication, distribution or sales of works and other protected subject matter, and whose activities have not been included in the core copyright industries. Industries included in this category include general wholesale and retailing; general transportation; and telephony and Internet. Clearly these industries play a very important part not only in our everyday lives but in national economies in general. Of course the new technology especially the development of information technology is challenging the set norms.[12] Similarly copyright-based industries played a very important role in other economies including India where it contributed about 5% of the GNP with film industry, book industry and computer software industry taking the lead. Clearly from above as of date the role of copyright in economic development need not be further highlighted. We will now discuss the role of copyright industries in the national economy of India with respect to few sectors and also briefly highlight the challenges faced by them as of date. Some of these sectors are:

1. Software Industry
2. Entertainment Industry
3. Publishing Industry.

9 Computer Software Industry

The rapid development of the software industry has caused it to be identified as a key resource for economic development. Though compared to some other economies, the Indian software industry is still considered to be in its infancy though as per the provided by National Association of Software and Services Company (NASSCOM) the industry was worth US $ 22 billion in the year 2004–05. Also over a million people are employed in this industry and with a rapid expansion rate approximately at 30% annually has ensured that the IT industry's dominant role in the national economy. The Standard Industrial Classification Codes (SIC) of the United States Government lists nine industries as part of computer software industry i.e. Custom Computer Programming Services, Pre-packaged Software, computer Integrated Systems Design, Data Processing and Preparation, Information retrieval Services, Computer Facilities Management, Computer rental and Leasing, Computer Maintenance and repair and Computer related Services. Of the above segments, Custom Computer Programming Services, custom Designing Services and Pre-Packaged Software can be described as the "Core" Software industry.

[12] The important role of copyright industries in the GDP of a national economy can be simply gauged from the statistical figures as follows: In the United States Economy "total" copyright industries accounted for an estimated $1.38 trillion or 11.12% of GDP in 2005, up from 11.09% of the U.S. GDP ($1.3 trillion) in 2004. In terms of employment the "total" copyright industries employed 11.3 million workers in 2005 (8.49%), up from 11.2 million workers in 2004 (8.53%). In the fifteen member European Union copyright based industries contributed about 5.27% of the GDP in the year 2004. In Singapore copyright based industries generated about 8.7 billion, i.e. about 5.7% of the GDP. In Australia in the year 2006/2007 Australia's copyright industries employed about 8% of the nation's workforce and generated about $97.7 billion in economic activity, i.e. 10.3% of GDP.

10 Protection Under the Copyright Law

Under the Act, computer programs are included in the definition of 'literary work.' The term 'computer' includes any electronic or similar device having information processing capabilities, and 'computer program' means a set of instructions expressed in words, code, schemes or in any other form including a machine readable medium, capable or causing a computer to perform a particular task or achieve a particular result. The TRIPs Agreement[13] vide Article 10(1) mandates that 'computer programs', whether in source or object code, shall be protected as literary works under the Berne Convention (1971)'. Further the WCT states that 'computer programs are protected as literary works within the meaning of Article 2 of the Berne Convention. In brief, the need for protection of rights in computer programs was first felt in 1970s with the development of microprocessors and consequently cheap personal computing machines. Owing to such developments it became possible to make copies of computer programs cheaply and easily. Since the costs of creation of software was high and the cost of copying in comparison was almost negligible a need was felt for a law that could adequately protect legitimate interests of the creators of the software. Thereafter, the WIPO Model Provisions on the protection of Computer Programs, 1978 (the Model Provisions) provided a framework to protect computer programs within the existing intellectual property rights regime. The Model Provisions though never were formally implemented found expression in the TRIPs Agreement and WCT[14] wherein computer programs are protected as stated above. In literary works, copyright protection extends to computer programs and to instructions encoded on silicon chips. The words "*schemes or in any other form*" in the definition of the term 'computer program' would seem to indicate that the source code and object code of a computer program are entitled to copyright protection. To emphasize, we go back to Article 10 (1) of the TRIPs Agreement, which clearly states that computer program whether in source or object code shall be protected as literary works. Of course copyrightability is subject to the normal requirements of originality in a literary work as discussed previously. It should be stated that predominantly, the courts are in favour of extending copyright protection to the object code of a computer programme and have extended protection beyond the program's literal code to their structure, sequence and organization.

11 Challenge of Piracy

Software piracy is the theft of software through illegal copying of programmes or through counterfeiting and distribution of imitation software products or unauthorized versions of software products. Technological advancements, particularly,

[13] Sreenivasulu 2013.

[14] Sreenivasulu 2013.

faster transmission online transmission speeds, sophisticated compression software and faster Internet connections have facilitated the emergence of the Internet as an international piracy facilitator. Globally, piracy has increased to such a level that for every two dollars of software bought legally, one dollars worth is obtained illegally. Clearly, piracy is a challenge to the software industry and it has been found that the problem is endemic in large as well as small Indian companies while the problem at retail and wholesale level is a regular practice. With the software piracy rate in India estimated to almost 74%, clear impact is being felt at all levels of the industry. Therefore, an effective intellectual property regime helps to fight such a menace. A research study conducted by IDC titled *Expanding Global Economies: The Benefits of Reducing Software Piracy* estimates that even a 10% reduction in piracy rate will create 50,000 new high tech jobs and add an additional USD 92 million in tax revenues. The study also indicates that reduction in piracy rates by even 10% would ensure the global IT sector grow at 49%. Example is being given of United Arab Emirates where with an intellectual property regime, piracy rate has come down making the country a sort after IT hub. Apart from civil remedies, the Indian Act also contains penal provisions to fight piracy, the industry suggested further amendments to ensure stricter enforcement of copyrights with respect to software. Some amendments have been suggested namely:

1. Ensuring continuous trial of infringement cases and speedy disposal of cases.
2. Increase the penalties with substantial penal sanctions and a comprehensive implementation plan.
3. To address the issue of Internet piracy in the Act.
4. To address the issue of circumvention of copyright protection technologies and to specifically make such circumvention a criminal offence.
5. Optical Disc regulations be enforced wherein manufacturers of CD's/Optical Discs are required by statute to be licensed and registered with an appropriate government authority.
6. To sensitize officers of the enforcement regime with respect o the serious nature of the offence and the consequences arising thereof and other suggestions.

12 Entertainment Industry

The Indian entertainment industry consists of film, music, television, radio and live entertainment.[15] The Indian entertainment industry has many segments. The software segment comprises of films, music and programmes, which are basically involved in the creation of content. The hardware segment includes studios and

[15] According to a report released by CII-KPMG146, the size of the Indian entertainment industry with an annual growth rate of about 18% would be about Rupees 588 Billion by 2010. The report also suggests that television industry will form the largest chunk overtaking the film industry, and constitute over 60% of its revenues.

other services that support the creation of entertainment software. The services segment encompasses distribution, exhibition, film procurement and banking services. Finally, the front-end media segment, which includes film magazines, videocassettes and theatres, act as an interface between the entertainment industry and the audience. Each of the above mentioned segments has a stake in the success of the entertainment industry and more so with the content creation segment. In the year 2001, film was accorded industry status by the Central Government thus making it eligible for film financing from banks and financial institutions.[16] The Indian entertainment industry is today in the midst of a paradigm shift where the largely unregulated industry is increasingly adopting business systems and processes to provide a corporate like structure with a focused eye on the financial aspects of entertainment. The Indian film industry is showing signs of transformation at the operating level as it begins to embrace corporatization and organized business structures. New technology is another peg contributing to rapid expansion. The key driver for the entertainment industry in next decade would be technology. In the new converged paradigm, its boundaries will be merged with those of the telecommunications and information technology segments. This will give rise to a host of value added features for consumers and new revenue streams with the players in cash segment. Mobile entertainment with its abilities to dissect the boundaries of time and space will be the biggest growth driver. The main drivers to growth of the entertainment industry are the addition of new platforms in different segments such as satellite radio and DTH for the television industry.

13 Protection Under the Copyright Law

Copyright plays an important role in the entertainment industry and the Act provides comprehensive protection to various categories of works namely—musical works, sound recordings, and cinematograph films. The Act also extends protection to performers and broad casting organisations. Apart from protection to the economic rights, the Act also envisages protection to the moral rights, i.e. the right of paternity and right of integrity. Clearly the Indian Act is in conformity with the TRIPs Agreement and is one of the most modern statutes. The courts too have strictly dealt with infringement or any violation of copyright in the entertainment industry. In *R.G. Anand* v. *Deluxe Films*[17] the Supreme Court commented that "it seems to us that the fundamental idea of violation of copyright or imitation is the violation of Eighth Commandant: '*Thou shalt not steal*', which forms the moral basis of the protective provisions of the Copyright Act."

[16] The Industrial Development Bank of India (IDBI) set up the country's first film fund worth Rs. 100 crores.

[17] 1978 AIR 1613, 1979 SCR (1) 218.

14 The Problem of Piracy

However amidst all the brouhaha is the monster of piracy, which is arguably the biggest challenge, facing the Indian entertainment industry. US-India Business Council (USIBC) in its study titled 'The Effects of Counterfeiting and Piracy on India's Entertainment industry' states that the industry loses some 820,000 jobs and about USD 4 billion every year to piracy.[18] Though piracy is a non-bailable cognizable offence under the Act, its enforcement is, to say the least, tardy. Another problem in tackling piracy stems from advancement of technologies such as Digital Versatile Discs (DVD). For instance 30,000 copies of DVDs appeared in the American market barely a week after the theatrical release of film Devdas there. Similarly, pirated cassettes of Indian films appear in the Pakistani market barely 2 or 3 days after they are released internationally. Malaysia is another big centre for piracy of Indian films.[19] Courts in India have been strict with infringement and piracy activities and have generally recognised the role of stringent copyright laws in combating piracy. In *State of Andhra Pradesh* v. *Nagoti Venkataramma*[20] the Supreme Court while commenting upon the 1984 amendments in the Act held that:

> The object of amending the Copyright Act was to prevent piracy which became a global problem due to rapid advances in technology. The legislature intended to prevent piracy and punish the pirates, protecting copyrights. The law therefore, came to be amended introducing Section 52-A. Thereafter, the piracy of cinematograph films and of sound recordings etc. could be satisfactorily prevented." The court went on to add that, "it is unnecessary for the prosecution to track on the trace out the owner of the Copyright to come and adduce evidence of infringement of copyright. The absence thereof does not constitute lack of essential element of infringements of copyright. If the particulars on video films etc. as mandated under Section 52-A do not find place, it would be infringement of copyright.

In India, video/cable piracy is on the rise and takes away significant portions of revenues from the producers of films and records and also the access to the legitimate markets of copyright holders. The judiciary has been proactive in granting injunctions against such activities. In *Mirabai Films Pvt. Ltd. v Siti Cable Network,*[21] the Delhi High Court granted a temporary injunction restraining telecasting/screening/exhibiting of the film 'Monsoon Wedding' on cable networks. In *Entertaining Enterprises v State of Tamil Nadu,*[22] the unauthorized exhibition of a film through videotapes was held to be violative of the copyright in the

[18] The CII-KPMG report estimates losses due to piracy at about Rupees 4.3 Billion which amounts to over 40% of the industry's total revenues.

[19] The International Intellectual Property Alliance 2005 Special Report 301 states that pirated VCDs, DVDs, and CD-Rs containing U.S. motion pictures cause severe damage in the markets in India. Most are available in major cities well before the local theatrical release of the title (so-called "pre-release" piracy).

[20] 1996 INSC 991 (20 August 1996).

[21] 2003 (26) PTC 473 Del.

[22] AIR 1984 Mad 278.

cinematograph film. Recent developments in the USA need to be looked at, where new modes of copyright infringement are emerging, with which both law and technology must keep pace. In the case of *MGM Studios Inc.* v. *Grokster Ltd.*,[23] the rule pronounced by the US Supreme Court was that "it is illegal to distribute a device (including software), with the object of promoting its use to infringe copyright, as shown by clear expression or other affirmative steps taken to foster infringement." However, the problem of piracy looms large over the Indian entertainment industry and various industry forums and initiatives have made representations to the government to bring in reforms in the copyright laws and its enforcement. Some of the suggestions made are as follows:

- Ensuring continuous trial of infringement cases and speedy disposal of cases.
- Mandatory punishment of convicted offenders with the minimum sentence of six months imprisonment.
- Requiring the infringer to pay statutory damages to the concerned owner of the copyright.
- To address the issue of Internet piracy specifically in the Act.
- Appointment of a special Public Prosecutor in relation to software related offences.
- Addressing Internet Piracy and ratifying the WIPO Treaties.

15 Publishing Industry

The publishing sector of India is the seventh largest in the world with about 70,000–80,000 titles and includes books, newspapers, magazines, periodicals and academic journals being published every year and the industry growth rate is estimated between 10 and 30%. The value of the publishing market in India is estimated to be about Rs. 11,000 crores of which publications in English are 40%, followed by Hindi at 25% and thereafter in other regional languages. There are about 16,000 publishers, many of them small, publishing in about 30 languages. Publishing in India however is fragmented and there are no real figures available anywhere. It should be stated that the growth in the publishing sector is also indicative of the economic growth, increase in the children going to schools and colleges, increase in the literacy rates, better standards of education and better marketing and retailing of books.[24] Also with an improvement in paper quality and printing, there is a growing market for outsourcing publishing and high-end pre-press work, which includes editing, typesetting, proofing and printing in India.

[23] 545 U.S. 913.

[24] There is ample scope for growth in educational books, as the world average for enrollment in higher education is 35% whereas in India it is only 10% of the population.

Also, digital technology is revolutionizing publishing industry. E-publishing has opened up channels for self publishing and entrepreneurs who encourage new authors to come to light and reach wider audience.

16 Piracy Issues

The Indian statute is one of the most modern statutes in the world and is in conformity with the TRIPs Agreement and other Treaties and Conventions on the subject. However, piracy is emerging as one big challenge in this sector as well. According to the IIPA report of 2009, rampant piracy of trade books, textbooks, professional books (scientific, technical and medical), and scholarly journals continues to plague the publishing industry, despite the fact that prices for legitimate titles in India are among the lowest in the world. All varieties of pirate books, from poor quality cover to- cover photocopies and obviously pirated cheap reprints, to hardbound, high quality copies of medical reference volumes, remain readily available. The marketing of trade books at stoplights in New Delhi has reached epidemic proportions, despite repeated complaints to the Delhi authorities. It should be stated that book piracy, in India, primarily depends on two factors, namely, the price of the book and its popularity. These two factors positively contribute to piracy. Piracy is generally confined to foreign and good indigenous books. The reason is that these books are demanded in large quantities and are also priced very high. The types of books pirated mostly are medical, engineering and other professional books, encyclopedia and popular fictions.

The piracy is also wide spread with respect to books published by National Council of Educational Research and Training (NCERT), National Open School and Board(s) of Secondary Education. These books even if priced low are having large demand. In terms of percentage, it is believed that about 20–25% of books sold (in number) in the country are pirated. Also, piracy by unauthorized photocopying remains a severe problem for the academic and professional sectors of the industry. Increasingly, sophisticated techniques are allowing photocopy shops to tap into high-end medical markets more than ever before. Raids in 2008 revealed use of high-quality scanning techniques to produce color copies of medical titles, printed straight from the electronic file created on the shop's computer. This allows for clearer reproduction of drawings and figures for students, and such reproductions have been marketed to medical colleges in Madhya Pradesh, Maharashtra, Karnataka, Rajasthan, Delhi, Mumbai and elsewhere. Copying continues at educational institutions as well, sometimes even condoned by the institutions. Wholesale copying of entire books is increasingly complemented or replaced by use of unauthorized compilations in the form of course packs, or "self instructional material" (SIM). These are used both for classroom teaching and distance learning, while the materials for the latter are sometimes found in electronic form. Clearly, the loss to the sector due to rampant piracy is huge and authorities are taking strong actions against such activities.[25] However, enforcement in universities is rare. Clearly not just in India but world over piracy is emerging as one big challenge to the copyright industries and the Internet is further compounding the problem. It has been suggested that a national anti-piracy strategy be formed at the central government level, with the ability to link in the State governments (IPR enforcement is a state responsibility in the Indian federal system,) in a meaningful, enforceable way. Such a strategy could start with a National Anti-Piracy Task Force with a membership that includes judges, prosecutors and police coupled with significant technical training. Most challenging, however, would be judicial reform. Piracy levels will remain essentially unchanged in India without the creation of efficient and deterrent judicial remedies. Recommendations would certainly include the need for reinvigorating the IP cells, setting up special IP prosecutors in each state and establishing specialized IP courts or appointing specialized IP judges. The principal objectives of such courts or judges would be to:

- ease backlogs (IP judges or courts should begin free of backlogs);
- enforce deadlines for adjudication/resolution of piracy cases, and prevent unjustified continuances;
- encourage completion of a set number of "model" cases with deterrent penalties to deliver a message to the Indian public about piracy;
- adopt case management techniques (we understand progress has been recently made on this and on instituting plea bargaining); and,
- Treat piracy as a serious economic crime.

17 Inferences

The objective of the intellectual property regime is to promote and protect innovation and creation and reward innovative and creative activities.[26] For the functioning of the economy in an effective way, innovation and creation are essential. Especially in the competitive free market economy innovations and creations keep the upsurge of the economy guaranteed. In this context, innovation and creation are very much required for economic growth and prosperity. The perspective that individuals are able to acquire property right over the result of their investment is encouraging individuals and enterprises to invest in research and development.[27] These property rights would be granted to one who can economically maximize profits.[28] Intellectual property rights, enhances economic development of the nation.

[25] The year 2008 saw several notable seizures of outward bound shipments by Indian Customs as well as good cooperation from courier and postal services in this respect.

[26] US Council for International Business 1985.

[27] Lunn 1985.

[28] Lehmann 1989.

References

Arena CM, Carreras EM (2008) The business of intellectual property. Oxford University Press, New York

Chisum DS (1998) Cases and materials on principles of patent law. Foundation press, New York, p 35–44

Ducker P (1969) The age of discontinuity: guidelines to our changing society. New York Harper and Row, p 264

Florida R, Kenny M (1991) The new age of capitalism. Futures 25(6):637

Lehmann (1989) Property and Intellectual property-property rights as restrictions on competition in furtherance of competition. IIC 1 at 11 as cited in Holyoaks and Torremans IP Law, 2nd ed. Butterworths, London 1998, p 15

Lunn (1985) The roles of property rights and market power in appropriating innovative output. J Legal Stud 423:425

Sreenivasulu NS (2011) Intellectual property rights, second revised and enlarged edition. Regal Publications, New Delhi, p 6

Sreenivasulu NS (2013) Law relating to Intellectual property, 1st edn. Penguin-Partridge Publications, Bloomington, Indiana, USA

US Council for International Business: A New MTN: Priorities for Intellectual Property (1985), p 3

Jurisprudential Analysis of the Rights of the Users in Copyrighted Works

Yashomati Ghosh

Abstract The advent of Internet and digital technology has revolutionized the way in which people enjoy and access different forms of entertainment. The traditional television, movies, music, radio and book industries have all undergone transformation in the past 10 years through the process of digitization. But in spite of the growing popularity of online distribution of copyrighted works, there is a critical gap in the legal regime applicable to consumers of such works. The traditional protections which consumers of copyrighted works enjoyed in the form of first sale doctrine, consumer rights and fair use rights are denied to them in the digital environment. By means of various technological protection measures as well as fear of litigation, the copyright based industries are controlling the fundamental right of an individual to access such works as well as her ability to creatively deal with it. Such control mechanisms are having a chilling effect on individual freedom as well as on the cultural growth of a society. In order to sustain the benefits of Internet and other advanced technologies, and promote the growth of online market it is necessary to protect the interest of the copyright holders as well as internet consumers. It is important to confer certain rights and freedoms to the consumers so that they will have adequate confidence to take full advantage of the various benefits of online technology and participate fully in the online marketplace. Conferring the consumers with specific rights and freedoms would give them the authority to demand access to new technologies for better enjoyment of Internet without fear of adverse actions. The present era of user-generated culture and the transformation of passive consumers to active users of creative work makes it necessary to grant legal recognition and protection to the rights of users from a social, legal, commercial and humanitarian perspective. In this chapter the jurisprudential foundation of copyright law has been intrinsically deliberated for the purpose of establishing the legal premise for the rights of the users in copyrighted works. The principle the-

Y. Ghosh (✉)
National Law School of India University, Bangalore, India
e-mail: yashomati@nls.ac.in

M.K. Sinha and V. Mahalwar (eds.), *Copyright Law in the Digital World*,
DOI 10.1007/978-981-10-3984-3_3

oretical arguments are derived from the jurisprudential basis of copyright law, consumer law jurisprudence, right to access cultural works based on the human rights argument and the fundamental right arguments.

1 Introduction

Internet was created to facilitate human interactions by means of sharing and communication. The purpose of internet was to create universal platform where individuals from across the world could participate and freely express themselves. Internet and related technologies have provided multiple opportunities for the people to translate their various activities from the physical world to the online world thereby connecting the different facets of human life with the touch of a button. The online connectivity has facilitated the performance of different traditional activities like conducting business, education, communication, watching movies, listening to music etc in the cyber world, but at the same time it has given rise to several problems which are unique to the cyber world and thereby challenging the legal system. Among the different sectors which have been affected by the growth of internet, the copyright based industries are at the forefront. The copyright protection granted to the copyright holders had been adversely affected by the working of the internet because the prevention of unauthorized reproduction which is the core of the copyright law stands significantly challenged by the new technology. Several attempts had been made to deal with the online challenges by enacting new technology specific laws, use of technological protection measures, stringent legislations against copyright infringement and by developing new business models. But these measures in general failed to achieve the desired objective because the aim of all these efforts was to singularly protect the interests of the copyright holders and did not take into consideration the needs and desires of the consumers of the new technology.

In the present era of user-generated culture and the transformation of passive consumers to active users of creative work makes it necessary to grant legal recognition and protection to the rights of users from a social, legal, commercial and humanitarian perspective. In this chapter, the jurisprudential foundation of copyright law has been intrinsically deliberated for the purpose of establishing the legal premise for the rights of the users in copyrighted works. The chapter has been broadly divided into five parts. Part I deals with the analysis of the major jurisprudential theories of intellectual property law for establishing the purpose and objective of copyright law. Part II highlights the opinion of the few leading socio-political thinkers on the social relevancy of copyright law. Part III discusses the judicial interpretations of rights of the copyright holders and the applicability of the doctrine of fair use in some leading jurisdictions. Part IV emphasizes upon the growing recognition of the rights of the internet users in the European Court of Justice and Part V discusses the human rights perspective of copyright law and the need to recognize the rights of the users of intellectual works.

2 Jurisprudential Theories and Copyright Law

The philosophical argument for giving recognition to intellectual and creative works as a form of property is largely derived from the traditional jurisprudential theories of property. Modern scholars have restructured the *labour theory* of John Locke to advocate for copyright law protection.[1] Other jurisprudential theories such as *welfare theory* and the *cultural theory* have also been developed in recent time to advocate for a legal regime of copyright law which balance the claims of the copyright holders with the social interest of members of the community.

2.1 Labour Theory of Property

The foundational basis of the labour theory was laid by John Locke in his *Second Treatise of Government.*[2] In Chap. 5 of the book Locke had discussed the origin and recognition of physical property in human society. He recognized the necessity to legalize the concept of private property for the purpose of bringing in peace, stability and progress in society. He built his argument from the biblical origin of human society. According to him, in the state of nature God gave to men in common the access to all the natural resources for their survival. In such a state of nature, it was the duty of men to preserve themselves and live in comfort by using natural resources like water, fruits and animal. All such resources were freely available and for the common use of all. But these resources could only be used by men by means of exerting labour onto them. Labour added some value to the goods which enhanced the level of human enjoyment of those goods. The concept of private property arose with the recognition of the fact that 'every man has a property in his own person'[3] and no one but himself has right to it. When a person uses his own limbs and puts in his own labour onto the natural resources, he thereby imposes his right on to it and makes it part of his private domain.

> Though the earth, and all inferior creatures, be common to all men, yet every man has a property in his own person: this no body has any right to but himself. The labour of his body, and the work of his hands, we may say, are properly his. Whatsoever then he removes out of the state that nature hath provided, and left it in, he hath mixed his labour with, and joined to it something that is his own, and thereby makes it his property.[4]

Since the physical labour of a person is an integral part of his individual property, the use of such labour on any natural resources excludes those resources from the common heritage of society and makes it the exclusive private property of

---

[1] Fisher 2001.

[2] Locke 1860–1690.

[3] *Id* at Chap. V, Sect. 27.

[4] *Id.*

the individual. The private property extends not only to the fruit borne or the crop grown on the land but also on the land itself wherein the person has put in his labour to till, plant, improve and cultivate the land. Thus, a barren piece of land wherein a man puts his own hard labour and cultivates a crop, the ownership of the man not only extends to the crops produced by the sweat of the man but also to the land on which the cultivation takes place. Such man assumes the proprietorship of the land as well as the crops as a reward for the labour put in by him. Locke proposed that when an individual put in his own 'pain, toil, sweat and labour'[5] in the available resources then he is entitled to the ownership of such property as his reward. By recognition of property rights, society at large is benefited by the increase in the '*common stock of mankind'* and a greater availability of useful resources for the enjoyment of mankind.

> ……he who appropriates land to himself by his labour, does not lessen, but increase the common stock of mankind: for the provisions serving to the support of human life, produced by one acre of inclosed and cultivated land, are (to speak much within compass) ten times more than those which are yielded by an acre of land of an equal richness lying waste in common. And therefore he that incloses land, and has a greater plenty of the conveniences of life from ten acres, than he could have from an hundred left to nature, may truly be said to give ninety acres to mankind[6]

The basic proposition of Locke is that since performance of labour is an undesirable act, society should reward acts of labour with property rights as token of appreciation for the benefits which society at large has derived from the laborious acts of the individual.

Locke's original theory was in relation to physical property, different modern scholars claim that his propositions are more relevant and suitable in justifying the creation of non-physical properties, like intellectual property. The most significant aspect of Locke's theory was the identification of the concept of 'commons' in the state of nature. The 'commons' was the universal resource base from which every individual could collect the requisite resources and create a value-added product which would not only benefit the individual but also the society at large. This newly created value-added product was recognized as the property of the creator as recognition of the labour and efforts put in by the creator. Application of this theory in the field of intellectual property implies identification of the state of commons with the notion of 'ideas'. Unlike in the case of physical property and the available natural resources in the state of commons, 'ideas' form the common resource base in the case of all intellectual properties. Ideas are infinite and available in abundance in the world. An individual can pick an idea, put his own labour and create a piece of work. Such of piece of work becomes the property of the creator by virtue of the labour put in by him. Justin Hughes justifies propertizing ideas under Locke's approach with three propositions: Firstly, the production of ideas requires a person's labour; secondly, that these ideas are appropriated from a 'common' which is

---

[5] *Id* at S. 43.

[6] *Id* at S. 37.

not significantly devalued by the removal of the idea; and thirdly, ideas can be made property without breaching the non-waste or spoilage condition.[7]

The labour theory of intellectual property based on Locke's notion of property is relevant in identifying the relationship between the creators and society. The labour-reward theory along with the notion of commons helps to create a platform whereby the necessity to reward or encourage a person for the labour which he puts in, creates the philosophical justification for recognizing a set of exclusive rights in favour of the creator and at the same time the notion of 'common of ideas' and the 'no-waste' principle makes it mandatory that the grant of exclusive rights to the copyright holders should not affect the interest of society and other users to acquire knowledge and progress with easy access to ideas and information. The intellectual property regime is based on the notion that the legal rights granted to the creators of intellectual works are a way for society to recognize the contribution of the creator, without undermining society's access to the work and the common pool of ideas. In the present day digital world, the principle of balance between the creators and the consumers is being put to challenge by means of various legal and technological measures. But it is implicit that the traditional notion of balance between creators and other consumer needs to be protected and reiterated in the digital environment so as to ensure that true knowledge based progress takes place in the globalized world. Locke's unique notion of common of ideas charters the path towards creation of a balanced intellectual property system between the users and the creators.

2.2 *Welfare Theory of Property*

The welfare theory of property is derived from the utilitarian principles of Jeremy Bentham and from the writings of John Stuart Mill. However the principle scholarship in developing the welfare theory of property is the writing of William M. Landes and Richard A. Posner in their leading essay on copyright law—*An Economic Analysis of Copyright Law.*[8] The theoretical premise of the argument is based on the idea that conferring of property rights should be based on the principle of 'maximization of net social welfare'[9] and it is the primary task of the law makers 'to strike an optimal balance between, on one hand, the power of exclusive rights to stimulate the creation of inventions and works of art, and on the other, the partially offsetting tendency of such rights to curtail widespread public enjoyment of those creations.'[10]

Landes and Posner have argued that since intellectual property is a *public good* the 'cost of creation' of copyrighted works is much higher than the 'cost of

[7] Hughes 1988.

[8] Landes and Posner 1989.

[9] Fisher 2001, *Supra* note 2.

[10] *Id.*

reproduction' of the same work thereby facilitating cheaper and easier copying of works and depriving the creator his ability to recover the cost of creation of the work, it is necessary to 'strike the correct balance between access and incentives' while granting copyright protection.[11] The cost of producing a copyrightable work involves the cost of creation i.e. author's time and effort in creating the work and the cost of publication, production, distribution, promotion of individual copies of the work. For the purpose of incentivizing the author to create further new works, it is necessary that the expected return from the sale of copies of the created work should exceed the expected cost of production of that work. It is necessary for the market to ensure to the author the fair return of the production costs because in the absence of it the author will lack necessary incentive to produce new works and the society will be deprived from accessing new creative works. Copyright law helps in achieving this objective by securing to the author the ability to ensure fair returns of the work created. However, such protection should be optimal so that copyright protection does not act as a factor in increasing the cost of expression and adding to the cost of production. It should be limited in nature and try to balance the needs of authors for copyright protection as well as adequate access to pre-existing works.

Landes and Posner have justified the recognition of fair use as an exception to copyright protection by means of their economic theory based arguments. Firstly, they argue that the transaction costs involved between the user of a copyrighted work and the owner of such work in negotiating the terms of minimal usage are prohibitively high. In such circumstances, the fair use privilege helps the user in obtaining a general permission to use the work without injuring significantly the interests of the copyright holder. Also, if such usages were made subject to legal protection then the cost and time involved in legal proceedings, keeping in view the enormous number of users, and the small amount of compensation to be recovered in return would deter all litigations. Also, establishing a compulsory licensing regime would not resolve the issue because the high transaction costs involved and the need of a huge administrative body to implement the program will adversely affect the cost efficiency factor. Denial of fair use exception will largely affect the growth of new creative works in society. Use of a copyrighted work by a user may be in the nature of *productive fair use* or *reproductive fair use.*[12] *See* Landes and Posner (1989) at 360. It is necessarily a desirable social goal to encourage productive fair use of a work which will facilitate further creations of new works and requirement of prior permission from the copyright holder will not only stifle such creative productions but also increase the cost of production of intellectual works.

The fair use principle also helps in achieving higher societal interests in areas like book review and parody works. Permissibility to a reviewer for free access to limited

[11] Landes (1989), *Supra* note 9 at 326.

[12] A productive use is one that lowers the cost of expression and tends to increase the number of works, while a reproductive one simply increases the number of 'copies' of a given work, reduces the gross profits of the author, and reduces the gross profits of the author, and reduces the incentives to create works.

portions of literary work through review work helps the author in gaining publicity for his work and also helps the readers in getting a general prior idea about the nature of the book before they actually buy or read the book. This mutually beneficial relationship helps in justifying the free access to literary works to the reviewers instead of demanding individual negotiations between the authors and the reviewers for determining the terms and conditions of review. Also, any prior contractual relation between the reviewer and the author will create an apprehension of biasness in the minds of the readers that the probable outcome of the review will not be an independent evaluation of the work but rather an element of favouritism towards the author by the reviewer. These factors along with the high transaction costs involved in individual costs between authors and reviewers justify the fair use exception of review works. Similarly, parody works fulfil the social goals of fair criticism and social ridicule. It is essential to allow the readers to comment and critique on a literary or musical work. The necessity to seek prior approval from the author before indulging in parody compositions will limit the opportunity of making fair criticism because the author may not desire ridiculing of his work and thereby stifle freedom of speech and expression. Justifying the limited duration of copyright protection, Landes and Posner have argued that firstly, limited time period reduces the amount and scope of potential monopoly profits, secondly, it reduces *tracing costs* i.e. the time, effort and money required to track the copyright holder and the heirs of a copyrighted work over many generations and seek permission before using such works, and thirdly, the longer duration of copyright protection would limit the number of available works in the public domain and thereby increase the cost of production of new copyrightable works due to higher transaction costs and consequently reduce the number of new creative works in society.

The welfare theory of copyright law as advocated by Landes and Posner has provided a strong foundational basis for justifying the rights of the consumers in copyrighted works in the digital environment. It is essential to ensure that the protection of copyrighted works should not add to the cost of expression and production of new works in the online environment. Internet has provided the consumers with the easy ability to have proper access to pre-existing work which will ensure freedom of expression and promote the production of new works. The attempts by the copyright holders to limit and regulate the access to copyrighted works through technological and other means will impose huge financial burdens on the consumers of copyrighted works thereby reducing the number of creative works produced in the society. Landes and Posner had argued that the economic justification for imposing *idea/expression* dichotomy in the copyright law was to prevent unnecessary expenditures. Attempt to prevent 'independent duplication of works' will impose huge investment of time and money on the copyright holders to find out and prohibit all works incorporating similar ideas. It will also impose an immense responsibility on the judiciary to draw the permissible limits of every idea in each and every case of creative creation. Additionally 'borrowing or building on materials from prior body of works and adding new and original expression to it' will require huge investment of time and money from each and every individual for the purpose of creating independent new work and result in 'rent-seeking' by the copyright holders. The problem of rent-seeking has become a reality in the digital world with the development of technological protection measures which empowers the copyright holders to regulate each and every use of their copyrighted works in the online environment and thereby imposing a huge expenditure on society for the production of new cultural works. In the absence of recognition of the rights of the consumers to access ideas and create new works in the digital environment the growth of culture will be adversely affected and retard progress. Similarly, it is essential to ensure grant of fair use rights to the consumers in the online environment. Imposing liability on the consumers to pay every time a minimum cost for accessing and using a copyrighted work will impose a huge financial expenditures on the users and create immense logistic problems when every user has to find out the true identity of each and every creator of a work living in different parts of the world and seek their prior permission for any creation or re-creation of their works. The costs involved in such acts are prohibitively high and also affect the spread of culture in society. In addition, the recommendations for imposing a compulsory license mechanism in the digital environment for grant of permission to use a copyrighted work, is unfeasible. The cost for setting up of a global administrative body to regulate the system of compulsory licensing of all musical works will involve huge manpower, expenditure and high level of technology. Such investments will be required for ensuring that all copyrighted works circulated on the internet are registered with the licensing body and also a regularly updated list of the copyright holders and heir are maintained by the body for the proper distribution of the money generated. A universal license fee structure has to be drafted and maintained so that every consumer can pay the requisite compulsory license fee and seek necessary permission for using the copyrighted work. Also, a proper tracking system is to be developed and maintained properly to keep a tab on all the different usages of the copyright work by the users across the world and also have a strong administrative support system to ensure proper and timely payment of fees by the internet users. Hence, it is argued that the rights of the consumers to enjoy the fair use privileges should be granted so as to ensure proper functioning of the copyright system in the digital world without imposing unnecessary financial, technical and administrative burden on the working of the internet. Another justification for recognizing the fair use rights of the consumers is to encourage the growth of free and fair productive fair use in the digital environment by promoting the conducting of works like writing review, critique, making parodies, satires etc. In the absence of such privileges, users would have to seek the permission of the copyright holders and pay for their access prior to making any comments, reviews or critiquing the work. Such payment and prior permission will restrict free expression of ideas and views because on one hand copyright holders will refuse to grant permission for fear of negative comments and on the other hand the neutrality in the review of the work done will be lost for public perception because of prior payment. In light of all these justifications, as argued by Landes and Posner, it is essential that the rights of the consumers should be equally respected in the digital world along with the rights of the copyright holders.

2.3 Cultural Theory of Property

The premise of this theory is based on the objective that the goal of copyright is to promote the creation of 'a just and attractive culture'.[13] Some of the advocates of this theory are William Fisher, Rosemary Coombe, Keith Aoki and Neil Netanel. The fair use justifications in copyright law permitting acts of criticism, commentary, education, parody, satire etc. are based on the principle of promoting free speech and expression in society and thereby ensuring the growth of culture. According to Fisher, the principal proponent of this theory, the creation of an intellectual culture is based on promoting consumer welfare, access to wide range of information and ideas, encourage artistic creativity, distributive justice, sociability and respect towards others.[14] The notion of consumer welfare implies making members of the society happy by encouraging and incentivizing them to produce creative works and at the same time encouraging others to use and disseminate the cultural works. The attempt should be made to balance the rights of the creators with the rights of the users so to maximize happiness in society. The goal of consumer welfare can be achieved by promoting wide access to information, ideas and different forms of entertainment among the citizens and make their lives much more enriching. Access to cultural works will also promote self-determination and self-expression among the citizens by enabling them to develop their own personalities. It will further enhance the growth of a cultural diversity in society by encouraging creativity among the citizens. However equal access to information, ideas and cultural work is essential for artistic and cultural growth in society, but such growth becomes sustainable when members of the society actively participate in the creation of cultural items and other works and are not mere passive receivers of intellectual works created by others.[15] Thus, it is essential to create an environment of semiotic democracy in society by promoting a culture of respect towards each other work and sociable environment for intermingling.

The cultural theory or social planning theory is based on the idea that the promotion and protection of intellectual properties is essential for the purpose of promoting the welfare of the members of society. Access to intellectual creations helps the individuals to develop their intellect as well as add on to their emotional and happiness quotient. It also helps the individual to become better participant in the social activities and the democratic process in the community. Thus access to cultural works have become equally important in the digital environment because majority of the younger generation have adopted and adapted the internet as their primary mode of communication and living their social life. The use of different forms of cultural work has become an essential part in their expressions and communications, and the creation of user-generated works is a process of out-letting their creative instincts. The fundamental premise of cultural theory of copyright law justifies the rights of the users to access copyrighted materials in the digital environment.

---

[13] Fisher 2001, *Supra* note 2.

[14] *Id.*

[15] *Id.*

These jurisprudential theories are of great relevance in the modern day. The importance and relevance of these theories are reflected in the judicial decisions of different countries. The interpretation of the copyright laws and the judgments of the courts of different countries are guided by the varied jurisprudential principles of fairness, incentives, reward, mark of personality, culture-shaping of society, contribution to society etc while delivering their decisions. However, the underlying guiding principle of copyright law is the balance between the interests of creators of intellectual works and the benefit which the society derives from such work.

3 Socio-Political Thinkers and Their Response to Copyright Law

Lord Macaulay and Sir Thomas Jefferson had made arguably two of the most significant speeches relating to the social welfare objective of copyright law. A brief look at the opinion of these leading thinkers will help to illustrate the purpose and objective behind enactment of the copyright law.

3.1 Lord Macaulay's View on Copyright Law

Lord Thomas Babington Macaulay had made one of the most important speeches on the purpose and objective of copyright in the annals of legal history. The speech was made on January 1841 before the British Parliament during the debate on extension of copyright period to 60 years from the death of the author.[16] His argument was based on public welfare rationale or citizen centric approach to copyright law. He challenges the labour-desert theory of copyright law by denying the absolute applicability of law of nature theory which gave '*every man a sacred and indefeasible property in his own ideas, in the fruits of his own reason and imagination.*'[17] He argued that the law of property, including intellectual property is a state conferred privilege which is granted on the basis of the principle of welfare of mankind. The term of property law, including copyright law should be enacted by the parliament in light of the greatest advantage to the society rationale. Grant of copyright protection is the most convenient way to ensure supply of goods in society and remunerating the authors by means of copyright protection is the most unobjectionable way of doing it. For the purpose of ensuring regular supply of intellectual works based on deep contemplation and research, it is essential to remunerate the authors for their 'literary labour'. Such grant of remuneration is possible by either means of patronage or by copyright protection. Grant of patronage has an adverse impact on the freedom of the author to freely

[16] Macaulay 1841.

[17] *Id.*

express himself because of his constant dependence on the whims of kings and noblemen for patronage hence copyright protection is the only applicable option. But copyright law has its own limitations because of the monopolistic nature of the system. Some of the important consequences of monopolistic trade is to *'make articles scarce, to make them dear, and to make them bad'* and grant of monopoly right of copyright law will also give rise to these negative tendencies in the production of cultural works hence the grant of monopoly protection in the form of copyright law should be minimal in terms of its duration. In the words of Lord Macaulay, *"It is good that authors should be remunerated; and the least exceptionable way of remunerating them is by a monopoly. Yet monopoly is an evil; but the evil ought not to last a day longer than is necessary for the purpose of securing the good."*[18] He further observes,

> The principle of copyright is this. It is a tax on readers for the purpose of giving a bounty to writers. The tax is an exceedingly bad one; it is a tax on one of the most innocent and most salutary of human pleasures; and never let us forget, that a tax on innocent pleasures is a premium on vicious pleasures. I admit, however, the necessity of giving a bounty to genius and learning. In order to give such a bounty, I willingly submit even to this severe and burdensome tax. Nay, I am ready to increase the tax, if it can be shown that by so doing I should proportionally increase the bounty.[19]

He argues the financial gain if any arising out of long copyright period does not come to vest in the family members of the author but is enjoyed by the publisher of such work for his successful speculation. The family members of the author after 60 years of his death will be difficult to identify and may enjoy very little in the share of the economic gain. Most often long duration of copyright protection grants monopoly power to the publishers to determine the availability of a copyrighted work, the number of copies which should be published and the price at which it shall be used. Such monopolistic power adversely affects the interests of the members of the society who are required to pay exorbitant prices to access the copyrighted works and there is no corresponding benefit to the authors and their families. He concluded by arguing that the proposal for the extension of the copyright term should be rejected on the ground of causing grievous injury to the public without conferring additional advantage to the author.[20]

3.2 Thomas Jefferson on Ideas and Intellectual Property[21]

Thomas Jefferson in his letter to Isaac McPherson analyzing the constitutional provision on intellectual property in the US Constitution argues that traditionally there has been no natural right to property but under the universal law, a property

---

[18] *Id.*

[19] *Id.*

[20] *Id.*

[21] The Founders' Constitution 1813.

may temporarily belong to the person who occupies it and the moment he relinquishes the occupation, the right of property goes with it. The entire notion of property is a creation of human society. In such a situation, ideas developed in the human minds cannot be conferred with the property rights protection because of the universal nature of ideas. Inventions developed by human beings cannot be granted property rights protection but such individuals may be granted the right to profits arising out of such works as an encouragement to produce more works of utility for society. However, such grants of exclusive rights or monopoly rights may not be an ideal method for encouraging growth of inventions and useful arts in society and other alternative methods may be equally beneficial in society. Grant of any exclusive property or profit making rights to inventors and creators should be determined on the ultimate touchstone of society's welfare and well being. In the words of Jefferson,

> If nature has made any one thing less susceptible than all others of exclusive property, it is the action of the thinking power called an idea, which an individual may exclusively possess as long as he keeps it to himself; but the moment it is divulged, it forces itself into the possession of every one, and the receiver cannot dispossess himself of it. Its peculiar character, too, is that no one possesses the less, because every other possesses the whole of it. He who receives an idea from me, receives instruction himself without lessening mine; as he who lights his taper at mine, receives light without darkening me. That ideas should freely spread from one to another over the globe, for the moral and mutual instruction of man, and improvement of his condition, seems to have been peculiarly and benevolently designed by nature, when she made them, like fire, expansible over all space, without lessening their density in any point, and like the air in which we breathe, move, and have our physical being, incapable of confinement or exclusive appropriation. Inventions then cannot, in nature, be a subject of property. Society may give an exclusive right to the profits arising from them, as an encouragement to men to pursue ideas which may produce utility, but this may or may not be done, according to the *will and convenience of the society*, without claim or complaint from anybody.[22]

4 Copyright Law and the Doctrine of Fair Use

4.1 United Kingdom

The Statute of Anne 1710 was the first copyright statute of the world.[23] Analysis of the legislation clearly identifies the objective of the law as *an act for the encouragement of learning*.[24] The law granted authors of books, the exclusive right to authorise the printing, reprinting and publishing of books for a limited period of 14 years, which was extendable for another period of 14 years during the lifetime of the author. In case of any unauthorised printing, publishing, selling of books, the

---

[22] *Id.*

[23] *See* The History of Copyright: A Critical Overview, *1710*.

[24] Preamble of the statute.

unauthorised copies would be seized and such publisher or seller would be subjected to imposition of fine. But, the statute contained several provisions dealing with people's right to access literary works. The authors were required to register the title of their works in the Register-Book of the Company of Stationers so as to enable a book seller or printer to inspect and identify the author of the work and obtain his permission for the purpose of publication. Any failure by the author to register his work would deprive him of seeking legal remedies under the statute in case of any infringement of his rights. In case of unreasonable or high price charged on a book, complaint under the statute could be brought before the specified authorities after due examination could reform and redress the pricing by limiting and settling the price of a book from time to time based on the just and reasonable judgment. In case of price revision the person complaining would be entitled to receive all the costs and expenditures which he spent for the purpose and pursuance of complaining and, the new limited and settled price would be published in the Gazette. All book sellers and printers would be legally bound to sell the book at the new settled price and any failure to do so would result in imposition of fine by the State. The statute also required that nine copies of the published books were to be submitted to the Warehouse-Keeper of the Company of Stationers for the purpose of being distributed to the libraries of different educational institutions and to be made part of their collection. Any failure to do so would result in imposition of penalty by the State.

After the passing of the Statute of Anne 1710, several amendments to the copyright law took place because of the need to make the legislation more suitable and contemporary to the changing needs of the people. The different copyright legislations which were introduced were the Copyright Act 1842, the Copyright Act 1911, the Copyright Act, 1956 and the Copyright, Designs and Patents Act of 1988. In these different amendments, the term of the copyright protection was increased and also the scope of the copyright law was widened to include a large variety of works like sound recordings, photographs, cinematographic works, software programs etc. Under the present Copyright, Designs and Patents Act 1988 (CDPA) proprietary rights is granted to a large category of original works like literary, dramatic, musical or artistic works, sound recordings, films or broadcasts etc.[25] Legal protection is granted from the time of creation of the work without any necessity to comply with any procedural norms.[26] The statute recognizes a set of exclusive rights to do certain acts in relation to the copyright work like right to copy the work; right to issue copies of the work to the public; right of renting or lending copies of the work to the public; right to communicate the work to the public; right of distribution; right of performance; right of adaptation etc. These rights have been granted to the copyright holders under the statute and are known as economic rights of the copyright holder. The Act also grants a set of 'moral rights' in favour of the copyright holder. These rights include the right to be identified as the author of the

[25] CDPA Section 1(1).

[26] Garnett et al. 2005.

work, the right to object to derogatory treatment of copyright works, the right to object to having a work falsely attributed to oneself and the right of privacy in respect of any photographs which were commissioned for private and domestic purposes. These rights have been granted for a period of 70 years after the death of the author. In cases of sound recordings, computer generated works etc. the protection is granted for a period of 50 years from making or making the work available to the public. Unauthorised violation of these rights constitutes copyright infringement and is liable for legal actions under the statute. Both civil and criminal remedies are available under the statute. The act imposes certain limitations on the exercise of the exclusive rights granted to the copyright holders by recognizing a number of fair dealing exceptions for non-commercial research and private study, criticism or review, and reporting current events.

Traditionally, the objective of copyright law in the United Kingdom has been premised on the economic and social justifications of copyright law. The necessity to protect the labour and hard work of the authors by encouraging protection of the creative works has been considered as an essential objective in copyright laws, but the need 'to encourage dissemination of ideas and knowledge to the general public' has been considered to be an equally important objective.[27] The copyright legislation and the judiciary have attempted to balance the interest of the copyright holders on the one hand, with the interests of the public at large in accessing the creative works. In the leading case of *Walter* v. *Lane*[28] the court recognised these justifications for the grant of copyright protection. In this case, Earl of Rosebery had delivered public speeches on matters of public importance on different occasions. Some of the reporters from The Times newspaper, who attended the public gatherings, wrote down the speeches in shorthand, then subsequently wrote the entire speeches, corrected, revised and punctuated the speeches. The contents of the speeches were verbatim of the words spoken by Lord Rosebery. The written speeches were published in The Times. The respondent, based on the published speeches wrote a book called *Appreciations and Addresses: Lord Rosebery*, containing those speeches without obtaining permission from the appellants. The appellant newspaper brought a legal action against the respondents on the ground of copyright violation. It was argued that by making notes of the speeches, transcribing them and publishing them verbatim in the newspaper confer authorship to the reporter with reference to the published work and entitled him to copyright protection. The respondents argued that there was no element of originality in the work created by the appellant hence not entitled for copyright protection. The House of Lords upholding the claims of the appellants held that the reporter was the author of the report of the speech under the Copyright laws. It was observed *"The speaker has a common law right of property in the speech before it is delivered to the public and may prevent its publication by any one else but Lord Rosebery "abandoned his ideas and words to the use of the public at large, or in other words*

[27] *Id* at 27.

[28] [1900] A.C. 539.

has himself published them."[29] It was deemed that the great hardships will be suffered if protection was not given to works which are produced after great expenditure of time, money and toil. In the leading case of *Donaldson* v. *Beckett*[30] the House of Lords dealt with the legality of statutory enacted copyright law in the UK. The judges in majority held that there was no copyright protection in perpetuity granted to the authors under the common law. In the words of Baron Eyre,

> A right to appropriate ideas was a right to appropriate something so ethereal as to elude definition! so intellectual as not to fall within the limits of the human mind to describe with any tolerable degree of accuracy. Ideas, if convertible into objects of property, should bear some faint similitude to other objects of property; they did not bear any such similitude, they were altogether anomalous. They could not pass by descent to heirs; they were not liable to bequest; no characteristic marks remained whereby to ascertain them; and, were such incorporealities not subject to one of the conditions which constituted the very essence of property original or derivative; were such incorporealities liable to exclusive appropriation by any right founded in the common law?

Lord Camden while delivering the opinion of the House, was extremely critical about the attempt by the publishers and book sellers to create a common law theory of literary property in perpetuity by authors. Prior to the invention of printing there was no notion of literary property in England or in Europe.

4.2 *United States*

The US Constitution is one of the very few constitutions in the world which has recognized the importance of science and arts in the progress of society and mankind. Article 1, Section 8, Clause 8 of the US Constitution has empowered the US Congress 'to promote the progress of Science and Arts, by securing for limited Times to Authors and Inventors the right to their respective writings and discoveries.'[31] This constitutional provision is also popularly known as the 'intellectual property clause' or the 'progress clause'. The clause is the basis for the enactment of the US Copyright laws and the Patent laws and, the fundamental objective of these laws was 'to promote the progress of science'. The provision is considered to be 'both a grant of power and a limitation' for the purpose of granting incentive to the authors to encourage them to be engaged in creative and useful activities.[32] In the case *Mazer* v. *Stein* the court upheld the objective of limited copyright protection for the purpose of promoting science and art in society.[33] The court observed *"The economic philosophy behind the clause empowering Congress to grant patents and*

---

[29] *Id* at 541.

[30] *Donaldson* v. *Beckett* (1774) 2 Brown's Parl. Cases 129, Decided on February 22, 1774, http://www.copyrighthistory.com/donaldson.html (last visited Dec 25, 2015).

[31] US Constitution.

[32] Graham v. John Deere Co. of Kansas City, 383 US 1, 5-6 (1966).

[33] 347 US 201, 219 (1954).

copyrights is the conviction that encouragement of individual effort by personal gain is the best way to advance public welfare through the talents of authors and inventors in 'Science and useful Arts.'"[34] In one of the earlier cases *Pennock* v. *Dialogue*, the court while recognising the rights of the users, had observed that the main objective of copyright law could be best achieved 'by giving the public at large a right to make, construct, use, and vend the thing invented, at as early a period as possible, having a due regard to the rights of the inventor.'[35] The leading case dealing with the interpretation of the copyright clause of the US Constitution was the case of *Eldred* v. *Ashcroft*.[36] Justice Ginsburg while delivering the opinion of the highest court of the US interpreted the scope of the constitutional provision relating to copyright law clause with reference to the extension of the duration of the copyright term by 20 years by the enactment of the Copyright Term Extension Act. Recognising the scope of copyright protection it was observed that *"the copyright gives the holder no monopoly on any knowledge. A reader of an author's writing may make full use of any fact or idea she acquires from her reading."*[37] In addition, the court recognized the built-in limitations on the rights of the copyright holders for the purpose of protecting the interests of the users. Firstly, by denying protection to 'ideas, procedure, process, system, method of operation, concept, principle, or discovery' the copyright law promotes freedom of speech and expression without compromising with the economic and other rights of the authors. Secondly, the 'fair use' exceptions enable the users to use the copyright protected expressions in certain specified circumstances like criticism, comment, news reporting, teaching, scholarship and research. Justice Breyer has recognized a large number of potential users of copyrighted works like 'music lovers, historians, scholars, teachers, writers, artists, database operators and researchers of all kinds' who use the copyrighted works for their own purposes or for the purposes of others.[38] Copyright law generally inhibits the ability of the users to achieve their objectives hence should be minimal in scope. Promoting and protecting the interests and welfare of the society is the primary objective of copyright law.

The Copyright Act of 1976 is the primary copyright legislation in the United States.[39] The Act recognizes rights of a copyright holder. Section 102 of the Act grants copyright protection to *'original works of authorship fixed in any tangible medium of expression, now known or later developed, from which they can be perceived, received, or otherwise communicated, either directly or with the aid of machine or device.'* The different categories of work protected under the Act are literary work, musical works including lyrics, dramatic works, pantomimes and choreographic works, motion pictures, sound recordings, pictoral, graphic and

---

[34] *Id* at 219.

[35] 2 Pet.1, 18 (1829), discussed by Justice Stevens in the case of *Eldred* v. *Ashcroft*.

[36] 186 (2003) 239 F.3d.

[37] *Id.*

[38] *Id.*

[39] The Copyright Act of 1976.

sculptural works etc. Section 106 of the Act recognizes five exclusive rights to copyright holders; the right to reproduce the work into copies and phonorecords; the right to create derivative works of the original work; the right to distribute copies and phonorecords of the work to the public by sale, lease, or rental; the right to perform the work publicly; and the right to display the work publicly. Recognizing the constitutional goal of promoting the progress of science and useful arts in society, the copyright law has imposed a number of limitations and recognized exceptions to the list of exclusive rights granted to the authors. The first category of exception is the fair use defense recognized under Section 107 of the Act. The common law recognised doctrine of fair use exception was codified under the Act and includes the application of four factors for the purpose of determination of the exception. The four factors are—(1) the purpose and character of the use, (2) the nature of the copyrighted work, (3) the amount and substantiality of the portion of the original work used; and (4) the effect of the use upon the market for the original work. The other limitations on the exclusive rights of the copyright holders are reproduction by libraries and archives under Section 108 of the Act. Section 109 of the Act enables 'the owner of a particular copy or phonorecord lawfully made under this title, or any person authorized by such owner, is entitled, without the authority of the copyright owner to sell or otherwise dispose of that copy or phonorecord.' However, such right does not include the right of rental, lease or lending for commercial purposes. The law extends the protection to acts of rental, lease, or lending of the phonorecord for non-profit purposes to a library or a nonprofit educational institution. The act further recognizes additional limitations on the exclusive rights in Sections 110,[40] 111[41] and 112.[42] Under Section 121 of the Act, limitations on the exclusive rights have been imposed for the benefit of blind and other people with disabilities.

In the case of *Sony Corporation of America* v. *Universal City Studios*[43] which is popularly known as the Sony Betamax case, the US Supreme Court dealt with the issue of fair use principle in a copyright infringement suit for the first time. In this case, a number of television production companies, including Universal Studios and the Walt Disney, had sued Sony for violating their copyright protection. It was alleged that the home video recording devices, known as Betamax video tape recorders manufactured by Sony, enabled the users to copy copyrighted television programs for subsequent watching. Ability to record television programs infringed the television production companies' right to regulate and control the manner of watching their programs and also deprived them of a potentially lucrative market for recorded television programs. The television companies did not sue individual

---

[40] S.110—Limitations on exclusive rights: Exemptions of certain performances and displays.

[41] S.111—Limitations on exclusive rights: Secondary transmissions of broadcast programming by cable.

[42] S.112—Limitations on exclusive rights: Ephemeral recordings.

[43] 464 US 417 (1984).

users of Betamax recorders, but sued Sony on the ground of vicarious liability and contributory infringement of copyright law.

Stevens J. while delivering the opinion for the majority recognized the social welfare objective of copyright law. The principle aim of copyright law was to ensure public good and reward the authors for their labour and contribution to social good. Hence, copyright holders were not granted all the rights relating to their created work but a number of exceptions for social good were recognised through the fair use principles. Accordingly, the court justified private recording of television programs on the ground of time-shifting, i.e. delaying the time of viewing a television program which a viewer was invited to watch free of charge did not amount to copyright infringement. It was argued that time-shifting increased the number of viewers and fell within the ambit of fair use exception. It allowed the viewer ambit of to view two simultaneous television broadcasts by watching one live and recording the other for subsequent viewing.[44] The machine also enabled the viewer to pause or fast-forward the recorded programs. The Court further denied the claim of contributory liability of Sony corporation on three grounds—(1) Sony did not supply the viewers with copyright infringing materials, but only provided them with a recording device. The relationship between Sony and its users ended with the delivery of the recording device across the sale counter. Thus, there was no direct involvement of Sony with the activities of its users. (2) Mere knowledge of the fact that its users may make unauthorized copies of copyrighted materials or knowledge that some users were making unauthorized copies was not adequate to make Sony Corporation vicariously liable. (3) On the basis of doctrine of staple article of commerce, any equipment even if it was being used by some users for infringing purposes, so long as it was capable of other legitimate and unobjectionable purposes i.e. substantial non-infringing usages such articles should not be held liable for copyright infringement. The court while discussing the objective of copyright law observed that—

> The monopoly privileges that Congress may authorize are neither unlimited nor primarily designed to provide a special private benefit. Rather, the limited grant is a means by which an important public purpose may be achieved. It is intended to motivate the creative activity of authors and inventors by the provision of a special reward, and to allow the public access to the products of their genius after the limited period of exclusive control has expired.[45]

It was acknowledged that rewarding of the copyright owners was the secondary consideration of copyright law whereas the 'general benefits derived by the public' was the primary concern. On the scope of fair use it was observed that

> [T]he Copyright Act grants the copyright holder "exclusive" rights to use and to authorize the use of his work in five qualified ways, including reproduction of the copyrighted work in copies. § 106. All reproductions of the work, however, are not within the exclusive domain of the copyright owner; some are in the public domain. Any individual may

---

[44] *Id* at 422.

[45] *Id* at 429.

> reproduce a copyrighted work for a "fair use"; the copyright owner does not possess the exclusive right to such a use.[46]

Hence, any person making a fair use of the work will not be deemed to be a copyright infringer with reference to that work. It has been acknowledged that the decision of the US Supreme Court in upholding the principle of substantial non-infringing uses and the staple article of commerce doctrine has correctly balanced the demand of copyright holders' claim for effective protection of their monopoly rights and the rights of the users to use advanced technologies for the betterment of their lives.

In *Harper & Row Publishers* v. *Nation Enterprises*[47] the court had recognized the importance of *free speech* and held that copyright law merely protected a 'specific form of expression' and did not restrict the access of individuals to different ideas or facts contained in the copyrighted works. It was further held that the copyright protection granted to the specific expressions, was also limited by the 'fair use' exceptions. The Court observed that 'The Framers intended copyright itself to be the engine of free expression. By establishing a marketable right to the use of one's expression, copyright supplies the economic incentive to create and disseminate ideas.'[48] The US Supreme Court applied the four factor test under Section 107 to determine the applicability of fair use exception. The fair use principle is recognized as 'a privilege in others than the owner of the copyright to use the copyrighted material in a reasonable manner without his consent.'[49] In this case, the court negated the applicability of the fair use defence on the grounds that the publication was made primarily for commercial purposes as opposed to non-profit activities and lacked good faith by publishing unpublished materials.

After a gap of 20 years, the US Supreme Court revisited the Sony Betamax decision in the leading case of *MGM* v. *Grokster*[50] case in light of the controversy relating to users rights *vis-a-vis* copyright holder's right to control the Internet and other related digital technologies. The Grokster and other companies had distributed free software in the Internet which enabled the internet users to easily share electronic files between computers through the peer to peer network (P2P network). The recording industry, film industry and television companies alleged that a large number of internet users were using the Grokster and Streamcast facilitated P2P networks to share a large number of copyright infringing materials like music files, movie files etc. The principle debate in this case revolved between the rights of copyright holders to retain control over their creative works and the rights of the users to use new and beneficial technologies. On one hand strictly upholding of the copyright holders' rights would limit the development of beneficial technologies and adversely affect the scientific progress in society and on the other hand, easy

[46] *Id* at 433.
[47] 471 US 539 (1985).
[48] *Id* at 558.
[49] *Id* at 549.
[50] 545 US 913 (2005).

copying through Internet and other advanced technologies had the ability to adversely affect the rights of the copyright holders and limit their creative incentive, thereby retarding the social and cultural progress of society. In spite of the strong arguments of the petitioners requesting the need to reconsider the Sony decision, the US Supreme Court reiterated the validity of their earlier ruling in Sony case and upheld the 'substantial non-infringing use' theory on the basis of staple article of commerce doctrine as the correct test to be adopted for determining the legality of new technologies. However, the Court correctly introduced the 'inducement theory' in copyright jurisprudence in this case. If a technology, irrespective of the fact that it has both infringing and non-infringing usages, is distributed and promoted with the objective of copyright infringement it will give rise to liability for the person distributing the device for acts of infringement by third parties. In this case, the Court recognized the beneficial aspects of P2P networks, but held Grokster and Streamcast liable for positive acts undertaken by it to encourage copyright infringement by its users. Unlike Sony in the *Sony Betamax case,* the Grokster and Streamcast had intentionally and actively encouraged its users to infringe copyright laws and participate in unauthorized distribution of copyrighted materials. Thus, the US Supreme Court recognized the competing claims of the copyright holders and the consumers at large and correctly tried to balance the both. Such an approach has been appreciated as the right approach when deciding issues of emerging technologies which have both potential advantages and disadvantages.

4.3 India

One of the important social goals recognized by the Indian Constitution is promoting the liberty of thought and expression amongst the different members of the community.[51] The fundamental rights chapter of the Constitution for the purpose of fulfilling this objective has granted every citizen the right to freedom of speech and expression.[52] It has also recognized the right to personal liberty of every individual in the society which cannot be encroached without proper procedure established by law.[53] For the purpose of achieving these objectives, the Constitution has imposed duties on the State as well as the citizens '*to value and preserve the rich heritage of our composite culture*' and '*to develop the scientific temper, humanism and the spirit of inquiry and reform*'.[54] Copyright law has played an important role in fulfilling these constitutional goals in society. The grant of exclusive rights to the authors of creative work is essential to encourage and incentivize them to create

[51] The Constitution of India—Preamble: *"We.....Liberty of thought, expression, belief, faith and worship..."*.

[52] *Id* at Article 19(1)(a).

[53] *Id* at A. 21.

[54] *Id* at Part IVA, Fundamental Duties, Article 51A (f) and (h).

more intellectual works for the benefit of society and mankind, but it is equally important to impose certain limitations on the exclusive rights so that members of the community could enjoy the creative works and participate actively in further creation of intellectual and creative works. The limitations on the scope of copyright protection is necessary to promote free speech, liberty of thought and expression and encourage the development of intellectual and creative thinking in men and women.

The Supreme Court of India in various judgments has recognized the welfare objective of copyright law and the necessity to shelter the interests of society without adversely affecting the interests of the authors and other copyright holders. In the leading decision of *Eastern Book Company* v. *D.B. Modak*[55] the Supreme Court observed—

> The copyright, protection finds its justification in fair play. When a person produces something with his skill and labour, it normally belongs to him and the other person would not be permitted to make a profit but of the skill and labour of the original author and it is for this reason the Copyright Act, 1957 gives to the authors certain exclusive rights in relation to the certain work referred in the Act. The object of the Act is to protect the author of the copyright work from an unlawful reproduction or exploitation of his work by others. Copyright is a right to stop others from exploiting the work without the consent or assent of the owner of the copyright. A copyright law presents a balance between the interests and rights of the author and that of the public in protecting the public domain, or to claim the copyright and protect it under the copyright statute. One of the key requirements is that of originality which contributes, and has a direct nexus, in maintaining the interests of the author as well as that of public in protecting the matters in' public domain. It is a well-accepted principle of copyright law that there is no copyright in the facts per se, as the facts are not created nor have they originated with the author of any work which embodies these facts. The issue of copyright is closely connected to that of commercial viability, and commercial consequences and implications.[56]

In the subsequent case of *Entertainment Network* v. *Super Cassette Industries Ltd.*, the Supreme Court while discussing the essential features of copyright law had further observed—

> The Act seeks to maintain a balance between the interest of the owner of the copyright in protecting his works on the one hand and the interest of the public to have access to the works, on the other. The extent to which the owner is entitled to protection in regard to his work for which he has obtained copyright and the interest of the public is a matter which would depend upon the statutory provisions. Whereas the Act provides for exclusive rights in favour of owners of the copyright, there are provisions where it has been recognized that public has also substantial interest in the availability of the works. The provisions relating to grant of compulsory license must be viewed having regard to the aforementioned competing rights where for an appropriate balance has to be stuck. For the said purpose, we may notice the broad features of the Act.[57]

---

[55] (2008) 1 SCC 1.

[56] *Id.* para 8.

[57] (2008) 13 SCC 30, para 61.

Thus based on these goals and objectives the Copyright Act has identified certain statutory restrictions on the rights of the copyright holders.

The Copyright Act has upheld the constitutional obligation of creating an environment of freedom for speech and expression, liberty of thoughts and promoting the growth of culture in society by recognizing a number of acts as permissible in nature and not falling within the scope of exclusive rights granted to the right holders under the copyright statute. Section 52 of the statute has identified and specified these acts and granted them independent legal status. This section stands out with reference to the fair use exceptions recognized under the copyright legislations of other jurisdictions. Section 52 has granted legal rights to the users of the creative works to use the copyrighted work in a certain manner and for certain purposes, and which will not amount to copyright infringement under Section 51. The permissible acts under Section 52 are not considered as an exception to the general rule under Section 51, on the contrary the scope of Section 52 is deemed to be outside the scope of Section 51. In the leading case of *Academy of General Education, Manipal* v. *B. Malini Mallya*[58], the Supreme Court had observed—

> Section 52 of the Act provides for certain acts which would not constitute an infringement of copyright. When a fair dealing is made, inter alia, of a literary or dramatic work for the purpose of private use including research and criticism or review whether of that work or of any other work, the right in terms of the provisions of the said Act cannot be claimed. Thus, if some performance or dance is carried out within the purview of the said clause, the order of injunction shall not be applicable. Similarly, appellant being an educational institution, if the dance is performed within the meaning of provisions of clause (i) of Sub-Section (1) of Section 52 of the Act strictly, the order of injunction shall not apply thereto also. Yet again, if such performance is conducted before a non-paying audience by the appellant, which is an institution if it comes within the purview of amateur club or society, the same would not constitute any violation of the said order of injunction.[59]

Similarly in an earlier decision of the Allahabad High Court in *S.K. Dutt* v. *Law Book Co.*[60] it was held that for the purpose of copyright infringement there must be substantial infringement of the work because a mere fair dealing of a work falls outside the scope of exclusive rights granted to the copyright holder, hence it is outside the mischief of copyright law.

The essential acts not amounting to copyright infringement under Section 52 and are deemed relevant to the users of musical works are—(a) fair dealing with any work for private or personal use, including private or personal use, research, criticism or review, reporting of current events or of a lecture made in public; (b) making of copies or adaptation of a computer program by the lawful possessor of such program from such copy in order to use it for the purpose it was supplied or for making back-up copies for the temporary protection against loss, destruction or any damage to the program; (c) doing of any act which is necessary to obtain information for the purpose of understanding the interoperability of a computer

[58] 2009 (39) PTC (SC).

[59] *Id* at para 20.

[60] AIR 1954 All 570.

program with other programs; (d) observing, studying or testing the functioning of the computer program to determine the ideas and principles underlying the program; (e) making copies or adaptation of the computer program from a personal and legally obtained copy for making non-commercial personal use; (f) the transient and incidental storage of a work or performance for the technical process of electronic transmission or communication to the public, or for purposes like electronic links, access or integration; (g) reproduction of any work for the purposes of judicial proceeding, legislative purposes or for any other legal purposes; (h) publication in a collection composed of non-copyrighted matter bona fide intended for instructional use; (i) reproduction of any work for instructional purposes, examination purposes, preparation of key answers etc; (j) the performance of a musical work or sound recording or cinematographic film in an educational institution by the staff and students of the institution and the audience limited to parents and guardians of students and other people associated with the institution; (k) causing a sound recording to be heard in an enclosed room or hall meant for the common use of residents in any residential premises as part of amenities for usage among the residents, or for the activities of a club, society or organization which has not been established for profit making purposes, or the performance of a musical work by an amateur club or society for non-paying audiences; (l) the storing of a work in any medium by electronic means by a non-commercial public library for preservation purposes when the library already has a non-digital copy of the work; (m) making three copies of a book under the instructions of a person in charge of non-commercial library if such book is not available for sale in India; (n) reproduction of an unpublished literary, dramatic or musical work kept in a library, museum or other institution to which the public has access for the purposes of research and private study so long as the identity of the author is not known or 60 years have passed from the date of death of the author; (o) the making of an ephemeral recording by a broadcasting organization of a work which it has the right to broadcast and the retention of such recording for archival purposes on the ground of exceptional documentary character; (p) the performance of a musical work or the communication to the public of such work or of a sound recording for the bona fide purposes of religious ceremony, marriage procession and other social festivities associated with marriage as well as for official ceremonies of the Central and State government or local authority; and (q) adaptation, reproduction, issuing of copies or communication to the public of any work in a format suitable for the use of persons suffering from different forms of disabilities and are unable to enjoy the creative works in their ordinary format. All the different permitted acts recognized under Section 52(1) are equally applicable for all translated or adapted works of literary, dramatic, artistic or musical in nature.[61]

Section 39 of the Copyright Act makes exceptions to the general rule recognizing the rights of the performers under Section 38. It provides that making of sound recording for the private use of the person making such recording or for the

---

[61] *Id* at S. 52 (2).

purposes of bona fide teaching or research will not be deemed to be infringement of the performer's rights. It is also provided that any uses which are consistent with the fair dealing provisions under the statute and for purposes like excerpts of a performance, reporting of current events, bonafide review, teaching, research or for the purpose of making any adaptation or modification necessary for the performance of any act specified under Section 52 will not be deemed to be infringement of the performer's rights.

The Copyright (Amendment) Act of 2012 has recognized the importance of music lovers recreating their favourite music by producing their cover versions. Section 31C enables a person to make cover version recordings of a sound recording which have been previously made after a period of 5 years by giving prior notice of his intention to make such recording and providing the copyright owner with the advance copies of all the covers or labels of the sound recordings and pay in advance to him such royalties which are fixed by the Copyright Board. The Amendment Act has also introduced Section 52(1)(zb) for protecting the rights of persons suffering from disability by enabling the making of adaptation, reproduction, issuing of copies or communicating to the public in a format which will be useful for persons suffering from different types of disabilities and enable them to enjoy the creative work. Section 31B has further provided for issuing of compulsory licenses for the publication of creative works for the benefit of disabled persons. The section provides that a registered organization working for the benefit of disabled persons can apply to the Copyright Board for obtaining compulsory licenses for the publication of a work in which copyright exists.[62] Section 31D has been introduced for granting licenses to radio and other broadcasting organizations for communicating to the public by way of broadcasting or by way of performance of a literary work, musical work and sound recording which was previously published.

One of the significant impacts of the Amendment Act 2012 is the introduction of Technological Protection Measures by copyright holders and the protection of Rights Management Information. These measures have been introduced in the Indian copyright law to make it compatible with the copyright laws of other countries and for fulfilling the international obligations under TRIPs agreement as well as WIPO Copyright Treaty and WIPO Performer's Treaty. Under Section 65A copyright holders have been granted the authority to use different technological measures for the purpose of protecting the different rights provided under the statute. Any person circumventing these technological measures will be liable for punishment with imprisonment of a term extendable to 2 years and will also be required to pay fines.[63] However, the rule has made certain exceptions like—(a) doing anything for a purpose which is not prohibited under the statute, (b) conducting encryption research using a lawfully obtained encrypted copy, (c) conducting any lawful investigation, (d) doing anything necessary for the purpose of

[62] *Id* at S. 31B.

[63] *Id* at S. 65A(1).

testing the security of a computer system or a computer network with the authorization of its owner, (e) operator, (f) doing anything for identification or surveillance of a user, or (g) taking measures necessary in the interest of national security.[64] Under Section 65B any person knowingly removing or altering the rights management information without necessary authority is likely to be punished with imprisonment of maximum 2 years and also liable to pay fines.[65] It is further provided that if any person unauthorizedly distributes or imports for distribution, broadcasts or communicates to the public copies of a work or performance knowing that the electronic rights management information has been removed or altered without authorization will also be subjected to similar punishments.[66] The copyright holder can also exercise the civil remedies.

Thus, the different provisions of the copyright law have taken into consideration the rights of the copyright holders and the interests of members of the society. The Copyright (Amendment) Act of 2012 has furthered the cause of consumers as well as authors of copyrighted works by making a number of changes in the existing law, but it is essential to recognize these rights in the nature of consumers rights in the field of copyrighted works.

5 Rights of Internet Users and European Court of Justice

The *Charter of Fundamental Rights of the European Union* was drafted by the European Commission in 2000.[67] The Charter was drafted with the intention to recognize the importance of indivisible and universal values of human dignity, freedom, equality and dignity for the purpose of implementing democratic principles and the rule of law notion. The main objective of the resolution was to 'place the individual at the heart of its activities' by establishing freedom, security and justice.[68] The Charter has acknowledged the necessity of internet based telecommunications as an integral part of human life and has consequently identified the right of every individual to access communications.[69] It has further recognized the right to freedom of expression which includes the 'freedom to hold opinions and to receive and impart information and ideas without interference by public authority and regardless of frontiers'.[70] Acknowledging the importance of intellectual properties, Article 17(2) of the Charter has also recognized the necessity to protect

---

[64] *Id* at S. 65A(2).

[65] *Id* at S. 65B(i).

[66] *Id* at S. 65B(ii).

[67] Charter of Fundamental Rights of the European Union (2000/C 364/01).

[68] *Id* at Preamble.

[69] *Id* at A.7—Everyone has the right to respect for his or private and family life, home and communications.

[70] *Id* at A. 11.

intellectual properties as part of the Fundamental Rights.[71] Thus European Union has made conscious efforts to acknowledge and recognize the rights of the internet users without limiting the rights of the copyright holders in the digital environment. This balancing approach has also been adopted by the European Court of Justice in its various decisions involving the interests of the copyright holders and concerns of the general members of the society. The importance of internet as an essential medium for human interactions and for exercising the right to freedom of expression and information has been recognized by the European Court of Human Rights in a number of important judgments. Some of the important judgments have been briefly discussed.

5.1 Ahmet Yildirim v. Turkey[72]

In this case, the applicant Ahmet Yildirim was a Turkish national and he owned and ran a website which was hosted by the Google Sites service. On June 2009, the Denzeil Criminal Court of Turkey had ordered the blocking of an internet site which contained materials which were deemed offensive to the memory of Mustafa Kemal Ataruk, the founding father of modern Turkey. The blocking order was submitted for execution to the Telecommunications Directorate but the Directorate requested the court to extend the scope of the order by blocking access to Google Sites because it was the only technical way to block the infringing website. The action of the Directorate resulted in the blocking of several sites hosted by Google Sites, including the website of the applicant who was unable to access his own website. The applicant challenged the decision before EHCR on the ground that the measure had infringed his right to freedom to receive and impart information and ideas, Article 10 of the Convention. The court upheld the right of the individual to access the internet and prohibited the wholesale blocking of online contents like Google by state authorities. It was held that the action taken by the Turkish authorities to block internet access to Google sites violated Article 10 of the Convention and violated the rights of the individuals to access the internet and denied them access to an essential means of expression and information.[73] It was recognized that internet had become 'one of the principal means of exercising the right to freedom of expression' in modern society and such right could only be infringed if 'it was prescribed by law, pursued one or more legitimate aims and was necessary in a democratic society to achieve such aims.'[74] A restriction on the access to information was permissible under the Convention only if a strict legal

[71] *Id* at A. 17(2)—Intellectual property shall be protected.

[72] Ahmet Yildirim v. Turkey Application no. 3111/10, http://hudoc.echr.coe.int/webservices/content/pdf/003-4202780-4985142 (last visited Dec 25, 2015).

[73] Voorhoof 2013.

[74] Yildirim, *Supra* note 73.

framework was established to regulate the ban imposed and provide an opportunity for judicial review of the order for the purpose of preventing any possible abuses. It was held that the order of the domestic court failed to provide the applicant a degree of protection which he was entitled to under the rule of law in a democratic society, hence was arbitrary in nature.[75]

5.2 *Scarlet v. Sabam*[76]

The ECHR has attempted to balance the different human rights enshrined in the Conventions and various protocols. It has made attempts to balance the importance of copyright law on the internet with other rights of the individuals. In the leading case of *Scarlet* v. *Sabam*, the ECHR tried to balance the rights of the copyright holders with the varied rights of the members of the society. SABAM was a management company representing the authors, composers, editors of musical works in authorizing the use of their copyrighted works by third party users whereas Scarlet is an internet service provider which provides customers with access to internet services without providing another services like downloading or file sharing.[77] In 2004, SABAM came to know that internet users subscribing to the Scarlet services were indulging in downloading of copyrighted works without paying royalties or seeking authorization from the members of SABAM by means of P2P network. SABAM brought a legal action against Scarlet claiming that as an ISP it was in the best position to take action against subscribers who indulged in copyright infringement. It sought court order instructing Scarlet to block or prevent internet users for sending music files through the P2P network without the permission of the copyright holders. Scarlet refused to install a system for the purpose of filtering electronic communications which use file sharing software based on P2P network so as to prevent distribution of copyright infringing materials on the internet and challenged the legal action. The President of the Tribunal de premiere ordered that Scarlet should take measures to prevent unauthorized distribution of music files. The decision was challenged before the Court of Appeals by Scarlet on the ground that 'it was impossible for it to comply with that injunction since the effectiveness and permanence of filtering and blocking systems had not been proved and that the installation of the equipment for so doing was faced with numerous practical obstacles, such as problems with the network capacity and the impact on the network. Moreover, any attempt to block the files concerned was, it argued, doomed to fail in the very short term because there were at that time several peer-to-peer software products which made it impossible for third parties to check

---

[75] *Id.*

[76] Scarlet Extended SA v. Société belge des auteurs, compositeurs et éditeurs SCRL (SABAM), European Court of Justice, 24, November 2011, C-70/10.

[77] *Id* at para 15–16.

their content.'[78] It was further argued that such actions were in contravention to provisions relating to protection of personal data and the secrecy of communications because the process of blocking or filtering will demand a general surveillance of the entire communication system.[79] In order to ensure that the demand for internet filtering were in compliance with the provisions of the European Union Law, the matter was referred to the European Court of Justice. The court considered the relevant provisions under the EC Directive on certain legal aspects of information society services, in particular electronic commerce, in the Internal Market (E-commerce directive), EC Directive on the harmonisation of certain aspects of copyright and related rights in the information society (Digital Copyright Directive), EC Directive on the enforcement of intellectual property rights, and EC Directive on concerning the processing of personal data and the protection of privacy in the electronic communications sector (Privacy and Electronic Communications directive). The court looked into the issue of whether 'an injunction imposed on ISP to introduce a system for all electronic communications passing via its services, in particular those involving the use of peer-to-peer software; which applies indiscriminately to all its customers; as a preventive measure; exclusively at its expense; and for an unlimited period, which is capable of identifying on that provider's network the movement of electronic files containing a musical, cinematographic or audio-visual work in respect of which the applicant claims to hold intellectual property rights, with a view to blocking the transfer of files the sharing of which infringes copyright' is permissible under the EC regulations. The court observed that the copyright holders had the authority to apply for injunctions against ISPs whose services were being used for copyright infringing activities to prevent such acts of copyright infringement under the existing rules. But such authority did not extend to require an ISP to install a filtering mechanism which would actively monitor all communication and exchange of data between the subscribers, identify within the information traffic those particular digital files on which the copyright holders claim to have legal ownership and also determine which of those files were being distributed and shared unlawfully and thereafter block all such illegal file sharing.[80] The court further observed that the right to intellectual property as enshrined in Article 17(2) of the Charter of Fundamental Rights of the European Union is important but is not inviolable and does not enjoy absolute protection under the legal system.[81] The rights associated with the protection of intellectual property rights have to be balanced with the protection of other fundamental rights.[82] It was further observed that 'in the context of measures adopted to protect copyright holders, national authorities and courts must strike a fair balance between the protection of copyright and the protection of the

[78] *Id* at para 24.

[79] *Id* at para 25–26.

[80] *Id* at para 40.

[81] *Id* at para 43.

[82] *Id* at para 44.

fundamental rights of individuals who are affected by such measures'.[83] The demand of the copyright holders to install a filtering system by the ISPs to monitor all the communications made through the network will on one hand violate the right of the ISPs to conduct their business and on the other hand, adversely affect the right of the internet users. The demand on the ISPs to install a 'complicated, costly, permanent computer filtering system' would violate Article 3(1) of the EC Directive on the Enforcement of Intellectual Property Rights which provided that the measures to be adopted for the purpose of protecting intellectual properties should not be 'unnecessarily complicated or costly'. The demand by the copyright holders requesting the installation of such expensive and complicated filtering system failed to ensure fair balance between the copyright holders and ISPs. Similarly, the procedure to monitor all the electronic communications violated the right of the users to 'protect their personal data and their freedom to receive or impart information' which are provided under Articles 8 and 11 of the Charter.[84] The technological procedure would also have adverse impact on the freedom of information because the filtering machine would generally fail to make a distinction between lawful and unlawful content, and thereby end up blocking genuine and lawful communications. Such filtering mechanism would also block all forms of permissible usages of copyright works which are contained under the exception clauses of copyright laws and thereby deny the users and society the essential rights granted by the copyright law for the promotion of culture, knowledge and information in society.[85] The court was also concerned with the fact that the filtering procedure may deny the users access to works which are in the public domain or which have been freely posted and circulated by the authors. Thus the court analyzed that the use of technological measures to protect the rights of the copyright holders had infringed upon important rights of the other members of the society, including the rights of the users. The technological procedures had failed to strike a fair balance between *'the right to intellectual property on one hand and the freedom to conduct business, right to protection of personal data and the freedom to receive or impart information, on the other.'*[86]

5.3 Ashby Donald v. France[87]

In the recent decision of the ECHR in the case of *Ashby Donald* v. *France*, the court dealt with the issue of conflict between the two important rights of copyright law and freedom of speech and expression. In this case, three fashion photographers, Robert

[83] *Id* at para 45.

[84] *Id.*

[85] *Id* at para 52.

[86] *Id* at para 54.

[87] Ashby Donald v. France Application no. 36769/08.

Ashby Donald, Marcio Madeira Moraes and Olivier Claisse had published photographs from a fashion show on their website without obtaining necessary permission from the fashion houses which claimed copyright on the clothes and the designs. The Court rejected the argument of the fashion photographers that the publication was protected under the copyright exception clause of French copyright law relating to news reporting and information purposes. It was held that the publication was for commercial purposes and not protected under the exception clause of copyright law. The court for the first time recognized that 'restrictions on the use of copyright protected works and sanctions based on copyright law ultimately can be regarded as interferences with the right of freedom of expression and information.'[88] It recognized that copyright protection may conflict with right to freedom of expression and information but every breach of human rights (a) has to be prescribed by law, (b) has to pursue a legitimate aim and (3) has to be considered necessary in a democratic society. The decision implied that a case or decision on copyright infringement must be in accordance with the three conditions specified in the second paragraph of Article 10 of the European Convention. In this case there was no violation of Article 10 as the publication of the picture was only for a commercial purpose and had no social utility. This decision of the ECHR is deemed landmark because of its effort to balance the rights of the copyright holders and the society at large. It enables a copyright claim to be justified in infringing an essential human right when such interference is prescribed by law and pursues a legitimate aim.[89] Failure to justify a copyright claim on the ground of 'necessary in a democratic society' will imply violation of right to freedom of speech and expression. Thus the decision provided that it was no longer sufficient to justify a copyright infringing claim and restricting another individual's right to freedom of expression simply by arguing that copyright law provision was infringed. The decision is significant attempt to protect the interests of the society and the users of copyrighted works by granting an additional protection to expressions and contents which are of general public importance and essential in society.

5.4 Fredrik Neij and Peter Sunde Kolmisoppi (the Pirate Bay) v. Sweden[90]

The applicants Fredrik Neij and Peter Sunde Kolmisoppi were involved with different aspects of The Pirate Bay, the largest file sharing service networks in the world. In 2008, the applicants along with two other persons were charged for committing copyright infringement under the Copyright Act 1960 before the

---

[88] Voorhoof, *Supra* note 74.

[89] Marjolein van der Helde, 2013.

[90] European Court of Human Rights, Fredrik Neij and Peter Sunde Kolmisoppi (The Pirate Bay) v. Sweden Application no. 40397/12.

District Court of Sweden. It was alleged that the defendants had facilitated the commission of copyright infringement by providing users the opportunities to upload torrent files and also search and download other available torrent files through the tracker function of The Pirate Bay. It was argued by the applicants that they were not liable for copyright infringement because of factors like they were merely service providers and were not involved with copyright infringing activities of the internet users. The District Court convicted the applicants for complicity to commit copyright infringement and imposed damages of Euro 3.3 million for facilitating and furthering the crimes in violation of Copyright Act. The ECHR on appeal analyzed the merits of the case in light of the constitutional guarantees relating to freedom of expression and information. The Swedish Constitution provides that *"Every citizen shall be guaranteed the following rights and freedoms in his relations with the public institutions: (1) freedom of expression: that is, the freedom to communicate information and express thoughts, opinions and sentiments, whether orally, pictorially, in writing, or in any other way; (2) freedom of information: that is, the freedom to procure and receive information and otherwise acquaint oneself with the utterances of others."*[91] Such rights of the citizens are subjected to limitations of Sections 21 and 23 of Chap. 2 of the Constitution. According to Section 21 *'limitations may be imposed only to satisfy the purposes acceptable in a democratic society'* and under Section 23 the specific grounds of restriction are *'security of the Realm, the national supply of goods, public order and public safety, good repute of the individual, sanctity of the private life and prevention and prosecution of crime'*[92] Article 10 of the European Convention provides that everyone has the right to freedom of expression and the freedom to receive and impart information and ideas without state intervention. Recognizing the importance of internet the court observed that *'the Internet plays an important role in enhancing the public's access to news and facilitating the sharing and dissemination of information generally.'*[93] The scope of protection under Article 10 extends *'not only to the content of the information but also to the means of transmission or reception since any restriction imposed on the means necessarily interferes with the right to receive and impart information'*.[94] In addition, the right under Article 10 is granted to 'everyone' irrespective of the fact whether the activity involved was for profit-making purposes or not. The court held that—

> In the present case, the applicants put in place the means for others to impart and receive information within the meaning of Article 10 of the Convention. The Court considers that the actions taken by the applicants are afforded protection under Article 10 Section 1 of the Convention and, consequently, the applicants' convictions interfered with their right to freedom of expression. Such interference breaches Article 10 unless it was "prescribed by

---

[91] Swedish Constitution, Chap. 2, Sect. 1.

[92] *Id.* Chap. 2, Sects. 21 & 23.

[93] Pirate Bay, *Supra* note 164.

[94] *Id.*

law", pursued one or more of the legitimate aims referred to in Article 10 Section 2 and was "necessary in a democratic society" to attain such aim or aims.[95]

By applying the facts of the case to the applicable legal provisions the Court held that the limitations imposed by Copyright law were 'prescribed by law' and were for the legitimate purpose of protecting the rights of the copyright holders and such protection was deemed necessary in a democratic society, hence the decisions of the District Court of Sweden were justified for the purpose of restricting the rights of the applicants. The genuine and effective protection of the rights of the copyright holders is dependent on not only the State's duty not to interfere but also on the demand for adopting positive measures by the State. In this case the court adopted the balancing test between competing interest groups by holding that *"the Court must take into account various factors, such as the nature of the competing interests involved and the degree to which those interests require protection in the circumstances of the case"* for the purpose of determining that the interference was 'necessary in a democratic society'.[96] States have been granted a wide margin of appreciation to determine the scope of protection granted to the different interest groups.

Thus, the ECHR has given due importance to the rights of the consumer as well as the rights of the copyright holders in the digital environment and recognized that internet plays a very significant role in disseminating and sharing of information among the people and any restriction imposed on the internet will infringe the rights guaranteed to the internet users under Article 10 of the Convention and can only be justified on equally competing grounds. Protection of political expression and debates should be given paramount importance in society.

6 Human Rights Perspective and the Law of Copyright

The Universal Declaration of Human Rights was drafted in the year 1948 after a long deliberation under the auspices of the United Nations. The main objective of the Declaration was to protect the dignity of all human beings across the societies and recognize certain inalienable rights in the nature of human rights which are deemed essential for the protection of freedom, justice and peace in the world. These attainment and protection of these rights are considered to be 'highest aspiration of the common people' as they promote the dignity and worth of human persons, equal rights of men and women and ensure social progress and better standards of life.[97] An important element of human life is the ability to participate in the cultural and social activities in a community and UDHR has recognized the

[95] *Id.*

[96] *Id.*

[97] UDHR, Preamble.

right of individuals to participate in the cultural life and enjoy different forms of artistic and creative works as an essential part of human rights.

Article 27 recognizes the right of every individual to participate in different forms of cultural life.[98] It recognizes the 'right of an individual to enjoy culture and to advance culture and science without interference from the state' as a human right.[99] The term 'culture' narrowly implies the creative, artistic or scientific activities which an individual might indulge in, whereas the broad connotation of the term refers to the total sum of all human activities including values, knowledge and practices.[100] The right to culture includes a set of rights like right to take part in cultural life; right to enjoy the benefits of scientific progress; right of individual to benefit from the protection of the moral and material interests resulting from any scientific, literary or artistic production of which he is author; and the right to freedom from the interference of the state in scientific or creative pursuits. It imposes an obligation on the State authorities to promote and protect cultural activities and artefacts. Professor Vernon Van Dyke in his seminal work *The Cultural Rights of the Peoples* has analysed the importance of the right to culture and the deep inter-relationship which it has with other essential elements of the society like self-government and political participation; language; education; religion; movement, residence and property; and freedom of expression.[101] The essence of Article 27 has been adopted in other international and regional instruments like the International Covenant on Economic, Social and Cultural Rights (1966).[102]

The Committee on Economic, Social and Cultural Rights which was established by the UN Economic and Social Council in 1985 for the purpose of monitoring the implementation of the convention. Other international instruments relating to cultural rights are the Declaration of the Principles of International Cultural

---

[98] Article 27 of the Declaration provides that—

(1) Everyone has the right freely to participate in the cultural life of the community, to enjoy the arts and to share in scientific advancement and its benefits.
(2) Everyone has the right to the protection of the moral and material interests resulting from any scientific, literary or artistic production of which he is the author.

[99] Right to Culture.

[100] Symonides 1998.

[101] Van Dyke 1980.

[102] Article 15 of ICESCR provides—

1. (a) To take part in cultural life; (b) To enjoy the benefits of scientific progress and its applications; (c) To benefit from the protection of the moral and material interests resulting from any scientific, literary or artistic production of which he is the author.
2. The steps to be taken by the States Parties to the present Covenant to achieve the full realization of this right shall include those necessary for the conservation, the development and the diffusion of science and culture.
3. The States Parties to the present Covenant undertake to respect the freedom indispensable for scientific research and creative activity.
4. The States Parties to the present Covenant recognize the benefits to be derived from the encouragement and development of international contacts and co-operation in the scientific and cultural fields.

Co-operation (1966), Limburg Principles on the Implementation of the International Covenant on Economic, Social and Cultural Rights (1986), Maastricht Guidelines on Violations of Economic, Social and Cultural Rights (1997), Convention on the Rights of the Child (1989), Convention Concerning the Protection of the World Cultural and Natural Heritage (1972) and Convention for the Protection of Cultural Property in the Event of Armed Conflict (1954). International organizations like the United Nations Educational, Scientific and Cultural Organization (UNESCO) has the responsibility to collaborate among nations through education, science and culture and promote respect for universal values like justice, rule of law, human rights and fundamental freedoms amongst the people across the world.

The cultural rights are deemed important in today's society and are considered as 'empowering rights' because the recognition of cultural identity of human beings are essential for the maintenance of human dignity and protection of human rights. Janusz Symonides has observed that 'without the recognition of cultural rights, cultural plurality and diversity, fully democratic societies cannot function properly.'[103] However, in the present debates relating to intellectual properties in general and copyright law in particular have largely concentrated on the scope and application of copyright laws and the permissible usages under the 'fair use' exceptions contained in the copyright law based on the principles of transformative and non-commercial usages, and the importance and relevance of the cultural rights in the intellectual property debates have been largely ignored by the judiciary and the policy makers. Eminent scholar Rosemary Coombe has observed, "*Cultural rights have largely been ignored in contemporary debates about the extension of intellectual property rights and the endangerment of the public domain.*"[104] The copyright based industries dominated by the US have often ignored the importance of the International Covenant on Social, Economic and Cultural Rights and the UNESCO.[105]

The inclusion of the right to culture in the copyright debates would widen the scope of the rights of the consumers by broadening the scope of public domain, free speech and fair use. The right to culture demands that not only new principles are developed recognizing the rights of the general people to use the cultural heritage of the world but also to create an environment wherein the different forms of cultural creativity can be developed and promoted. In the words of Coombe,

> In a global environment where opportunities for cultural representation are so unequally distributed, vague fears about "copyrighting culture" cannot ethically be met with mere assertions of individual liberty or the importance of the undifferentiated public circulation of culture. We should be working toward cultural policies that enable more peoples with distinct traditions to participate in the cultural life of their own communities, in new and emergent forms of cross-cultural dialogue, and in a more inclusive public domain."[106]

---

[103] Symonides, *Supra* note 101.

[104] Coombe 2005.

[105] *Id.*

[106] *Id.*

It is deemed essential to balance the rights of the intellectual property holders with the right of individuals to freely express their creativity. An effort has been made by the international community to recognize the right to access to intellectual properties as part of the human rights through various international and regional human rights instruments. The right to access cultural works and the right to participate in the cultural life of the society is an important human right which every individual is entitled to enjoy. With the advancement of technology and development of internet, it is necessary to extend the scope of the cultural rights and apply them on the digital environment. It is important to recognize the cyber world as an extension of the living space of the people wherein people use the digital media to express themselves and gather information. Access to cultural works like musical works is essential for the promotion and development of the online environment hence recognition of the right of the users to cultural works is of utmost importance in the digital environment.

7 Conclusion

Internet has become an integral part of human life and the cyberspace has assumed a second life for the younger generations. Easy access to information and materials are necessary for the well functioning of this system. In such an environment, it is important to ensure that internet remains equally accessible to all members of the society. Protection of intellectual works is important for the growth of culture and science in society and grant of copyright protection to the authors of creative works is an attempt towards achieving this objective. In the digital environment, attempts have been made to enhance the scope of copyright protection to prevent unauthorised distribution of copyrighted materials and facilitate the growth of copyright based industries. But in the absence of recognition of the rights of the consumers of copyrighted works in the digital environment true growth of user friendly internet will not take place. In this chapter the theoretical premise for creating a user friendly digital environment was laid down by analyzing different justifications like copyright jurisprudence, human rights principles, digital rights theory and constitutional arguments. In light of the analysis made, it is asserted that the recognition of the rights of the consumers in the online environment is not only a legal and economic necessity but is also imperative from the perspective of human rights and citizenship rights.

References

Coombe R (2005) Cultural rights and intellectual property debates—human rights dialogue: 'Cultural Rights'. Carnegie Council for Ethics in International Affairs, April 22, 2005. http://www.carnegiecouncil.org/publications/archive/dialogue/2_12/section_3/5152.html (last visited Dec 25, 2015)

Fisher W (2001) Theories of intellectual property. In: Munzer S (ed) New essays in the legal and political theory of property. Cambridge University Press, pp 168–199

Locke J (2015) Two treatises on Government (1860–1690). The Laws of Nature and Nature's God. http://www.lonang.com/exlibris/locke/ (last visited Dec 25, 2015)

Hughes J (1988) The philosophy of intellectual property. 77 Geo. L.J.287 300

Landes WM, Posner RA (1989) An economic analysis of copyright law. J Legal Stud 18(2): 325–363

Macaulay TB (2015) Speech delivered in the house of commons on the 5th of February 1841. http://www.kuro5hin.org/story/2002/4/25/1345/03329 (last visited Dec 25, 2015)

The Founders' Constitution (2015) Thomas Jefferson to Isaac McPherson, Article 1, Section 8, Clause 8, 13 August 1813. http://press-pubs.uchicago.edu/founders/documents/a1_8_8s12.html (last visited Dec 25, 2015)

The History of Copyright: A Critical Overview, The statute of Anne 1710. http://www.copyrighthistory.com/anne.html (last visited Dec 25, 2015)

Garnett K, Davies G, Harbottle G (2005) Copinger and Skone James on copyright. Sweet & Maxwell 23, vol I

Voorhoof D (2015) ECHR: copyright vs. freedom of expression. Kluwer Blogger, 25.01.2013, http://kluwercopyrightblog.com/2013/01/25/echr-copyright-vs-freedom-of-expression/ (last visited Dec 25, 2015)

Symonides J (1998) Cultural rights: a neglected category of human rights. Int Soc Sci J 158:559, 14p, 2bw. http://www.iupui.edu/~anthkb/a104/humanrights/cultrights.htm (last visited Dec 25, 2015)

Van Dyke V (1980) The cultural rights of peoples. Universal Human Rights 2(2):1–21

Marrakesh Treaty to Facilitate Access to Published Works for Visually Disabled: Putting an End to Global Book Famine

V.K. Ahuja

Abstract The access to knowledge opens the door to a good education, successful employment and a fruitful and independent personal life. The right to education remains unachievable for blind, visually impaired and print disabled persons due to absence of reading material in accessible formats, such as braille, large prints, audio cassettes, etc. The visually impaired persons do not have adequate access to the published works, due to which they fail to achieve equal opportunities in society. In order to facilitate access to published works for the aforesaid persons, the Marrakesh Treaty to Facilitate Access to Published Works for Persons who are Blind, Visually Impaired or Otherwise Print Disabled was adopted on 27 June, 2013 at WIPO. The Treaty obligates Contracting Parties to provide limitation or exception to the right of reproduction, the right of distribution, and the right of making available to the public in their national laws to facilitate the availability of works in accessible format copies for beneficiary persons. Such limitation or exception is to permit changes needed to make the work accessible in the alternative format. India is the first country to ratify the Marrakesh Treaty. The Marrakesh Treaty, which came into force on 30th September 2016, is a welcome step towards the realization of human rights of the beneficiaries. The Treaty aims at improving access for the beneficiaries to publish works in the formats such as Braille, Daisy, large print text, audio books, etc. The Treaty is just first step towards the ending of book scarcity for the beneficiaries. The States will have to show their will by becoming party to this Treaty and to amend their laws accordingly.

V.K. Ahuja (✉)
Faculty of Law, University of Delhi, Delhi 110007, India
e-mail: vkahuja2002@yahoo.co.in

M.K. Sinha and V. Mahalwar (eds.), *Copyright Law in the Digital World*,
DOI 10.1007/978-981-10-3984-3_4

1 Introduction

The access to knowledge opens the door to a good education, successful employment and a fruitful and independent personal life.[1] The right to education has been recognized as human rights in several international human rights instruments, most particularly in Universal Declaration of Human Rights, 1948; International Covenant on Economic, Social and Cultural Rights, 1966; Convention on Rights of Child, 1989; and Convention on the Rights of Persons with Disabilities, 2006. The right to education remains unachievable for blind, visually impaired and print disabled persons due to absence of reading material in accessible formats, such as braille, large prints, audio cassettes, etc. Less than 10% of all published materials are available in accessible formats and most of these are available in English alone.[2] Of the estimated 6 million children around the globe with a visual impairment, some 4.4 million of them live in under-resourced settings and do not receive an education.[3] Majority of persons with visual impairments or with other print disabilities live in developing and least-developed countries. It is estimated that around 90% of those living with print disabilities reside in developing countries.[4]

The visually impaired persons do not have adequate access to the published works, due to which they fail to achieve equal opportunities in society. Therefore, the lack of education due to unavailability of published work in accessible format, results in the further denial of their other human rights, most particularly the right of employment. Their freedom of expression, including the freedom to seek, receive and impart information and ideas of all kinds on an equal basis with others, as well as their enjoyment of the right to education, and the opportunity to conduct research is adversely affected. It is important for the international community to enhance opportunities for everyone to participate in the cultural life of the community, to enjoy the arts and to share scientific progress and its benefits. A fair deal to visually impaired persons will be possible only when they will have access to published work like normal persons.

In order to facilitate access to published works for the aforesaid persons, the Marrakesh Treaty to Facilitate Access to Published Works for Persons who are Blind, Visually Impaired or Otherwise Print Disabled was adopted on 27 June, 2013 at World Intellectual Property Organization (WIPO). The Marrakesh Treaty was adopted recalling "the principles of non-discrimination, equal opportunity, accessibility and full and effective participation and inclusion in society, proclaimed in the Universal Declaration of Human Rights and the United Nations Convention

[1] Jewell 2015.

[2] *Id.* at 16.

[3] *Id.* at 19.

[4] Jewell 2014.

on the Rights of Persons with Disabilities."[5] The Treaty required the deposit of 20 instruments of ratification or accession from the eligible parties[6] for coming into force. The treaty came into force on September 30, 2016.

2 Meaning of "Accessible Format Copy"

According to Article 2(b) of the Marrakesh Treaty, "accessible format copy" means a copy of a work in an alternative manner or form which gives a beneficiary person access to the work, including to permit the person to have access as feasibly and comfortably as a person without visual impairment or other print disability. The term has been defined broadly so as to include any format which makes a book accessible to the beneficiaries. The term may include e.g. Braille, Daisy, large print, talking books, digital formats etc.

The accessible format copy is to be used exclusively by beneficiary persons. It must respect the integrity of the original work, taking due consideration of the changes needed to make the work accessible in the alternative format and of the accessibility needs of the beneficiary persons.

3 Who Is a Beneficiary Person?

According to Article 3, a beneficiary person means a person who—(i) is blind; (ii) has a visual impairment or a perceptual or reading disability which cannot be improved to give visual function equivalent to a normal person and so is unable to read the printed works; or (iii) is otherwise unable, through physical disability, to hold or manipulate a book or to focus or move the eyes to the extent that would be normally acceptable for reading. Article 3, thus defines the term beneficiary person in a broader manner and includes any physical disability that comes in the way of effective reading. According to Article 3, the beneficiaries include blind, visually impaired, reading disabled (e.g. persons having dyslexia), and others who have a physical disability that obstruct them to hold a book, turn pages or focus.

---

[5] See Preamble of Marrakesh Treaty to Facilitate Access to Published Works for Persons Who Are Blind, Visually Impaired, or Otherwise Print Disabled (June 28, 2013).

[6] In addition to Member States of WIPO, any intergovernmental organization and the European Union may also become party in accordance with Article 15 of the Marrakesh Treaty.

4 Limitations or Exceptions in National Copyright Laws

The Treaty obligates Contracting Parties to provide limitation or exception to the right of reproduction, the right of distribution, and the right of making available to the public in their national laws to facilitate the availability of works in accessible format copies for beneficiary persons. Such limitation or exception is to permit changes needed to make the work accessible in the alternative format.[7]

Further, at the discretion of Contracting Parties, limitation or exception to the right of public performance may also be provided to facilitate access to works for beneficiary persons. This provision is discretionary and not obligatory.[8]

By imposing limitation or exception in national law, the Parties may permit the authorized entities[9] to make an accessible format copy of a work, obtain from another authorized entity an accessible format copy, and supply those copies to beneficiary persons by any means, including by non-commercial lending or by electronic communication by wire or wireless means.

Such an entity may also undertake any intermediate steps to achieve these objectives, when—(i) it has lawful access to that work; (ii) the work is converted to an accessible format copy, which may include any means needed to navigate information in the accessible format; (iii) such accessible format copies are supplied exclusively for beneficiary persons; and (iv) the activity is undertaken on a non-profit basis.

In addition to above, a beneficiary person himself, or someone acting on his behalf, may make or assist him in making of an accessible format copy of a work for his personal use where the beneficiary person has lawful access to that work.[10]

A Contracting Party may provide other limitations or exceptions in its national copyright law pursuant to Articles 10 and 11 of the Marrakesh Treaty. A Contracting Party may confine limitations or exceptions to works which, in the particular accessible format, cannot be obtained commercially under reasonable terms for beneficiary persons in that market. The Treaty leaves it to the Parties to determine whether limitations or exceptions are subject to remuneration.[11]

Article 10 enables Contracting Parties to fulfill their rights and obligations through limitations or exceptions specifically for the benefit of beneficiary persons, other limitations or exceptions, or a combination thereof, within their national legal system and practice. These may include judicial, administrative or regulatory

[7] Marrakesh Treaty, Article 4(1)(a).

[8] *Id.* Article 4(1)(b).

[9] *Id.* Article 2(c) defines "authorized entity" to mean "an entity that is authorized or recognized by the government to provide education, instructional training, adaptive reading or information access to beneficiary persons on a non-profit basis. It also includes a government institution or non-profit organization that provides the same services to beneficiary persons as one of its primary activities or institutional obligations".

[10] *Id.* Article 4(2).

[11] *Id.* Article 4(3)–(5).

determinations for the benefit of beneficiary persons as to fair practices, dealings or uses to meet their needs consistent with the Contracting Parties' rights and obligations under the Berne Convention, other international treaties, and Article 11.

According to Article 11, the Contracting Parties may exercise their rights and have to comply with their obligations under the Berne Convention, the Agreement on Trade-Related Aspects of Intellectual Property Rights (TRIPs Agreement) and the WIPO Copyright Treaty (WCT). The Marrakesh Treaty makes it obligatory for the Contracting Parties to comply with the three-step test obligations under these treaties. The three-step test obligations have been laid down in the following manner.

In accordance with Article 9(2) of the Berne Convention, a Contracting Party may permit the reproduction of works in certain special cases provided that such reproduction does not conflict with a normal exploitation of the work and does not unreasonably prejudice the legitimate interests of the author. Similarly, in accordance with Article 13 of the TRIPs Agreement, a Contracting Party is to confine limitations or exceptions to exclusive rights to certain special cases which do not conflict with a normal exploitation of the work and do not unreasonably prejudice the legitimate interests of the rightholder.

Further, in accordance with Article 10(1) of the WCT, a Contracting Party may provide for limitations or exceptions to the rights granted to authors under the WCT in certain special cases, that do not conflict with a normal exploitation of the work and do not unreasonably prejudice the legitimate interests of the author. Apart from that, in accordance with Article 10(2) of the WCT, a Contracting Party is to confine, when applying the Berne Convention, any limitations or exceptions to rights to certain special cases that do not conflict with a normal exploitation of the work and do not unreasonably prejudice the legitimate interests of the author.

Thus, according to three-step test, any exception or limitation—(1) shall cover only certain special cases; (2) shall not conflict with the normal exploitation of the work; and (3) shall not unreasonably prejudice the legitimate interests of the rightholder.

The copyright limitations and exceptions for the benefit of beneficiary persons other than those provided under this Treaty may also be implemented by Contracting Parties in their national laws. This may have regard to their economic situation and social and cultural needs. Further, these limitations and exceptions are to be in conformity with their international rights and obligations. In the case of a least-developed country, these limitations and exceptions are to be implemented by taking into account its special needs and its particular international rights and obligations and flexibilities thereof. This Treaty is without prejudice to other limitations and exceptions for persons with disabilities provided by national law.[12]

---

[12] *Id.* Article 12.

5 Distribution of Accessible Format Copies Abroad

According to Article 5, an accessible format copy made in lawful manner in one Contracting Party may be distributed or made available by an authorized entity to a beneficiary person or an authorized entity in another Contracting Party. However, when an authorized entity in a Contracting Party which does not have obligations under Article 9 of the Berne Convention, receives accessible format copies, it will ensure, consistent with its own legal system and practices, that the accessible format copies are only reproduced, distributed or made available for the benefit of beneficiary persons in that Contracting Party's jurisdiction.

Article 6 enables a Contracting Party to permit a beneficiary person, someone acting on his behalf, or an authorized entity to import an accessible format copy for the benefit of beneficiary persons without the authorization of the rightholder, to the extent to which that Party permits them to make an accessible format copy of a work.

6 Obligations Concerning Technological Measures

In the digital environment, the rightholders take the support of technological measures to exploit the work on Internet. Thus, no rights in respect of digital uses of works may be applied efficiently without the support of technological measures. Technological measures cover various devices and electronic tools, which consist of systems allowing and monitoring the access to protected material and information. These systems include passwording, encryption, digital envelopes, etc.[13] Ordinarily, the States provide legal protection against the circumvention of technological measures. The technological measures work as "digital padlock". They are being used by the rightholder on a digital book to prevent people from having unauthorised access to such works. This is a widespread measure to prevent infringement of copyright. The States provide civil and criminal remedies against the circumvention of these technological measures. However, it has also been observed that sometimes this padlock inadvertently block legitimate access by print disabled people, for instance those using "screen-reading text-to-speech software".[14]

In order to overcome the aforesaid problem and to facilitate the access to published works for the beneficiaries, the Marrakesh Treaty obligates the Contracting Parties to take appropriate measures to ensure that when they provide adequate legal protection and effective legal remedies against the circumvention of effective technological measures, this legal protection does not prevent beneficiary persons

[13] Ahuja 2015.

[14] The Treaty of Marrakesh explained, available at: http://www.worldblindunion.org/english/news/Pages/The-Treaty-of-Marrakesh.aspx.

from enjoying the limitations and exceptions provided for in this Treaty.[15] In other words, it shall not be illegal to circumvent the technological measures for the aforesaid purpose.

7 Cooperation to Facilitate Cross-Border Exchange

Article 9 obligates the Contracting Parties to endeavor to foster the cross-border exchange of accessible format copies by encouraging the voluntary sharing of information to assist authorized entities in identifying one another. The International Bureau of WIPO is to establish an information access point for this purpose. Article 9 does not imply mandatory registration for authorized entities nor does it constitute a precondition for authorized entities to engage in activities recognized under this Treaty. It provides for a possibility for sharing information to facilitate the cross-border exchange of accessible format copies.

8 Indian Position

India is the first country to ratify the Marrakesh Treaty. It is noteworthy that India amended its Copyright Act, 1957 in 2012, even prior to the adoption of the Treaty to incorporate new provisions for the facilitating the access of disabled persons to the published materials in the accessible format.

8.1 Reproduction of Work in Accessible Format for Disabled Persons in India

The 2012 amendment to Copyright Act incorporated Section 52(1)(zb), which allows adaptation, reproduction, issue of copies or communication to the public of any work by any person in any accessible format to facilitate persons with disability to access to works including sharing with any person with disability of such accessible format for private or personal use, educational purpose or research.

Where normal format prevents the enjoyment of any work by disabled persons, any organization[16] working for their benefits are also allowed to adapt, reproduce,

---

[15] Marrakesh Treaty, Article 7.

[16] "Any organization" includes an organization registered under Section 12A of the Income-tax Act, 1961 and working for the benefit of persons with disability or recognized under Chapter X of the Persons with Disabilities (Equal Opportunities, Protection or Rights and Full Participation) Act, 1995 or receiving grants from the government for facilitating access to persons with disabilities or an educational institution or library or archives recognized by the Government.

issue copies or communicate to them such work in accessible format. "Accessible format" includes Braille, Daisy, large print, talking books, digital formats and all other formats that can be used by persons with disabilities.[17]

The copies so made in the accessible format are to be made available to the disabled persons on a non-profit basis. However, the person/organization making such copies can recover the cost of production only. The organization making such copies shall ensure that such copies are used only by disabled persons. The organization shall also take reasonable steps to prevent their entry into ordinary channels of business.

The organization intending to adapt, reproduce, issue of copies or communication to public of any work in any accessible format shall maintain at its principal place of business a register containing the following details, namely—(i) the name of the work, author or owner or publisher along with year of publication; (ii) the details of the accessible format in which the work is produced; (iii) the nature of activity such as adaptation, reproduction, issue of copies or communication to the public; (iv) total number of copies made, list of persons with disabilities to whom copies have been distributed; and (v) price, if any, charged on the copies.[18]

This is a welcome provision in the Copyright Act and fulfils the longstanding demand of the disabled persons. The provision rules out the possibility of making profits by persons or organization who provide copies of the work in accessible format to disabled persons.

8.2 Compulsory Licence for the Benefit of Disabled Persons

As per Section 31B, any person working for the benefit of persons with disability on a profit basis or for business may apply in the prescribed manner to the Copyright Board for a compulsory licence to publish any work in which copyright subsists for the benefit of such persons. It should not be a case to which the aforesaid provisions of Section 52(1)(zb) applies. The Copyright Board shall dispose of such application preferably within a period of 2 months. The Copyright Board may make necessary inquiry to establish the applicant's credentials and satisfy itself that the application is made in good faith.

After giving to the owners of rights in the work a reasonable opportunity of being heard and after holding necessary inquiry, if the Copyright Board is satisfied that a compulsory licence needs to be issued to make the work available to the disabled, it may direct the Registrar of Copyrights to grant to the applicant such a licence to publish the work.

The compulsory licence is to specify the means and format of publication, the period during which the compulsory licence may be exercised and in the case of issue of copies, the number of copies that may be issued including the rate or royalty.

---

[17] The Copyright Rules, 2013, explanation to rule 77.

[18] *Id.* rule 76.

However, where a compulsory licence has been issued, the Copyright Board may, on a further application and after giving reasonable opportunity to the owners of rights, extend the period of compulsory licence and allow the issue of more copies as it may deem fit.

8.2.1 Procedure for the Grant of Licence

A copy of application is to be served by registered post on the owner of copyright and if the owner of such copyright is not known or is not traceable, a copy of the application shall be served by registered post on the publisher whose name appears on the work. The Board shall give an opportunity of being heard to the owner of the copyright and the applicant and also, wherever practicable, to any person claiming any interest in the copyright of the work, and shall take such evidence in respect of the application, as it deems fit.

If the Board is satisfied that the licence for publication of the work in the format applied for may be granted to the applicant, or if there are more applicants than one, to such of the applicants as in the opinion of the Board would best serve the interest of the disabled persons, it shall direct the Registrar of Copyright to grant licence accordingly.

The licence granted under Section 31B is to specify: (a) the period within which such work shall be published; (b) the medium and format in which the work shall be produced and published; (c) the number of copies that shall be produced; (d) the rate at which royalties in respect of such copies shall be paid to the owner of the copyright in the work; and (e) the person to whom such royalties shall be payable.[19]

While determining royalties, the Board shall take into consideration—(a) the proposed price at which a copy of such work shall be made available to disabled persons; (b) the prevailing standards of royalties in regard to such works; (c) the cost involved in making the accessible formats for the disabled person; and (d) such other matters as may be considered relevant by the Copyright Board.[20]

On an application, the Board may extend the period of licence, if it is satisfied that the licensee for sufficient reasons was unable to produce and publish the work within the specified period.

The Board may, after giving an opportunity of being heard to the licensee, cancel the licence on the grounds—(a) that the licensee has failed to produce and publish such work within the time specified in the licence or within the extended time; (b) that the licence was obtained by fraud or misrepresentation as to any essential fact; (c) that the licensee has contravened any of the terms and conditions of the licence; or (d) the owner of the copyright has satisfied the requirement of the disabled person by publishing in the same format with same or lower price for which the compulsory licence was granted.[21]

---

[19] *Id.* rule 18.

[20] *Id.* rule 19.

[21] *Id.* rule 21.

9 Role of Accessible Books Consortium (ABC)

The Accessible Books Consortium (ABC), which was launched in June 2014, is an alliance consisting of WIPO, the World Blind Union, the DAISY Consortium, the International Federation of Library Associations and Institutions, the International Authors' Forum, the International Federation of Reproduction Rights Organizations and the International Publishers Association.[22] The ABC, being a practical initiative to support the goals of the Marrakesh Treaty, seeks to provide the printed materials in the accessible format in greater number. It is involved in three major activities—(i) building capacity; (ii) the promotion of "born accessible" publishing (inclusive publishing); and (iii) an international book exchange known as TIGAR Service.[23]

As far as the activity of building capacity is concerned, the ABC trains print disability support organizations, local publishers and government services in the latest accessible format publishing technologies. The purpose is to increase the number and range of books. In 2014, in comparison to 184,084 accessible format books held by US National Library Service for the Blind and Physically Handicapped, India had around 18,000 books.[24] One of the priorities of the ABC is to create an environment in developing countries by capacity building in which the publishers should feel confident to share their printed materials with the organizations which are working for the cause of visually impaired people.

As far as TIGAR service of ABC is concerned, it supports broader access by facilitating the cross-border exchange of printed materials in accessible formats. In 2014, there were 12 participating organizations from different countries, which were part of the TIGAR service. The TIGAR service helps in avoiding duplication of the material in the accessible formats. If a book has been converted into an accessible format at one place, it should be shareable among various organizations in different countries to reach the end users. The avoidance of duplication helps in saving resources which are utilized in converting other books in accessible formats.

10 Conclusion

The Marrakesh Treaty is a welcome step towards the realization of human rights of the beneficiaries. The Treaty aims at improving access for the beneficiaries to publish works in the formats such as Braille, Daisy, large print text, audio books, etc. The Contracting Parties shall be required to bring their copyrights laws in conformity with the provisions of this Treaty by providing limitations or exceptions for this purpose. The Treaty empowers the State Parties to exchange, import or export the published materials in the accessible format. The Treaty is just first step

[22] Jewell, February 2015.

[23] Jewell, August 2014.

[24] *Id.* at 22.

towards the ending of book scarcity for the beneficiaries. The States will have to show their will by becoming party to this Treaty and to amend their laws accordingly. The governmental efforts may not be adequate. The educational institutions and libraries must make efforts to achieve this goal. A greater responsibility also lies on the NGOs, particularly those working for the welfare of disabled persons. It is, however, important for the States to ensure that the provisions meant for the benefits of beneficiaries in their national copyright laws are not misused and the work so converted does not enter into ordinary channels of business, causing serious harm to the copyright owner.

References

Ahuja VK (2015) Law of copyright and neighboring rights: National and international perspectives, pp 268–269 (Lexis Nexis, New Delhi, 2nd edn 2015)

Jewell C (2014) Accessible books consortium: Breaking down barriers to accessibility. 4 WIPO Magazine 19, Aug 2014

Jewell C (2015) Removing barriers to literacy: How the Marrakesh VIP Treaty can change lives. 1 WIPO Magazine 19, Feb 2015

Reproduction Right in Digital Medium and Free Use for Educational Purpose—An Analysis of National and International Obligations of India to Provide Education to All Viz. a Viz. Protecting Copyright

Poonam Dass

Abstract India is party to human rights conventions which provides for right to education and equality in education apart from giving right to get benefit for creativity. The Berne convention on literary and artistic works, TRIPs agreement and WIPO copyright treaties provide rights to the authors for copyrighted works and balance these rights with certain free uses for public. India provides for certain exclusive rights to owners of copyright and certain free uses for educational and other purposes, in order to fulfill its international and constitutional obligations. The reproduction right in copyrighted works can be affected by use of reprographic techniques like photocopying or by other similar means. Before the advent of digital technology, reprography was limited to photocopying but now there are many means through which copying is possible like scanning, digital copies, print copies etc. There are provisions in the copyright law which permit free uses for educational purposes like fair dealing in any work for research, private study etc. The other being 'reproduction of any work by a teacher or a pupil in course of instruction'. It makes no express limitation as to length and number of copies to be made. One of the questions to be analysed is whether this provision allows reproduction in institutional teaching or in any other form of teaching including digital education, and does it make any implied restriction to length and number of copies to made. Does the provision require balancing and hence be subject to three step test of Berne. Whether the legalization of use of technology like encryption and making its circumvention penal, affects such free use of work. Finally, whether the developing country like India should continue permitting free reprographic uses for educational purposes in order to achieve its goals of education to all and access to quality education.

P. Dass (✉)
Faculty of Law, University of Delhi, Delhi, India
e-mail: pd_70_70@yahoo.com

M.K. Sinha and V. Mahalwar (eds.), *Copyright Law in the Digital World*,
DOI 10.1007/978-981-10-3984-3_5

1 Introduction

The Universal Declaration of Human Rights, 1948 (UDHR) and the Covenant on Economic, Social and Cultural rights, 1966 (CESCR) recognises the human right to education and equality in education. These instruments also recognise the literary and artistic productions of authors and rights of the public to freely enjoy these works and share its benefits. The treaties on copyright like the Berne convention on literary and artistic works, the Trade Related Intellectual Property agreement, 1994 (TRIPs) and the WIPO Copyright treaty, 1996 (WCT) provide exclusive rights to the owners of copyrighted works and also incorporate certain free uses for the public. These treaties try to balance an individual's right to education and right of authors to benefit from their creativity. India is party to human rights covenants, Berne Convention and TRIPs agreement. To enable authors to benefit from their creativity the Copyright Act, 1957[1] was passed which provides for certain exclusive rights to owners of copyright and certain free uses for public including educational use. In order to fulfill its international obligations and constitutional goals to provide right to education, India has made certain constitutional amendments. It has further enacted the Right to Education Act, 2009[2] to achieve universal access to quality education for all.

India being a developing country has given primacy to education. It has implemented the National Policy on Education, 1992 which is a guide to educational development in India and whose main objective is to provide education to all. In order to achieve the goals, apart from institutional teaching it has used other means of education like open schools, distance education and digital education. These require reproduction of copyrighted material in course of instruction which in turn affects the right of owners of copyrighted works not only in real world but also in virtual world.

The reproduction right in copyrighted works can be affected by use of reprographic techniques like photocopying or by other similar means. Before the advent of digital technology, reprography was limited to photocopying but now there are many other means through which copying is possible like scanning, digital copies, print copies etc. There are provisions in the copyright law which permit free uses for educational purposes like fair dealing in any work for research, private study etc. The other being 'reproduction of any work by a teacher or a pupil in course of instruction'. One of the questions to be analysed is whether this provision make any restrictions to length of the work to be used and number of copies to be made. Does it require balancing and hence be subject to three step test of Berne. Secondly, whether it applies to all forms of teaching i.e. institutional teaching or in any other form of teaching including digital education, and at all levels whether primary, secondary and higher education. Thirdly, does the developing country like India should permit free reprographic uses for educational purposes in order to achieve its

[1] Act 14 of 1957.

[2] The Right of Children to Free and Compulsory Education (RTE) Act, 2009 (Act 35 of 2009).

educational goals namely education to all and access to quality education and material. Finally, whether the legalization of use of technology like encryption and prohibiting its circumvention, affects free use of work for education.

2 Right to Reproduction of Copyrighted Works and Its Limitations for Educational Purposes-International Position

2.1 Berne Convention—1886–1948

The Berne Convention, 1886 protected 'literary and artistic works'. The expression included every production whatsoever in the literary, scientific, or artistic domain which can be published by any mode of impression or reproduction.[3] It did not provide for any explicit right to reproduction. It only provided for 'translation[4]' right. However the convention prohibited certain reproduction or translation of non political material published in newspapers and periodicals if expressly forbidden by authors or publishers, in country other than the publishing country. This provision exempted articles of political discussion, news of the day and other miscellaneous information.[5] It further prohibited certain illicit reproductions through indirect appropriations in same or other form without essential alterations, additions, or abridgments, so as not to present the character of a new original work. For a liberty of extracting portions for publication, destined for educational and scientific purposes the convention provided that the effect of legislations or of special

[3] The Bern Convention, 1886, Article 4—The expression 'literary and artistic works' shall include books, pamphlets, and all other writings; dramatic or dramatico-musical works, musical compositions with or without words; works of drawing, painting, sculpture and engraving; lithographs, illustrations, geographical charts; plans, sketches, and plastic works relative to geography, topography, architecture, or science in general; in fact, every production whatsoever in the literary, scientific, or artistic domain which can be published by any mode of impression or reproduction., *available at:* http://keionline.org/sites/default/files/1886_Berne_Convention.pdf (last visited on Dec. 3, 2015).

[4] *Id.* Article 5—Authors who are subjects or citizens of any of the countries of the Union, or their lawful representatives, shall enjoy in the other countries the exclusive right of making or authorizing the translation of their works until the expiration of ten years from the publication of the original work in one of the countries of the Union.

[5] *Id.* Article 7—Articles from newspapers or periodicals published in any of the countries of the Union may be reproduced in original or in translation in the other countries of the Union, unless the authors or publishers have expressly forbidden it. For periodicals it shall be sufficient if the prohibition is indicated in general terms at the beginning of each number of the periodical.

This prohibition cannot in any case apply to articles of political discussion, or to the reproduction of news of the day or miscellaneous information.

arrangements existing or to be concluded between the convention countries, will not be affected by this Convention.[6]

The Paris Additional Act, 1896 provided protection for photograph.[7] Further addition was made in Article 7 where it was stipulated that the serial stories, including tales, published in the newspapers or periodicals cannot be reproduced in original or its translation, by other member countries without the consent of the authors.

The Berne Convention as revised in Berlin in 1908 provided protection to choreographic works[8] in addition to works already protected under 1886 convention.[9] The cinematographic productions[10] were also included in literary and artistic work. It enhanced the rights of authors of literary, artistic and scientific work to make cinematogarphic work.[11] The authors of musical works were given right of authorising the adaptation of those works to instruments which can reproduce them mechanically and the public performance of the their works by means of these instruments. The reservations and conditions could be provided by domestic legislation for this provision and the article was specifically made retroactive.[12] The Berlin Act prohibited reproduction of serial stories, tales and all other works published in newspaper or periodicals without the consent of author, however the other exemptions provided for newspapers and periodicals remained same as

---

[6] *Id.* Article 8—As regards the liberty of extracting portions from literary or artistic works for use in publications destined for educational or scientific purposes, or for chrestomathies, the effect of the legislation of the countries of the Union, and of special arrangements existing or to be concluded between them, is not affected by the present Convention.

[7] The Paris Additional Act, 1896, Article 2, *available at:* http://keionline.org/sites/default/files/1896_additional_acts_and_Interpretative_declaration.pdf (last visited on Dec. 4, 2015).

[8] The Bern Convention, 1908 (Berlin Act)., Article 2, *available at:* http://keionline.org/sites/default/files/1908_Berne_Convention.pdf (last visited on Dec. 3, 2015).

[9] *Id.* Article 3.

[10] *Id.* Article 14—Authors of literary, scientific or artistic works shall have the exclusive right of authorizing the reproduction and public representation of their works by cinematography.

Cinematograph productions shall be protected as literary or artistic works, if, by the arrangement of the acting form or the combinations of the incidents represented, the author has given the work a personal and original character.

Without prejudice to the rights of the author of the original work the reproduction by cinematography of a literary, scientific or artistic work shall be protected as an original work.

The above provisions apply to reproduction or production effected by any other process analogous to cinematography.

[11] *Ibid.*

[12] *Id.* Article 13, The authors of musical works shall have the exclusive right of authorizing: (1) the adaptation of those works to instruments which can reproduce them mechanically; (2) the public performance of the said works by means of these instruments.

Reservations and conditions relating to the application of this Article may be determined by the domestic legislation of each country in so far as it is concerned; but the effect of any such reservations and conditions will be strictly limited to the country which has put them in force.

The provisions of para 1 shall not be retroactive, and consequently shall not be applicable in any country of the Union to works which have been lawfully adapted in that country to mechanical instruments before the coming into force of the present Convention.

provided in 1886 Act. The legal consequences of the breach of this obligation had to be determined by the laws of the country where protection is claimed.[13] Unlawful reproduction through indirect appropriation of work was also not permitted under the Berlin Act[14] just as in the 1886 Act. For educational purposes the liberty of extracting portions for publication remained the same.[15]

The Rome Act, 1928[16] apart from providing what was given in Berlin, 1908 provided to authors of literary and artistic works right to communication to public by 'radiodiffusion'[17] under Article 11bis. The right could be limited through national legislations by putting conditions. The conditions could not in any case prejudice the moral right (*droit moral*) of the author as provided under Article 6bis, nor the right which belongs to the author to obtain an equitable remuneration that shall be fixed by the competent authority, in case the agreement fails (Article 11bis (2)). The right of public representation of dramatic and dramatico musical works and public representation of its translation was provided under this Act,[18] apart from public performance of musical works[19] and adaption through mechanical instruments and public performance through such instruments,[20] remained same as in Berlin Act. The unauthorised indirect reproduction of work in same or other form without alterations was kept as it is in the Article 12. With regard to reproduction of work in newspapers, periodicals, the articles on current economic, political or religious topics were permitted to be reproduced by the press unless the reproduction thereof is expressly reserved. The source of these articles had to be clearly indicated. For educational purposes, the provision of extracting portions of works in a publication the legislation of the member countries and special arrangements between them were not affected by the convention.

The Convention was revised in 1948 at Brussels, wherein certain additions were made to the Rome Act. The cinematographic work was protected as original work.[21] The right to public recitation of literary work was created.[22] The permission granted by the authors of literary and artistic works to communicate to the public by radiodiffusion and by any other means of wireless diffusion of signs, sounds or images, did not include permission for recording on instruments, excluding

[13] *Id.* Article 9.

[14] *Id.* Article 12.

[15] *Id.* Article 10.

[16] The Bern Convention, 1928 (Rome Act), *available at:* http://keionline.org/sites/default/files/1928_Rome_revisions_Berne.pdf (last visited on Dec. 2, 2015).

[17] Radiodiffusion is a French word which means radio broadcasting in English. See My Dictionary.net, *available at:* www.mydictionary.net/French-english/radiodiffusion.html (last visited on Nov. 17, 2015).

[18] *Supra* n. 14, Articles 11(1), 11(2).

[19] *Id.* Article 11(1).

[20] *Id.* Article 13(1).

[21] The Bern Convention, 1948 (Brussels Act), Article 14(2), *available at:* http://www.wipo.int/wipolex/en/treaties/text.jsp?file_id=278722 (last visited on Dec. 2, 2015).

[22] *Id.* Article 11ter.

ephemeral recording wherever permitted by national legislations.[23] The use of short quotations from newspaper articles, etc. for the press summaries was permitted.[24] The use of excerpts of literary and artistic works for publication of works in educational or scientific publications or in chrestomathies[25] was similar to the previous Act with the addition of words "as justified for the purpose". The determination of conditions under which recording, reproduction, and public communication of short extracts from literary and artistic works may be made for the purpose of reporting current events by means of photography or cinematography or by radio diffusion was left to the national legislations.[26]

The only means of reproduction available till Brussels Act was printing press as there was no photocopiers or computers. Hence there was no explicit right of reproduction but there were certain prohibitions not to reproduce for certain purposes in publications. Taking short excerpts or quotations to be used in newspapers, periodicals, and press summaries by mentioning source was permitted. The use of excerpts in publications for educational and scientific purpose as justified for the purpose was left to be determined by national legislations. Therefore, for educational purposes every member State had liberty according to its needs to provide for use of literary and artistic works.

2.2 Intergovernmental Copyright Committees—1961, 1965, 1968, 1971 and 1975

The reprography in the form of photocopying became rampant in 1960s and 1970s. The Brussels, 1948 had no provision for controlling it. [In 1961 a joint meeting of the Intergovernmental Copyright Committee was organised by UNESCO to look at copyright-related matters and on its agenda was a photographic reproduction of copyright works by or for libraries, documentation and scientific institutions. The resolution was passed to prepare a report for the next joint session.[27]][28] In 1965 a meeting was held for the purpose which included matter relating to photocopying, micro-form reproduction and analogous procedures.[29] It found variations in the national legislations as regard this matter was concerned. However, since it was

[23] *Id.* Article 11(bis)(3).

[24] *Id.* Article 10(2).

[25] *Id.* Article 10(1).

[26] *Id.* Article 10 bis.

[27] Intergovernmental Copyright committee, 6th session (23–30 Sep. 1961), UNESCO/CUA/112 Paris (30 Nov. 1961), Resolution No. 43(VI) p. 17, *available at:* http://unesdoc.unesco.org/images/0012/001275/127535EB.pdf (last visited on Nov. 10, 2015).

[28] *See* Wiseman 2012.

[29] Intergovernmental Copyright Committee IGC/VIII/16, *available at:* http://unesdoc.unesco.org/images/0014/001455/145589eb.pdf (last visited on Nov. 10, 2015).

thought to revise the Berne Convention the same were deferred. In 1968 after the Stockholm revision took place, the committee made certain recommendations with respect to reproduction for personal use of the reproducer, reproduction for various purposes by non commercial libraries, and *reproduction for educational purposes* e.g. by a student or teacher on personal request. *In such non commercial uses reproduction without payment of royalties were recommended* and if the use is by profit making library the payment of royalties was required.[30] In 1971 in the 11th session the 1968 report was annexed and it was stated that the matter is complex and technical and report need to be reviewed again. It needs the reconciliation of interests of users and authors and their assignees and the matter should be considered in 1973 along with the revised recommendations. The instrument can be non binding and in the form of model in the States.[31] In 1973 the *WIPO working group 1973* also looked into the 1968 recommendations and gave their *revised recommendations*[32] viz. *the personal use, use by instructors in educational institutions for teaching purposes, use for a library, were free uses, especially for developing countries as they were not to pay remuneration in such cases and they were left to adjust their regulations relating to reprography according to their needs.*[33] Reprographic reproduction according to the committee included any system or technique by which facsimile reproductions are made in any size or form.[34] However, the committee recommended desirability of an international instrument.[35] The subcommittee on the Intergovernmental Copyright Committee in 1975 adopted a resolution whereby they left to the concerned States to resolve the problem according to their requirements.[36]

2.3 Stockholm 1967 and After

The Stockholm conference was held for revision of Berne, taking into consideration the problems of developing countries for providing certain exceptions for them. The

---

[30] Advisability of adopting an international regulation concerning the photographic reproduction of copyrighted works, UNESCO Doc 17C/23, *Report of desirability of an International Regulation Concerning the photographic reproduction of copyright works* Annex paras 18–35, *available at:* http://unesdoc.unesco.org/images/0000/000014/001477eb.pdf (last visited on Nov. 10, 2015).

[31] Nature of International instrument proposed, *Id.* Annex p. 8 paras 53–58.

[32] WIPO Working Group on Reprographic Reproduction of works Protected by Copyright, 1973, Doc. UNESCO/WIPO/RP.2/6 (21 Sep. 1973) Annex A paras 1–8, *available at* http://unesdoc.unesco.org/images/0000/000058/005848eb.pdf (last visited on Nov. 10, 2015).

[33] *Id.* Annex A para 6.

[34] *Id.* para 7.

[35] *Id.* para 8.

[36] Annex to report on Sub-Committee of the Intergovernmental Copyright Committee on Reprographic Reproduction, Washington D.C., (June 16–21, 1975) *See* Copyright—review of the WIPO 11th year, No. 8 August 1975 at p. 175, *available at:* http://www.wipo.int/edocs/pubdocs/en/copyright/120/wipo_pub_120_1975_08.pdf (last visited on Nov. 10, 2015).

text of the Stockholm Conference was incorporated in Paris Act, 1971. The Stockholm Act, 1967 for the first time provided for the reproduction right. The national legislations were allowed to provide limitations and exceptions to reproduction right. They could permit in certain special cases reproduction of the work provided that such reproduction does not conflict with a normal exploitation of the work and does not unreasonably prejudice the legitimate interests of the author commonly known as three step test.[37]

The discussion of the Stockholm conference with respect to the reproduction right, gave an example of photocopying for explaining the three step test:

> A practical example might be photocopying for various purposes. If it consists of producing a very large number of copies, it may not be permitted, as it conflicts with a normal exploitation of the work. If it prejudice the legitimate interests of the author, provided that, according to national legislation, an equitable remuneration is paid. If a small number of copies are made, photocopying may be permitted without payment, particularly for individual or scientific use.[38]

The Act laid down certain exceptions to the reproduction right. The Article 10(1) permitted to make quotations from any work provided that their making is compatible with fair practice, and their extent does not exceed that justified by the purpose.

The WIPO Standing Committee on Copyright in its 9th session in 2003 gave dictionary meaning to the word 'quotation' as

> the taking of some part of a greater whole–a group of words from a text or a speech, a musical passage or visual image taken from a piece of music or a work of art–where the taking is done by someone other than the originator of the work[39]

---

[37] The Bern Convention, 1967 (Stockholm Act), Article 9—Authors of literary and artistic works protected by this Convention shall have the exclusive right of authorizing the reproduction of these works, in any manner or form.

(2) It shall be a matter for legislation in the countries of the Union to permit the reproduction of such works in certain special cases, provided that such reproduction does not conflict with a normal exploitation of the work and does not unreasonably prejudice the legitimate interests of the author.

(3) Any sound or visual recording shall be considered as a reproduction for the purposes of this Convention, *available at:* http://www.wipo.int/wipolex/en/treaties/text.jsp?file_id=287756 (last visited on Dec. 4, 2015).

[38] *Records of the Intellectual Property Conference of Stockholm (1967),* June 11–July 14, 1967 Vol II 85 p. 292, *available at:* http://global.oup.com/booksites/content/9780198259466/15550029 (last visited on Dec. 4, 2015).

[39] Sam Ricketson, *WIPO Study on Limitations and Exceptions of Copyright and Related Rights in the Digital Environment*, WIPO Standing Committee on Copyright and related rights, 9th Session, Geneva (June 23–27, 2003) Doc. No. SCCR/9/7 p. 12 para 2, *available at:*

http://www.wipo.int/edocs/mdocs/copyright/en/sccr_9/sccr_9_7.pdf (last visited on Dec. 2, 2015).

With respect to length of quotation it gave examples as below:

> In some instances, it … may make lengthy quotations from a work, in order to ensure that it is presented correctly, as in the case of a critical review or work of scholarship. It is also possible to envisage other circumstances where quotation of the whole of a work may be justified, as in the example given by one commentary of a work on the history of twentieth-century art where representative pictures of particular schools of art would be needed by way of illustration. Another might be cartoons or short poems where these are quoted as part of a wider work of commentary or review.[40]

Therefore, from above it can be interpreted that even though the meaning of quotation is taking some part of the greater whole still in some cases the whole work can be reproduced so long it is justified by the purpose and compatible with fair practice.

Article10(2) provides an exception for teaching purposes. It states:

> It shall be a matter for legislation in the countries of the Union, and for special agreements existing or to be concluded between them, to permit the utilization, to the extent justified by the purpose, of literary or artistic works by way of illustration in publications, broadcasts or sound or visual recordings for teaching, provided such utilization is compatible with fair practice.

The WIPO Standing Committee on Copyright Right and related right had provided some explanation to the above article. According to the committee what is utilization of work for teaching purpose has to be determined by national legislations, however, some limitation has been placed by article by using the words to the extent justified by the purpose by way of illustration, broadcast or sound or visual recording and compatible with fair practice. The committee stated that these do not reflect quantitative limitations. The illustration may appear to place some restriction, but would not exclude the use of the whole of the work in appropriate circumstances, for example, in the case of an artistic work or short literary work. The word fair practice does not imply quantitative restrictions.[41] The following statement expresses this view of WIPO standing committee:

> Article 10 (2) does not contain any restriction on the number of copies that may be made in the case of publications and sound or visual recordings that are made for teaching purposes. Just as no limitation is imposed in respect of the public which is reached by a broadcast intended for teaching purposes, so there can be no limitation on the number of copies that can be made for the same purpose. The only further qualification applied here is that the making of multiple copies must be compatible with "fair practice." Obviously, if this competes with the author's normal exploitation of his work and unreasonably prejudices, his legitimate interests, article 10 (2) should not apply.[42]

The above statement of WIPO standing committee that multiple copies must be compatible with fair practice, does it mean that balancing is required by application of second and third step of the three step test under Article 9(2) of the Berne,

---

[40] *Ibid.*

[41] *Id.* pp. 14–15.

[42] *Id.* p. 15, para 8.

viz. use should not conflict with a normal exploitation of the work and unreasonably prejudice the legitimate interest of the author.

When can use conflict with a normal exploitation of the work

The WTO Panel Report with regard to the United States, Section 110(5) of The US Copyright Act, referred to the interpretation of 'normal exploitation' under Article 13 of the TRIPs agreement[43] whereby it stated that

> …in our view, not every use of a work, which, in principle, is covered by the scope of exclusive rights and involves commercial gain, necessarily conflicts with a normal exploitation of that work. If this were the case, hardly any exception or limitation could pass the test of the second condition and Article 13 might be left devoid of meaning, because normal exploitation would be equated with full use of exclusive rights.[44]

The Panel further stated:

> We believe that an exception or limitation to an exclusive right in domestic legislation rises to the level of a conflict with a normal exploitation of the work (i.e., the copyright or rather the whole bundle of exclusive rights conferred by the ownership of the copyright), if uses, that in principle are covered by that right, but exempted under the exception or limitation, enter into economic competition with the ways that right-holders normally extract economic value from that right to the work (i.e., the copyright) and thereby deprive them of significant or tangible commercial gains.[45]

Therefore, the WTO panel clearly states that every use that involves commercial gain may not conflict with normal exploitation of the works. The 'normal exploitation' does not mean full exploitation. The conflict may occur if it enters into economic competition with the ways which deprive the right holders of significant or tangible commercial gain. Hence making a copy of the work for teaching purpose cannot be considered to be in conflict with the normal exploitation of the work unless one enters into the economic competition with right holder.

When can use unreasonably prejudice the legitimate interests of the right holder?

With regard to the *third condition* that *it does not unreasonably prejudice the legitimate interests of the right holder,* WIPO Standing committee on Copyright was of the view that the legitimate interest will include both economic and non economic interests. In case of reproduction right where large number of copies are made it depends on whether the copies made are proportionate or excessive. If the use is not proportionate or unreasonable than it will be a subject matter of compulsory license.[46]

The WIPO standing committee differentiated between Articles 9(2) and 10(2) and stated that limitations and exceptions to rights of authors in certain non

---

[43] The TRIPs agreement, 1994, Article 13—"Members shall confine limitations and exceptions to exclusive rights to certain special cases which do not conflict with a normal exploitation of the work and do not unreasonably prejudice the legitimate interests of the right-holder".

[44] WTO Panel, *Report on United States—Section 110(5) of The US Copyright Act* p. 48, para 6.182, *available at:* https://www.wto.org/english/tratop_e/dispu_e/1234da.pdf (last visited on Dec. 1, 2015); *Supra* n. 38 at p. 24.

[45] *Id.* p. 48, para 6.183.

[46] *Id.* p. 27 last para.

economic public considerations were permitted for a long time and balancing had already been done by successive revision conferences. The Article 9(2) will be applicable to future exceptions created to the reproduction right and the domestic laws which have already created exceptions in favour of public, it would be in vein to suppose that at this stage they will abolish these exceptions. It stated:

> the Berne Convention contains, and has contained for a long time, a series of provisions that acknowledge that limitations and exceptions to authors' rights may be made in certain specified circumstances that are justified by other non-economic "public policy" considerations: see, for example,... criticism and review (article 10 (1)), educational purposes (article 10 (2)). ... The only difference between these provisions and article 9 (2) is that the former embody (to a greater or less extent), in the text of each provision, the results of the balancing process that has been achieved by the successive revision conferences that have adopted them, whereas article 9 (2) is consciously framed as an omnibus or umbrella provision that is prospectively applicable to all exceptions to the reproduction right.[47] This interpretation furthermore is consistent with what is to be found in the preparatory work for the Stockholm Conference, a legitimate supplementary aid to treaty interpretation. It will be recalled here that the Conference programme contained the comment, "that it should not be forgotten that domestic laws already contained a series of exceptions in favor of various public and cultural interests and that it would be in vain to suppose that countries would be ready at this stage to abolish these exceptions to any appreciable extent."[48] Furthermore, the records of the Conference and the various amendments proposed by delegates indicate that they were seeking to reach some general description of the purposes for which exceptions might be made that would accommodate the existing public interest exceptions in national laws.[49]

Extension of teaching exception to digital environment

The WIPO Copyright Treaty applies the Articles 1–21 of the Berne Convention (the Paris Act, 1971) in the digital environment. It also created new rights of distribution (Article 6), communication to public (Article 8) and rental rights (Article 7) to be applied in a digital environment. For limitations and exceptions the treaty provides for 3 step test under Article 10(1) and for Berne rights under Article 10(2).[50] The test is similar to the one provided in Berne for limitations and exceptions to the reproduction right.

With regard to the application of educational exceptions under Bern the one of the objectives of WCT as stated in the preamble is

---

[47] *Supra* n. 39 p. 25.

[48] *Records* 1967, Vol. I, pp. 112 (Doc S/1) *Id.* p. 25.

[49] *Supra* n. 39 p. 25.

[50] The WIPO Copyright Treaty, 1996, Article 10—**Limitations and Exceptions-**(1) Contracting Parties may, in their national legislation, provide for limitations of or exceptions to the rights granted to authors of literary and artistic works under this Treaty in certain special cases that do not conflict with a normal exploitation of the work and do not unreasonably prejudice the legitimate interests of the author.

(2) Contracting Parties shall, when applying the Berne Convention, confine any limitations of or exceptions to rights provided for therein to certain special cases that do not conflict with a normal exploitation of the work and do not unreasonably prejudice the legitimate interests of the author.

> *Recognizing* the need to maintain a balance between the rights of authors and the larger public interest, particularly education, research and access to information, as reflected in the Berne Convention

Further, Article 1 clearly states that this (1) treaty shall not have any connection with treaties, other than the Berne Convention, nor shall it prejudice any rights and obligations under any other treaties and (2) nothing in this Treaty shall derogate from existing obligations that Contracting Parties have towards each other under the Berne Convention for the Protection of Literary and Artistic Works. The clause (4) states that the Contracting Parties shall comply with Articles 1–21 and the Appendix of the Berne Convention.

The agreed statement to Article 1(4) provides that reproduction right exceptions or limitations under Berne fully apply in the digital environment.[51] The para 2 of the agreed statement to Article 10 of WCT which states that Article 10(2) do not extend or reduce the scope of exceptions under the Berne Convention[52] reinforces the view that that educational exception under Berne cannot be further subject to three step test under WCT.

The next question is whether the educational exception of Berne can apply to all levels of education i.e. institutional, outside institutions, distance or digital education.

With regard to application of the article at all levels of education the Stockholm records showed that in the conference one of the view was as follows:

> The wish was expressed that it should be made clear in this Report that the word 'teaching' was to include teaching at all levels—in educational institutions and universities, municipal and State schools, and private schools. Education outside these institutions, for instance general teaching available to the public, but not included in the above categories, should be excluded.[53]

However, the Stockholm text used above does not expressly limit teaching only in educational institutions. Hence, the above restrictive view cannot be impliedly adopted by the Conference. The WCT further extends the teaching exceptions of the Berne in the digital environment. Therefore, utilization can not be limited to institutional teaching but will equally apply to online education.

The above discussion shows that for educational purposes the Stockholm Act does not provide any limitation as to length of work to be used and number of

---

[51] *Id.* agreed statement to Article 1(4), "The reproduction right, as set out in Article 9 of the Berne Convention, and the exceptions permitted thereunder, fully apply in the digital environment, in particular to the use of works in digital form. It is understood that the storage of a protected work in digital form in an electronic medium constitutes a reproduction within the meaning of Article 9 of the Berne Convention".

[52] *Id.* Agreed statement to Article 10, "It is understood that the provisions of Article 10 permit Contracting Parties to carry forward and appropriately extend into the digital environment limitations and exceptions in their national laws which have been considered acceptable under the Berne Convention. Similarly, these provisions should be understood to permit Contracting Parties to devise new exceptions and limitations that are appropriate in the digital network environment.

It is also understood that Article 10 (2) neither reduces nor extends the scope of applicability of the limitations and exceptions permitted by the Berne Convention".

[53] *Supra* n. 29, para 97.

copies to be reproduced for teaching purposes so long it is justified for the purpose. Article 10(2) can also not restrict copying of the whole of the work, subject to mentioning of source, as mentioned in Article 10(3). The article further does not restrict the number of copies to be made for teaching purposes. However, multiple copies must be compatible with fair practice i.e. the use should be proportionate. The TRIPs agreement and the WCT does not limit the scope of Berne teaching exceptions. The WCT rather extends the exception in digital environment.

Hence, the making of copies through reprographic techniques for teaching purposes digitally like scanning, taking print outs, copying on hard disks etc. is permissible under Berne so long the use justified for the purpose and is proportional and not excessive The teaching exception under Bern Convention cannot be restricted to institutional framework but can cover distance and online education, and teaching outside the institution.

3 Indian Position—Education Versus Copyright

3.1 Education in India

India is a developing country and the literacy rate as per 2011 census is 74.04% in comparison to developed countries which have almost attained 99% literacy. It is way behind its target of 100%. There are disparities in education in the society as regards women, minorities backward classes, and persons with disability are concerned. The inequality exists at all levels, whether primary, secondary or higher Education.

International Obligations

It has undertaken international obligations as far as education is concerned under the various conventions. The UDHR which has become part of customary international law which specifically states that there is right to education for everyone. Regarding access to education it provides for free and compulsory education at the elementary level and equally accessible higher education on the merits. It also lays down the goals of education stating that the education should be directed towards the full development of human personality.[54] The Covenant on Economic, Social and Cultural Rights, 1966 to which India is a party, apart from reiterating what has

[54] The Universal Declaration of Human Rights, 1948, Article 26—(1) Everyone has the right to education. Education shall be free, at least in the elementary and fundamental stages. Elementary education shall be compulsory. Technical and professional education shall be made generally available and higher education shall be equally accessible to all on the basis of merit.

(2) Education shall be directed to the full development of the human personality and to the strengthening of respect for human rights and fundamental freedoms. It shall promote understanding, tolerance and friendship among all nations, racial or religious groups, and shall further the activities of the United Nations for the maintenance of peace.

(3) Parents have a prior right to choose the kind of education that shall be given to their children.

been stated in the UDHR, it provides that *there should be the progressive introduction of free education at the secondary and higher education level.*[55] The Convention on Rights of Persons with Disability, 2006 recognise their right to education without discrimination and provided that they should not exclude from the general education system on the basis of disability at all levels of education.[56] Similarly the Convention on Elimination of all forms of Discrimination against Woman, 1979 (CEDAW) provides for elimination of discrimination of woman in order to ensure equal rights with men in the field of education.[57] The goal as provided by UNESCO in its post 2015 development agenda is "Member States should "Ensure equitable quality education and lifelong learning for all by 2030" as a possible overarching education goal, aiming to achieve just, inclusive, peaceful and sustainable societies".[58]

Constitutional Obligation

Our Constitution makers have in the Preamble set the goals of social justice, equality, maintaining dignity of the individual. For attaining social justice the inequalities in education have to be removed. The 86th amendment to the

---

[55] The Covenant on Economic, Social, and Cultural rights, 1966, Article 13—1. The States Parties to the present Covenant recognize the right of everyone to education. They agree that education shall be directed to the full development of the human personality and the sense of its dignity, and shall strengthen the respect for human rights and fundamental freedoms. They further agree that education shall enable all persons to participate effectively in a free society, promote understanding, tolerance and friendship among all nations and all racial, ethnic or religious groups, and further the activities of the United Nations for the maintenance of peace.

2. The States Parties to the present Covenant recognize that, with a view to achieving the full realization of this right:

(a) Primary education shall be compulsory and available free to all;

(b) Secondary education in its different forms, including technical and vocational secondary education, shall be made generally available and accessible to all by every appropriate means, and in particular by the progressive introduction of free education;

(c) Higher education shall be made equally accessible to all, on the basis of capacity, by every appropriate means, and in particular by the progressive introduction of free education;

(d) Fundamental education shall be encouraged or intensified as far as possible for those persons who have not received or completed the whole period of their primary education;

(e) The development of a system of schools at all levels shall be actively pursued, an adequate fellowship system shall be established, and the material conditions of teaching staff shall be continuously improved.

[56] The Convention on Rights of Persons with Disability, Article 24, *available at:* http://www.un.org/disabilities/convention/convention.shtml (last visited on Dec. 11, 2015).

[57] The Convention on Elimination of All forms of Elimination against Women, Article 10, *available at:* http://www.un.org/disabilities/convention/convention.shtml (last visited on Dec. 11, 2015).

[58] UNESCO *Position Paper on Education post 2015,* para 14, doc, no. ED-14/EFA/POST-2015/1, *available at:* http://unesdoc.unesco.org/images/0022/002273/227336E.pdf (last visited Dec. 5, 2015).

Id. Article 21A (Inserted by 86th Amendment, Act, 2002).

Id. Article 41.

Id. Article 46.

Constitution made right to free and compulsory education from 6 to 14 years of age as a Fundamental Right.[59] Further, within the economic capacity, the State has to make provisions for the right to work, education and public assistance in certain cases like disablement, old age etc.[60] The State has to promote educational and economic interests of weaker sections of society, SCs and STs.[61] The State has to protect the interests of minorities.[62] The minorities have been given the right to establish and administer the educational institutions.[63] The Supreme Court of India has held that dignity of the individual cannot be assured unless it is accompanied by right to education.[64] In *Unnikrishanan Case* this court held that the right to education is 'implicit in and flows from the right to life guaranteed under Article 21'.[65] In order to achieve the goal of universal access to quality education for all, the Right of Children to Free and Compulsory Education (RTE) Act, 2009 (Act 35 of 2009) was passed.

Governments Initiative to achieve quality education for all—National Policy on Education

The India's National Policy on Education, 1992 which is a guide for educational development in India stated that the reforms are required in the system to provide education to all. Education has to be reoriented to promote women's equality and education. There should be an element of gender sensitization in education. In order to achieve equity and social justice in education the education system has to be sensitive to the needs of SC, STs, backward classes, minorities and persons with disability. The universalisation of education requires literacy programmes for children at primary level, adult literacy, literacy for women, backward classes, minorities and person with disabilities. The State has to provide equality in education not only at the primary level, but also at secondary, higher education level, vocational education, language education and research and development. The policy provides for various schemes and strategy for implementation. The focus is on providing quality education to all and access to materials. The emphasis is not only on classroom teaching through institutional framework, but also through the establishment of open schools,[66] distance education and education by use of

---

[59] The Constitution of India, Article 21A (Inserted by 86th Amendment, Act, 2002).

[60] *Id.* Article 41.

[61] *Id.* Article 46.

[62] *Id.* Article 29.

[63] *Id.* Article 30.

[64] See *Mohini Jain* v. *State of Karnataka*, (1992) 3 SCC 666—"right to life (Article 21) is a compendious expression with all those rights which the courts must enforce because they are basic to the dignified enjoyment of life and that the dignity of an individual cannot be assured unless it is accompanied by the right to education".

[65] *Unnikrishnan* v. *State of Andhra Pradesh*, (1993) 1 SCC 645.

[66] The open universities are established for providing higher education, namely Indira Gandhi Open University. Many traditional universities also provide under graduate and post graduate correspondence courses where study material as per the syllabus is supplied.

electronic media[67] and use of computers in education. *The achievement of goals requires government to provide for infrastructure, teacher training, course curriculum, skill development, access to quality material for teaching purposes* etc.*; and this may sometimes conflict with the interest of the owners of copyright.*[68] The Annual Report of Ministry of HRD for the year 2013–14 and 2014–15 lays down the government efforts towards implementation of the policy in the year 2013–14 and 2014–15.[69]

---

[67] With regard to education through the use of information and communication technology the government has NMEICT scheme. For the implementation of scheme many projects have been undertaken and one of them being generation of e-content for the target groups covering all disciplines at higher education level, which provides e-learning through online Web and Video based courses in engineering, science and humanities. Over 329 courses are complete and made available in NPTEL website. More than 990 courses in various disciplines in engineering and science are getting generated in phase-II of NPTELFor UG courses; **Consortium of Educational Communication** (**CEC**) has been tasked for e-content generation. In phase-I, e-content for 19 UG subjects and in phase-II e-content for 68 subjects will be generated by the CEC in collaboration with its media centers. For 77 PG subjects, e-content generation activity has been assigned to **University Grants Commission** (**UGC**). The process of content creation has been initiated for 72 subjects.

The government also plans to launch direct to home educational channels 24 × 7. Teachers will deliver live Sessions. The students can seek answers to their queries instantaneously from the teacher during the transmission. The content delivered shall be converted into e-Contents and viewers can benefit watching the content on demand at their convenient time, place and pace. An educational portal Shakshat has been created for delivery of content. The aim is also to provide computers for building connectivity in colleges, universities and deemed universities. The National Library and Information Services Infrastructure for Scholarly Content (N-List) programme provide access to more than 3100 e-journals and 75,000 e-books to all degree colleges. Annual Report of Ministry of HRD 2013–14 *Technology Enabled Learning pp*. 97–98. Available at http://mhrd.gov.in/sites/upload_files/mhrd/files/document-reports/AR2013-14.pdf (last visited on Dec. 10, 2015).

[68] *See generally* National Policy for Education, 1992, *available at:* http://mhrd.gov.in/sites/upload_files/mhrd/files/document-reports/NPE86-mod92.pdf (last visited on on Dec. 10, 2015).

[69] The various programmes at different level include **Sarva Siksha Abhiyan** to achieve the goals of universal access and retention, bridging of gender and social gaps in enrolment levels and enhancement of learning levels of all children and **mid day meals** To enhance enrollment, retention and attendance and simultaneously improving nutritional levels among children at Primary level. For promotion of girls in education schemes like **Mahila samakhya** aims to create a collective awareness and understanding of rural, most-marginalised women's contexts and build their capacities to challenge it, **Kasturba Gandhi Balika Vidyalaya** (KGBV), **Rashtriya Madhyamik Shiksha Abhiyan** (RMSA) aims to create a collective awareness and understanding of rural, most—marginalised women's contexts and build their capacities to challenge it, Scheme for construction and running of **Girls' Hostel for students** of secondary and higher secondary schools The Scheme envisages construction of a hostel with the capacity of 100 girls in each of about 3,500 Educationally Backward Blocks (EBBs) in the country and many other schemes, **Inclusive Education of the Disabled at secondary stage (IEDSS)**—The aim of the scheme is to enable all students with disabilities, after completing eight years of elementary schooling, to pursue further four years of secondary schooling. The interventions at **higher education** level include: Indira Gandhi Scholarship for Single Girl Child for Pursuing Higher and Technical Education; Construction of Women's Hostels for Colleges; Development of Women's Studies in Universities and Colleges; Post-Doctoral Fellowships for Women; an Special Scheme of Construction of Women's Hostels for Colleges in North East States; for adult literacy the scheme

3.2 Copyright in India

International Obligations

The UDHR and the Covenant on Economic, social and cultural rights provides for protection of moral and material interests resulting from any scientific, literary or artistic production of which he is the author, and at the same time everyone has right to freely enjoy the arts and to share in scientific advancement and its benefits.[70] The article not only provides for protecting interests of authors in literary or artistic production but also gives right to public to freely enjoy and share the benefits of those productions. The Berne Convention on literary and artistic works to which India is party has tried to make a balance between the rights of authors and the rights of the public by providing certain free uses of work for certain purposes which includes educational purpose. The Berne rights, limitations and exceptions are extended to the TRIPs and WCT as discussed above.

Statutory Protection for the Copyright

The copyright is protected through a statute and hence is a statutory right unlike right to education which has a constitutional status and is declared as fundamental right.[71] The Parliament has enacted the Copyright Act, 1957 which has been amended from time to time to bring it in consonance with TRIPs and WCT. The Act provides for certain limitations to the reproduction right of the owners of work for the purposes of education, research, private study, criticism and review.

The first Act relating to copyright in India was The Copyright Act, 1847 which mainly dealt with the printing and sale of books and such print or sale without the consent of the proprietor was not permitted. It also dealt with grant of a compulsory license in case of suppression of books from public. The 1847 Act was replaced by

---

(Footnote 69 continued)

of **Saakshar Bharat** with main focus of the programme is on women, SCs, STs, minorities and other disadvantaged groups to impart functional literacy and numeracy to non-literate and non-numerate adults; **Rashtriya Uchchatar Shiksha Abhiyan** (**RUSA**) number of Centrally Funded Educational Institutions(CFEIs) have been set up. All such efforts has resulted in higher Gross Enrollment Ratio(GER) and as per the provisional report for All India Survey on Higher Education(AISHE) 2011–12, GER in higher education of the country is 20.4% with 28.5 million students in higher education. A **Centrally Sponsored Scheme** (**CSS**) for reforming the State Higher Education system, **polytechnics** for skill development; The **National Mission on Education through Information and Communication Technology** (NMEICT), utilization of available Education Satellite (EduSAT) and Direct to Home (DTH) platforms, training and empowerment of teachers to effectively use the new method of teaching learning etc. See Annual Report of Ministry of HRD 2013–14 available at http://mhrd.gov.in/sites/upload_files/mhrd/files/document-reports/AR2013-14.pdf; *see also* the recent programmes in the Annual Report of Ministry of HRD 2014–15 part I and part II, *available at*:http://mhrd.gov.in/sites/upload_files/mhrd/files/document-reports/Part1.pdf and http://mhrd.gov.in/sites/upload_files/mhrd/files/document-reports/Part2.pdf (last visited on Dec. 10, 2015).

[70] The Universal Declaration of Human Rights, Article 27; the Covenant on Economic, Social and Cultural Rights., Article 15(1) (a) and (b).

[71] *Supra.*

the Imperial Act of 1914 which gave certain rights to authors, namely the translation of the work, adaptation in literary, dramatic and musical works.[72] The only limitation on rights related to educational purpose was an act of publication in a collection of short passages from published literary works not themselves published for the use of schools in which copyright subsists: Provided that not more than two of such passages from works by the same author are published by the same publisher within five years, and that the source from which such passages are taken is acknowledged.[73] Another act was fair dealing with any work for the purposes of private study, research, criticism, review, or newspaper summary.[74]

The Act of 1914 was replaced by the Copyright Act, 1957. The 1957 Act protected original literary, dramatic, musical, artistic works; sound recordings and cinematograph films[75] and gave exclusive rights to the owners of work, namely the right of reproduction, including storing through electronic means, communication to public, issue of copies, performance of the work, to make adaptation and translation etc.[76]

Free Reprographic Uses for Educational Purpose

Reprography is defined under the Act making copies by photocopies or similar means. The similar means in the digital age can include microfilms, scanning, digital copies, computer printouts etc. All these affect the reproduction right of the author. The Section 52 of the Act provides certain free uses which include reproduction of work for educational purposes. This limits the right of reproduction of the owner of the copyright.

Firstly S. 52(1)(a) permits a fair dealing with any work, not being a computer programme, for the purposes of private or personal use, including research; criticism or review, the reporting of current events and current affairs, including the reporting of a lecture delivered in public. Further the explanation provides that the storing of any work in any electronic medium for the purposes mentioned in this clause, including the incidental storage of any computer programme which is not itself an infringing copy for the said purposes, shall not constitute infringement of copyright.

The word fair dealing has not been defined in the Act. The courts have to interpret whether the use amounts to fair dealing based on facts and circumstances of the case and overall impression carried by the court. Long extracts followed by short comments may in certain circumstances be unfair and, short extracts followed by long comments will be fair or unfair will again depend on circumstances of the case. The standard employed for discerning fair use is that of a fair minded and honest person. The courts have held that it should not include substantial copying. The substantial copying depends upon the quality of work used and not the

[72] The Copyright Act, 1914 (Act III of 1914), s. 1(2).

[73] *Id.* s. 2(1) iv).

[74] *Id.* s. 2(1)(i).

[75] The Copyright Act, 1957 (Act 14 of 1957), s. 13.

[76] *Id.* s. 14.

quantity.[77] The interpretation of the court of the word 'fair dealing' satisfies the test laid down in the Article 10(1) of the Berne convention as discussed above.

Another important provision which permits reprography for teaching purposes is S. 52(1)(i) which provides for reproduction of any work by a teacher or a pupil in the course of instruction.

The words teacher, pupil and course of instruction have not been defined anywhere. The ordinary meaning of teacher is one who imparts knowledge as how to do something and pupil is a person who is taught by another, i.e. a student in relation to teachers. The dictionary meaning of 'course of instruction' is 'imparting education through a series of lessons'.[78] There is no restriction as to the quantity of work to be reproduced it can be whole of the work or a part of it. It also does not limit the number of copies to be reproduced, but if the copies made are more than what is required for educational purpose, certainly the courts will not permit that. The text does not restrict the section to a teacher teaching in an educational institution in a classroom to a student, but it is wide enough to cover teaching even through distance education and online education through virtual classrooms. Further, it does not restrict levels of teaching that is primary, secondary or higher education.

The question that arises with respect to Section 52(1)(i) is whether this provision is in accordance with Berne convention.

The Berne convention itself allows certain free uses. One of them is, use for teaching or educational purposes under Article 10(2) which as has been extended to TRIPs as well as WCT. The article does not require any further balancing by applying three step test as balancing was done by the successive revision of Berne convention.[79] The article permits utilisation of work for teaching purposes but does not provide the manner of its utilization. It was left to be determined by member countries. Hence the member State can restrict any exclusive rights for teaching purposes. The article does not restrict that the utilization could be for institutional teaching, distance education or online education or for any level that is primary, secondary or higher education and it had to be decided as per the needs of the member countries of the Berne.

Under the Section 52(1)(i) only the exclusive right of reproduction has been restricted and on the type and level of teaching there is no restriction which Berne also permits. The only limitation in Berne is 'as justified by the purpose' and 'compatible with fair practice'. It does not restrict the length and number of copies to be made. The Section 52(1)(i) limits reproduction by the teacher or pupil in course of instruction. So whatever length has been copied has to be as per the requirements in course of instruction i.e. the series of lessons which need to be taught. That satisfies the test of 'justified by the purpose' of the Berne exception.

---

[77] *Super Cassettes Industries Ltd.* v. *Hamar Television Network Pvt. Ltd.*, 2011 (45) PTC 70 (Del).

[78] *Available at:* http://www.thefreedictionary.com/course+of+instruction (last visited on 10 Nov. 2015).

[79] *Supra* discussion on Article 10(2) of Berne Convention (Stockholm Act).

If the requirement of course of instruction is to copy whole of work, it is permissible in the section so as in the Berne depending on the purpose and the context in which the work has been used for teaching purposes. The Berne does not restrict who should copy; but the Indian law further limits reproduction by teacher or pupil which implies that it is not for mixing the copies in the normal business channels. The section makes no limitation as to number of copies to be made. The Berne also permits that so long the multiple copies made are proportionate.[80]

Hence, the above sub section is in accordance with Berne teaching exception which itself cannot be further subjected to three step test as balancing of that provision was done by the successive revisions of Berne convention. Secondly the sub section was included in Act 12 of 1957 much before the explicit right to reproduction was included in the Berne. The Stockholm discussion provides that the Article 9(2) has to be applied to future exceptions and not the one which already exist in the national legislations. Therefore, view of some right holders that Section 52(1)(i) should be subject to three step does not appear to be appropriate.

S. 52(1)(zb) which permits reproduction has been introduced by the amendments made in 2012 in the Copyright Act, 1957 for persons with disability. It limits not only the right of reproduction, but even the right to issue copies, communication to the public any work in an accessible format to facilitate person with disability, including sharing with any person for private or personal use, educational purpose or research. It also permits any organization working in the benefit of such persons provided copies are made available on a non profit basis and they have taken reasonable steps to prevent its entry into ordinary channels of business. The organization can be the one receiving grant from the government or an educational institution or a library or one registered under Section 12A of the Income Tax Act.[81] Such restriction of rights is permitted by Berne Convention. The Convention

---

[80] *Ibid.*

[81] *Id.* s. 52(1)(zb) (inserted by Act 27 of 2012)—the adaptation, reproduction, issue of copies or communication to the public of any work in any accessible format, by—

(i) any person to facilitate person with disability to access to works including sharing with any person with disability of such accessible format for private or personal use, educational purpose or research; or

(i•) any organisation working for the benefit of the persons with disabilities in case the normal format prevents the enjoyment of such works by such persons:

Provided that the copies of the works in such accessible format are made available to the persons with disabilities on a non-profit basis but to recover only the cost of production:

Provided further that the organisation shall ensure that the copies of works in such accessible format are used only by persons with disabilities and takes reasonable steps to prevent its entry into ordinary channels of business.

Explanation.—For the purposes of this sub-clause, "any organisation" includes and organisation registered under Section 12A of the Income-Tax Act, 1961 and working for the benefit of persons with disability or recognised under Chap. X of the Persons with Disabilities (Equal Opportunities, Protection or Rights and full Participation) Act, 1995 or receiving grants from the government for facilitating access to persons with disabilities or an educational institution or library or Archives recognised by the Government.

on Rights of Persons with Disability obliges contracting states to provide work in accessible formats to facilitate effective education.[82]

This clause does not make any restriction as to level of education or type of education and the free use is allowed not only by a teacher or pupil, but is much wider by any person or organization working for the purpose mentioned in the section. There is no restriction to the number of copies to be made or length of work to be reproduced. But certainly the copy should not reach the ordinary channels of business. This satisfies the requirement of the Article 10(2) of the Berne 'justified by the purpose' and 'compatible with fair practice'.

Hence, Indian legislation permits reprography for teaching purposes irrespective of level of education or type of education whether institutional, distance or online. There is no limitation on length of work to be reproduced or number of copies to be made so long as the purpose is educational and the copies do not get into the normal business channels. The exceptions are in consonance with the Bern Convention as they permit reproduction only for educational purpose without mixing copies in normal business channels.

The teaching exceptions under the Copyright Act are applicable in the digital environment also. The only point to be mentioned is that use of work in course of instruction by a teacher or a pupil in case of online education, the right holder's two rights are simultaneously being affected, reproduction as well as communication to the public. Since the Berne leaves how the utilization has to be done, to be determined by member countries, the exception can be introduced to restrict the right for teaching purposes.

The Copyright Act, 1957 as amended in 2012 provided for certain limitations for online reproductions, which do not infringe the right of copyright holders. Firstly, the transient or incidental storage of work in the technical process of electronic transmission or communication,[83] secondly for the purpose of providing electronic links, access or integration, where such links, access or integration is not expressly prohibited by the right holder.[84]

The need of providing quality education in India where the literacy level is low and also where there are inequalities in education in the society, the State has to devise certain methods to provide free access to educational material. One of method chosen is permitting reprography/reproduction for the teaching purposes under the Copyright Act. India being a developing country, has to continue with the present exceptions created for educational purposes for attaining the goals of social justice and achieving 100% literacy.

The other question that arises with respect to online reproduction is whether legalization of use of technology like encryption affects free use of digital material for teaching purposes.

---

[82] *See generally* the Convention on Rights of Persons with Disability, 2006, Article 24 on education.

[83] *Id.* s. 52(1)(b).

[84] *Id.* s. 52(1)(c).

The WIPO Copyright Treaty obliges the Contracting States to provide for legal remedies for circumvention of effective technological measures used by the authors to exercise their rights under the copyright law.[85] The article does not provide whether the technological measure used for preventing access control or copy control by the author. The author can restrict the act of reproduction by totally preventing the access to work even beyond the term of protection as the act of circumvention is not linked to infringement of rights. This will also take away the basic right of public of reading and browsing. Though the article specifically provides to exempt uses permitted by law however still an ordinary person having only basic knowledge of technology cannot take advantage of this exception. Hence, the provision tilts the balance in favour of authors. Certain public uses like fair dealing in work or educational use will be effected by this.

The Copyright Act, 1957 has made the act of circumvention of effective technological measure, applied for protecting exclusive rights, as penal.[86] If any one circumvents such technology with the intention of infringement of the rights of the owners will be liable under the section. The section links circumvention with infringement unlike WCT which does not do so. The WCT further limits technological measures applied by author as it uses the words 'technology used by author' in the article, whereas the section is much wider as it uses the words 'effective technological measure applied for the purpose of protecting any of the rights conferred by this Act'. Hence section implicitly will include anybody holding exclusive rights. The proviso to the section states that it does not apply to acts not expressly prohibited by the Act or encryption research. The third party who facilitates circumvention will not be liable for intervention.[87] The proviso will not be of any use to

---

[85] The WIPO Copyright Treaty, Article 11,—Contracting Parties shall provide adequate legal protection and effective legal remedies against the circumvention of effective technological measures that are used by authors in connection with the exercise of their rights under this Treaty or the Berne Convention and that restrict acts, in respect of their works, which are not authorized by the authors concerned or permitted by law.

[86] The Copyright Act, 1957, s. 65 A (1),—Any person who circumvents an effective technological measure applied for the purpose of protecting any of the rights conferred by this Act, with the intention of infringing such rights, shall be punishable with imprisonment which may extend to two years and shall also be liable to fine.

[87] *Id. s.* 65 A(2) Nothing in sub-Section (1) shall prevent any person from,

(a) doing anything referred to therein for ·a purpose not expressly prohibited by this Act:

Provided that any person facilitating circumvention by another person of a technological measure for such a purpose shall maintain a complete record of such other person including his name, address and all relevant particulars necessary to identify him and the purpose for which he has been facilitated; or (b) doing anything necessary to conduct encryption research using a lawfully obtained encrypted copy; or

(c) conducting any lawful investigation; or

(d) doing anything necessary for the purpose of testing the security of a computer system or a computer network with the authorisation of its owner; or

(e) operator; or

(f) doing anything necessary to circumvent technological measures intended for identification or surveillance of a user; or

those who have only basic knowledge of such technologies as they will not be able to access or reproduce for the uses permitted under the Copyright Act unless he hires any skilled person for the purpose of circumvention. Further, the technology can prevent access or copying of work even after the expiry of the term of copyright. Hence the provision is a hindrance for use of work for educational purposes.

4 Conclusion

India has a major goal of achieving social justice. Education promotes social justice, by removing inequalities in society, maintaining the dignity of the individual and removing poverty. The Copyright is a monopoly right but it benefits society by providing creative works to it. India is a developing nation where literacy level is very low as compared to developed nations and therefore its needs are different. Hence India has not only to give priority to education but at the same time protect the rights of owners of copyright by balancing individual's right to education with exclusive rights of the individual in his copyrighted work.

Reprographic use affects the reproduction right of owners of works. However Indian law permits reproduction of work for teaching and research purposes without any quantitative limitations so long there is fair dealing in the work or the work is reproduced by teacher or pupil in the course of instruction, or for persons with disability. There is no restriction as to level of teaching i.e. primary, secondary or higher education or type of education whether institutional or online education. There is no limitation as to the number of copies to be made so long it is for teaching purposes and do not mix with normal business channels. The only drawback is while reproducing online the right of communication to the public is affected simultaneously with the reproduction right. Therefore, the exception can be created for on line education whereby communication to public in the course of instruction may also be permitted. Further the acts of transient and incidental storage of work purely for technical process of electronic transmission and for providing links for electronic transmission, access or integration not expressly prohibited by right holder are already permitted acts under the Copyright Act, 1957.

The teaching exceptions under the copyright Act, 1957 are in consonance the Berne, which provide for utilization of works for teaching purposes, to the extent justified by the purpose and are compatible with fair practice. It has been left to national legislations to determine the utilizations by limiting the rights of the owners. The purpose has to be educational and can be provided for all of level teaching and all types including online education. There is no restriction as to the number of copies to be made so long it is proportionate for the purpose of education and does not enter into economic competition with right holders for commercial gains. Further

(Footnote 87 continued)

(g) taking measures necessary in the interest of national security.

the Intergovernmental Copyright Committee had made the recommendations in 1968 that personal use, use by instructors in educational institutions for teaching purposes or for a library, to be considered as free uses, especially for developing countries, as they were not to pay remuneration in such cases and further recommended for an international instrument. But, in 1975 by a resolution the countries were left to adjust their regulations relating to reprography according to their needs.

The solution to reduce reprography can be to provide educational material at affordable prices and also to promote education by free uses. This will create new works for future markets and more royalties for right holders. However the application of access control or copy control technology will not allow an ordinary skilled person to take benefit of the educational exceptions under the copyright law unless he hires a third person to circumvent the technology. This tilts the balance in favour of the right holder. In India where a person cannot pay for educational material it cannot be expected that he will pay a third person who is skilled in that technology to circumvent technological measures. We cannot forget that India has an international obligation under the Covenant on Economic Social and Cultural rights for not only providing free education at primary level but *also progressive introduction of free education at the secondary and higher education level.*

Reference

Wiseman L (2012) The reprographic crisis: towards an international solution. Monish UL Rev 38 (1):60–77. Available at: http://www.austlii.edu.au/au/journals/MonashULawRw/2012/4.pdf. (Last visited on 10 Nov. 2015).

'Minor Exemptions' Doctrine in National Copyright Law: Guidance from the WTO Jurisprudence

R. Rajesh Babu

Abstract The limitations and exceptions to the exclusive use of copyright have largely remained an "unregulated space" despite over a century of international norm-setting in copyright. This is particularly true of the "minor reservations" or "minor exemptions" doctrine, a concept closely linked to the notion of "fair use" or "fair dealing" in the TRIPs Agreement. Minor exceptions provide states with flexibility to limit the exclusive use of copyright. This chapter attempts to understand the emerging jurisprudence on the TRIPs Agreements, specifically in the area of "minor exemptions" under the international copyrights law. More specifically, the paper shall analyse select WTO dispute settlement cases where the WTO panels and the Appellate Body has had the opportunity to clarify and interpret the consistency of the national copyright law in the context of obligations assumed under the TRIPs Agreement and the Berne Convention 1971. The chapter addresses the issue of "minor exemption" which has direct implications on the private proprietary claims and the broader public interest. The Indian law and policy makers could take useful guidance of the emerging jurisprudence in structuring their national policy while addressing their national priorities.

1 Introduction

The "limitations and exceptions" to the exclusive use of copyright has largely remained an "unregulated space" despite over a century of international norm setting in copyright.[1] This is particularly true of the "minor reservations" or "minor exemptions" doctrine. This concept is closely linked to the notion of 'fair use' or 'fair dealing' in the TRIPs Agreement that provides states with flexibility to limit the exclusive use of copyright. However, unlike fair dealing exceptions, "minor

[1] Hugenholtz and Okediji 2008.

R. Rajesh Babu (✉)
IIM Calcutta, Kolkata, India
e-mail: rajeshbabu@iimcal.ac.in

M.K. Sinha and V. Mahalwar (eds.), *Copyright Law in the Digital World*,
DOI 10.1007/978-981-10-3984-3_6

exemptions" have remained as "implied exceptions" in the Berne Convention for the Protection of Literary and Artistic Works 1971 (*hereinafter* Berne Convention). In other words, minor exceptions are "implied" limitations or exceptions which are in addition to the "explicit" exceptions found in the Berne Convention.[2] The minor exemption was originally intended to be inserted in the Bern Convention to allow Member States to retain any limitations existing in their national laws. During the Revision of the Berne Convention attempted at the Brussels and the Stockholm Conferences, the Member States invoked the "minor reservations" doctrine to justify the maintenance in their national laws of existing exceptions of minor importance.[3] Owing to fear that "such a provision would 'positively incite' those States which had not such exceptions to incorporate them in their laws", a decision was made to finally rejected the "explicit" mention of these minor exemptions in the Bern Convention.[4] Thus, these implied exceptions have no explicit basis in the Bern Convention, nor are they part of the Conventions itself.[5]

The minor reservations or minor exemption doctrine as embedded in the Berne Convention, carried over to in the TRIPs Agreement permits states to exempt by national laws, acts of public performance or reproduction of copyrighted materials.[6] More specifically, these minor reservations (or "minor exemptions") doctrine are yet to be codified and exists only in state practice. The international legal basis of these reservations are only found in the formal declaration made in the final Report of the Brussels Conference which recognised the right of states to provide in national laws minor reservations to the right of public performance (communication to the public) that are in conformity with the Bern Convention. It falls into two categories: (i) those in relation to performing, recitation, broadcasting, recording and cinematographic rights, and (ii) those in relation to translations. It was further said that the minor reservations are usually concerned with *de minimis* uses, for instance, use of works during religious ceremonies, or use by military bands or the needs of the child and adult education.[7] There has been no clarity as to whether the examples of minor reservations mentioned in these review conference report are exhaustive. The States have however maintained the view that they are allowed to maintain or introduce other minor exceptions than those addressed in these Reports, as long as they qualify as 'minor reservations' and are truly of minor importance. In other words, the international copyright law has broadly left the discretion to the national legislators to decide the 'legitimate' interest of the author and to what extent it can be prejudiced such that it is not 'unreasonable' under the law and does not conflict with the normal exploitation of the work.[8] Of course this does not mean

---

[2] 110(5) Panel Report, at 18. See also Henry (2001).

[3] Okediji 2005. See also, Senftleben 2004.

[4] Ricketson 2003.

[5] Reinbothe and Lewinski 2015.

[6] Ibid.

[7] Hugenholtz and Okediji 2008.

[8] Agarwala and Prasad 2009.

that national 'minor reservations' may be of any kind and scope. They must be "of a restricted character" and must comply with test laid down under the Berne Convention and the TRIPs Agreement.

Given the uncodified nature of the "minority exemptions" in both, the Berne Convention as well as the TRIPs agreement, several questions remained ambiguous in terms of policy interventions at the national level and its compatibility with the international norms. For instance, to what extent the Berne Convention *acquis* form part of the WTO legal system? Or can new minor exception could be introduced or are they frozen? Or what are the criteria to determine whether a particular "minor" exemption is permissible? More important is the question on the balance that must be preserved between private right of the copyright holder and public interest of the community at large. Some of these questions came up for scrutiny in the WTO Dispute Settlement Body (DSB) in the context of the newly introduced "minor reservations" incorporated by the US in the Copyright Act of 1976, as amended by the Fairness in Music Licensing Act of 28 October 1998, which entered into force on 26 January 1999. The European Communities (EC) challenged the maintainability of the "minor exemptions" under the WTO TRIPs Agreement and the Bern Conventions, as it conflicted substantially with the right of the copyright holder. The WTO DSB established Panel got the opportunity to elaborate on the nature and scope of the "minor exemptions", throwing some light on an otherwise uncodified exception.

Accordingly, this chapter is an attempt to understand the emerging jurisprudence on the TRIPs Agreements, specifically in the area of "minor exemptions" under the international copyright law. More specifically, this chapter shall analyse some WTO dispute settlement cases where the panels and the Appellate Body has had the opportunity to clarify and interpret the consistency of the national copyright law in the context of obligations assumed under the TRIPs Agreement and the Berne Convention 1971. The chapter addresses the issue of "minor exemption" which has direct implications on the private proprietary claims and the broader public interest. The Indian law and policy makers could take useful guidance of the emerging jurisprudence in structuring their national policy while addressing their national priorities.

2 WTO TRIPs and the Copyright Regime

The WTO Agreement on Trade Related Intellectual Property Rights (TRIPs Agreement) lays down the minimum standard that the members' countries provide for the protection of IPRs.[9] Apart from bringing together a broad range of IPRs within its ambit, the Agreements also incorporates pre-existing obligations found in

[9] "The TRIPs Agreement is unique in the WTO context in that it prescribes precise and justifiable minimum standards for the legislative, administrative and judicial protection of private rights which apply to both domestically-produced as well as imported intellectual property". Petersmann 1997.

the Berne, Paris and Rome conventions.[10] Specifically, in the copyright area, TRIPs sets forth the "Berne-plus" minimum standard of protection.[11] In other words, by signing the TRIPs agreement which is part of the single undertaking, the WTO member states agreed to be bound by all the obligations presented in those agreements, with the exception of moral rights. The member states are not permitted to make any reservations from these minimum obligations. Even if states have made reservation in the earlier convention, the same shall not apply in the context of the TRIPs obligations. More importantly, these set of obligations must be incorporated into the domestic legal system of all the countries, with appropriate enforcement mechanisms which provides for an effective remedy. The failure of a member state to adhere to such requirement of national framework could result in the invocation of the WTO dispute settlement understanding (DSU) by the affected member. In short, the compliance requirement with the minimum obligations under the TRIPs agreement is absolute and any deviation from the same could be the subject of twin judicial actions, one at the national level judical process, and the other at the international level through the WTO DSU. Both remedies could be pursued independent of each other.

The invocation of the WTO dispute settlement system is not limited to a non-implementation of a domestic legal framework, but also against any interpretation that may be developed by the national executive or judicial bodies. More specifically, the divergent interpretations of the treaties and their domestic law and practices could be subject to challenge through the WTO DSS and the frequency of such challenges would increase substantially against the laws of other states that offer less IPR protection or indulge in restrictive interpretation of the IPR.[12] Thus, the emerging jurisprudence in the WTO, specifically on the clarification and interpretation of the panel and Appellate Body assumes considerable significance in creating an international standard on the global understanding of the IPRs concerned. Such interpretation and clarification by the panels and the Appellate Body of the WTO DSB informs of the rights assumed under the TRIPs agreements and any derogation from such standard could be met with challenge from other WTO member states.

The substantive standards of copyright protection are laid down in the TRIPs Agreement Articles 9–13, Section 1, Part II entitled "Copyright and Related Rights". In addition to these substantive obligations, the Berne Convention administered by the World Intellectual Property Organization (WIPO) has been incorporated in the TRIPs agreement vide Article 9.1 of the TRIPs Agreement. This Article obliges WTO Members to comply with Articles 1–21 of the Berne Convention (1971) (with the exception of Article 6bis on moral rights and the rights

[10] Berne Convention for the Protection of Literary Works, 1886 (revised on 1967); Paris Convention for the protection of Industrial Property 1883 (revised on 1967) and International Convention for the Protection of Performers, Producers of Phonograms and Broadcasting Organizations, 1962; Berne Convention for the Protection of Literary and Artistic Works 1971.

[11] 'Copyright Enforcement under the TRIPs Agreement' IIPA Paper, October 2004, p. 1.

[12] Helfer 1998.

derived therefrom) and the Appendix thereto. Through their incorporation, the substantive rules of the Berne Convention, including the provisions of its Articles 11bis(1)(iii) and 11(1)(ii), have become integral part of the TRIPs Agreement and as provisions of that Agreement have to be read as applying to WTO Members.[13]

Over the years, there have been 10 disputes that relate to copyright which have been brought before the WTO DSB for adjudication.[14] However, most of the cases have not moved beyond the consultation stage. Of these cases, only two have proceeded to the panel stage and a ruling which was adopted by the DSB. They are: *United States—Section 110(5) of US Copyright Act* of 26 January 1999 (DS160), a complainant initiated by the European Communities; *China—Measures Affecting the Protection and Enforcement of Intellectual Property Rights* (DS362), a complainant initiated by the US. In this paper, we shall focus on the first case wherein the Panel interpreted and clarified the nature and scope of the 'minor exceptions' doctrine.[15] The case assumes importance as for the first time an international tribunal has clarified the scope of the 'Minor exceptions' doctrine that provides states to flexibility to limited the exclusive use of copyright under the TRIPs Agreement, thereby establishing an international benchmark.

3 *United States—Section 110(5) of the US Copyright Act*: The Case in Context

This case was initiated by the EC on 26 January 1999, against the US amendment of Section 110(5) of the US Copyright Act as amended by the "Fairness in Music Licensing Act" enacted on 27 October 1998. The amendment imposed "limitations"

---

[13] *Section 110(5) of US Copyright Act*, Panel Report, para 6.18.

[14] *Japan—Measures Concerning Sound Recordings* (Complainant: United States) 9 February 1996 mutually satisfactory solution (DS28); *Japan—Measures concerning Sound Recordings* (Complainant: European Communities) 28 May 1996 mutually satisfactory solution (DS42); DS82 *Ireland—Measures Affecting the Grant of Copyright and Neighbouring Rights* (Complainant: United States) 14 May 1997 mutually satisfactory solution; DS83 *Denmark—Measures Affecting the Enforcement of Intellectual Property Rights* (Complainant: United States) 14 May 1997 mutually satisfactory solution; DS86 *Sweden—Measures Affecting the Enforcement of Intellectual Property Rights* (Complainant: United States) 28 May 1997 mutually satisfactory solution; DS115 *European Communities—Measures Affecting the Grant of Copyright and Neighbouring Rights* (Complainant: United States) 6 January 1998 mutually satisfactory solution; DS124 *European Communities—Enforcement of Intellectual Property Rights for Motion Pictures and Television Programs* (Complainant: United States) 30 April 1998 mutually satisfactory solution; DS125 *Greece—Enforcement of Intellectual Property Rights for Motion Pictures and Television Programs* (Complainant: United States) 4 May 1998 mutually satisfactory solution; DS160 *United States—Section 110(5) of US Copyright Act* (Complainant: European Communities) 26 January 1999; DS362 *China—Measures Affecting the Protection and Enforcement of Intellectual Property Rights* (Complainant: United States).

[15] *United States—Section 110(5) of the US Copyright Act, Panel Report*, WT/DS160/R 15 June 2000.

in the form of "home-style" and "business" exemptions on the exclusive rights provided to owners of copyright in respect of certain performances and displays. The EC challenged the US measures as incompatible with the obligations undertaken under Article 9.1 of the TRIPs Agreement together with Articles 11(1)(ii) and 11bis(1)(iii) of the Berne Convention (1971) and that the same cannot be justified under any "express" or "implied" exception or limitation permissible under the Berne Convention or the TRIPs Agreement. On the other hand, the US argued that the TRIPs Agreement and, the Berne Convention which was incorporated in the TRIPs Agreement, allowed States to place minor limitations on the exclusive rights of copyright owners and the current amendment is justifiable under such limitation. The EU estimated the actual annual losses to EC rights holders at $53.65 million whereas the US estimated the amount at less than $500,000 annually because of this exemption.[16]

To be compatible with the TRIPs Agreement and judge the appropriateness of the "home-style and business exemptions" (minor exemptions as claimed by the US), they must meet the standard set under Article 13 of the TRIPs Agreement.[17] After a detailed analysis, the WTO Panel found the "minor exception", specifically business exemption, incompatible with the TRIPs Agreement as it found the public retransmission of broadcast music in commercial premises (bars, shops, restaurants etc.) without royalties being paid an exceedingly broad derogation from the exclusive right of authors to authorise the public communication of their works. The WTO DSB adopted the report on 27 July 2000. On June 23, 2003, the US and the EU reached a mutually satisfactory temporary arrangement pursuant to which, the US agreed to pay a lump-sum payment of $3.3 million to the EU, "to a fund established to finance activities of general interest to music copyright holders, in particular awareness-raising campaigns at the national and international level and activities to combat piracy in the digital network."[18] There is no report on the compliance of the US with the DSB report.[19]

[16] United States—Section 110(5) of US Copyright Act, (WT/DS160/5 of 16 April (1999), p. 84.

[17] Australia, Brazil, Canada, Japan and Switzerland reserved their rights to participate in the panel proceedings as third parties.

[18] USTR, Section 110(5) of US Copyright Act, Dispute Settlement Proceedings <https://ustr.gov/issue-areas/enforcement/dispute-settlement-proceedings/united-states-%E2%80%94-section-1105-us-copyright-ac>. The WTO Arbitration process on November 9, 2001, had determined that the value of the benefits lost to the EU as $1.1 million per year. *United States—Section 110(5) of the US Copyright Act Recourse to Arbitration under Article 25 of the DSU*, WT/DS160/ARB25/1, 9 November 2001.

[19] *Status Report Regarding Implementation of the DSB Recommendations and Rulings in the Dispute United States—Section 110(5) of the US Copyright Act (WT/DS160)*, WT/DS160/24/Add.99, 15 March 2013.

We shall now consider in detail the analysis and the reasoning of the Panel while arriving at this conclusion. The US Copyright Act under Section 106 provides the owner of copyright exclusive rights to any of the following:

> "...
>
> (4) in the case of literary, musical, dramatic, and choreographic works, pantomimes, and motion pictures and other audio visual works, *to perform the copyrighted work publicly*;
>
> (5) in the case of literary, musical, dramatic, and choreographic works, pantomimes, and pictorial, graphic, or sculptural works, including the individual images of a motion picture or other audiovisual work, *to display the copyrighted work publicly*; and ...".[20]

To perform[21] or display a work "publicly" means:

(1) to perform or display it at a *place open to the public* or at any place where a *substantial number of persons outside of a normal circle of a family and its social acquaintances is gathered*; or
(2) to transmit[22] or otherwise communicate a performance or display of the work to a place specified by clause (1) or to the public, *by means of any device or process*, whether the members of the public capable of receiving the performance or display receive it in the same place or in separate places and at the same time or at different times.

The amendment in question was the Section 110(5) of US Copyright Act (as amended by the Fairness in Music Licensing Act 1998) which introduced certain limitations on these exclusive rights of the copyright owner by exemption of certain performances and displays. Broadly this exemption was classified into:

"Homestyle" exemption[23]: The objective of the homestyle exemption was "to exempt from copyright liability of anyone who merely turns on, in a public place, an ordinary radio or television receiving apparatus of a kind commonly sold to members of the public for private use."[24] The clause imposed liability only where the proprietor has a *commercial 'sound system'* installed or converts a standard home receiving apparatus into equivalent of a commercial sound system.[25] This clause also exempt a *small commercial establishment* "which was not of sufficient size to justify, as a practical matter, a subscription to a commercial background music service".

---

[20] Section 106: Exclusive rights in copyrighted works, The Copyright Act.

[21] The Act also goes on to define the term "to perform a work" to mean to recite, render, play, dance, or act it, either directly or by means of any device or process or, in the case of a motion picture or other audiovisual work, to show its images in any sequence or to make the sounds accompanying it audible.

[22] The Act defines the term "To transmit a performance or display" as to communicate it by any device or process whereby images or sounds are received beyond the place from which they are sent.

[23] Section 110(5) (A) US Copyright Act.

[24] *Section 110(5) of US Copyright Act*, Panel Report, para 2.5.

[25] Ibid.

Business exemption[26]: Business exemption added by the 1998 amendment, on the other hand, exempted under certain conditions, communication by an establishment of a transmission or retransmission embodying a performance or display of a *nondramatic* musical work intended to be received by the general public, originated by a radio or television broadcast station licensed as such by the US Federal Communications Commission, or, if an audiovisual transmission, by a cable system or satellite carrier.[27] The beneficiaries of the business exemption are divided into two categories:

- establishments other than food service or drinking establishments ('retail establishments'), and food service and drinking establishments. In each category, establishments under a certain size limit are exempted, regardless of the type of equipment they use. The size limits are 2,000 gross square feet (186 m^2) for retail establishments and 3,750 gross square feet (348 m^2) for restaurants.[28]
- if the size of an establishment *is above the limits*, the exemption applies provided that the establishment does not exceed the *limits set for the equipment used*. The limits on equipment are different as regards, on the one hand, audio performances, and, on the other hand, audiovisual performances and displays. The rules concerning equipment limitations are the same for both retail establishments and restaurants above the respective size limits.[29]

The types of transmissions covered by both homestyle and business exemptions include 'original broadcasts' over the air or by satellite, 'rebroadcasts' by terrestrial means or by satellite, cable retransmissions of original broadcasts, and original cable transmissions or other transmissions by wire. However, it does not apply to the use of recorded music, such as CDs or cassette tapes, or to live performances of music.[30] While examining these exceptions, the Panel interpreted communication to the public of works transmitted over the "Internet" also as part of homestyle exemption.

The question that was raised by the EC before the WTO Panel was whether the 'homestyle' and 'Business' exemption provided by the US can be justified under the WTO TRIPs Agreement and the Berne Convention. More specifically, whether the US law falls within the ambit of permissible implied "minor" exemptions.

---

[26] Section 103 (B), US Copyright Act.

[27] *Section 110(5) of US Copyright Act*, Panel Report, para 2.9.

[28] Studies estimates that in 1999, 70% of eating establishments and 73% of drinking establishments fell under the 3,750 square feet limit, and that 45% of retail establishments fell under the 2,000 square feet limit (Dun & Bradstreet, Inc. study) (2.12). The studies conducted by the National Restaurant Association (NRA) concerning its membership indicate that 36% of table service restaurant members (those with sit-down waiter service) and 95% of quick service restaurant members are less than 3,750 square feet.

[29] *US—Section 110(5) Copyright Act*, Panel Report, para 2.14.

[30] Ibid, para 2.15, 2.16.

4 Legal Status and Scope of the "Minor Exceptions" Doctrine Under the TRIPs Agreement

Before considering where the US exemptions could be justified as "minor exemptions" under the TRIPs Agreement, the Panel addressed the critical questions: (i) to what extent the "minor exceptions" doctrine forms part of the Berne Convention (1971) *acquis*; and (ii) whether the "minor exceptions" doctrine, if it forms part of the Berne Convention, has been incorporated into the TRIPs Agreement, by virtue of Article 9.1 of that Agreement. Only if these two questions are answered in the affirmative, the Panel needs to proceed further.

On the question of the legal status of the "minor exceptions" doctrine and whether it forms part of the Berne Convention *acquis*, the panel answered in the affirmative. The Panel noted that, historically, the Berne Convention had provided for both 'explicit' and 'implicit' minor exceptions to the exclusive rights, allowing member countries to provide limitations and exceptions to certain rights.[31] This existence of minor exceptions doctrine was confirmed from the successive revision conferences of the Berne Convention (which is reflected in the Reports), the state practice as reflected in the national copyright laws of Berne Convention members, as well as of the WTO Members before and after the date that the TRIPs Agreement became applicable to them.[32] The General Report of the Brussels Conference of 1948 specifically refers to "religious ceremonies, military bands and the needs of the child and adult education" as examples of situations in respect of which minor exceptions may be provided. However, the panel noted that the state practice on the treatment of minor exceptions varies between different countries. For instance, India exempts performances at amateur clubs or societies. New Zealand exempts public performance of musical works at educational establishments. The Philippines exempts public performances for charitable and educational purposes, conventions and fairs. South Africa exempts public performances in the context of demonstrations of radio or television receivers and recording equipment by dealers of or clients for such equipment.[33]

Interpreting the Berne Convention, the panel further reached the following significant conclusion on the nature and scope of the minor exemptions:

---

[31] Ibid, para 6.48.

[32] Ibid, para 6.55.

[33] For example, Australia exempts public performance by wireless apparatus at premises of, *inter alia*, hotels or guest houses. Belgium exempts a work's communication to the public in a place accessible to the public where the aim of the communication is not the work itself, and exempts the performance of a work during a public examination where the purpose is the assessment of the performer. Finland exempts public performance in connection with religious services and education. Finland and Denmark provide for exceptions where a work's performance is not the main feature of the event, provided that no fee is charged and the event is not for profit. Brazil allows free use of works in commercial establishments for the purpose of demonstration to customers in establishments that market equipment that makes such use possible.

1. The 'minor exemptions' are not confined to limitations or exceptions of exclusively "non-commercial character". The EC had argued that the "minor exemption" doctrine is permitted only in the case of exceptions that are exclusively of non-commercial character.
2. The panel also rejected the contention that "it may under no circumstances justify exceptions to uses with a more than negligible economic impact on copyright holders".[34]
3. The lists of 'minor exemptions' found in the records (General Report) are only illustrative in character. The EC has argued that "minor exemptions" cannot be expanded and allowed countries to "maintain" existing national exceptions. The panel rejected the EC's contention of the "grandfathering" theory and the interpretation that the lists of examples found in the records are only illustrative in character.
4. The panel also disagreed with the EC's contention that the coverage of the minor exemption was "frozen" in 1967 and new minor exemptions can be introduced by member states as long as they meet the criteria.

4.1 Berne *Acquis* Part of TRIPs Agreement

The Panel then turned to the question of where the Berne *acquis* on "minor exemption" is part of the TRIPs Agreement by virtue of Article 19.1. Article 9.1 of the TRIPs Agreement obligates WTO Members to comply with Articles 1–21 of the Berne Convention with the exception of Article 6bis on moral rights and the rights derived therefrom. The panel noted that Article 9.1 of the TRIPs agreement neither does expressly exclude the incorporation of Articles 11 and 11*bis* of the Berne Convention that includes the entire *acquis* of these provisions, nor exclude the possibility of providing minor exceptions to the respective exclusive rights.[35] They based their argument and confirmation of their interpretation on the "preparatory works" of the GATT Uruguay Round negotiations on the TRIPs Agreement which mentions "minor exemptions" doctrine as forming part of existing international standards.[36] Based on this, the panel concluded that Article 9.1 of the TRIPs Agreement has incorporated not only the text of Articles 1–21 of the Berne Convention (1971), but the entire Berne *acquis* relating to these articles.

---

[34] 6.58.

[35] "We note that Article 30 of the Vienna Convention on the application of successive treaties is not relevant in this respect, because all provisions of the TRIPs Agreement—including the incorporated Articles 1–21 of the Berne Convention (1971)—entered into force at the same point in time." *US—Section 110(5) Copyright Act*, Panel Report, para 6.41.

[36] *US—Section 110(5) of US Copyright Act*, Panel Report, paras. 6.64–66.

5 The US "Minor Exceptions" and Triple Test Under TRIPs Article 13 Standard

Having found the applicability of the Berne *acquis* to the TRIPs agreement, the panel turned to the question of compatibility of the US "minor exceptions"—homestyle exemption and business exemption—provided under the Section 110(5) of the US Copyright Act falling within the ambit of Article 13 standard. Article 13 provides for the general 'limitations and exceptions' applicable to exclusive rights of the holders of copyright. It provides that:

> Members shall confine limitations or exceptions to exclusive rights to certain special cases which do not conflict with a normal exploitation of the work and do not unreasonably prejudice the legitimate interests of the right holder.

This provision provides the standard by which to judge the appropriateness of limitations or exceptions, including the "minor exceptions" doctrine. In other words, Article 13 of the TRIPs Agreement clarifies and articulates the scope of the minor exceptions doctrine in the TRIPs Agreement. "No limitation, not even those that belong in the category of minor reservations, may exceed the limits set by the three-steps test". The three-step found in Article 9(2) of the BC was introduced in international copyright law at the 1967 Stockholm Conference, as a companion to the formal recognition of the general right of reproduction in Article 9(1) of the Berne Convention. The three-step test reappeared in TRIPs Article 13 and subsequently in WCT Article 10.[37] Hugenholtz and Okediji (2008) notes that with the "transformation from a norm of international copyright to a norm of international trade law, the focus of the test has shifted from the interests of the author to those of the right holder", with the WTO emphasising more on the commercial interests of intermediaries, while downplaying the interests of the authors.

The three conditions contained in Article 13 of the TRIPs Agreement require that minor exemptions to exclusive rights:

(1) be confined to certain special cases,
(2) do not conflict with a normal exploitation of the work, and
(3) do not unreasonably prejudice the legitimate interests of the right holder.

These three conditions are to be applied on a cumulative basis, each being a separate and independent requirement that must be satisfied. Failure to comply with any one of the three conditions would result in the Article 13 exception being disallowed.[38] In other words, the three-step test has been designed to defend

[37] Variants of the test also appear in various regional instruments, such as the European harmonization directives, or in bilateral treaties, such as the US–Australia FTA (Article 17.4(10)). Hugenholtz and Okediji 2008.

[38] *US—Section 110(5) of US Copyright Act*, Panel Report, para 6.97.

authors' rights against wholesale exemptions without clear justifications and against acts of use which undermine the economic value of these rights.[39]

The **first condition** of Article 13 that must be satisfied is about confining the "minor exemption" to "certain special cases". This would require the limitation or exception to be "clearly defined" in national legislation and should be "narrow in its scope and reach" (of limited application). However, an exemption may be compatible with the first condition even if it pursues a special purpose whose underlying legitimacy in a normative sense cannot be discerned.[40] The panel found the homestyle and business exemption to be "clearly defined". Applying this test in the context of "homestyle exception", the panel rejected the EC's argument that the criteria under subparagraph (A) are ambiguously worded because the expression "a single receiving apparatus of a kind commonly used in private homes" is in itself imprecise and a "moving target" due to technological development.[41] Further, it was found that the coverage of the "homestyle exception" with respect to eating, drinking and other establishments was (a) 16% of all US eating establishments; (b) 13.5% of all US drinking establishments; and (c) 18% of all US retail establishments. Since the potential users are limited to a comparably small percentage, the panel concluded that the exemption is specific enough to meet the standard set under Article 13. However, the primary contention between the parties was whether the "business" exemption can be considered as a "special" case within the meaning of Article 13. It was found that in the US, approximately 73% of all drinking, 70% of all eating, and 45% of all retail establishments are entitled to get exemption under "business" exemption. Since a substantial majority of eating and drinking establishments and close to half of retail establishments are covered by the exemption contained in "business" exemption (Section 110(5)(B), US Copyright Act), the panel concluded that the exemption does not qualify as a "certain special case" within the meaning of the first condition of Article 13.[42]

The **second condition** under Article 13 of the TRIPs Agreement requires that the "minor exemption" do not conflict with a "normal exploitation" of the work. "Exploitation" of musical works refers to "the activity by which copyright owners employ the exclusive rights conferred on them to extract economic value from their rights to those works". The term "normal" exploitation for the panel clearly means something "less than full use of an exclusive right" to "extract economic value from" a copyright holder's works.[43] If the scope of exclusive rights covers every use of a work involving commercial gain, necessarily conflicts with a normal exploitation of that work, then "hardly any exception or limitation could pass the test of the second condition and Article 13 might be left devoid of meaning, because

---

[39] Reinbothe and Lewinski 2015.

[40] *US—Section 110(5) of US Copyright Act*, Panel Report, para 6.112.

[41] Ibid, para 6.137.

[42] *US—Section 110(5) Copyright Act,* Panel Report, para 6.133.

[43] *US—Section 110(5) Copyright Act,* Panel Report, p. 44.

normal exploitation would be equated with full use of exclusive rights".[44] The panel noted that an "exception or limitation" to an exclusive right can be considered to be in conflict with a normal exploitation if

> uses that are covered by that exclusive right but exempted under the exception or limitation, *enter into economic competition* with the ways that right holders normally extract economic value from that right to the work (i.e., the copyright) and thereby deprive them of significant or tangible commercial gains.[45]

The Panel created a dual test to judge whether or not an exception or limitation interferes with a copyright holder's normal exploitation. Quantitative Step—The first part of the test involves a quantitative "economic analysis of the degree of market displacement in terms of forgone collection of remuneration by right owners caused by the free use of works due to the exemption at issue."[46] Qualitative Step involved the question of whether or not the uses allowed by the exemption compete with the author's uses in an economically significant or practically important way.[47] The Panel's evaluation of the actual and potential effects was based on current market conditions, as well as the market conditions ("technological developments" and "changing consumer preferences") as they are likely to evolve in the near future.[48] In other words, it is the potential actual effect of the exception on the market at a given point in time that determines the market conditions that would be the benchmark for defining the normative connotation of normal exploitation. For this purpose, the panel noted that communication to the public would include not only radio and television broadcasts, and recorded music (CDs and tapes) when assessing what is a normal use of musical works.[49]

The panel found that since a large percentages of business reached by the business exemption interfered with a significant portion of a potentially large economic market for copyright holders, "business exemption" in subsection (B) cannot pass the second condition set under Article 13, regardless of whether or not copyright holders commonly utilized this market.[50] In the case of the "home-style exemption" of subparagraph (A), the basic rationale of this clause is that the secondary use of the transmission by turning on an ordinary receiver in public is so remote and minimal that no further liability should be imposed. In other words, the provision is intended to define the borderline between two situations:

[44] Ibid, para 6.182.

[45] Ibid, para 6.183 (emphasis added).

[46] Henry 2001.

[47] *US—Section 110(5) Copyright Act,* Panel Report, p. 47.

[48] Ibid, p. 50.

[49] Ibid, para 6.207.

[50] Henry 2001, p. 17.

- a situation where one listens to the radio or watches the television (which is not covered by the scope of copyright and, hence, outside normal exploitation of works), and
- a situation where one uses appropriate equipment to cause a new public performance of music contained in a broadcast or other transmission.

This borderline is defined by laying emphasis on "turning on an ordinary receiver", albeit that member of the public might also hear the transmission.[51] The panel concluded that this act does not "have economic or practical importance of any considerable dimension for the right holders of musical works"[52] and therefore, concluded that the "homestyle exemption" does not conflict with a normal exploitation of works within the meaning of the second condition of Article 13.

The **third condition** that Article 13 imposes is that the minor exemption should not "unreasonably prejudice the legitimate interests of the right holder". For the Panel, the crucial question was the degree or level of "prejudice" that may be considered as "unreasonable", given that, a certain amount of "prejudice" has to be presumed justified as "not unreasonable".[53] In the Panel's view, prejudice reaches "an unreasonable level if an exception or limitation causes or has the potential to cause an unreasonable loss of income to the copyright owner". Thus, the analysis of the third condition implies determining, first, what are the "interests" of right holders at stake and which attributes make them "legitimate"; and interpretation of the term "prejudice" and what amount of "prejudice" reached a level that should be considered "unreasonable".[54]

After taking a precise analysis of the figures provided by the parties, and taking account of the actual as well as the potential prejudice caused by the exemptions, the panel found that "business exemption" is likely to reduce the amount of income that may be generated from restaurants and retail establishments for the use of recorded music or commercial background music services.[55] The panels noted that the US, in whom the burden of proof lies, has also not demonstrated that the business exemption does not unreasonably prejudice the legitimate interests of the right holder.[56] Accordingly, it arrived at the conclusion that the business exemption does not meet the requirements of the third condition of Article 13 of the TRIPs Agreement. However, in the cases of "homestyle exemption", the panel observed that playing music by the small establishments by means of homestyle apparatus has never been a significant source of revenue collection for collective management

[51] *US—Section 110(5) Copyright Act,* Panel Report, para 6.214.

[52] Ibid para 6.219.

[53] Gaubiac 2001.

[54] *Section 110(5) of US Copyright Act,* Panel Report, para 6.222.

[55] Gaubiac 2001 p. 11.

[56] *Section 110(5) of US Copyright Act,* Panel Report, para 6.265.

organizations (CMOs),[57] and therefore the homestyle exemption does not cause unreasonable prejudice to the legitimate interests of the right holders within the meaning of the third condition of Article 13. For panel: the playing of dramatic works through homestyle apparatus [was concerned] the panel failed to see how these would 'acquire such economic or practical importance that it could cause an unreasonable prejudice to the legitimate interests of rights holders.'[58]

6 National Policy Implications

In short, the Panel found that the US copyright provisions allowing music broadcasting without payment by small businesses as inconsistent with the TRIPs obligations. However, the 'homestyle' exception was regarded as one of the "special cases which do not conflict with a normal exploitation of the work" permitted by TRIPs Article 13. The finding was based on the broader interpretation of the TRIPs obligations that limitations and exceptions under the minor exceptions doctrine is (i) primarily concerned with *de minimis* use, (ii) its application is not limited to the examples contained in the reports of the Berne Convention revision conferences held in Brussels and Stockholm (not limited to religious ceremonies, military bands and the needs of the child and adult education), but shall be determined on a case to case basis, (iii) minor exemption is not exclusively for non-commercial uses, but also allowed for commercial use but with an "economic impact" threshold, or (iv) to exceptions in national legislation that existed prior to 1967, that is, the exemptions are not frozen in 1967.[59] The panel also interpreted the "minor" exemption as part of the Berne *acquis*, which in turn has become part of the WTO TRIPs agreement.

Member States must have the policy space and flexibility to determine the nature of minor exception that suits their national public interest, be it child education or adult education. The panel recognised this flexibility while negating the EC's argument that the "minor exemption" is only available for non-commercial use and is not "frozen" in 1967. This interpretation would help member states to put in place their own "minor exceptions", that suits their domestic conditions, however, within the limits set by Article 13 of the TRIPs Agreement. At the same time, by interpreting the whole of the Berne *acquis* within the WTO framework, the panel's ruling has the consequence of enhancing the rights and obligations of the member states neither envisaged by the covered agreements nor negotiated during the Uruguay round of trade negotiations. The interpretation has made the WTO

[57] Holders of copyright in musical works (composers, lyricists and music publishers) normally entrust the licensing of nondramatic public performance of their works to collective management organizations ("CMOs" or performing rights organizations). Revenues are distributed to individual right holders through the CMOs that represent the right holders in question. *Section 110(5) of US Copyright Act*, Panel Report, para 2.17.

[58] *Section 110(5) of US Copyright Act*, Panel Report, p. 84.

[59] *Section 110(5) of US Copyright Act*, Panel Report, para 6.93.

members who were never party to the Berne Convention, now bound by not just the text of the Convention, but also of the state practice of the Convention, of which the WTO member States had never acknowledged or agreed to.

In addition, the panel established the "economic impact" test as the sole test to determine whether such unlicensed use of the exception is legitimate and TRIPs compliant. According to this interpretation, once that unlicensed use reaches a certain economic threshold, no exemption will be permitted against the exclusive rights of a copyright holder. "It will matter not whether that use is being offered as a public service by a not-for-profit provider, or for entirely commercial reasons. Neither would the relative needs, or wealth of the potential beneficiaries of such free access, enter the equation."[60] This "over-reliance on economic data as the determinative factor under each of the three parts of the Article 13 test" was considered by Henry as "an unworkable strategy for assessing such exceptions: at best, it gives wealthier nations an advantage over poorer ones; at worst it makes an a priori prediction of such exceptions' permissibility under TRIPs nearly impossible."[61] Henry also points to the fact that the Panel's narrow interpretation of the Article 13 test may serve to invalidate existing member nations' exceptions, or to restrict their scope so much that the underlying policy objectives are thwarted.

> The fact that these possibilities exist suggests that the Panel's decision has, in effect, changed the playing field of TRIPs compliant exceptions. Countries wishing to become TRIPs compliant have adopted entire bodies of affirmative law through a detailed negotiation process.

Thus, if one go by the strict interpretation developed by the panel, some of the exceptions adopted by the states may no longer be acceptable. For example, Henry considers a passage from Bulgaria's copyright law, which is contained in a section, entitled "Permissible Free Use":

> reproduction by copier or other similar means of parts of published works or of small works, as well as the recording of parts of films and other audio-visual works on audio or video media by educational Institutions (sic) and their use for educational purposes.[62]

This provision may not pass even the first test of the Article 13, that an exception must be clearly defined and narrow in scope and reach.

The WTO decision was also criticised on the ground that the Panel did not bring clarity on the core question of the scope of "non-commercial use" of intellectual property. More specifically, the panel avoided the discussion on the need to balance private proprietary claims and the broader public interest (reconcile commercial and non-commercial values), that lies at the heart of public policy concerning the protection of intellectual property.[63] Raising a point with respect to the significance

---

[60] Henry (2001).

[61] Ibid.

[62] Copyright and Neighbouring Rights Act of 1993 (as amended in 1994 and 2000), State Gazette Vol. 4. No. 28, Apr. 2000, Chapter 5, Article 23(2). (Republic of Bulgaria) in Henry 2001.

[63] Shrybman 2000.

of economic impacts associated with certain non-commercial uses, Shrybman, wonders what would be the threshold were the "economic impacts for a copyright owner be so great as to negate the societal benefits associated with making information freely available for such non-commercial purposes as adult and childhood education?" "Should the balance of these competing interests shift with the character of either the rights holder, or the beneficiaries of making certain IP freely available", he wonders. For example, should the line be drawn in the same place when the rights holder is a large media corporation and the users, students in a developing country? Shrybman notes that the panel showed scant awareness of the policy framework which should have at least informed, if not guided, its deliberations.

> Rather it ignored the public interest dimension of arguments made by the EC and supported by other intervening nations, choosing instead to simply reduce the issues before it—to ones involving the competing claims among private commercial users. Thus less than two paragraphs of its very lengthy decision are devoted to addressing the issue of non-commercial use.

He notes that this is largely in sync with the "pattern with trade dispute resolution under the WTO—panels have shown such a myopic preoccupation with the trade liberalization goals of the regime, that all other competing policy perspectives are scarcely considered."

7 Conclusion

In short, the panel has brought some clarity to an area (minor exemption) which is otherwise not being address in any international adjudication process. It has legitimised the non-static nature of the "minor exemptions", however at the same time, problematizing the applicability of the Berne *acquis* in the WTO legal system. The panel benchmarked "economic analysis" as the criteria for determining the validity of the "minor exception", which seems to considerably narrow down the scope of the exception, taking away the public interest element in the process. More importantly, the panel lost a key opportunity to address the public policy issue in maintaining a minor exception, on the one hand, the proprietary right of the copyright holder. The ruling has been consciously not appealed to the Appellate Body, which may to a certain extent diminish its value in the WTO jurisprudence. The developing countries like India must use their policy space to pursue their public interest goals by testing the boundaries of the exceptions and limitations, specifically the minor exemptions which give larger leeway then established exceptions.

References

Agarwala A, Prasad A Copyright law desk book: knowledge, access & development

Gaubiac Y (2001) Exceptions and limitations to copyright within the meaning of Article 13 of TRIPS: WTO rules on copyright exemptions. Commun Commer Electron 1

Helfer LR (1998) Adjudicating copyright claims under the TRIPs agreement: the case for a European human rights analogy. Harvard Int Law J 39(2):361

Henry SE (2001), The first international challenge to U.S. Copyright law: what does the WTO analysis of 17 U.S.C. ß 110(5) mean to the future of international Harmonization of copyright laws under the TRIPS agreement? Penn State Int Law Rev 20:301

Hugenholtz PB, Okediji RL (2008) Conceiving an international instrument on limitations and exceptions to copyright, Final Report March 06, 2008, Institute for Information Law University of Minnesota and University of Amsterdam Law School

Okediji RL (2005) Welfare and digital copyright in international perspective. In Reichman JH, Maskus K (eds) International public goods and transfer of technology under a globalized intellectual property regime, Cambridge University Press

Petersmann E-U (1997) *The GATT/WTO Dispute Settlement System: International Law, International Organizations and Dispute Settlement* 13–14

Reinbothe J, Lewinski SV (2015) The WIPO treaties on copyright: a commentary on the WCT, the WPPT, and the BTAP, p 161

Ricketson S (2003) WIPO study on limitations and exceptions of copyright and related rights in the digital environment, SCCR/9/7, 5 Apr 2003

Senftleben M (2004) Copyrights, limitations and the three-step-test Kluwer Law International, pp 198–201

Shrybman S (2000) Information, commodification and the world trade organization remarks prepared for the IFLA conference, Jerusalem, Aug 2000. http://www.vcn.bc.ca/bclaip/globalization/shrybman3.htm#_ftnref9

Universal Law Publishers (2009), p 142

Copyright and Human Rights: The Quest for a Fair Balance

Vandana Mahalwar

Abstract Human Rights and copyright are two distinct and contrary arenas of law, which intersect each other at various points. Copyright is regarded as a means of incentivizing the creation of new works and as a source of dissemination of work. While, on the other hand, the human rights framework of intellectual property in the UDHR and ICESCR aims to offer individuals, the well-merited protection of their moral and material interests in their intellectual creations. Article 27(2) of the UDHR recognizes everyone's right to the protection of the moral and material interests resulting from any scientific, literary or artistic production of which he is the author. Dichotomy of rights in Article 27 portrays internal conflict between access to benefits of arts and scientific advancements and moral and material interests. Article 15(1)(c) of the ICESCR also requires each state party of the Covenant to recognize the right of everyone to benefit from the protection of the moral and material interests resulting from any scientific, literary or artistic production. There are two distinct approaches to the copyright-human rights interface. The first approach views the copyright and human rights in fundamental conflict with each other, while the second approach considers both to be compatible with each other but still striving to trade-off between access and incentives. This chapter explores the internal and external clashes between copyright and human rights and also addresses the challenges in giving a human rights framework to copyright.

1 Introduction

Human rights and copyright, two bodies of law that were once unfamiliar to each other, are attempting to harmonizing for last few decades. For decades the two arenas have developed in virtual isolation from each other. But in the last few years,

V. Mahalwar (✉)
The Indian Law Institute, New Delhi, India
e-mail: vandana.mahalwar@gmail.com

M.K. Sinha and V. Mahalwar (eds.), *Copyright Law in the Digital World*,
DOI 10.1007/978-981-10-3984-3_7

international standard setting activities have begun to map the previously uncharted intersections between intellectual property law on the one hand and human rights law on the other. Copyright is usually looked upon not only as a means of incentivising the creation of new works but also as a source of dissemination of work while maintaining its integrity. Though copyright law is seen on the flipside of the freedom of expression, yet, if we trace the history back, it suggests that initial copyright statues were enacted to assert and better protect the author's freedom of expression to overcome the stationer's control in England. US Supreme Court stated in 1985 in *Harper and Row* v. *Nation Enterprises*[1] that

> It should not be forgotten that the Framers intended copyright itself to be the engine of free expression. By establishing a marketable right to use of one's expression, copyright supplies the economic incentive to create and disseminate ideas.

The idea of the US Supreme Court of copyright as 'an engine of free expression' gained a shape at international level also. Copyright plays this role in three ways. Firstly, it plays the production function by conferring the economic incentives for the creativity. The U.S. Supreme Court also expressed in *Mazer* v. *Stein*[2] that "the economic philosophy behind the clause empowering Congress to grant patents and copyrights is the conviction that encouragement of individual effort by personal gain is the best way to advance public welfare through the talents of authors and inventors in science and useful arts." Secondly, it plays the structural function by supporting the authors who want the economic sustenance and independence from governmental influence. Thirdly, it plays the expressive role, it motivates the authors by bolstering the importance of author's creative contribution to public.[3]

The basic objective of copyright law is to protect the property rights of the author and to exclude the world from making use of the work without authorization from the author. But, when another author has to use the first author's expression, he has to seek his permission. And here, two contrary interests intersect each other.

This clash was addressed by Lord Phillips M.R., in *Ashdown* v. *Telegraph Group Ltd*[4]

> Copyright is antithetical to freedom of expression. It prevents all, save the owner of the copyright, from expressing information in the form of the literary work protected by the copyright.[5]

There is a need to explore and recognise the idea that respect for freedom of expression can not sustain without respect for an author's literary or artistic creativity, as a basic human right.

---

[1] 471 US 539 (1985).

[2] 347 U.S. 201(1954).

[3] Gendreau 2004.

[4] [2001] 4 All ER 666.

[5] *Id.*, para 30.

2 International Legal Framework

Article 27(2) of the Universal Declaration of Human Rights states explicitly that "everyone has the right to the protection of the moral and material interests resulting from any scientific, literary or artistic production of which he is the author." Article 15(1)(c) of the International Covenant on Economic, Social and Cultural Rights requires each state party to the Covenant to "recognize the right of everyone to benefit from the protection of the moral and material interests resulting from any scientific, literary or artistic production of which he [or she] is the author." Both intellectual property law and human rights law try to strike a balance between public and private rights and, in this sense, the two are not in direct conflict with each other. This chapter aims to discourse the conflict between Copyright and freedom of expression under human rights.

3 UDHR

The national laws for copyright vis-a-vis freedom of expression and education vary considerably from state to state. It was neither feasible nor practical to harmonise national legislation to solve this problem of diverse nature of National legislations, so some provisions were incorporated in International Treaties with an emphasis on basic human freedoms and rights, where the author's rights are expressly mentioned.

Article 27 of the United Nations Declaration on Human Rights[6] reads:

(1) Everyone has the right freely to participate in the cultural life of the community, to enjoy the arts and to share in scientific advancement and its benefits.
(2) Everyone has the right to the protection of the moral and material interests resulting from any scientific, literary or artistic production of which he is the author.

Article 27, as a human right is of universal nature and vests in every human being. Furthermore, the human rights that are embodied in UDHR are to exist independently of such right's recognition in legal systems or customs or enforcement in their own country. Article 27 of UDHR has historic roots. Dichotomy of rights in Article 27 presents a divide between access to benefits of arts and scientific advancements and moral and material interests.[7] Right to Education is not merely an important right, it is more crucial as it is supporting other human rights.

Article 27 of UDHR gives rise to a paradoxical juxtaposition of public right of access to scientific advancements and private right to protection of scientific, literary and artistic production of which he is author. Hence, Article 27

[6] Adopted on December 10, 1948.

[7] Nickel 1987.

accommodates both, private and public interests at same place. Article 27 characterises a clear conflict between an author's right and right to education. Also, Article 27(1) while taking count of right to freely participate in cultural life of community and right to have access to art and scientific advancements, applies to communities as well as individuals.[8] However, it is silent as to the ambit of community that whether the right extends to participate in global community or merely domestic community.

This dichotomy within Article 27 complicates the human rights of everyone with human rights of 'creators' as 'moral and material interests'.

Article 27(2), as a declaration of author's moral and material interests as human rights, incorporates the attributes of property rights. It restricts the states on putting obstacles to impede the ability of individuals to exercise these rights.

This gives rise to the questions and concerns regarding the appropriateness of incorporation of author's 'moral and material interest' in UDHR. The drafting history of Article 27 shows that many were reluctant to the idea of incorporating moral and material interests. René Cassin, a delegate from France, who was delegated the work of revision of Humphrey draft of UDHR in June 1947,[9] believed that everyone has the ability and desire to engage in creative activity.[10] He believed that such aspirations to develop intellectual and creative activities from which copyright works may result is found in every human being.[11] Hence, it needs the recognition and protection in the same manner as other basic human rights.

Moreover, the term 'free' in first clause of Article 27 was inserted upon a suggestion by José Encinas, a Peruvian delegate. Encinas believed that it was not enough for the declaration to state that everyone has the right to participate in cultural, artistic and scientific life of the community.[12] He stressed that Article 27 needs to provide that "the right to do so in that complete freedom without which there could be no creation worthy of man."[13] Encinas envisioned a link between freedom of thought and freedom to create. While proposing to insert the word "freely" in Article 27, he stated "An earlier article … had dealt with freedom of thought, it seemed pertinent now to recognize freedom of creative thought, in order to protect it from harmful pressures which were only too frequent in recent history."[14] This amendment was picked up by a vote of 30 to zero, with two abstentions.[15]

---

[8] Eide et al. 1992.

[9] Morsink 1999.

[10] Helfer and Austin 2011.

[11] Chapman 2001.

[12] *Supra* note 10 at 224.

[13] *Id.* at 184.

[14] *Supra* note 9 at 218.

[15] *Ibid.*

The drafting history of Article 27 reveals 27(2) to be more contentious as there was no much debate on inclusion of right to enjoy the arts and scientific advancements in Article 27(1) but there was more disagreement about incorporation of moral and material interests in Article 27(2). The French delegation were more emphatic on the special character of moral rights as they expressed that, in addition to material or economic rights, the creators should have a right over work that would not cease to exist even when the work has entered the public domain.[16] Article 27(2) of UDHR gives moral and material interest, the status of human rights.[17] On April 29, 1959, the Court of Appeal in Paris conferred Charlie Chaplin, a British national, french rights regarding his moral rights based on Article 27(2) when he opposed the unauthorised addition of a sound track to one of his motion picture.[18]

4 Article 15 of the ICESCR

Article 15 of the ICESCR reflects the soul and language of Article 27 of the UDHR. It also talks of everyone's right:

(1) to take part in culture;
(2) to enjoy the benefit of scientific progress and its applications; and
(3) to the benefits from protection of the moral and material interests resulting from any scientific, literary or artistic production of which he is an author.

The drafting of Article 15 had much of debate on incorporation of intellectual property provisions.[19] There was a disagreement among the members regarding whether the bill should be in the form of a covenant or a declaration.[20]

---

[16] *Id,* at 219–220.

[17] Foster 2015.

[18] *Société Roy Export Company Establishment et Charlie Chaplin* v. *Société Les Films Roger Richebé*, 28 R.I.D.A. 133 (1960).

[19] *Supra* note 10 at 178.

[20] Yu 2006–2007; *supra* note 9 at 13. Johannes Morsink stated:

> Most of the delegations felt that the phrase *international bill of rights* meant no less than a covenant, while the two superpowers, the U.S. (most of the time and the USSR (all the time), insisted that all the Council had meant was for them to draw up a declaration or manifesto of principles without any machinery of implementation attached to it.

The smaller member states of United Nations wished for a covenant that would bind all the large and small nations in the same manner.[21] Because Article 15 of ICESCR proceeds onto the footsteps of Article 27, a few delegates were unwilling to reiterate what is already there in Article 27 of UDHR.[22]

During the drafting meetings, the right to take part in cultural life and to enjoy the benefits of scientific progress were not in controversy.[23] But, there was no disagreement on inclusion of right to benefit from cultural and scientific advances.[24] The provisions relating to these two rights were adopted by fifteen to zero votes, with three abstentions.[25]

On the other hand, the inclusion of the rights to the protection of interests in intellectual property was more contentious.[26] The United Nations Educational, Scientific and Cultural Organisation (UNESCO hereinafter) and french delegates were the ones who were in favour of inclusion of author's rights in the covenant. The French delegates emphasised that its inclusion is must for the protection of author's moral and material rights.[27] The U.S. was enthusiastic in its inclusion in

---

[21] *Id.* at 15.

[22] *Ibid.* Danish delegate Max Sorensen expressed,

> It would clearly be undesirable merely to transpose the relevant sections from the Universal Declaration to the draft Covenant, for to do so would weaken the authority of the former, and lead to unwarranted conclusions about the significance of those of its provisions which were not reiterated in the latter.

Also, Eleanor Roosevelt, the US delegate while highlighting the fundamental difference between two documents stated,

> The [Declaration] consisted of a statement of standard which countries were asked to achieve.... But...a covenant was a very different kind of document, since it must be capable of legal enforcement. The task of drafting such an instrument was wholly unlike that of setting out hopes and aspirations relating to the rights and freedoms of people.

[23] *Supra* note at 1062.

[24] *Ibid.* Maria Green stated:

> From the beginning, there seems to have been little dissension over the notion of including a right to benefit from cultural and scientific advances.

Jacques Havet, an UNESCO official noted:

> The right of everyone to enjoy his share of the benefits of science was to a great extent the determining factor for the exercise by mankind as a whole of many other rights.... Enjoyment of the benefits of scientific progress implied the dissemination of basic scientific knowledge, especially knowledge best calculated to enlighten men's minds and combat prejudices, coordinated efforts on the part of States, in conjunction with the competent specialized agencies, to raise standards of living, and a wider dissemination of culture through the processes and apparatus created by science.

[25] *Id.* at 1063.

[26] *Supra* note 17 at 347.

[27] *Id.* at 348.

the draft covenant because it was already under consideration for the soon to be signed Universal Copyright Convention.[28]

Ultimately, this provision of right of protection interest in intellectual creations was rejected by seven to seven votes, with four abstentions.[29]

Again, in May 1952, the issue was introduced with a good support from French delegation and UNESCO.[30] United States, United Kingdom and Yugoslavia still opposed the inclusion of author's interests, stating that the issue is too complicated to be covered in covenant, rather it should be dealt with in some other instrument.[31] Valenzuela, a Chilean delegate, while stating the reasons for voting against the author's interest in covenant, gave relevant reasons providing that "there was also need to protect the under-developed countries, which had greatly suffered in the past from their inability to compete in scientific research and to take out their own patents."[32]

The Australian delegation expressed that it was "inadvisable to provide for the protection of the author without also considering the rights of the community"

Pierre Juvigny, a French delegate disagreed with and responded to Chilean delegate by stating that monopolies in the field of intellectual property do not give such risk; furthermore, absence of such provision would not be a remedy to the poor position of such under-developed countries.[33] Albeit, the provision was again rejected, by a vote of seven to six with four abstentions.[34]

Hence, when the draft Covenant was submitted to the twelfth session of the Third Committee of General Assembly by the Commission on Human Rights in the autumn of 1957, it had no Article 15(1)(c) regarding protection of moral and material interests of authors and creators. With respect to Article 15(1)(a) and

---

[28] Universal Copyright Convention (adopted on Sept. 6, 1952); supra note 20 at 1063–1064. As Roosevelt stated:

> In her delegation's opinion the subject of copyright should not be dealt with in the Covenant, because it was already under study by UNESCO which... was engaged on the collation of copyright laws with the object of building up a corpus of doctrine and in due course drafting a convention. Until all the complexities of that subject had been exhaustively studied, it would be impossible to lay down a general principle concerning it for inclusion in the Covenant.

[29] *Supra* note 17 at 348.

[30] The French delegation expressed:

> The draft covenant included provisions for the protection of the property and emoluments of professional workers and should therefore be completed by a provision for the protection of the moral and material interests resulting from scientific, literary or artistic production.... It was not a matter only of material rights; the scientist and artist had a moral right to the protection of his work, for example against plagiarism, theft, mutilation and unwarranted use (at page 1064, reconceptualising).

[31] *Supra* note 20 at 1064.

[32] *Id.* at 1065.

[33] *Ibid.*

[34] *Supra* note 10 at 178.

Article 15(1)(a)(b),[35] there was good support from the all the delegations but slightest discussion on the creator's interests. With regard to the debate on right to protection of creator's interest, this time, the proposal to include this right in the covenant came from Costa Rican and Uruguayan, not by French delegation.[36]

Tejera, a Uruguayan delegate substantiated the proposal by contending that intellectual property rights provision would rather complement the public rights provision in the covenant.[37] The Chinese delegate, Chang, underscored the importance of this proposed provision by stating that protection of author's rights would assure the authenticity of the works to public.[38] Like earlier, UNESCO remained in support of the restoration of intellectual property rights.

Some delegations, who were initially against the idea of intellectual property rights protection, changed their minds by the time Third Committee of the General Assembly assembled.[39] One of the major reason for the same can be Universal Copyright Convention, which was entered into effect on September 16, 1955. The Universal Copyright Convention was important for the reason that United States, who was not a member of the Berne Convention,[40] became a member of it. United States of America and USSR did not become members of the Berne Convention because of its high level of protection. The movement for a universal convention came from a newly founded cultural organisation, UNESCO, which intended to invite the countries without forcing them to lower their standard of protection.[41]

---

[35] Maria Green, International Anti-Poverty Law Centre., " Drafting History of the Article 15(1)(c) of the International Covenant," para 34, U.N. Doc. E/C.12/2000/15 (Oct. 9, 2000).
As Green noted,

> The only reference to that passage was by D'Souza, the Indian representative, who mentioned that 'undoubtedly scientific discoveries should benefit not only all individuals, but also nations, regardless of their degree of development.

[36] *Supra* note 20 at 1066; *supra* note 35, para 35.
Tejera, a Uruguay delegate observed,

> [A] reference to authors' copyright was imperative. For lack of international protection, literary and scientific works, for example, were frequently pirated by foreign countries which paid no royalties to the authors.

[37] *Ibid.* Moreover, Tejera stated that

> the right of the author and the right of the public were not opposed to but complemented each other.

[38] *Supra* note 20 at 1067.

[39] *Ibid.* The major reason for the same can be Universal Copyright Convention, which was entered into effect on September 16, 1955.

[40] Berne Convention for the Protection of Artistic and Literary Works (adopted on September 9, 1886).

[41] Bogsch 1972.

The Universal Copyright Convention was independent in its operation from the Berne Convention.[42]

Britain, who earlier was in the support of the United States, now emphasised that it was "essential to include a provision corresponding to that in Article 27, para 2, of the UDHR in the Covenant."[43] Likewise, one Chilean delegation, who initially opposed the incorporation of IP provision, now stated that "as one of the signatories of the Universal Copyright Convention, which was fully in accordance with its own legislation, Chile had no difficulty in supporting that amendment."[44] Sweden, Israel, and the Dominican Republic were also in the favour of inclusion. Indonesia and the Eastern bloc countries were opponents for the reason that strengthening the private property would lead to an interference with "government control over science and art, and scientists and artists."[45] In last, the provision was adopted by a vote of thirty nine to nine with twenty four abstentions.[46] In 1966, ICESCR was ultimately adopted.

5 General Comment No. 17: An Overview

The ambiguity in the language of Article 15 because of conflicting interests between authors and human rights demanded a clarity on the provision of the covenant. General Comments provide a general interpretation on any specific article.[47] General Comment No. 17 is a long and thickly formulated document of 57 paragraphs comprising 6 parts.

The interpretation of Article 15(1)(c) in General Comments provide that the ambit of author's rights is much more circumscribed than the rights guaranteed in public international law.[48] The General Comment clarifies that the 'moral and material interests' of authors in Article 15(1)(c) do not coincide with intellectual property rights under domestic or international law. General Comment, also marks out the difference between human rights and intellectual property rights. It provides that human rights are inherent to human beings because human beings enter the world with such rights but intellectual property rights are the incentives which are

[42] Universal Copyright Convention, Paris Text, 1971, Article XVII(1) reads as:

> The Convention shall not in any way affect the provisions of the Berne Convention for the Protection of Literary and Artistic Works or membership in the Union created by the Convention.

[43] *Supra* note 20 at 1067.

[44] *Supra* note 35, para 37.

[45] Id., para 42. The Indonesian delegation expressed the concern that

> the matter could not be treated adequately in a short provision and that authors' rights had to be considered in the light of the claims of the public in all countries.

[46] *Supra* note 17 at 349.

[47] *Supra* note 10 at 188.

[48] *Ibid.*

given by the states to the creator for creativity and states preserve the integrity of scientific, literary and artistic productions for the benefit of the society as whole. Then, the intellectual property rights have the temporal limitations because they are protected only for a limited period of time, on expiration of which they enter the public domain, while human rights, on the other hand, are "the timeless expressions of fundamental entitlements of the human person".[49] Also, intellectual property rights can be revoked, assigned and licensed to any person. The General Comment asserts that Article 15(1)(c) "safeguards the personal link between authors and their creation".[50] The General Comment provides that Article 15(1)(c) does not extend to legal persons such as "Corporations" and "other business associations". The Committee asserts that only the author, whether man or woman, individual or group of individuals of scientific, literary or artistic productions can claim a moral and material right as a creator or an author.[51]

More importantly, the area where protection of intellectual property rights and human rights get converged with each other, is the protection of moral rights of authors. The Committee, in regard to moral interests, asserts that it encompasses the right "to object to any distortion, mutilation or other modification of, or other derogatory action in relation to, their productions that would be prejudicial to their honour or reputation."[52] This assertion goes squarely consistent with Article 6bis of the Berne Convention.[53]

The conflict between Article 15(1)(b) i.e. right to enjoy the benefit of scientific progress and its applications and Article 15(1)(c) i.e. right to benefit from protection

---

[49] Sub-Commission on Human Rights Resolution 2000/7, E/CN.4/Sub.2/2000/7, para 2, August 17, 2000 General Comment, para 2; The Committee on Economic, Social and Cultural Rights, General Comment No. 17: The Right of Everyone to benefit from Protection of the Moral and Material Interests Resulting from any Scientific, Literary or Artistic Production of which He or She is the Author (Article 15(1)(c)), U.N. Doc. E/C.12/GC/17, January 12, 2006, *available at:* http://hrlibrary.umn.edu/gencomm/escgencom17.html (last visited on March 23, 2016).

[50] *Ibid.*

[51] *Supra* note 10 at 196; *supra* note 17 at 350.

[52] *Supra* note 49, para 13.

[53] Berne Convention for Protection of Literary and Artistic Works, 1883, Article 6bis reads as:

(1) Independently of the author's economic rights, and even after the transfer of the said rights, the author shall have the right to claim authorship of the work and to object to any distortion, mutilation or other modification of, or other derogatory action in relation to, the said work, which would be prejudicial to his honour or reputation.

(2) The rights granted to the author in accordance with the preceding paragraph shall, after his death, be maintained, at least until the expiry of the economic rights, and shall be exercisable by the persons or institutions authorized by the legislation of the country where protection is claimed. However, those countries whose legislation, at the moment of their ratification of or accession to this Act, does not provide for the protection after the death of the author of all the rights set out in the preceding paragraph may provide that some of these rights may, after his death, cease to be maintained.

(3) The means of redress for safeguarding the rights granted by this Article shall be governed by the legislation of the country where protection is claimed.

of the moral and material interests resulting from any scientific, literary or artistic production of which he is an author demands somewhat balanced approach. Also, the quantum of conflict may vary from state to state. A State that implements and over-respects the human rights of 'moral and material interests' of authors would fail to achieve its human rights targets in completion because copyright, though not expressly mentioned in Article 15, but literary work's authors have got certain rights for their creations. Copyright functions as a natural limitation on freedom of expression. Over highlighting of the moral and material interest as human right may dominate and take over the core human rights such as freedom of expression and right to education.

6 The Agreement on Trade-Related Aspects of Intellectual Property Rights

In 1994, the Agreement o Trade-Related Aspects of Intellectual Property Rights (TRIPs hereinafter) entered into force. The Agreement is highly controversial because the standpoint of the developed and less developed countries on the protection of Intellectual Property Rights stand far apart.[54] The TRIPs aims to protect only the "material interests" human rights of the authors, leaving the moral interests approach totally unaddressed and unidentified. As the Preamble to the Agreement, states clearly that it aims to promote effective and adequate protection of intellectual property rights, it primarily concerns itself with private economic rights over public human rights including right to education and freedom of expression expanding the sphere of conflict between the both.[55] The agreement also makes it clear in its Preamble that intellectual property rights are private rights. The membership in World Trade Organisation required complying with the minimum standards laid down in TRIPs. So, if developing states want to reap the benefits of a free trade, they had to agree to the TRIPs requirements in order to enjoy the free and open trade benefits.

There are many points of intersection between human rights and TRIPs.[56] At this point, it becomes noteworthy that TRIPs is different from earlier intellectual property conventions, because non-compliance of its provisions by states can be challenged through WTO's dispute resolution system. Also, there exists a conflict between human right to education and TRIPs provisions relating to copyright. Article 9 of Berne Convention incorporates Article 1 through 21 except moral right given under Article 6bis.[57] This article has not made it mandatory for member states to recognize it, hence, it is a 'berne-minus provision'.

---

[54] Yu 2009.

[55] *Supra* note 17 at 351.

[56] Helfer 2003.

[57] *Supra* note 40, Article 9.

The most striking feature of TRIPs with respect to international copyright protection is its non-dynamic character. The drafters of the agreement merely adopted the existing provisions of copyright from Berne Convention, instead of creating a new international copyright protection.[58]

TRIPs Agreement, with a Berne baseline, just adds to and subtracts from this Berne baseline in different ways. To start with what it subtracts, TRIPs has clearly excluded moral rights given in Article 6bis of Berne Convention.[59] Moral rights are one of the major reasons of divergence between common law and civil law approaches on copyright protection. Some additions have also been made to Berne Convention, TRIPs protects computer programs[60] as literary works and it also protects the copyright in databases because of the selection and systematic arrangements of data.[61] TRIPs also makes it clear that copyright protection extends only to 'expressions and not to the ideas, procedures, methods of operation or mathematical concepts as such.'[62]

Article 13 of TRIPs attempts to strike a balance between exclusive rights and public interests by laying down the three-step test on the limitations to the exclusive rights.[63] It asks the member states to confine limitations or exceptions to exclusive rights:

(i) to certain special cases;
(ii) which do not conflict with a normal exploitation of the work; and
(iii) do not unreasonably prejudice the legitimate interests of the right holder.

An instance, where this three-step test of Article 13 would apply, would be where a compulsory licence is granted on the ground of unreasonable high prices charged by the copyright owner which prevented a person from accessing the educational material.[64] This test fulfils two purposes; first, it specifies the areas for which copyright owners do not require rights to boost their profits; second, it puts forth a compensation mechanism for the limitations that are in public interest but can highly impact the economic interests of copyright holders.[65]

The drafting history of three-step test discloses that this provision was incorporated to act as a balancing tool to achieve the socio-economic needs of public.[66] When for the first time, the three-step test was introduced at the international copyright level in Article 9.2 of the Berne Convention in 1967, it aimed to counter

---

[58] Helfer 1998.

[59] The main proponent of the exception contained in Article 9.1 of TRIPs Agreement was the US.

[60] The Agreement on Trade-Related Aspects of Intellectual Property Rights, adopted on April 15, 1994 (*hereinafter* TRIPs), Article 10.1.

[61] The subject matter of protection under Article 10.2 of TRIPs Agreement is 'compilation of data or other material'.

[62] TRIPs, Article 9.2.

[63] *Id.*, Article 13.

[64] Correa 2007.

[65] Gervais 2015.

[66] Geiger et al. 2014.

the exclusive economic right to reproduction, of the copyright owner.[67] On a discourse on the text of Article 9.2, the original text 'in certain *particular* cases where the reproduction *is not contrary* to the legitimate interests of the author' was replaced by 'in certain *special* cases where the reproduction *does not unreasonably prejudice* the legitimate interests of the authors' at the proposal of the United Kingdom.[68] This indicates that the primary aim of TRIPs and Berne Convention is to protect the private interest of copyright owner while the public interests like human right to education are always placed as exceptions to material rights.

The three-step test of TRIPs Agreement also conforms to the objectives and principles laid down in Articles 7 and 8. This analysis is completely in harmony with Article 31(1) of the Vienna Convention on the Law of Treaties, which provides that "a treaty shall be interpreted in good faith in accordance with the ordinary meaning to be given to the terms of the treaty in their context and in the light of its *object and purpose*".[69]

Article 7 of TRIPs provides that

> The protection and enforcement of intellectual property rights should contribute to the promotion of technological innovation and to the transfer and dissemination of technology, to the mutual advantage of producers and users of technological knowledge and in a manner conducive to social and economic welfare, and to a balance of rights and obligations.

Article 7 aims to strike a balance between the economic private rights and public interests by highlighting the goal of advancing not only economic development, but social welfare as well.[70] Various developing countries stressed upon the importance of Article 7 for the better interpretation and implementation of the Agreement.[71] This article serves as an aid while interpreting the provisions of TRIPs by indicating that a sheer economic outlook should not be followed leaving out other social values and objectives.[72]

With the similar object, Article 8 states that:

> 1. Members may, in formulating or amending their laws and regulations, adopt measures necessary to protect public health and nutrition, and to promote the public interest in sectors of vital importance to their socio-economic and technological development, provided that such measures are consistent with the provisions of this Agreement.
> 2. Appropriate measures, provided that they are consistent with the provisions of this Agreement, may be needed to prevent the abuse of intellectual property rights by right holders or the resort to practices which unreasonably restrain trade or adversely affect the international transfer of technology.

---

[67] *Id.*, at 584.

[68] *Ibid.*

[69] Vienna Convention on the Law of Treaties, concluded on May 23, 1969, Article 31.

[70] *Supra* note 66 at 598.

[71] See the submission to the Council of TRIPs by the African Group, Barbados, Bolivia, Brazil, Dominion Republic, Ecuador, Honduras, India, Indonesia, Jamaica, Pakistan, Philippines, Peru, Sri Lanka, Thailand, and Venezuela, IP/C/W/296, 19 June 2001.

[72] Ruse-Khan 2011.

Article 8.1 of TRIPs allows member states to adopt measures for the promotion of "the public interest in sectors of vital importance to their socio-economic and technological development." Moreover, the Preamble to the TRIPs Agreement concentrates not just on the aim of promoting adequate protection mechanisms but, also addresses the "underlying public policy objectives of national systems" and, with regard to least-developed countries, the needs "in respect of maximum flexibility in the domestic implementation.[73]

The upshot remains that Articles 7 and 8.1 ask the members to implement the obligations given under Agreement in a way coherent with public policy encouraging the social and economic welfare.[74]

Having analysed the intellectual property provisions in international instruments, one might infer that copyright has a very weak claim to human rights status as it is clearly demonstrated by much debated and controversial inclusion of intellectual property provisions in international human rights instruments.[75] The said provisions were included in these international instruments with an intention to protect the human rights in a better way.

7 Analysing the Conflict

There are two distinct schools of thoughts to look at the so far unchartered intersection between copyright and freedom of expression. Both the schools are founded on squarely opposite views.[76] The first approach views strong intellectual property protection leading to the erosion of human rights, especially the economic, social and cultural rights.[77] This school proposes to acknowledge the supremacy and domination of human rights over intellectual property rights, wherever the two rights clash in any treaty.[78]

The second school of thought uses the same lens for both the rights and aims to define the "*appropriate scope of private monopoly power that gives authors and inventors a sufficient incentive to create and innovate, while ensuring that the consuming public had adequate access to the fruits of their efforts.*"

This school views both the rights as compatible with each other and proposes to balance wherever exclusive right discords with the accessibility rights.[79]

Before resolving the debate between conflict and coexistence, it is significant to mark out the actual areas of conflict between human rights and copyright. There

[73] *Supra* note 66 at 598–599.

[74] *Supra* note 64 at 103.

[75] Torremans 2007.

[76] *Supra* note 56 at 47–48.

[77] *Ibid.*

[78] *Ibid.*

[79] *Ibid.*

seems no definite conflict between copyright and freedom of expression, because the limited term of protection of property right to the author entitles people to freely use the work when it enters the public domain. Besides, the idea-expression dichotomy facilitates the public to work upon the ideas shared by authors. There are some exceptions and limitations also including fair use and licence provisions, which consent to the public's freedom of expression.[80]

Having considered that, there are two more areas where the copyright and freedom of expression diverge. First, the author's right of divulgation which authorises an author to decide under what conditions and at what time his work shall be published for the first time. This right entitles the author to keep his work private till any time. This right is also termed as right to disclosure. Second, the right to withdraw work from public at any point of time. This right authorises the author to discontinue its exploitation at any time when he believes that work no longer relates to his beliefs.[81] Hence, the right to education, as guaranteed under Article 26 of UDHR and Article 13 of IESCR may get upset as the use of copyright is extensively needed in accomplishment of these guarantees.

8 The Internal Conflict

The internal conflicts arise when different provisions within any document clash with each other. To be precise, in UDHR, Articles 26[82] and 27[83] create room for conflict as between right to compulsory and accessible education, and moral and material interests of authors.

---

[80] Minero 2015.

[81] *Id.* at 177.

[82] Universal Declaration of Human Rights, adopted on December 10, 1948, Article 26 reads as:

(1) Everyone has the right to education. Education shall be free, at least in the elementary and fundamental stages. Elementary education shall be compulsory. Technical and professional education shall be made generally available and higher education shall be equally accessible to all on the basis of merit.

(2) Education shall be directed to the full development of the human personality and to the strengthening of respect for human rights and fundamental freedoms. It shall promote understanding, tolerance and friendship among all nations, racial or religious groups, and shall further the activities of the United Nations for the maintenance of peace.

(3) Parents have a prior right to choose the kind of education that shall be given to their children.

[83] (1) *Id.*, Article 27 reads as: (1) Everyone has the right freely to participate in the cultural life of the community, to enjoy the arts and to share in scientific advancement and its benefits.

(2) Everyone has the right to the protection of the moral and material interests resulting from any scientific, literary or artistic production of which he is the author.

In ICESCR, Articles 13[84] and 14[85] stand against Articles 15(1)(c).[86] Articles 13 and 14 recognise everyone's right to free education at primary level. The two provisions also aim to make the secondary level education accessible to all. While Article 15(1)(c) embraces the concerns for the protection of moral and material interests ensuing the personal link stable between creator and the creation.

In TRIPs, Article 9 sets the minimum standards to be maintained by states in order to protect copyright of owners while Article 7 determines the objectives of TRIPs agreement. Article 7 states:

---

[84] International Covenant on Economic, Social and Cultural Rights, adopted on December 16, 1966, Article 13 reads as:

1. The States Parties to the present Covenant recognize the right of everyone to education. They agree that education shall be directed to the full development of the human personality and the sense of its dignity, and shall strengthen the respect for human rights and fundamental freedoms. They further agree that education shall enable all persons to participate effectively in a free society, promote understanding, tolerance and friendship among all nations and all racial, ethnic or religious groups, and further the activities of the United Nations for the maintenance of peace.
2. The States Parties to the present Covenant recognize that, with a view to achieving the full realization of this right:
   (a) Primary education shall be compulsory and available free to all;
   (b) Secondary education in its different forms, including technical and vocational secondary education, shall be made generally available and accessible to all by every appropriate means, and in particular by the progressive introduction of free education;
   (c) Higher education shall be made equally accessible to all, on the basis of capacity, by every appropriate means, and in particular by the progressive introduction of free education;
   (d) Fundamental education shall be encouraged or intensified as far as possible for those persons who have not received or completed the whole period of their primary education;
   (e) The development of a system of schools at all levels shall be actively pursued, an adequate fellowship system shall be established, and the material conditions of teaching staff shall be continuously improved.
3. The States Parties to the present Covenant undertake to have respect for the liberty of parents and, when applicable, legal guardians to choose for their children schools, other than those established by the public authorities, which conform to such minimum educational standards as may be laid down or approved by the State and to ensure the religious and moral education of their children in conformity with their own convictions.
4. No part of this article shall be construed so as to interfere with the liberty of individuals and bodies to establish and direct educational institutions, subject always to the observance of the principles set forth in paragraph I of this article and to the requirement that the education given in such institutions shall conform to such minimum standards as may be laid down by the State.

[85] Each State Party to the present Covenant which, at the time of becoming a Party, has not been able to secure in its metropolitan territory or other territories under its jurisdiction compulsory primary education, free of charge, undertakes, within two years, to work out and adopt a detailed plan of action for the progressive implementation, within a reasonable number of years, to be fixed in the plan, of the principle of compulsory education free of charge for all.

[86] *Id.*, Article 15(1)(c) reads as: The States Parties to the present Covenant recognize the right of everyone:

(c) To benefit from the protection of the moral and material interests resulting from any scientific, literary or artistic production of which he is the author.

> The protection and enforcement of intellectual property rights should contribute to the promotion of technological innovation and to the transfer and dissemination of technology, to the *mutual advantage of producers and users* of technological knowledge and in a manner conducive to *social and economic welfare*, and to a *balance of rights* and obligations.

The phrase '*in a manner conducive to social and economic welfare*' demonstrates that the recognition and enforcement of intellectual property rights are subject to public interest. This statement gets substantiated by Article 8.1 of TRIPs.[87] The human rights and intellectual property conflict has also been acknowledged by UN Commission on Human Right.[88]

Article 9 of TRIPs states that the member states shall not have any rights or obligations in respect of rights conferred under Article 6bis of the Berne Convention. Hence, both the paternity and the integrity rights, being the author's special rights, have not been kept in TRIPs.[89] TRIPs Agreement had an intention to absolutely exclude the moral rights from Article 9.1. This assertion gets strength from the fact that Article 9.1 uses not only 'the rights conferred *under* Article 6bis of the berne convention', but also 'the rights derived *therefrom*'.[90] It conveys that what has been excluded in Article 9.1 of TRIPs is not merely whatever is given in Article 6bis[91] of Berne, but all those rights which derive their authority from the moral rights principle. Therefore, the right of divulgation and right to withdraw the work from public, which are reputation based rights, do not even find their mention in Article 6bis of Berne Convention, also stand outside the ambit of Article 9.1 of TRIPs because of their moralistic stand.

---

[87] TRIPs, Article 18.1 reads as:

Members may, in formulating or amending their laws and regulations, adopt measures necessary to protect public health and nutrition, and to promote the public interest in sectors of vital importance to their socio-economic and technological development, provided that such measures are consistent with the provisions of this Agreement.

[88] Sub Commission on the Promotion and Protection of Human Rights, 'The impact of the Agreement on Trade-Related Aspects of Intellectual Property Rights on human rights', E/CN.4/Sub.2/2001/13, June 2001.

[89] Gervais 2008.

[90] Supra note 64 at 118.

[91] Berne Convention, Article 6bis reads as:

(1) Independently of the author's economic rights, and even after the transfer of the said rights, the author shall have the right to claim authorship of the work and to object to any distortion, mutilation or other modification of, or other derogatory action in relation to, the said work, which would be prejudicial to his honor or reputation.
(2) The rights granted to the author in accordance with the preceding paragraph shall, after his death, be maintained, at least until the expiry of the economic rights, and shall be exercisable by the persons or institutions authorized by the legislation of the country where protection is claimed. However, those countries whose legislation, at the moment of their ratification of or accession to this Act, does not provide for the protection after the death of the author of all the rights set out in the preceding paragraph may provide that some of these rights may, after his death, cease to be maintained.
(3) The means of redress for safeguarding the rights granted by this Article shall be governed by the legislation of the country where protection is claimed.

It would be rational to express that by leaving out the moral rights which are rooted in natural law, TRIPs Agreement has dwindled the balance between economic and moral interests of copyright.[92]

9 A Need to Balance the Conflicting Interests

As Audrey R. Chapman put it:

> To be consistent with the full provisions of Article 15 [of the International Covenant on Economic, Social and Cultural Rights], the type and level of protection afforded under any intellectual property regime must facilitate and promote cultural participation and scientific progress and do so in a manner that will broadly benefit members of society both on an individual and collective level.[93]

On one hand, it is utmost required to protect the private interests of author to foster the creativity, for which a variety of monopoly rights are conferred on the author for making use of the work, on the contrary, it is the need of the society to make use of that copyrighted work for the over-all progress of the society.

The language of Article 15 of ICESCR also suggests for the act of balancing interests as it requires the States to recognize the right of everyone to benefit from the moral and materialistic interests. There is a world of difference between *enjoying the benefits from* such protection and enjoying an absolute and unrestricted monopoly rights over intellectual property rights.[94] States, at their own domestic levels, strive to ensure this balance by providing for fair use exceptions, temporal limitations and licensing provisions. Article 4 of ICESCR also speaks for the balancing act by stating that:

> The States Parties to the present Covenant recognize that, in the enjoyment of those rights provided by the State in conformity with the present Covenant, the State may subject such rights only to such limitations as are determined by law only in so far as this may be compatible with the nature of these rights and solely for the purpose of promoting the *general welfare in a democratic society.*

With a purpose to further the objectives of this balancing paradigm, few scholars have advanced some logical approaches to strike the balance between public and private interests by proportionately interfering with an individual's property rights. The principle of proportionality demands that the interference with core human rights of a person must not go beyond what is required to attain a legitimate public policy. The different approaches include:

(1) The Fair Remuneration Approach
(2) The Core Minimum Approach
(3) The Progressive Realisation Approach.

---

[92] *Supra* note 84 at p. 14.

[93] *Supra* note 11 at 5.

[94] Torremans 2015.

10 The Fair Remuneration Approach

This approach works in cases of conflicting interests regarding intellectual property and freedom of expression. The approach is squarely founded on the idea that exclusive property rights are vested in the author of the work but there are some visible limits on such exclusive exploitation by the author that meet the requirement of general welfare of the society. But, such limitations on the exploitation rights of the author may substantially impact the profits that would generate from the exclusive use of such copyrighted work.[95] To neutralise such impact, the legislature is the competent authority to ensure that authors require fair remuneration for such exempted use.

General Comment No. 17 provided that[96]:

> The imposition of limitations may, under certain circumstances, require compensatory measures, such as payment of adequate compensation for the use of scientific, literary or artistic productions in the public interest.

Fair Remuneration Approach entitles public to exploit the creative works by payment of adequate compensation to the author. This approach balances the conflicting interests by granting compulsory licence on the ones who need to have access to it (not a free licence) and fair remuneration to the author (not an absolute control). Legislatures of different countries have adopted this approach.

This approach runs parallel to the objectives of the Berne Convention since Article 9.2 of Berne provides, with much concern towards both the contradictory interests, that:[97]

> It shall be a matter for legislation in the countries of the Union to permit the reproduction of such works in certain special cases, provided that such reproduction does not conflict with a normal exploitation of the work and *does not unreasonably prejudice the legitimate interests of the author.*

In the three-step test, the last prong i.e. the legitimate interest is context-dependent. Though, the legitimate interest is not limited merely to equitable remuneration but, it embraces a significant connotation of it.[98]

But, it would be noteworthy that the fair remuneration approach would position differently in diverse jurisdictions because the impact of such limitations on copyright would be different to some extent, in developed and developing countries. A related line of reasoning would be that if the remuneration is fixed so elevated then this balancing act would be mere sham as it would keep the masses away from their core human rights. The whole concept is conditioned on *just* and *fair* compensation to the right holders so that other folks of society may exercise their human rights.

---

[95] *Supra* note 20 at 1096.

[96] The Right of Everyone to Benefit from the Protection of the Moral and Material Interests Resulting from Any Scientific, Literary or Artistic Production of which He Is The Author, Article 15(1)(c)) para 4, U.N.Doc.E/C12/GC/17 (Jan. 12, 2006).

[97] Berne Convention, Article 11bis, 13.

[98] *Supra* note 66 at 596.

11 Core Minimum Approach

The Core Minimum Approach provides on minimum essential level of protection a state has to offer to comply with its human rights obligations.[99] As General Comment No. 3 stated[100]:

> A minimum core obligation to ensure the satisfaction of, at the very least, minimum essential levels of each of the rights is incumbent upon every State party. Thus, for example, a State party in which any significant number of individuals is deprived of essential foodstuffs, of essential primary health care, of basic shelter and housing, or of the most basic forms of education is, *prima* facie, failing to discharge its obligations under the Covenant. If the Covenant were to be read in such a way as not to establish such a minimum core obligation, it would be largely deprived of its *raison d'etre*. By the same token, it must be noted that any assessment as to whether a State has discharged its minimum core obligation must also take account of resource constraints applying within the country concerned. Article 2(1) obligates each State party to take the necessary steps "to the maximum of its available resources". In order for a State party to be able to attribute its failure to meet at least its minimum core obligations to a lack of available resources it must demonstrate that every effort has been made to use all resources that are at its disposition in an effort to satisfy, as a matter of priority, those minimum obligations.

The comment shows how the different human rights are mutually-reliant. It clears that the division of the rights need not be in accordance to their priority, but each right must be appreciated to the extent that it provides for the essential needs of every individual in society. When there are limitations of resources, state can not make a choice with human rights that it wants to bring to fruition, rather it has to fulfil the 'minimum essential levels' of protection of all the human rights.

It is significant how this approach is advantageous to interests of creators and authors. Even when state needs resources to realize other human rights, it provides authors with the minimum essential level of protection.

There are various limitations associated with this approach, it is one thing to say that there is core content of every human right and another, to determine precisely that how much protection a state is required to offer under core minimum approach.[101]

12 The Progressive Realization Approach

Having roots in UDHR and ICESCR, this approach seeks how the states can use additional resources to enhance the level of human rights protection. Unlike the core minimum approach, this approach provides that intellectual property rights

[99] Supra note 10 at 1095.

[100] CESCR, *General Comment No. 3: The Nature of States Parties Obligations (Article 2, para 1)*, 10, U.N. Doc. E/1991/23 (Dec. 14, 1990).

[101] *Supra* note 11 at 314–315.

must not only enable but should facilitate access to benefits of creativity.[102] This approach is extensively used to augment the human rights protection. Helfer says '*where intellectual property laws help to achieve human rights outcomes, governments should embrace it. Where it hinders those outcomes, its rules should be modified (but not necessarily restricted)*'[103] States, regardless of what amount of resources they have at their disposal, must take instant steps within their means towards the fulfillment of these rights.[104] It provides that realisation of human rights by states shall be a continual process, not merely instant achievement.

13 Authors Guild, Inc. v. Google, Inc.[105]: An Overview

This landmark copyright infringement lawsuit came with a final dictum after more than 10 years of its filing.[106] The second circuit pronounced for the Google, ruling that Google's unauthorised digitization of copyright protected works and display of snippets from test are non-infringing fair uses.[107] Google Inc. started its Library Project and Google Books Project, by entering into bi-lateral agreements with world's major research libraries under which Google Inc. makes and retains digital copies of the books submitted to it by major libraries which they legally would not have been able to do themselves and in return, it permits the libraries to download and retain the digital copies of those books. However, this Google search function permits to view only limited text. Further, it displays just three snippets (small passages) and one snippet is an eight of a page, in size. Google also makes one out of ten pages completely unavailable to be viewed by user, Google terms this process as "blacklisting". This program basically aimed at allowing the public to search the texts of digitally copied books and find the snippets of text on Google search engine.

Earlier, the US second circuit court of appeals rejected the plaintiff's contention in a summary judgment in favour of Google.

Guild's most important argument was that Google's act did not comprise 'transformative use', rather it was substitutive and its ultimate commercial profit motivation and its derivation of revenue from its dominance of the wide internet search preclude a finding of fair use. Authors Guild major submission was that the digital revolution should not be at the cost of author's property right. Further, there is a necessity to ensure that the next generation of authors and other creators

[102] *Ibid.*

[103] Helfer 2007.

[104] Progressive Realisation and Non-regression, ESCR-Net, *available at:* https://www.escr-net.org/resources/progressive-realisation-and-non-regression (last visited on March 27, 2016).

[105] 13-4829-cv (2d Cir. Oct. 16, 2015).

[106] Plaintiffs brought this suit on September 20, 2005.

[107] *Supra* note 105.

get alike opportunities as those who came before them. Court started the testing of searching and snippet function of Google against all the four components of fair use given under Section 107 of the US Copyright Act. While bridging the gap between educational fair use and transformative use jurisprudence, court provided that in this case, Google aimed to provide public with access to information that they otherwise would have not been able to access.

Having considered the arguments from both sides, Court expressed that

> While authors are undoubtedly important intended beneficiaries of copyright, the ultimate, primary intended beneficiary is public, whose access to knowledge copyright seeks to advance by providing rewards for authorship.[108]

Court went on to state the importance of copyright for masses by providing that

> For nearly three hundred years, since shortly after the birth of copyright in England in 1710, courts have recognised that, in certain circumstances, giving authors absolute control over all copying from their works would tend in some circumstances to limit, rather than expand, public knowledge.[109]

A closer reading, however, reveals that court has foregrounded the public interest over copyright. The most significant role of the court in this case is in rationalising the human rights centric constructions. In this principled judgment, the court marshalled the duty to achieve the social justice as it goes in complete consonance with Article 27 of UDHR, Article 15 of IESCR and Article 7 of TRIPs.

14 Conclusion

Copyright comes with an inherent dichotomy of public interests i.e. right to education, freedom of expression on one hand and private interests i.e. exclusive economic interests vested in reproduction rights, on the other hand. It might not be affordable to expand the intellectual property protection at the cost of human rights, nor can it be reasonable to appreciate the human rights by restricting the intellectual property rights. As different international instruments very evidently demonstrate that general welfare has to be borne in mind while protecting the moral and material interest of authors, nations should form the equilibrium and balance the conflicting interests, proportionately and adequately, while keeping in mind not to use a hammer to break the nut where knife can efficiently serve the purpose. Interests invoked by authors and right holders must be weighed against the rationales justifying the use privilege. Further, this balancing test would vary in all the jurisdictions and more importantly, it can not remain same for all the coming times, it would require modifications from time to time. Also, a harmonious solution is

---

[108] *Id.* at 13.

[109] *Ibid.*

desired to adequately balance the conflicts between copyright and exceptions. Another problem that springs out is that international human rights regime lacks coherence and is not centralised which reduces chances of incorporation of such international rules into domestic laws. Judges too, at times, may not be firmly sure of the authority because of lack of comprehensive normative hierarchy at international level. Hence, a harmonious solution is obligatory to fill the human rights-copyright interface with coherent, consistent, and balanced legal norms that enhance both individual rights and social welfare.

References

Bogsch A (1972) The law of copyright and the universal convention, 3rd edn. Sijthoff Leyden Bowker, p 4

Chapman AR (2001) Approaching intellectual property as a human right (obligations related to Article 15(1)(c)). XXXV Copyright Bulletin 5. Available at: http://unesdoc.unesco.org/images/0012/001255/125505e.pdf (last visited on 20 March 2016).

Correa CM (2007) Trade related aspects of intellectual property rights: a commentary on TRIPS agreement. Oxford University Press UK, p 146

Eide A, Alfredsson G, et al (eds) (1992) The universal declaration of human rights: a commentary. Scandinavian University Press, Oslo, p 430 (with collaboration of Theresa Swinehart)

Foster SE (2015) The conflict between the human right to education and copyright. In: Torremans PLC (ed) Intellectual property law and human rights, 3rd edn. Wolters Kluwer, p 347

Geiger C, Gervais D, et al (2014) The three-step test revisited: how to use the test's flexibility in national copyright law. Am U Int'l L Rev 29:582

Gendreau Y (2004) Copyright and freedom of expression in Canada. In: Torremans P (ed.) Copyright and human rights: freedom of expression, intellectual property, privacy, 1st edn. Kluwer Law International, Hague, p 21

Gervais DJ (2008) Intellectual property and human rights: learning to live together. In: Torremans PLC (ed) Intellectual property and human rights. Kluwer, Netherlands, p 12

Gervais DJ (2015) How intellectual property and human rights can live together: an updated perspective. In: Torremans PLC (ed) Intellectual property law and human rights, 3rd edn. Wolters Kluwer, p 347

LR Helfer (1998) Adjudicating copyright claims under the TRIPS agreement: the case for a European human rights analogy. Harv Int'l LJ 39:378

LR Helfer (2003) Human rights and intellectual property: conflict or coexistence? Minn Intell Prop Rev 5:47

Helfer LR (2007) Towards a human rights framework for intellectual property. UC Davis L Rev 40:1018

Helfer LR, Austin GW (2011) Human rights and intellectual property: mapping the global interface, 1st edn. Cambridge University Press, New York, p 183

Minero G (2015) Intellectual property rights: coinciding and cooperating. In: Torremans PLC (ed) Intellectual property law and human rights, 3rd edn. Wolters Kluwer, p 176

Morsink J (1999) The universal declaration of human rights: origins, drafting and intent. University of Pennsylvania Press, Philadelphia, p 220

Nickel JW (1987) Making sense of human rights: philosophical reflections on the universal declaration of human rights, 1st edn. University of California Press, Berkeley, p 3

Ruse-Khan H (2011) Assessing the need for a general public interest exception in the TRIPS agreement. In: Kur A, Levin M (eds) Intellectual property in a fair world trade system—proposals for reforming trips. Edward Elgar Publication, p 167

Torremans PLC (2007) Is copyright a human right? Mich St L Rev 2007:280.

Torremans PLC (2015) Copyright (and other intellectual property rights) as a human rights. In: Torremans PLC (eds) Intellectual property law and human rights, 3rd edn. Wolters Kluwer, p 237

Yu PK (2006–2007) Reconceptualizing intellectual property interests in a human rights framework. UC Davis L Rev 40:1059

Yu PK (2009) The objective and principles of the TRIPS agreement. Hous L Rev 46:797

Copyright, Access and Information Society

Anirban Mazumder

Abstract Copyright law is mandated to make a balance between conflicting issues like incentive and access. This article will try to explore how copyright law can make an attempt to increase access and contribute in the making of information society. In the process of doing it, the article will examine interaction of copyright law with public or private interest. This article will also try to establish link between copyright and free speech which will facilitate role of copyright in strengthening access to information.

Keywords Copyright · Information · Access

1 Copyright Protection and Public/Private Interest

Information is an invaluable social resource. Before information is given a strenuous legal protection, it must be made sure that protection is warranted and carefully delineated. The mechanism to stimulate dissemination and use of new knowledge is an important incentive for generating knowledge. Access to information is an issue which concerns various categories of users. Information which are in public domain, information where database constitutes the only source of that information, information relating the academic and scientific research and other information of public interest are always sensitive to monopolization and consequent restriction in use. There are databases like databases on remote sensing activities which are by their nature unique and cannot be reproduced independently

This chapter has been derived from the author's previous publication in 2016 by Springer, titled "Database Law: Perspectives from India".

A. Mazumder (✉)
National University of Juridical Sciences, Kolkata, India
e-mail: animazum@hotmail.com

M.K. Sinha and V. Mahalwar (eds.), *Copyright Law in the Digital World*,
DOI 10.1007/978-981-10-3984-3_8

by third parties and in these cases possibility of monopoly becomes greater.[1] By introducing intellectual property rights in non-original databases, private rights will be created in the information contained in the databases which would seriously damage the content of public domain in the domain of scientific, educational and legal information.[2]

Any increase in the cost of accessing databases will have a chain reaction in the society as the research is likely to compensate the higher cost with another source of revenue based on the result of the research either through patenting or other means of exclusion of research output. This has been indicated by the increase of private involvement in collection and generation of data. This can also lead to a strategy of scientific collaboration in the model of 'open science'.[3] There is an increasing demand for consumer's access to information like weather data, maps, and statutory registers.

Copyright protection for a compilation is confined to selection and arrangement of information and reproducing selection and arrangement will infringe either copyright in compilation or database. Information recorded in a work qualifying for copyright protection may be used and re-expressed till reuse does not amount to reproduction of substantial part of it and to this extent underlying information in a copyrighted work remains in public domain.[4]

Digital technology has created considerable tension for traditional concepts of copyright law. Digital Millennium Copyright Act in the United States and Information Society Directive in the European Union have affected freedom of expression as it does not recognize the right of private copying.[5] The apprehension is that information published in copy protected form, without having any other source shall be effectively monopolized. ALLEA (All European Academics) expressed concern that scientific research would be affected because of the Directive as the Directive limits the access to data for research and scientific purposes.[6]

---

[1] The Association of Research Libraries have noted that prices of such journals rose by 115% between 1986–1994 which was the result of a market which was monopolistic and controlled by a small group of publishers. M. Maurer, Raw Knowledge: Protecting Technical Databases for Science and Industry, Workshop on Promoting Access to Scientific and Technical Data for the Public Interest: An Assessment of Policy Options, National Academy of Sciences, January, 1999.

[2] Maurer and Scotchmer 1999.

[3] Baron 2001.

[4] In Elanco Product Ltd v. Mandops Ltd 1980 RPC 213. Patent on herbicide expired. The defendant marketed it with an accompanying leaflet with detailed instruction as to use the herbicide. Much of the information was in public domain. The plaintiff-the original inventor alleged that the leaflet infringed their copyright in the leaflet they provided with the tin. The court granted injunction and held that defendant could not use plaintiff's skill and judgment to save themselves the trouble and cost of assembling literature.

[5] Arrest of Russian programmer on criminal charges for developing software to circumvent Adobe's copy-protection technology for digital book. http://www.epccentral.org/dmca.html. See also Cathrine Colston 2001.

[6] First Evaluation of Directive 96/9/EC on Legal Protection of Databases, Commission of The European Communities, Brussels, 12th December 2005. p. 21.

Christophe Geiger thinks that sui generis protection for database has the potential for monopolization of information and creating multiple intellectual property rights over same subject matter, affects access to information.[7] This possibility arises only in cases where database is the only source of particular information. Compulsory licensing and broad exceptions will be better balancing factors. The lengthy process of litigation in case of competition law does not make a certain remedy for denial of access.[8] The possibility of perpetual protection for database right can also jeopardize the human rights in general and public's right to information in particular.

2 Copyright and Access to Information

Does copyright prevent free access to information? The Library of Alexandria felt that money or a lack of infrastructure was not the main problem of information in society; rather the greatest problem was copyright.[9] OECD also emphasized on reconciliation between effective IPR protection and the need for access to information.[10] The increasing perception among the academic community is that copyright hinders access to knowledge.[11] Considering the negative impacts of copyright, it is important to ensure free access to information.[12] This issue becomes more pertinent in case of developing countries. Intellectual property is justified to preserve for the authors the fruits of their work as well as to disseminate ideas. Authors are encouraged to create new works and there by contribute in disseminating new ideas. Copyright law should be drafted in such a way so as to maintain balance between protection of the author and interest of the society.[13]

'The Framers of the U.S. Constitution intend copyright itself to be the engine of free expression. By establishing a marketable right to the use of one's expression,

[7] Book Review of Christophe Geiger 2006 E.I.P.R. 357.

[8] Apart from high degree of litigiousness due to a legislation on competition, it only solves the problem of undue appropriation by competitors and not by users, recourse to unfair competition is available only ex post, it does not solve the problem of information Samaritan who for non-economic reason extracts data and then make it available to public for free, the legislation does not give any exclusive or transferable right and the concept of unfair competition varies from country to country. The Impact of Protection of Non-Original Databases on the Countries of Latin America and the Caribbean, WIPO, Standing Committee on Copyright and Related Rights, Eights Sessions, Geneva, 2002. p. 15.

[9] Christophe Geiger 2006.

[10] OECD Report on the Scientific Publishing Industry, Digital Broadband Content 2005.

[11] Christophe Geiger 2006.

[12] Hugenholtz 1996, as cited by Christophe Geiger 2006.

[13] 'The Congress shall have the power securing for limited times to Authors and Inventors the exclusive right to their respective writings and discoveries'. Article 1§ 8, American Constitution.

copyright supplies the economic incentive to create and disseminate ideas.[14] Principles of natural law, constitutional principles and norms of international law have influenced principles of copyright law to emerge.[15] Two conflicting but important issues are to be carefully balanced through copyright legislation—on author's side, property right and right of personality and on the user's side, freedom of expression and freedom of information.[16]

The exclusive right created by copyright works under different limitations to ensure free access to information. These are like, ideas themselves are not protected, but expressions which have originality are protected. Protection is for a limited period, protected expressions can be used if it is required in public interest, protected expressions can also be used for private purpose, teaching and research. These principles are recognized by international instruments like Berne Convention, TRIPs and WCT.[17]

In information society, knowledge has become a contributing factor in economy and thus attempts have been made to reserve the use of information through intellectual property right and as a result the difference between idea and expression is becoming blurred. This situation is reflected in cases of sole source database and business method patent.[18] The technical development in copying and distributing attained a new height through digital technology and it affected investors negatively as it allowed users to copy and share documents quite easily. To challenge these threats investors took resort to technical device that prevents copying and circumventing measures were considered as illegal.[19] These technical devices would not be in a position to appreciate the legitimacy of purpose and decide accordingly. Thus investors would like to regulate access through technology instead of through law.

"The question, in cases of whether a statute pre-empts a claim, is whether the two can be regarded as "*equivalent rights*" (Nimmer, pp. 1–51), i.e. whether, in terms of Section 16, the right sought to be asserted is a "*copyright or any similar right in any work*" (emphasis supplied). Indeed, such preclusion, and the test of equivalence, must necessarily be the import of Section 16 to give effect to the words "*any similar right*".[20]

Technology will always have effects—positive and negative. Internet being a huge source of information can play a pivotal role in education and research and at the same time Internet poses threat for fundamentals of copyright. Public domain should be defined in clear terms to include matters like essential public information, official documents and texts. States are given discretion to decide the ambit of

---

[14] Griffiths and Suthersanan 2005, as cited by Christophe Geiger 2006.

[15] Fundamental Rights, Universal Declaration of Human Rights, European Convention on Human Rights.

[16] Christophe Geiger 2006.

[17] Articles 7 and 10 of Berne Convention, Article 9 of TRIPs, Article 2 of WCT.

[18] Christophe Geiger 2006.

[19] WCT 1996.

[20] Akuate Internet Services v. Star India, CM Appl.4665/2013, Delhi High Court.

public domain; so States should make full use of it like patentable subject matter.[21] While defining, public domain should have space to accommodate technical and social changes. The definition can also include works of social, cultural and economic importance to keep them outside the purview of exclusive right.[22]

Anything corollary to the exception can also be enforced against the right holder and thus if a technical measure hinders the user from enjoying the use permitted by law, then the user can enforce that hindrance.[23] But this right is made available to only limited situations and it does not cover rights like digital private copy or quotation right. The Directive[24] provides that appropriate measure can be taken to enforce functioning of limitations but no explanation has been given to describe what constitutes appropriate measure. If Article 8[25] and Article 9[26] are considered to ensure access to information, it may be found that they do not constitute sufficient means to reach the objective as it all depends on the interpretation of the term 'lawful user'.[27] A careful observation indicates that the exception to sui generis right in Article 9 for private purpose and teaching and research allows only extraction and not re-utilization.

Principles of copyright must ensure that rights of the users are balanced with rights of authors. In digital environment, private copying has not been recognized but exception has been made to allow copy for scientific purpose to ensure access to information.[28] This should be coupled with enforceable right to overcome technical barrier. Every author is a researcher and user at the first place. The author takes note of the existing literature at the time of creating work. Thus denying private copy would negatively affect the creative process of the author. Here the purpose of copy

---

[21] Article 27, TRIPs.

[22] Following Article 3a(1) European Directive 97/36 (on television)—'Member States may take measures ... to ensure that broadcasters under its jurisdiction do not broadcast on an exclusive basis events which are regarded by the Member States as being of major importance for society in such a way as to deprive a substantial proportion of public ... of possibility of following such event via live coverage or deferred coverage on free television'.

Article 9, Convention of Council of Europe on Transfrontier Television, 1989, '...to examine and where necessary, take legal measure... to avoid right of public to information being undermined due to exercise of exclusive right'. These can be sports, cultural and other events as well.

[23] Section 95b(2) German Copyright Act, user is entitled to demand from the right holder support required for exercise of certain legitimate uses, as cited by Christophe Geiger, Copyright and Free Access to Information: For a Fair Balance of Interest in a Globalize World 2006 E.I.P.R. 370.

[24] Article 6.4.

[25] The maker of a database which is made available to the public in whatever manner my not prevent a lawful user of the database from extracting and/or reutilizing insubstantial part of the contents evaluated qualitatively or quantitatively for any purpose whatsoever.

[26] Lawful user of a database which is made available to public in whatever manner may without authorization of the maker of the database, extract or reutilize a substantial part of its content in case of extraction for private purpose of the content of a non-electronic database, in case of extraction for teaching and scientific research for non commercial purpose, in case of extraction for administrative or judicial purpose.

[27] Thakur, Database Protection in the European Union and the United States, 2001IPQ 100.

[28] Section 53(2)(1) German Copyright Act.

becomes important. Copy for consuming music may not be allowed but copy for producing a literary work may be allowed, knowing very well the practical difficulty of cross checking it one might require to copy a piece of music in order to get information about it and it may not be necessary that one plays the music every time to enjoy it. User's right management is more desirable than digital right management.[29] To balance both sides private copying should be continued along with equitable remuneration which will satisfy both the author and user.

3 Copyright and Free Speech

Copyright does not restrict free speech as it offers the author the exclusive right to specific expression and it does not protect the idea and also it permits fair use of the expression.[30] The Copyright Term Extension Act 1998 extended duration of copyrighted works by 20 years period. The United States Supreme Court held that the Copyright Term Extension Act 1998 was not unconstitutional as it did not restrict free speech.[31] The copyright patent clause of the US constitution provides, 'Congress shall have power to promote Progress of Science and Useful Arts by securing to Authors for limited times the exclusive right to their writing'.[32]

US Supreme Court in Eldred v. Ashcroft[33] did not find anything in the text and history of the constitution which prevents limited term of copyright being extended by another limited term. The word 'limited time' in copyright clause does not mean inalterable but rather it means confined within certain limits. So extension of copyright term by 20 years which was confined within certain limits did not violate constitutional mandate. The benefit of the extension of copyright term was given to existing and future work, so that all of them could be governed evenhandedly.

In 1993 European Union extended copyright term to life plus 70 years and made a provision not to allow this extended protection to the works of non—EU countries who did not offer similar extended term. So for the interest of reciprocity, the copyright term extension was justified. The extended term of protection would encourage more investment in creating more copyrightable works. Copyright Term Extension Act 1998 did not change the contours of copyright. The First Amendment secures freedom to make or decline to make one's speech. Thus the First Amendment of Copyright Term Extension Act 1998 is unwarranted.

[29] Christophe Geiger, Copyright and Free Access to Information: For a Fair Balance of Interest in a Globalize World 2006 E.I.P.R. 371.

[30] Eldred v. Ashcroft 537 US 186.

[31] Eldred v. Ashcroft 537 US 186.

[32] Article 1 § 8 cl 8, US Constitution.

[33] Eldred v. Ashcroft 537 US 186.

Justice Breyer in his dissenting judgment in Eldred v. Ashcroft[34] quoted from Walterscheid[35] 'the economic effect of this 20 year extension—the longest blanket extension since the Nation's founding—is to make the copyright term not limited but virtually perpetual. Its primary legal effect is to grant the extended term not to authors, but to their heirs, estates or corporate successors. And most importantly, its practical effect is not to promote but to inhibit, the progress of 'Science'—by which word the Framers meant learning or knowledge'.

Even the personality approach can justify extension of copyright protection by inclusion of adaptation works but it may suffer difficulty in including work of information as personality in low authorial information works is less than apparent and thus does not qualify for copyright protection. The personality approach also expanded the scope of copyright protection by liberating it from any particular form and thereby allowing work irrespective of form to come under copyright protection.

But the question still remains whether copyright at all should protect functional, commercial works as the Court denied copyright protection to price catalogue of bathroom fixtures in J.L. Mott Iron Works v. Clow[36] and observed 'We discover nothing original in the treatment of the subject, it is merely the picture of the bath tub in ordinary use. The question, therefore which confront us is, were such things intended to be protected by the constitutional provision in question? The object of that provision was to promote the dissemination of learning, by inducing intellectual labour in works which would promote the general knowledge in science and the useful arts. It is not designed as a protection to traders in the particular manner in which they might shot their wares. It sought to stimulate original investigation, whether in literature, science, or arts, for the betterment of the people, that they might be instructed and improved with respect to those subjects'.

4 Copyright and Incentive for Investment

The value of information in the commercial world is well understood and the informational works well fit into the principles of copyright law as it protects works like directories, calendars and statistical reports. If these works are valuable enough to be the target of piracy, they should be important enough to be protected. Commercial value of low authorial works can support justification for copyright protection. In Bleistein v. Donaldson Lithographing Co,[37] Justice Holmes observed 'if they command the interest of any public, they have a commercial value—it would be bold to say that they have not an aesthetic and educational value—and the taste of any public is not to be treated with contempt'.

---

[34] 537 US 186.

[35] Walterscheid 2000.

[36] 82 F. 316 (7th Cir. 1897).

[37] 188 U.S 239 (1903).

According to Justice Holmes, copyright can be awarded to both works with creative value and with commercial value. There can be two complimentary rationales for copyright protection—copyright protects against appropriation of both authorial personality present in a work and the labour and resource invested in it. When right in derivative work borrows justification from personality theory, the same cannot support low authorial work and the labour theory can support the hard work of second comer who adds his own labour to existing information to claim copyright. 'The doctrine of new and different use which permit copying of information in illustration of new and original proposition or for any other purpose not substantially the same as the plaintiff's use. There is no recognized principle which will prevent a subsequent compiler from copying common material from an existing compilation and combining them in a new form or using them for a different purpose'.[38]

In high authorship work, right to control adapted versions flow from personality right of self determination, that is to control manifestation of himself in various forms. Statutory expansion does not any more support a similar claim of hard work by a second comer in case of dramatization or translation works. The continuing emphasis on protection of author's labour and investment in the making of informational works reflect the influence of expanded scope of high authorship copyright and along with that diminishing effect of new toil defense by the second comer in case of low authorial work is also reflected. This is closely linked with the existing standard of technology as when mere copying is costly and time consuming, addition of independent material to existing material can justify as significant contribution but the same may not be true if technology makes copying more simple and an easy job. As reproduction and dissemination of information became cheaper and faster, ability of the second comer to compete with the initial compiler increased.

The new technology helped the second comer to save time and money by copying the previously compiled information and thus pressure increased to protect information. With this faster and better means of copying, the quantum of copying leading towards infringement has been reduced. The new copying and distributing technology may force the Court to stretch copyright protection for low authorial work even to non-competing appropriation.

The modern view regarding copyright principle supports more the personality concept of original authorship rather than labour theory. The Courts may like to extend copyright protection to low authorial works depending on uniqueness of selection and arrangement. The reluctance of the court in this regard is mainly due to threat of monopolizing the facts and thus copyright protection often emphasizes on the need for keeping data free. Two other factors which influence the decision in these cases are economic harm of the first compiler and opportunity to reprimand the free rider. The new technology helps copying and developing derivative works

[38] Drone 1879.

in such a way that scope of copyright protection for low authorial works becomes very limited and can offer very little protection in a meaningful manner.

It turned out to be original work of authorship included compilations if compilations as a whole constituted an original work of authorship. The emphasis was on original authorship which was not defined by statute but discussed through judicial decisions which created more controversy than clarifying it. As a result original authorship could cover a wide range of low authorial works—those whose investment of labour justified protection and those whose selection and arrangement justified protection.

Professor Goreman observed 'Court should resolve the problem of full copyright protection under the rubric of infringement and fair use rather than of copyright-ability. This in turn will offer greater flexibility, enabling the court to label as infringement those works which interfere with the monopoly of the copyright holder without bringing a commensurate benefit to the public'.[39]

Sweat is a strong argument for original authorship but should the personality concept be considered exclusively for the purpose of authorship? It is possible that considering the technological development sweat for informational work has in fact become a very little endeavor and hence loses the justification for copyright protection. This argument does not in any way affect labour intensive work of authorship. This technological superior position has not only challenged copyright-ability of low authorial work but also raised doubts about the maker of compilation. Who should be the author of computer assisted database—maker of the software who assists the database or the person who takes initiative to make the database?[40]

The problem of substantial labour pre-requisite for copyright-ability is the assessment of quantum of labour that justifies copyright protection. How much of labour is required? And whether all labour is to be treated alike or there are some efforts which generate more sweat than others. A work by work analysis will require the court to differentiate between works which genuinely generates more sweat and socially useful work like map created from original survey, for which copyright incentive is presumed to be essential and works which are collected rather easily such as maps created from data collected from variety of published sources, for which copyright would arguably be superfluous.

The social benefit theory justifies copyright protection by noting that social benefits will not follow in the absence of copyright. Address list, law reports, maps remains to be as useful as it was in the last century and as they are socially beneficial even today, copyright in these works should continue as it was in the last century. Even if court could indicate criteria to decide on social value, the standard cannot be predictable. No doubt the question will still remain whether copyright is the most appropriate means to ensure production of these works.

---

[39] Gorman 1963.

[40] Samuelson 1986.

References

Baron P (2001) Back to future: learning from the past in the database debate. Ohio State L J 62:880

Colston C (2001) Sui generis database right: ripe for review. J Inf Law Technol 3. http://www.elj.warwick.ac.uk/jilt/01-3/colston.html

Drone ES (1879) A treatise on the law of property in intellectual productions in great Britain and the united states. Little Brown & Co, Boston, p 424

Geiger C (2006) Copyright and free access to information: for a fair balance of interest in a globalize world. Eur Intellect Property Rev 366

Gorman (1963) Copyright protection for the collection and representation of facts. Harvard Law Rev 76:1569

Griffiths J, Suthersanan U (2005) Copyright and free speech. Oxford University Press

Hugenholtz P (1996) Adapting copyright to the information superhighway. The Future of Copyright in a Digital Era', Kluwer

Maurer SM, Scotchmer S (1999) Intellectual property rights: database protection: is it broken and should we fix it? Science 284:789

OECD Report on the Scientific Publishing Industry (2005) Digital broadband content: Scientific Publishing

Samuelson (1986) Allocating ownership right in computer—generated works. Univ Pitt Law Rev 47:1185

Walterscheid E (2000) The nature of the intellectual property clause in the historical perspective, p 125

Software Protection Under Copyright Law

V.K. Unni

Abstract Although copyright policy has been governed by the need to protect the interests of authors, it also attempts to protect the society's interests. Building upon the foundation provided by the international copyright treaties, which specify minimum standards of legal protection, the copyright system has evolved from being a rather vague area of the law into a system of central importance. Technological advances do have a huge impact upon the operation and effectiveness of copyright law. These advances spawn new industries and new methods for reproduction and dissemination of works of authorship, which will give new opportunities for authors. In the past seven decades, we have witnessed rapid developments in the field of communications and information technology which have exponentially expanded and extended the ability of human beings to communicate. The digital computer will stand out as one of the most important contributions to the great communication and information revolution which happened during the period. Undoubtedly, the scope of copyright protection for computer software is a major source of worry for both proprietary and open source software developers. This is because the scope of the program will ultimately determine what aspects of a program are forming part of the protectable core as copyrightable expression, and what features will be available for a future developer to copy. The analysis of the scope of copyright protection should be determined by delicately balancing the author's creative rights with the public interest in access. This chapter deals with the legal issues involved in protection of software by providing a comprehensive coverage of the important international developments.

V.K. Unni (✉)
IIM Calcutta, Kolkata, India
e-mail: krisunni1@gmail.com

M.K. Sinha and V. Mahalwar (eds.), *Copyright Law in the Digital World*,
DOI 10.1007/978-981-10-3984-3_9

1 Introduction

The copyright law is based on the charming notion that authors create something out of nothing and such works owe their origin to the authors who produce them.[1] More often those who argue for stringent copyright protection, base their logic on the premise that copyright should fine-tune the balance between highly creative people who bring new works into being and the unscrupulous public who would steal the fruits of their genius. The need to give authors an exclusive right to their writings is based on two reasons.

The first is that: copyright provides an incentive for authors to create and disseminate works of social value.[2] This is known as the instrumental justification. Thus by giving authors a monopoly over their works, copyright tries to correct the under incentive that might happen if free riders were allowed to share in the value created by an author's efforts. The second reason is that copyright rewards authors, who are eligible to be compensated for their contributions.[3] This is known as the desert justification. The rhetoric evokes sympathetic images of the author at work.[4] The instrumental justification brings to our mind the picture of an author struggling to avoid abandoning his creative skills to feed his family. By contrast, the desert justification invokes a genius irrevocably committed to his work.[5]

2 Technological Influences on Copyright

Copyright law is also a subtle and esoteric area that evolved in response to technological change.[6] Technological advances do have a huge impact upon the operation and effectiveness of copyright law. These advances spawn new industries and new methods for reproduction and dissemination of works of authorship, which will give new opportunities for authors. At the same time these technologies also create additional challenges. Copyright law has responded to those challenges, from the

[1] Litman 1990.

[2] In many cases the US Supreme Court has relied upon incentive justification for copyright. See, e.g., *Sony Corp.* v. *Universal City Studios*, 464 U.S. 417, p. 429 (1984), this essentially meant that copyright was intended to motivate the creative activity of authors and inventors by the provision of a special reward.

[3] This argument can be reflected in *Mazer* v. *Stein*, 347 U.S. 201, p. 219 (1954), sacrificial days devoted to such creative activities deserve rewards commensurate with the services rendered.

[4] Sterk 1996.

[5] *Ibid.*

[6] *Folsom* v. *Marsh*, 9 F. Cas. 342, 344 (1841).

days of printing press to digital audio recorders and everything in between photocopiers, radio, television, videocassette recorders, cable television and satellites.[7]

In the past seven decades we have witnessed rapid developments in the field of communications and information technology which have exponentially expanded and extended the ability of human beings to communicate. The digital computer will stand out as one of the most important contributions to the great communication and information revolution which happened during the period. These machines have opened new vistas for reproducing, recording, storing, and disseminating human thought and creativity.

3 Fundamentals of Computer Technology

A modern day computer consists of hardware which is the physical computing machine and software which is the computer program that runs the machine and does the data processing tasks for the person who uses the computer. Any computer's basic hardware is made of the central processing unit (CPU), internal memory storage, keyboard, disk drives, mouse and other devices for transferring data and programs into and out of the internal memory.[8] When commands are given by the user the software directs the hardware to perform various data processing tasks.

4 Fundamentals of Software

Computer software consists of set of instructions which can be utilised in diverse mundane tasks such as preparation of payrolls, monitoring vehicular movements on road, sea and air, recording and storing data, doing complex calculations for research, running assembly lines, and taking inventory. They are developed by the careful fixation of words, phrases, numbers, and other symbols in different media.[9] The main categories of computer software are operating systems and application programs. An operating system is a set of programs that manages the computer's internal functions and acts as an interface between the computer hardware, the application programs, and the computer user.[10] Application programs do specific

[7] *Intellectual Property and the National Information Infrastructure: The Report of the Working Group on Intellectual Property Right* (USPTO, 1995) 13.

[8] See generally Curran and Curnow 1984.

[9] See Report titled *National Commission on New Technology Uses of Copyrighted Works* (hereinafter CONTU Report) 22.

[10] Cook 1984.

data processing tasks for the user like book-keeping, inventory management, word processing etc.[11]

Basically there are two forms of software code: source code and object code. A computer programmer writes software in source code, using programming languages like Basic or C which can be read by human beings.[12] To be very simple, source code is the language that programmers employ to computers and command them to execute desired functions.[13] The programmer can differentiate the different steps and the instructions that program provides to a computer that helps the computer to finish the assigned task.

Interestingly the programmers never speak directly to computers because computers cannot understand a single word from the source code.[14] For a computer to process the source code, the source code must first be changed into object code which is known as "executable" or "machine readable" code. Object code is a series of ones and zeroes that a computer understands.[15]

Thus the said programs like C and Basic are the expressive medium through which programmers dictate the desired function of a program. Source code for a computer program is written in a high-level language, such as C or FORTRAN. Changes to the program are made to the source code, but the program is not run in its source code version.

A program called compiler is used to convert the source code into object code. Computer programs sold to the public, such as Microsoft Excel or Word contain only the object code. This mode of software distribution also prevents many programmers/users from modifying the code, as it is difficult, to understand the nuanced programming within a given piece of software without having access to the original source code.[16] Since the source code is more abstract, a few lines of source code can produce many lines of executable code. Thus if one were to write a line of source code that said "Walk to the bank," the resulting executable code might say, "Lift your right foot for 2 s then stop lifting it, slowly move it forward 30 inches. Keep it down." and so on until explicit commands for walking to the bank were made.[17]

During the initial days of programming in the 1960s and 1970s, sharing source code was the usual practice. Programmers were involved in building on and debugging each other's works, which led to higher quality software. Those were the days when software was sold along with the computer hardware marketed by companies like Bell Labs and Xerox, which had research facilities which facilitated

---

[11] Toong and Gupta 1982.

[12] Xuan-Thao N. Nguyen et al. 2006.

[13] Strasser 2001.

[14] In other words the programmers and computers never speak the same language.

[15] Nguyen supra note 12 at 504.

[16] Azzi 2010.

[17] McJohn 2000.

collaboration with others in the software community.[18] These companies which made their profits from the computer hardware they sold were distributing software free of charge.[19]

During the next phase when the computer industry experienced phenomenal growth software became a commodity in and of itself which prompted companies to focus more protecting innovations dealing with software, which had the effect of replacing the collaborative programming communities that helped sustain software development during the initial days of the digital computer revolution.[20] Today, a large number of mainstream computer technologies revolve around the software and companies do everything possible to protect the rights under software by relying upon the laws of contract, copyright, patent, and trade secret.

5 Legal Protection of Software

United States of America (US) was the first country to have a thorough debate on the various legal models which can be used to protect software. It was in 1974 that the US Congress set up the National Commission on New Technological Uses of Copyrighted Works to study the implications of the new technologies like software and suggest suitable changes to federal intellectual property law.[21] CONTU held extensive discussions with various stakeholders and consulted numerous experts and finally recommended that the intellectual work embodied in computer software should be protected through copyright law. CONTU opted for copyright as the most suitable mode of protection in spite of the fact that copyright cannot protect “any idea, procedure, process, system, method of operation, concept, principle, or discovery”.[22] CONTU was very well aware that it was impossible in 1978 to establish a clear demarcation between the computer program’s copyrightable expression and the uncopyrightable processes which are implemented by those programs.[23] CONTU’s recommendations were given effect by the US Congress in 1980 by making suitable amendments to the federal copyright law.

Markets for goods covering intellectual creations often face the “public goods” problem.[24] Public goods have two important characteristics (1) nonexcludability—it is difficult to keep out those who do not pay for the good from using it and (2) nonrivalrous competition—additional consumers of the good do not decrease the quantity of the good which can be given to others. The private market will

[18] Lerner and Tirole 2002.

[19] *Ibid.*

[20] *Ibid.* at 201.

[21] CONTU Report supra note 9.

[22] Copyright Act of 1976, 17 U.S.C. § 102(b) (1982).

[23] CONTU Report supra note 9 at 22–23.

[24] Arrow 1962.

always try to supply such goods in lesser quantity because producers cannot get the marginal value of their investment in supplying such goods.[25]

The information covering innovation in application programs was accepted by CONTU as a prime example of a public good which satisfied the two important characteristics mentioned above. CONTU observed that since application program creators could not reap the marginal value of their efforts under these circumstances, they would tend to undersupply new and better application programs if there was no incentive to innovate.[26] The CONTU recommended that copyright, with its low requirements for protection and lengthy duration, was in a better position to give protection to software. On choosing the most appropriate form CONTU was guided by the literary form of computer software rather than its utilitarian substance.[27]

However the most difficult issue was to pin-point the exact nature and scope of monopoly granted by copyright protection. Interestingly in most of the countries including US the Copyright Act specifically limits the scope of protection for all works by providing that *in no case does copyright protection for an original work of authorship extend to any idea, procedure, process, system, method of operation, concept, principle, or discovery, regardless of the form in which it is described, explained, illustrated, or embodied in such work.*[28] This means that the copyright protection shall be given only to the expression of an idea and not the idea per se. The idea-expression divide or idea-expression dichotomy is a concept which defines the appropriate function of copyright laws, which are generally designed to protect the fixed expression of an idea rather than the basic idea itself. The issue pertaining to idea-expression dichotomy and its implications involving copyright infringement involving software will be discussed later in this chapter

CONTU also considered alternative models like patent, trade secrets, misappropriation doctrine etc.[29] CONTU noted that Patent law was generally not seen as a practical option for the protection of most software as they do not manifest sufficient novelty or non-obviousness to be granted a patent.[30] Secondly the time and cost of obtaining protection under patent law might not be worth the effort, especially in circumstances when the software was not expected to have a long life cycle. Thirdly to obtain a patent, the inventor had to make an enabling disclosure to the Patent Office and ultimately to the public which the inventor might be reluctant as such disclosures would facilitate access by others to the inner workings of the

[25] Samuelson 1954.

[26] CONTU Report supra note 9 at 9–12.

[27] *Ibid.* at 19–23.

[28] Section 102(b) of Copyright Act.

[29] The misappropriation doctrine in US is a branch of unfair competition law which can be used to protect some aspects of intellectual work embodied in program code. In the famous case of *International News Service v. Associated Press*, 248 U.S. 215 (1918) the Supreme Court held that the gatherer of valuable information has a limited right to prevent competitors from copying such information.

[30] Davidson 1983.

patentee's invention and would destroy any trade secret claim.[31] On trade secrets CONTU did not recommend it as the secrecy element usually required that contractual or other means be used to limit dissemination of the valuable information. CONTU observed that even if trade secret protection was a possible option it was difficult for licensors of computer software, especially mass-marketed programs, to constantly monitor and enforce such agreements.[32]

The first round of copyright infringement disputes after the inclusion of software within the field of copyright dealt with whether and to what extent literal copying of computer software violates copyright law. Through these cases the courts interpreted the copyright law as one which will prohibit direct copying of all forms of computer software, whether in its object code or source code version, whether designed to perform specific data processing tasks for the user called as application programs or to manage the internal functions of computers called as operating systems.[33] In *Apple Computer, Inc.* v. *Franklin Computer Corp.*,[34] one of the most important cases during the initial days the court held that copyright law protected the exact coding of a computer operating system and that there was no merger of idea and expression as long as other methods of expressing the idea underlying the operating system program were not foreclosed as a practical matter.[35]

A second generation of copyright infringement suits which emerged subsequently deals with the extent to which non-literal forms of copying constitute copyright infringement. Many of the second generation cases dealing with copyright infringement of program code raised crucial questions on idea-expression dichotomy.

6 The Origins of the Idea-Expression Dichotomy

The origins of the idea-expression dichotomy in U.S.A can be traced to the Supreme Court case of *Baker* v. *Selden*[36] In the said case Charles Selden got a copyright in a book, which dealt with his particular book-keeping system.[37] The book consisted of an introductory essay explaining the system of book-keeping to which were annexed certain forms or blanks consisting of ruled lines and headings, which illustrated how the said system of book keeping had to be carried out.[38]

[31] Q-Co *Indus.* v. *Hoffman*, 625 F. Supp. 608, 617 (S.D.N.Y. 1985).

[32] Gilburne and Johnston 1982;

[33] Goldstein 1986, ALSO, *Apple Computer, Inc.* v. *Franklin Computer Corp.*, 714 F.2d 1240, 1251 (3d Cir. 1983), *cert. dismissed,* 464 U.S. 1033 (1984).

[34] 714 F.2d 1240 (3d Cir. 1983).

[35] *Ibid.* at 1253.

[36] 101 U.S. 99 (1880).

[37] The book's title was Selden's Condensed Ledger or Book-keeping Simplified.

[38] Supra note 36 at 101.

Later on Baker published a book on accounting, which made use of a similar plan so far as results were concerned; but made a different arrangement of the columns, and used different headings. Thus the allegation of complainant was that Baker had used Selden's system of accounting, however he did not allege that Baker had actually copied the particular forms contained in Selden's book.[39] Thus the main question before the court was whether the exclusive property in a system of book-keeping could be claimed, under the law of copyright, by means of a book in which that system was explained.[40]

The court noted that there was a clear distinction between the books, as such, and the art, which it was, intended to illustrate and explain. A treatise on the composition and use of medicines, even if they were old would be the subject matter of copyright. But at the same time no one could contend that the copyright of the treatise would give him the exclusive right to the art or manufacture described therein.[41] Thus the copyright of a book on book-keeping could not secure the exclusive right to make, sell, and use account-books prepared upon the plan set forth in such book. In the words of Justice Bradley "*that blank account-books are not the subject of copyright; and that the mere copyright of Selden's book did not confer upon him the exclusive right to make and use account-books, ruled and arranged as designated by him and described and illustrated in said book*".[42]

Interestingly the Court never used the words idea and expression to describe the distinction between unprotectable and protectable works. Instead it developed the distinction between the informational use of a work and the use of the work in practice.

7 Idea-Expression Dichotomy and the Abstraction Test

Even though many cases have discussed the concept of Idea-Expression dichotomy the most famous case which has covered this doctrine in detail is *Nichols* v. *Universal Pictures Corp.*[43] The plaintiff was the author of a play, "*Abie's Irish Rose*". The defendant produced a motion picture play, "*The Cohens and The Kellys*" which the plaintiff alleged was copied from his work. On the issue whether the defendant had infringed plaintiff's work, the court noted the following

[39] *Ibid.*

[40] *Ibid.*

[41] The court gave an example that the copyright of a work on mathematical science cannot give to the author an exclusive right to the methods of operation which he propounds, or to the diagrams which he employs to explain them, so as to prevent an engineer from using them whenever occasion requires.

[42] Supra note 36 at 107.

[43] 45 F.2d 119 (1930).

"Upon any work, and especially upon a play, a great number of patterns of increasing generality will fit equally well, as more and more of the incident is left out."[44]

The court found that the plot of the second play was too different to infringe, because the most detailed pattern which was common to both, eliminated so much from each that its content went into the public domain; and for that the mere subsection of a plot was not susceptible of copyright.[45] Thus the court held that the similarities in plot between the two works were not enough to find that protected expression had been taken. However there is no precise, predictable point where ideas end and expression begins. This decision made it very clear that idea behind a play could never be copyrighted and would always remain in public domain. This would make sure that many of the basic building blocks would not be subject to a monopoly.

8 Protection of Software and Idea-Expression Dichotomy

One of the landmark cases, which dealt with the issue of idea-expression dichotomy in the context of software, arose in the year 1986.[46] The said case, which was decided by the Court of Appeals, was presented with a copyright infringement action concerning a software program that was written to manage the operation of a dental laboratory. In the said case the appellant Jaslow Dental Laboratory, Inc. was a corporation in the business of manufacturing dental prosthetics and devices. Plaintiff Whelan Associates, Inc. was also a company the business of developing and marketing custom computer programs.[47]

Jaslow Lab wanted to computerise its operations and for doing so, it hired the Strohl Systems Group, Inc. a small corporation that developed custom-made software to develop a program that would run on Jaslow Lab's new IBM Series computer and take care of the lab's business needs. The person at Strohl responsible for the Jaslow Labs account was Elaine Whelan, an experienced programmer who was an officer and also half owner of Strohl.[48] The programmer made the said program after a series of visits to various dentals labs. Those visits really helped the programmer to understand the layout, workflow, and administration of dental laboratories generally. Ms. Whelan wrote a program called Dentalab for Jaslow Lab and it was written in a computer language known as EDL (Event Driven Language), so that it would work with IBM Series machines.[49]

---

[44] *Ibid.*

[45] *Ibid.*

[46] *Whelan Assocs.* v. *Jaslow Dental Lab.*, Inc., 797 F.2d 1222 (1986).

[47] *Ibid.* p. 1225.

[48] *Ibid.*

[49] *Ibid.* at 1225–1226.

Later on Ms. Whelan left Strohl to start her own business, Whelan Associates, Inc., which acquired Strohl's interest in the Dentalab program. Thereafter, Whelan Associates entered into negotiations with Jaslow Lab and made Jaslow Lab its marketing representative for the Dentalab program.

The parties' business relationship worked successfully during the initial period for about 2 years. Around this time Jaslow became more familiar with computer programming, and he found out that since Dentalab was written in EDL it could not be used on computers that many of the smaller dental prosthetics firms were using. He also thought that there might be a market for a program that served essentially the same function as Dentalab but could also be used in smaller dental prosthetics firms. Thus he developed a program in the BASIC language for such computers. The said program called the Dentcom PC program became the alleged infringing program in this case.[50]

Whelan Associates by filing the case in the District Court alleged that Dentcom programs infringed Whelan Associates' copyright in Dentalab. Jaslow denied the said argument stating that Jaslow had developed the Dentcom system independently, and therefore could not have violated Whelan Associate's copyright, even if Whelan's copyright were valid.[51]

The District Court held that Jaslow had not created the Dentcom system independently, and the Dentcom system, although written in a different computer language from the Dentalab, was substantially similar to Dentalab because its structure and overall organisation were substantially similar.[52] This substantial similarity, with Jaslow's acknowledged access to the Dentalab system, led the district court to conclude that each sale of the Dentcom program violated Whelan Associates' copyright on the Dentalab system and thus the court therefore awarded Whelan Associates damages for the copyright infringements, and enjoined Dentcom from selling any more copies of the Dentalab or Dentcom programs.[53] Against the said order of the District Court, Jaslow appealed before the Court of Appeals.

The Court of Appeals noted that the creation of a program often takes place in several steps, moving from the general to the specific. This was because programs were intended to accomplish particular tasks, and thus the first step in creating the program was identifying the problem that the computer programmer was trying to solve. In the said case the problem was record keeping for his business. Once the programmer learnt more about the problem, he would then outline a solution, which might be in the form of a flowchart, which will break down the solution into a series of smaller units called subroutines or modules.[54]

[50] *Ibid.* at 1226.

[51] *Ibid.* at 1227.

[52] *Whelan Associates* v. *Jaslow Dental Laboratory*, 609 F. Supp. 1307, 1321 (1985).

[53] *Ibid.* at 1322.

[54] Whelan supra note 46 at 1230, Program's efficiency mostly depended upon the arrangements of its modules and subroutines; although two programs could produce the same result, one might be more efficient because of different internal arrangements of modules and subroutines.

Court further observed that once the program structure was refined, the programmer had to decide about what data was needed, where the data should be introduced, how the data should be input, and how it should be combined with other data. Since the Dentalab program was intended to handle all of the business-related aspects of a dental laboratory, it had to accommodate and interrelate many different pieces and types of data including patient's names, dentist's names, inventory, accounts receivable, accounts payable, and payroll.[55] Once the detailed design of the program was over, the coding would begin and thereafter each of the steps identified in the design had to be turned into a language that the computer can understand. The programmer first would write in a source code, which might be in one of several languages, BASIC, FORTRAN, or EDL. Once the program was written in source code, it had to be translated into object code.[56]

Thus the court observed that the coding process was a comparatively small part of programming and a larger portion of the expense and difficulty in creating computer programs was attributable to the development of the structure and logic of the program. According to the court the main question confronted by it in the present case was whether mere similarity in the overall structure of programs can be the basis for a copyright infringement, or in other words whether a program's copyright protection covers the structure of the program or only the program's literal elements, *i.e.*, its source and object codes.[57] Interestingly the argument of Jaslow was that the structure of a computer program was the idea and not the expression of the idea, and therefore the structure could not be protected by the program copyright.

The Court of Appeals opined that the idea of the Dentalab program was the efficient management of a dental laboratory, which had significantly different requirements from those of other businesses. Since the said idea could be accomplished in a number of different ways with a number of different structures, the structure of the Dentalab program was part of the program's expression and not its idea.[58] The court affirmed the decision of the District Court, and held that there was ample evidence of substantial similarity between the structure, sequence, and organisation of the parties' programs. Thus the court held that the program's copyright protection also covered the structure of the program apart from the program's literal elements like source code. This decision had created a negative impact upon the public domain by covering the structure, sequence, and organisation of the computer program under the ambit of copyright protection.

---

[55] *Ibid.*

[56] *Ibid.*

[57] *Ibid. at* 1234.

[58] *Ibid. at* 1236.

9 Abstraction, Filtration, Comparison Test

After six years in Computer Associates, *International* v. *Altai*, Inc.,[59] the Court of Appeals was once again concerned with a similar case. Plaintiff created a computer program containing a sub-program that enabled the primary program to run on different operating systems. Defendant hired one of plaintiff's employees, who misappropriated copies of the source code for plaintiff's subprogram, which he then used to create a program for defendant. Upon knowledge of this copying, the defendant then rewrote its program leaving out those portions that had been copied from plaintiff's subprogram. Plaintiff sued for copyright infringement with respect to both versions of defendant's program.[60]

Lower Court found copyright infringement only with respect to first version of defendant's program and thus dismissed second claim and against this the plaintiff appealed. Appellant-plaintiff contended that despite Altai's rewriting of its programs code,[61] the resulting program was substantially similar to the structure of its program.[62] The structure of a program included its non-literal components such as general flow charts as well as the more specific organisation of inter-modular relationships, parameter lists, and macros.

The Court of Appeals opined that the approach of the court followed in the case of Whelan[63]; so as to separate idea from expression in computer programs relied too heavily on metaphysical distinctions and did not place enough emphasis on practical considerations. Instead of following the decision of *Whelan,* the court in this case enunciated an *Abstraction Filtration Comparison* test. Accordingly to ascertain substantial similarity a court would first break down the allegedly infringed program into its constituent structural parts. Then, the court had to examine each of these parts for such things as incorporated ideas, expression that is necessarily incidental to those ideas, and elements that are taken from the public domain, so that it could then sift out all non-protectable material. After filtering out these elements the remaining kernel, would be compared with the structure of an allegedly infringing program. The result of this comparison would determine whether the protectable elements of the programs at issue were substantially similar so as to warrant a finding of infringement.[64]

Thus by adopting the above three step analysis for substantial similarity between the non-literal elements of computer programs, the court attempted to do two things. Firstly it wanted to ensure that the programmers might receive appropriate copyright protection for innovative utilitarian works containing expression; and secondly it made sure that non-protectable technical expression remained in the

[59] 982 F.2d 693 (1992).

[60] *Ibid.* at 698–699.

[61] The defendant's program was named as Oscar.

[62] Appellant program was names as Adapter.

[63] Whelan supra note 46.

[64] Computer Associates supra note 59.

public domain for others to use freely as building blocks in their own work.[65] Thus the Computer Associates case gave a more narrow scope of copyright protection for a program's non-literal aspects. To quote the words of Justice Walker.

> At first blush, it may seem counter-intuitive that someone who has benefited to some degree from illicitly obtained material can emerge from an infringement suit relatively unscathed. However, so long as the appropriated material consists of non-protectable expression, this result is neither unfair nor unfortunate. it is the means by which copyright advances the progress of science and art.[66]

Thus it becomes clear that copyright for computer programs prevents not only literal copying, but also copying of "non-literal elements", such as the program's structure, sequence and organisation. These non-literal features can be protected only to the extent that they incorporate authorship in programmer's expression of original ideas, as distinguished from the ideas themselves.[67] The graphics, sounds and appearance of a computer program can also be protected under the category of audiovisual work; which means that even if no program code was copied the program's copyright can still be infringed.[68]

10 Copyrightability of Computer Program's User Interface

Ever since the advent of digital computers significant strides have been made in the field of "computer-human interaction," a branch of study that has become a crucial factor in most aspects of computer system design including the design of application programs.[69] According to this field there are five important factors which programmers should try to achieve while they are designing application programs. Those factors are (1) minimize learning time, (2) maximize speed of performance, (3) minimize rate of user errors, (4) maximize user satisfaction, and (5) maximize users' retention of knowledge over time.[70] Since application programmers try to implement these objectives in designing computer-human interfaces many of their design choices are dictated by principles of human factor analysis which have evolved over years of empirical research.[71]

Video-display is one important aspect of computer-human interfaces that falls under the scope of copyright. The common examples of video displays are menu status screens, game displays, and mathematical tables like spreadsheets. Here also

---

[65] *Ibid.* at 721.

[66] *Ibid.* at 706, finally the Court held that there was no infringement.

[67] Computer Associates supra note 59.

[68] *Stern Elecs Inc* v *Kaufman* 669 F. 2d 852, 855 (2d Cir.1982).

[69] See Shneiderman 1987.

[70] Menell 1989.

[71] *Ibid.* at 1055.

the crucial issue behind the scope of copyright protection for video displays is whether their content falls under the category of protectable expression or uncopyrightable idea. In one of the first cases involving the user interface of a program *Broderbund Software, Inc.* v. *Unison World*, Inc.[72] The plaintiff was the owner of copyright in an application program used in designing greeting cards, posters etc. which contained a series of menu-driven video displays that helped the user to navigate through the various design steps. The defendant's program, designed to work on a different computer system, copied the plaintiff's menu screens, input formats, and screen sequencing. The court relied upon Whelan and held that since other means of expressing the underlying idea of the plaintiff's program—a system for making greeting cards, banners, existed the "overall structure, sequencing, and arrangement of screens" in the plaintiff's program was protected.[73] Later on while deciding *Manufacturers Technology, Inc.* v. *CAMS*, Inc, which almost immediately followed Whelan and Broderbund, the court directly addressed the copyrightability of computer screen displays and held that the Broderbund approach was too expansive.[74]

In *Apple Computer, Inc.* v. *Microsoft Corporation*, the first case involving GUIs the court held that GUIs would receive very little copyright protection.[75] In this case, Apple registered the copyright for its own version of the personal computer GUI, and then issued licences to Microsoft and Hewlett-Packard. Later Microsoft and HP updated their own GUIs to create second versions of their software which contained non-licensed elements of Apple's GUI. Apple sued Microsoft and HP for copyright infringement.[76] Apple argued that Microsoft had copied 189 elements including: design and appearance of application windows; design and appearance of dialog boxes; menu design and appearance etc.[77] According to Apple the look and feel of the GUI was more important than the 189 elements taken.[78] The court, however, ignored Apple's look and feel argument and instead analyzed each element one by one to hold that out of the ten unlicensed elements of Apple not even one was copyrightable.[79] Court further held that "*Apple cannot get patent-like protection for the idea of a graphical user interface or the idea of a desktop metaphor*" under copyright law.[80] Scholars note that after the decision in *Apple* v. *Microsoft*, the software industry began to rely more on design patents for safeguarding their rights over GUIs.[81]

---

[72] 648 F. Supp. 1127 (N.D. Cal. 1986).

[73] *Ibid.* at 1133.

[74] 706 F. Supp. 984, 992 (D. Conn. 1989).

[75] *Apple Computer, Inc.* v. *Microsoft Corp.*, 35 F.3d 1435 (9th Cir. 1994).

[76] *Ibid.* at 1441–1442.

[77] *Apple Computer, Inc.* v. *Microsoft Corp.*, 717 F. Supp. 1428, 1433–1435 (N.D. Cal. 1991).

[78] Apple supra note 75 at 1442.

[79] *Ibid.* 1433–1435.

[80] *Ibid.* 1443.

[81] Stigler 2014.

Lotus Dev. Corp. v. *Borland International*[82] was the landmark case involving menu, command, hierarchy of a computer program. This case will be covered in detail as it reached the US Supreme Court. The main issue involved here was to determine whether the computer program's *menu command hierarchy* was a copyrightable subject matter. The district court held that appellant Borland International, Inc., had infringed the plaintiff's, copyright in Lotus 1-2-3, a computer spreadsheet program, when Borland copied the Lotus 1-2-3-menu command hierarchy into its Quattro and Quattro Pro computer spreadsheet programs.[83]

Lotus 1-2-3 is a spreadsheet program that enables users to perform accounting functions electronically on a computer. Users manipulate and control the program via series of menu commands, such as "Copy," "Print," and "Quit". Users choose commands either by highlighting them on the screen or by typing their first letter. In all, Lotus 1-2-3 has 469 commands arranged into more than 50 menus and submenus. Lotus 1-2-3, allowed users to write what were called *macros*.[84] By writing a macro, a user could designate a series of command choices with a single macro keystroke.[85] To put it in other words, Lotus 1-2-3 macros shortened the time needed to set up and operate the program.[86]

Borland released its first Quattro program to the public in 1987, and its objective was to develop a spreadsheet program far superior to existing programs, including Lotus 1-2-3. The district court found that Borland included in its Quattro and Quattro Pro version 1.0 a virtually identical copy of the entire 1-2-3-menu tree.[87] However it had to be noted that, Borland did not copy any of Lotus's underlying computer code; though it copied the words and structure of Lotus's menu command hierarchy. Borland included the Lotus menu command hierarchy in its programs in order to make them compatible with Lotus 1-2-3. Thus the spreadsheet users who were already familiar with Lotus 1-2-3 could easily switch over to the Borland programs without having to learn new commands or rewrite their Lotus macros.[88]

During the appeal, before the Court of Appeals, Borland did not dispute that it had factually copied the words and arrangement of the Lotus's menu command hierarchy. Instead the argument was that it had lawfully copied the unprotectable menus of Lotus 1-2-3 and submitted that the said menu command hierarchy was not copyrightable because it was method of operation that was foreclosed from

---

[82] 49 F.3d 807 (1996).

[83] *Ibid*, at 809.

[84] *Ibid*.

[85] Rather than typing the whole series each time, the user only needs to type the single pre-programmed macro keystroke, causing the program to recall and perform the designated series of commands automatically.

[86] Supra note 82 at 809–810.

[87] *Ibid*. at 810.

[88] *Ibid*.

copyright protection.[89] Thus the only issue in the appeal was to determine whether the Lotus's menu command hierarchy was a copyrightable subject matter.[90]

The court finally held that the Lotus *menu command hierarchy* was a method of operation.[91] According to the Court a "method of operation," referred to the means by which a person operated something.[92] Thus a text, which described how to operate something, would not extend copyright protection to the method of operation itself. The general public would be free to employ that method and to describe it in their own words. Similarly, if a new method of operation was used rather than described, other people would still be free to employ or describe that method.[93]

Coming to the present case the Court observed that Lotus menu command hierarchy provided the means by which users could control and operate Lotus 1-2-3. If users wanted to copy material, they used the "Copy" command, if they wanted to print material; they used the "Print" command etc. Users had to use the command terms to instruct the computer what to do.[94] Without the menu command hierarchy, users would not be able to access and control, or indeed make use of, Lotus 1-2-3's functional capabilities. Thus the court held that the said *menu command hierarchy* was an uncopyrightable *method of operation*.[95]

In other words the Lotus menu command hierarchy did not merely explain and present Lotus 1-2-3's functional capabilities to the user; further it also acted as the method by which the program was operated and controlled. Court carefully noted that, although Borland did not have to copy Lotus's underlying program code to allow users to operate its programs in substantially the same way as Lotus 1-2-3, Borland was forced to copy the Lotus menu command hierarchy to allow its users to operate the programs in substantially the same way.[96] This according to the court was a very crucial difference.[97]

The court was not persuaded by the reasoning that Lotus developers could have designed the Lotus menu command hierarchy differently since it was immaterial to the question of whether it was a *method of operation*. The court's main inquiry was whether the Lotus menu command hierarchy was a method of operation. The question was answered in the affirmative because the court found that all the users operated Lotus 1-2-3 by using the Lotus menu command hierarchy and that the entire Lotus menu command hierarchy was essential to operating Lotus 1-2-3. The

---

[89] *Ibid.* at 815, by relying upon 17 USC Section 102 (b) which states that "*in no case does copyright protection for an original work of authorship extend to any idea, procedure, process, system, method of operation, concept, principle, or discovery, regardless of the form in which it is described, explained, illustrated, or embodied in such work*".

[90] *Ibid.* at 813. Borland admitted that it had copied the Lotus menu command hierarchy.

[91] It did not consider whether it could also be a system, process, or procedure.

[92] It can be a car, television or a computer.

[93] Supra note 82 at 815.

[94] *Ibid.*

[95] *Ibid.*

[96] *Ibid.*

[97] *Ibid.*

expressive choices of what to name the command terms and how to arrange them could not alter the status of the uncopyrightable menu command hierarchy into copyrightable subject matter.[98]

In the words of Justice Stahl "In many ways, the Lotus menu command hierarchy is like the buttons used to control, say, a video cassette recorder ("VCR") … That the buttons are arranged and labeled does not make them a "literary work," nor does it make them an "expression" of the abstract "method of operating" a VCR via a set of labeled buttons Instead, the buttons are themselves the "method of operating" the VCR."[99]

11 Copyright Protection for Software in Other Jurisdictions

When the discussions began in the 1970's on the mode of protection for computer programs the international community wanted the creation of a sui generis right, which can cover all the special features of this new branch of human creativity.[100] The European Commission initiated its discussions in 1985 and at that time, several states had gone ahead to recognise computer programs as copyrightable subject-matter with Germany doing so with the Copyright Amendment Act of 1985, and the United Kingdom enacting the Copyright (Computer Software) Amendment Act of 1985.[101]

The regulative framework in EU comprises of two legislations Directive 91/250 on the legal protection of computer programs, which was repealed by Directive 2009/24 on the legal protection of computer programs and secondly, on general copyright law, Directive 2001/29 dealing with the harmonization of certain aspects of copyright and related rights in the information society.[102] Today almost all countries in the world protect software under the laws of copyright as a literary work. This can also be found in international agreements like the TRIPs Agreement.[103] In India from the year 1994 onwards computer programs have been afforded protection under the law of copyright.[104] Since the Indian law is very similar to the various other global legislations this chapter does not cover the Indian position in detail.

---

[98] *Ibid.*

[99] *Ibid.* at 817.

[100] Hilty and Geiger 2005.

[101] Guarda 2013.

[102] *Ibid.* at 446.

[103] TRIPs Agreement Article 10(1) deals with copyright protection of computer programs.

[104] Indian Copyright Act 1957, S. 2 (ffc). "computer programme" means a set of instructions expressed in words, codes, schemes or in any other form, including a machine readable medium, capable of causing a computer to perform a particular task or achieve a particular result;

12 Conclusion

Undoubtedly the scope of copyright protection for computer software is a major source of worry for both proprietary and open source software developers. This is because the scope of the program will ultimately determine what aspects of a program are forming part of the protectable core as copyrightable expression, and what features will be available for a future developer to copy. The analysis of the scope of copyright protection should be determined by delicately balancing the author's creative rights with the public interest in access. A narrow scope of protection, represented by the *abstraction, filtration, comparison* analysis, will definitely provide greater public access and will enrich public domain, whereas a broader scope of protection inhibits public access and diminishes the public domain.

Copyright protection gives the author of a software program a bundle of exclusive rights, including the right to make copies of the program, the right to make an adaptation, right to perform etc.[105] These rights are subject to some specific statutory limitations. These limitations represent a codification of the attempted balance between protection of the author's rights and the rights of the general public.[106] Again in the context of computer software, there are some decisions to the effect that decompilation of object code may be a fair use.[107] This process is very crucial for software programmers who write the code so as to make it interoperable with other programs. By decompiling the protected code of a software program, the programmer reveals its technical requirements and can create a program that will meet and work with these technical requirements.

References

Arrow KJ (1962) Economic welfare and the allocation of resources for invention. In The rate and direction of inventive activity: economic and social factors, p 609

Azzi RM (2010) CPR: How Jacobsen V. Katzer resuscitated the open source movement. Univ Ill Law Rev, pp 1271, 1275

Cook R (1984) Operating systems, Popular computing, p 111

Curran S, Curnow R (1984) Overcoming computer illiteracy: a friendly introduction to computers

Davidson DM (1983) Protecting computer software: a comprehensive analysis. Jurimetrics J, 23: 339, 357

Gilburne MR, Johnston RL, (1982) Trade secret protection for software generally and in the mass market. Computer/LJ, 3: 211, 255–263

Goldstein P (1986) Infringement of copyright in computer programs U Pitt L Rev, 47: 1119, 1126–1127

---

[105] Indian Copyright Act, S. 14.

[106] *Ibid.*, S. 52 deals with fair use provisions.

[107] *Sega Enters. Ltd.* v. *Accolade, Inc.*, 977 F.2d 1526 (1993), Decompilation, is the reversal of the process of compilation; that is, turning object code back into source code. Almost all jurisdictions, including India, have this exemption.

Guarda P (2013) Looking for a feasible form of software protection: copyright or patent, is that the question? Euro Intellect Property Rev, 35(8):445, 446
Hilty RM, Geiger C (2005) Patenting software? A judicial and socio-economic analysis. Int India Centre 36: 615, 619–622
Lerner J, Tirole J (2002) *Some* simple economics of open source, 50. J Indus Econ 197:200
Litman J (1990) The public domain. Emory LJ, 39: 965
McJohn SM (2000) The Paradoxes of free software. Geo Mason L Rev 9: 25, 26
Menell PS (1989) An analysis of the scope of copyright protection for application programs, Stan L Rev, 41: 1045, 1054–1055
Nguyen XTN et al. (2006) Intellectual property, software, and information licensing: law and practice, p 504
Samuelson PA (1954) The pure theory of public expenditure. Rev Econ & Statistics, 36: 387
Shneiderman B (1987) Designing the user interface: strategies for effective computer interaction pp 15–18
Stewart, SE (1996) Rhetoric and reality in Copyright Law. Mich Law Rev, 94: 1197
Stigler R (2014) Ooey GUI: The messy protection of graphical user interfaces, 12 Nw J Tech & Intell Prop, pp 215 37
Strasser M (2001) A new paradigm in intellectual property law? The case against open sources. Stan Tech Law Rev, p 4
Toong HD, Gupta A (1982), Personal computers, SCI pp 87, 88

Database Protection in India: Need for Reforms

K.D. Raju

Abstract Recently there is a spurt of database theft reported in India especially from the Business Processing Outsourcing (BPO) sector by employees in India. Database protection and data protection is not distinguished in any legislations in India clearly. Compilation of data is not protected in India under any sui generis legislation unlike in the developed country like EU. Now the protection can be given under "literary work" under the Copyright Act 1957. Courts in India held that compilation of databases are protected under the Copyright Act as "literary work" as held by the Delhi High Court in *Himalaya Drug Company* v. *Sumit*. The objective of this chapter is to explore database protection in India through various legal provisions, including Article 21 and 300A of the Indian Constitution, Copyright Act 1957, the IT Act, 2000 and various international agreements to which India is a party. Other country practices like in EU and US are examined to find out the possibility of adapting appropriate protection in India. The Indian jurisprudence is analyzed closely to understand the judicial opinion on this issue in the recent past. It closely analyses the question of applicability of copyright law to the protection of databases. The study concludes by suggesting appropriate ways of protection of databases in India.

Keywords Database protection · Copyright · India

K.D. Raju (✉)
Rajiv Gandhi School of Intellectual Property Law, IIT, Kharagpur, India
e-mail: rajukd@gmail.com

M.K. Sinha and V. Mahalwar (eds.), *Copyright Law in the Digital World*,
DOI 10.1007/978-981-10-3984-3_10

1 Introduction

A database is usually described as a compilation of works, data or a collection of other materials arranged in a systematic or methodical way.[1] The facts arranged with a certain level of creativity on the part of the author. The creativity is qualified for protection under the copyright provisions. Databases have always been commodities of both commercial value and social security in the modern digital era.[2] Electronic databases have become indispensable platforms in the information technology driven era. In the recent past the subject has got greater attention due to technological changes and legal regime to protect databases all over the world. Compilations were protected as "books" under copyright law of many countries. One theory of protection is the "sweat of the brow" and another one is the creativity of the author in compilations. Creativity is considered as a component of originality and provided protection. Innovations require incentives and copyright is the right given by law to the creators of literary, dramatic, musical and a variety of other works of mind. Commercial exploitation of copyright yields income to the creators and thus making pecuniary rewards to individual's creativity.[3] Under the Berne Convention databases constitute creative compilations which enjoy protection under copyright as literary works. The level of creativity required for such copyright protection is not defined by any international conventions. The "sweat of the brow" theory is prominent among countries and some kind of innovation, effort, investment or creativity is protected.

Copyright protection offers the indispensable incentives for the creation of new valuable works and the investment into production and distribution of cultural and information goods. The economic importance depends on the protection given to databases especially in the digital world. Protection of creativity has to be done through national legislations and other policies. Appropriate copyright or other sue generis system is indispensable for participation and co-operation in the international regimes. The advent of Trade Related Aspects of Intellectual Property Rights (TRIPs) Agreement under the World Trade Organization (WTO) regime.

The present chapter discusses about the current protection of databases under the international agreements. The second part of this chapter discusses various Indian legislations protects the database especially the Information Technology Act. The third part deals with database protection under the Indian Copyright Act and Indian court's decisions on the subject. The fourth part analyses the jurisprudence in other jurisdictions like the US and EU. The concluding part gives suggestion for a strong protection of database in India. It is argued that India requires a sue generis protection of database on the lines of EU for a stronger protection and easy and secure access to databases.

---

[1] Copyright and Databases.

[2] Report on Legal Protection for Databases.

[3] Study on Copyright Piracy in India.

2 Protection of Database Under TRIPs and Other International Agreements

Protection of database under the copyright laws of countries is problematic due to the development of technology and formats of data in the secured form. The basic principle of protection is the skill, labour and judgement of the author that is protected irrespective of the form in which the product appears e.g. whether one types a book on an old-fashioned typewriter or transforms it into a digitized form or in handwritten form. The collection of materials, assembly and arrangement of the pre-existing forms constitute original authorship under copyright protection.

Article 9 of the TRIPs agreement provides that "copyright protection shall extend to expressions and not to ideas." Article 10(2) of TRIPs facilitates the protection of computer programmes which reads, "Compilations of data or other material, whether in machine readable or other form, which by reason of the selection or arrangement of their contents constitute intellectual creations shall be protected as such. Such protection, which shall not extend to the data or material itself, shall be without prejudice to any copyright subsisting in the data or material itself."[4] It means that irrespective of the compilation in the form of machine readable or not, if there is an intellectual creation in the compilation, it can be protected under copyright protection. All the 164 WTO Members have to implement the provisions at the domestic level.

Article 2 of the Berne Convention for the Protection of Literary and Artistic Works 1886 (amended last in 1979) protects compilations of facts and factual databases. Article 2(5) specifically protects compilations or collections of literary or artistic works such as encyclopedias and anthologies on the reason for their selection and arrangement of contents constitute intellectual creations and thus it can be protected.

Article 5 of the WIPO Copyright Treaty 1996 provides protection to "compilations of data." It provides that "compilations of data or other material, in any form, which by reason of the selection or arrangement of their contents constitute intellectual creations, are protected as such. This protection does not extend to the data or the material itself and is without prejudice to any copyright subsisting in the data or material contained in the compilation."

WIPO has been discussing the introduction of protection of non-original database which presently does not come within the purview of copyright laws since 1996. The WIPO Diplomatic Conference on Certain Copyright and Neighboring Rights Questions which took place in Geneva from December 2 to 20, 1996 recognized that "databases are a vital element in the development of a global information infrastructure."[5]

---

[4] Article 10(2) of TRIPs, https://www.wto.org/english/tratop_e/trips_e/t_agm3_e.htm, visited on 21.02.2016.

[5] Existing National and Regional Legislation Concerning Intellectual Property in Databases.

In short, the Berne Convention, WIPO Copyright Treaty and the TRIPs agreement provides explicit provisions for the protection of compilation of databases. Even though the level of protection is different in domestic jurisdictions.

3 Database Protection in India

Article 21 of the Indian constitution provides for right to life and personal liberty. The Indian courts interpreted the provisions widely and included right to livelihood and right to privacy involved in the article as fundamental right. Property in the form of databases cannot be taken away by somebody without the due process of law. The State should take measures to protect and enjoy the right in a meaningful and effective way. Hence, protection of valuable databases are important in economic terms and protecting the rights of citizens in the absence of neither data protection law nor privacy law in India.

Indian Penal Code 1860 can also be effectively used against theft of data as "movable property." The information stored in computers in the form of databases can well be considered as movable property and nothing is excluding computer data from the definition. Misappropriation of such data can come within the purview of the penal law. Unauthorized access of such databases by employees can be considered as criminal breach of trust and penal provisions can be made applicable to such incidents happened in HSBC case.[6]

The Indian Contract Act 1872 also can be used for protection of databases in India. Strong database protection clauses can be incorporated into business and employment contracts for its breach. The data exporters and importers can protect their data under strong contract provisions. In case of breach, damages can be claimed and specific performance of the contract can also be enforced. These measures will boost the outsourcing industry in their business as well as protection of huge databases involves confidential data.

4 Information Technology Act 2000

Database protection involves a set of privacy laws, confidential information and other set of information which require stronger protection than copyright in India. Database protection in this chapter refers to compiled databases includes digital databases. There is no explicit law to protect privacy in India rather a set of provisions including constitutional provisions like Article 19(1)(a) and Article 21, right to life and personal liberty. The Information Technology Act, 2000 (IT Act) and Indian Contract Act, 1872 also deal with data protection.

[6] HSBC case.

Section 2(o) of the IT Act defines data as a representation of information, knowledge, facts, concepts or instructions which are being prepared or have been prepared in a formalized manner, and is intended to be processed, is being processed or has been processed in a computer system or computer network. It means that any kind of information prepared in a formalized manner is considered as "data."

Section 2(v) defines "information" to include data, text, images, sound, voice, codes, computer programmes, software and databases or micro film or computer generated micro fiche. Section 4 recognizes the legal recognition of electronic records as information and consequently "data."

Section 43(h) Explanation (ii) provides that "computer database" means a representation of information, knowledge, facts, concepts or instructions in text, image, audio, video that are being prepared or have been prepared in a formalized manner or have been produced by a computer, computer system or computer network and are intended for use in a computer, computer system or computer network. Section 43 imposes a penalty of INR 10 million for downloading data without consent.

Section 43A of the IT Act provides that where a body corporate, possessing, dealing or handling any sensitive personal data or information in a computer resource which it owns, controls or operates, is negligent in implementing and maintaining reasonable security practices and procedures and thereby causes wrongful loss or wrongful gain to any person, such body corporate shall be liable to pay damages by way of compensation, not exceeding five crore rupees, to the person so affected.

The Government of India had notified the Information Technology (Reasonable Security Practices and Procedures and Sensitive Personal Data or Information) Rules, 2011 under Section 43A of the IT Act, 2000. Rule 4 mandates that every body corporate that collects receives or stores personal information shall provide a privacy policy for handling and dealing with personal as well as sensitive personal data. Such policy has to be published in the website of the body corporate. Negligent use of such data, losing such data due to the lack of reasonable security practices, or wrongful gain to any person, such body corporate may be held liable to pay damages to the person so affected to the tune of five crores.

Section 72 of the IT Act provides that if any person concerned breaches such confidentiality and privacy, discloses such information or data to any other person shall be punished with imprisonment for a term which may extend to 2 years, or with fine which may extend to one lakh rupees or with both. Section 66 of the 2008 amendment provides that "if any person, dishonestly or fraudulently does any act referred to in Section 43, he shall be punishable with imprisonment for a term which may extend to three years or with fine which may extend to five lakh rupees or with both."

The IT Act defines and imposes responsibility on network service provider as an intermediary who is liable for any known misuse of third party information or data or for not exercising due diligence to prevent the offence. All the Business Process Outsourcing (BPO) companies in India are liable for any leak of information under "intermediaries." The IT Act covers offences committed outside India irrespective of the offender's nationality as far as the computer system is in India.

5 Information Technology (Reasonable Security Practices and Procedures and Sensitive Personal Data or Information) Rules, 2011

India came up with the Information Technology (Reasonable Security Practices and Procedures and Sensitive Personal Data or Information) Rules, 2011 in order to protect the data of corporates, data providers and government. Rule 3 protects sensitive personal data such as passwords, credit card information, medical and biometric records. It also includes a set of other data as well:

(1) password;
(2) financial information such as Bank account or credit card or debit card or other payment instrument details;
(3) physical, physiological and mental health condition;
(4) sexual orientation;
(5) medical records and history;
(6) biometric information;
(7) any detail relating to the above clauses as provided to body corporate for providing service; and
(8) any of the information received under above clauses by body corporate for processing, stored or processed under lawful contract or otherwise.[7]

Rule 4 provides that any body-corporate that collects, stores, passes, deals or handle any information shall provide a privacy policy for handling such information including sensitive data must ensure that the same are available only under a lawful contract. Rule 6 clearly restricts that such data can be only revealed with the prior permission from the provider of such information. Other than these rules there is no separate data protection rule in the country. These database collections are prone to theft and the Government came up with these rules after the HSBC Bank case involving theft of customer data by its employees in India. It involves the damage to the reputation of the bank as well as privacy violations of customers in other parts of the world.

IT Act 2000 provides civil and penal remedies in case of violation of databases or data theft which are not sufficient in the information technology age. Section 10A inserted by the amendment in 2008 to the IT Act validates online contracts made in an electronic form.

---

[7] Ministry of Communication, Government of India Notification dated 11 April 2011.

6 Indian Copyright Act and Database Protection

Tangible properties are protected under Article 300A of the Indian Constitution, but intellectual property is not protected under Indian Constitution. The intangible form of property makes it difficult to protect it by using the traditional mechanisms of protection. New legal mechanisms are required to ensure that such properties are not stolen. Copyright Act, 1957 protects copyright form of intellectual property rights. "literary work" protects computer databases as well. Copying a computer database or distributing a database amounts to infringement of copyright which is attractive of civil and criminal remedies. Data protection is meant to protect the privacy of information and individuals. This is mainly to protect creativity and "sweat of the brow."

Section 2(o) of the Copyright Act, 1957 provides that literary work includes "literary work" and computer programmes, table and compilations including *computer literary data bases* while Section 13(1)(a) defines an original literary work. The process of creating database includes huge investments and effort. The objective of commercial exploitation of such effort is quite natural and justified under the "sweat of the brow" doctrine. In the advent of technology, databases can be easily copied and lot of economic loss can happen to the copyright owner who created the database. The increased dependence of technology and computers can cause more danger and possibility of increased copying.[8]

Computer softwares and databases are protected under this provision after 1994 amendments to the Copyright Act. The skill, judgment and labour of the authors are protected irrespective of the form in digitalized or printed. Database owners solely rely on copyright protection for their literary works. In order to qualify the protection standards, the subject matter must show some creativity or originality in selection or arrangement of contents of the compilation. In *Eastern Book Company* v. *Desai*,[9] it was held that putting paragraph numbers and correcting mistakes of a court judgment were not enough creativity and there could not be copyright in the reproductions. But if the plaintiff prepares head notes with his own skill and labour, there can be copyright in such head notes. In cases like *McMillan* v. *Suresh Chunder Deb*,[10] *and Govindan* v. *E.M. Gopalakrishna*,[11] it was held that compilations like dictionaries developed through devotion of time, capital, energy, brain skill and labour, taken from a common source, even though the originality level is small, it can be considered as a literary work and can be protected under copyright. In both the decisions Indian courts followed the doctrine of "sweat of the brow." The Court held that in law books and in books as mentioned above there is very little amount of originality but the same is protected by law and no man is entitled

---

[8] Apar Gupta 2007.

[9] AIR 2001 (Delhi) 203.

[10] (1890) ILR 17 (Cal) 951, 961.

[11] AIR 1955 (Mad) 391.

to steal or appropriate for himself the result of another's brain, skill or labour even in such works. The Court further clarified that where there is a common source, the person relying on it must prove that he actually went to the common source from where he borrowed, employing his own skill, labour and brains and that he did not merely copied.

In *University of London Press, Ltd.* v. *University Tutorial Press, Ltd.*,[12] dealing with the meaning of the words 'original literary work' that the original does not mean expression of original or inventive thought. The Copyright Act is not concerned with the original ideas, but with the expression of thought. The originality which is required relates to the expression of thought and the Act does not require that the expression must be in original or novel form. The work must not be copied from any other work and it should originate from the author itself. It is clear that the compilation work need not be an original literary work. In *Ladbroke (Football) Ltd.* v. *William Hill (Football) Ltd.*,[13] the court held that, the concept of originality was considered on the basis of one's skill, judgment and/or labour in the context of compilation. The "skill and judgment" test is approved by the Supreme Court of India in *Eastern Book Company & Ors.* v. *D.B. Modak & Anr.*[14]

In *H. Blacklock and Co. Ltd.* v. *C. Arthur Pearson Ltd.*,[15] Joyce, J. observed that "Under the present Copyright Act, copyright subsists in every original 'literary work' which includes compilations; so that I suppose the list of names which forms or is contained in the index to Bradshaw is entitled to copyright as much as any other part of the publication."[16]

In *Burlington Home Shopping Pvt. Ltd.* v. *Rajnish Chibber and Anr.*,[17] after referring to the provisions of Section 17(c) of the Copyright Act which provides that if a work is made in the course of other's employment under a contract of service or apprenticeship it is the employer who is the first owner of the copyright therein in the absence of any agreement to the contrary, a reference has been made as to what can be 'compilations' that has to be included in literary works and such information would include a list of clients and their addresses.

In *Himalaya Drug Co.* v. *Sumit*,[18] the plaintiff's website was in respect of herbal database and the defendant infringed the database. They copied all the detailed information of the herbal database. The Delhi High Court ordered a permanent injunction against the defendant restraining from infringing upon the plaintiff's database. The Court found that the defendant has copied the entire herbal database of the plaintiff and has thereby infringed the copyright of the plaintiff. "The plaintiff has also been able to demonstrate that the defendants have attempted to pass off its

[12] [1916] 2 Chap. 601.

[13] [1964] 1 WLR 273 (HL).

[14] 12th December 2007.

[15] (1915) 2 Chap. 376.

[16] *Shyamlal Paharia & Anr* v. *Gaya Prasad Gupta 'Rasal,'* AIR 1971 All 192.

[17] 61 (1996) DLT 6.

[18] 126 (2006) DLT 23, 2006 (32) PTC 112 Del.

herbal database as and for that of the plaintiff's and have also violated the 'trade dress' rights that exist in respect of the plaintiff's herbal database." The court also awarded a punitive damages to the tune of Rs. 7,94,227/-.

In *Diljit Titus, Advocate & Ors.* v. *Alfred A Adebare & Ors.*,[19] Delhi High Court held that copyright in a database prepared by a junior advocate during his tenure with senior advocate is with the senior advocate and using his resources vest with the employer. Court relying on Section 17(1)(c) of the Copyright Act, observed that work carried out during the course of employment under a contract of service or apprenticeship, copyright is with the employer.

7 Database Protection in Other Jurisdictions

7.1 United States

Database in the US is generally protected as compilations under Copyright Act under literary and artistic works.[20] Compilations are defined as a collection and assembling of preexisting materials or of data that are selected in such a way that the resulting work as a whole constitutes an original work of authorship but not on the underlying material or data.[21] A database of selected quotations from the U.S. President which involves enough original and creative expression that it is protected by copyright even though such quotations as such are not protected. The database of facts are also protected as compilation which involves enough original expression to qualify for protection. However, facts as such are not copyrightable under Section 103. This is mainly because of the fact/expression dichotomy which exists in all works of authorship.[22]

In *Feist Publications, Inc.* v. *Rural Telephone Service Company, Inc.*,[23] the US Supreme Court held that, a compilation is not copyrightable per se, but is copyrightable only if its facts have been "selected, coordinated, or arranged in such a way that the resulting work as a whole constitutes an original work of authorship". In this case copying from a telephone directory was under question and both the lower courts held in favour of Rural Telephone, but the Supreme Court was of the opinion that Rural's white pages were not selected, coordinated, or arranged in such a way as to create an original work of authorship. Rural's selection of listings—subscribers' names, towns, and telephone numbers–was obvious and lacked the modicum of creativity necessary to transform mere selection into copyrightable expression. The Court confirmed the theory of "sweat of the brow" or "industrious

[19] 130 (2006) DLT 330, 2006 (32) PTC 609 Del.

[20] 17 U.S.C. § 101.

[21] 17 U.S.C. § 103(b).

[22] The Future of Database Protection in US Copyright Law 2001.

[23] 499 U.S. 340 (1991).

collection" test of copyrightability. The Court followed the 1918 common law rule in *International News Service v Associated Press*, that "copyright provides no protection for facts …".[24] In this case two competing news agencies were entangled in dispute over copying news items from the plaintiff during the First World War. Justice Pitney in a majority opinion found that AP had a quasi property right in the news gathered and the right exist against competitors. This the theory of unfair competition/misappropriation is confined to the INS case. Non-creative works may not be given protection, that may promotes duplication of databases.

In the case of *ProCD, Incorporated* v. *Matthew Zeidenberg and Silken Mountain Web Services, Inc.*,[25] the plaintiff has compiled information from more than 3,000 telephone directories into a computer database. The end user of the CD Rom extracted a large portion of the database and made available over internet in his web site to the public. The lower court rejected all copyright claims and found that the shrinkwrap license that controlled the end user's right to use the data was both unenforceable (as a shrink wrap license) and preempted by the Copyright Act. In an appeal to the 7th Circuit Court, it was acknowledged that the database might not be sufficiently original to be protected by copyright. As a result, there was no copyright infringement by the end-user. The Court also found that end-user to be guilty of breach of contract, since the shrink-wrap license for the CD ROM prohibited the end-user's conduct.[26]

But in *CCC Information Services* v. *Maclean Hunter Market Reports*,[27] the court found computer database to be protectable element. A larger market holder copied the car valuation of a smaller player, Red Book and many customers are shifted from Red Book to CCC Information. In this case the Court found creativity on the part of the respondent and held that the valuations are original creations, their logical arrangement, fitting for the needs of the market, does not negate their originality.[28]

In *Kregos* v. *Associated Press*,[29] it was held that "validity of Kregos's compilation copyright could not be rejected for lacking, as a matter of law, the requisite originality and creativity. It was also held that Kregos's forms did not evince a merger of idea and expression, because the potentially relevant data about pitching were numerous, and there were numerous means of expressing the idea of rating pitchers' performances. It was further held that the district court erred in holding the "blank form" doctrine barred copyright in this case, because Kregos's forms, unlike check stubs, or a blank diary, convey information." It means that "requisite originality and creativity" need not be completely proved.

---

[24] 248 US 215 (1918).

[25] United States Court of Appeals, Seventh Circuit, decided on 20th June 1996.

[26] Database Legal Protection.

[27] 44 F.3d 61 (2d Cir. 1994).

[28] Ibid.

[29] United States Court of Appeal, Kregos II, 937 F.2d at 710.

In *Key Publications, Inc.* v. *Chinatown Today Publishing Enterprises Inc.*,[30] the Second Circuit sustained the copyrightability of the yellow pages of a telephone directory for New York's Chinese-American community. The court found that the selection of entries in Key's directory was an addition, the arrangement of the directory into categories (e.g., Accountants, Bridal Shops, Shoe Stores, Bean Curd and Bean Sprout Shops) was, when "viewed in the aggregate," original, because it "entailed the *de minimis* thought needed to withstand the originality requirement".

In *Victor Lalli Enterprises, Inc.* v. *Big Red Apple, Inc.*,[31] the Second Circuit found insufficient creativity to support a copyright. The compilation at issue in *Lalli* was comprised of "lucky numbers" used in gambling, arranged in a grid with months along the vertical axis and days of the month along the horizontal axis. The numbers were computed according to a formula that was standard in that industry. The court found no originality in either the selection or arrangement of the data: "Lalli exercises neither selectivity in what he reports nor creativity in how he reports it." The compilation was therefore held to be non copyrightable. This position was confirmed in *Matthew Bender & Co.* v. *West Pub. Co.*,[32] in which it was ruled without written opinion that West's pagination of reported cases was not copyrightable, and it was held that West's editorial revision of cases themselves entails no copyrightable.

Creativity and judgment is core in the copyrightability of databases. In *Warren Pub., Inc.* v. *Microdos Data Corp.*,[33] plaintiff "did not exercise any creativity or judgment in 'selecting' cable systems to include in its Fact book, but rather included the entire relevant universe known to it." In spite of the fact that the copyrightability of the plaintiff's compilation was conceded by the defendant (and therefore not an issue on appeal), the court did not find any element of the plaintiff's work that it examined to be protectable. From a plaintiff's standpoint, this has the same effect as a finding of non-copyrightability, since the only conduct that arguably can be said to infringe is verbatim duplication of the entire work.

The doctrine of "soft facts" or "soft ideas" articulated by the Second Circuit in *CCC Information Servs., Inc.* v. *Maclean Hunter Market Reports, Inc.* In *CCC.*, the Second Circuit posited that there are facts or ideas that are "infused with the author's taste or opinion," as opposed to explaining phenomena or furnishing solutions to the problems. The court recognized that using the merger doctrine to rule out protection for the compilation itself by characterizing as "ideas" the criteria used to select or arrange its contents would render copyright for compilations "illusory." But copying of features such as positions of symbols and street alignments in a pectoral form did not constitute infringement.[34] So the standard of copyrightability is held clearly in *Mid America Title Co.* v. *Kirk*,[35] that "the element

[30] 945 F.2d at 513–514 (2d Cir. 1991)

[31] 936 F.2d 671 (2d Cir. 1991).

[32] 1997 U.S. Dist. LEXIS 6915.

[33] 115 F.3d 1509 (11th Cir. 1997).

[34] *Alexandria Drafting Co.* v. *Amsterdam*, 1997 U.S. Dist. LEXIS 8197.

[35] 991 F.2d 417.

of copyrightable originality in a compilation claim is often subtle, and therefore a determination at the pleading stage will often be impossible."

In the case of *Mead Data Central, Inc.*, v. *West Publishing, Corp.*,[36] the issue was whether the 'star-paging' feature of the LEXIS system infringed West's copyright in its case reporters. The court held that because the feature incorporated the page numbers of West's printed reporters, Mead had, in fact, taken copyrightable expression in the form of West's selection and arrangement of the reported opinions. The situation in Mead would seem to fall squarely within the first of our categories since the selection and arrangement found copyrightable by the court lied in the format of the reporters and not in the structure of an electronic database.

The US approach to database is very clear that it is eligible for copyright protection only if their selection and arrangement are sufficiently original.

8 European Union

The EU has adopted Directive on the legal protection of database in 1996.[37] EU adopted "sui generis" protection of databases irrespective of it being original or not.[38] The Directive is applicable to analogue and digital databases. Under the Directive, there is two tier protection available for databases, original and creative databases enjoy copyright protection. The very issue of whether modern databases form suitable subject matter for copyright protection is somewhat contentious in the digital age. This is mainly because in the digital age they may be copied and violate copyright protection. There are different opinions on the strict protection of copyright to such compilations in the EU. Hence, it adopted a two prone strategy and protection, firstly, copyright protection for original works and secondly, those data bases which fail to reach the threshold of originality protected under 15 year sui generis protection. But the maker of the database has to show "substantial investment" in the preparation of the database.

The EU directive defines "database" broadly as "a collection of independent works, data or other materials arranged in a systematic or methodical way and individually accessible by electronic or other means."[39] Databases are included whether it is electronic or other form. But the European Court held that "the collection should be contained in a fixed base, of some sort, and include technical means such as electronic, electromagnetic or electro-optical processes … or other means, such as index, a table of contents, or a particular plan or method of

[36] 799 F.2d 1219 (8th Cir. 1986), cert. denied, 479 U.S. 1070 (1987).

[37] Directive 96/9/EC, 1996.

[38] The EU Single Market.

[39] Article 1(2) of the Directive.

classification, to allow the retrieval of any independent material contained within it."[40] The sui generis right is available to the maker of a database where there has been qualitatively and quantitatively a substantial investment in obtaining, verification or presentation of the contents of the database.

Following the US Supreme Court decision in *Feist*, the Dutch Supreme Court in *Van Daele* v. *Romme*,[41] raised the concern of adequacy of copyright protection for databases in EU. In this case the plaintiff brought an infringement suit against the defendant who has copied the 230,000 key word entries in the plaintiff's dictionary into his electronic database and offered the database to crossword enthusiasts. The Utrecht District Court and the Amsterdam Court of Appeals both granted an injunction against the defendant, holding that the plaintiff's selection of keywords was original under Dutch compilation copyright law. However, in 1991, the Hoge Radd (Supreme Court) reversed this decision and held that a compilation of factual data does not meet the originality threshold and cannot be protected by copyright. But it was held that the dictionary itself is copyrightable as it reflected the personal view of the author regarding the nature of the current Dutch language. This case clearly put the boundaries of protection available to factual compilations in EU.

In 2004 the ECJ delivered a series of judgments concerning database directive in which the Court separated the investment made to create the data from the investment needed to obtain, verify, or present it.[42] The ECJ found that investment necessary to benefit from the sui generis right must be in obtaining, presenting, or verifying preexisting data. It means that database producer can benefit from the sui generis right only when investment is attributable directly to database protection. A qualitatively negligible part of the contents of a database may in fact represent, in terms of obtaining, verification or presentation, significant human, technical or financial investment.[43]

In the matter of digital database infringement in *Football Dataco* v. *Sportradar*,[44] the ECJ held that database infringement not only occurs at the location of the server where the data is sent from, but also in the place where the internet user accesses the data. In the present case the Court considered the possibility of protecting football league fixture lists on the basis of the 1996 Directive. The Court held that such fixture lists cannot, in principle, be protected on the basis of the 'sui generis' right provided for under the Directive. This judgment is important in the backdrop of digital databases and its vulnerability to piracy from anywhere in the world.

---

[40] *Fixtures Marketing Ltd.* v. *Organismos Prognostikon Agonon Podosfairou* EG (2004) ECR I-10549 (paras 29–30), C-444/02.

[41] Jan 4, 1991 - HR 04-01-1991, NJ 1991, 608.

[42] Case C-338/02, *Fixtures Marketing Ltd.* v. *Svenska Spel* AB, 2004 ECR I-10479; Case C-444/02, *Fixtures Marketing Ltd.* v. *Organismos Prognostikon Agonon Podosfairou*, 2004 ECR I-10549; *Fixtures Marketing Ltd.* v. *Veikkaus AB*, 2004 ECR I-10365; Case C-203/02, *British Horseracing Bd. Ltd.* v. *William Hill Org. Ltd.*, 2004 ECR I-10415.

[43] C-203/02, *British Horseracing Board Ltd.* v. *William Hill Org. Ltd.*, 2004 ECR I-10415, Judgment dated November 9, 2004.

[44] (C-173/11).

"They are costly to produce, but they are easy to reproduce or copy."[45] The "sweat of the brow" theory is very much prevalent in the UK as well with regard to the database protection.[46] If the author has used his labour and skill in the creation of the work, it is eligible for copyright protection irrespective of the originality of the work. But factual databases are not protected unless their "selection, organization and accumulation" has beyond the expertise of an average programmer.[47] But the "substantial investment" theory has prevailed after the EU directive on database in 1996.[48] The cost of collecting and maintaining current data on thousands of real estate properties was held to be "substantial investment" by a District Court of Hague.[49] At the same time it was held that newspaper headlines are mere "spin-off" and there is no substantial investment and cannot be copyrighted.[50] But the court held that newspaper articles were copyrightable works.[51] Deep links to newspaper articles and distributing headlines from newspapers were held to be liable for infringement of copyright.[52] Hence, all kind of databases are essential element of the continuous advances in human knowledge and productivity.[53]

In the case of *Ryanair Ltd* v. *PR Aviation BV*,[54] the court considered the question of usage of data for commercial purpose from the website of the complainant. The court held that "even assuming the digital information made public by Ryanair were covered by the protection of written materials ('geschriftenbeschering'), for the purpose of Article 10(1)(1) of the Auteurswet, PR Aviation had not infringed Ryanair's rights, given that its conduct corresponded to normal, within the meaning of Article 24a(1) of the Auteurswet, and therefore legitimate use of the Ryanair website."

In appeal also the Court held that no criterion other than that of originality is effective for the purposes of protection by copyright. Observing that it follows from the judgment of the *Gerechtshof te Amsterdam* that Ryanair's data set does not satisfy that criterion and cannot be protected.

The court in *Freistaat Bayern* v. *Verlag Esterbauer GmbH*,[55] confirmed the position in *Fixtures Marketing* and held that the "concept of database must be understood as applying to 'literary, artistic, musical or other collections of works or collections of other material such as texts, sound, images, numbers, facts, and data"

---

[45] *Mathew Bender & CO* v. *West Publishing Co.* See also Nelson 1999.

[46] *Waterlow Publishers Ltd v Rose* The Times 8 Dec 1989.

[47] *Incassoprogramm* decision of 9 May 1985 of German Federal Court.

[48] 96/9/EC, 11 March 1996.

[49] *NVM* v. *De Telegraaf*, Judgment dated 12 September 2000.

[50] *Algemeen Dagblad a.o.* v. *Eureka*, Judgment dated 22 August 2000.

[51] *Danish Newspaper Organization* v. *Newsbooster*, Copenhagen Court, Judgment dated 24 June 2002.

[52] *Copiepresse* v. *Google Inc.*, Court of First Instance, Brussels, Judgment dated 5 September 2006.

[53] Manap et al. 2012.

[54] C-30/14.

[55] C-490/14, judgment dated 29 October 2015.

and the protection granted thereunder relates both to electronic and non-electronic databases.

The EU sui generis and two tier protection is a unique one and "substantial investment" provision gives the core of the principles according to the 1996 directive. It also protects extraction of the database for a period of 15 years from the day of its creation subject to the 1996 directive. It is based on the "sweat of the brow" theory and subsequent "substantial investment" formula. Protection and safeguards must be given to digital databases which is a concern for the future.[56] The EU model is a strong economic base for the protection of original and non-original databases. It provides a dedicated balance between the creators of the database to protect their economic investments and the interests of users through secure access to information.[57]

9 Conclusion

The legal protection of database involves complex issues involving extraneous factors. The "sweat of the brow" doctrine is firmly prevalent in many countries. There must be provisions for protecting original and non-original databases so that all kind of compilation databases are protected in the digital era. Information technology has been developed as an indispensable tool as a means of information and knowledge exchange. Copyright protection of such comprehensive databases remains to be problematic especially when they are accessed through the internet, beyond territorial jurisdictions and legislations.

Adopting "sui generis" legislations like in the EU is most adaptable to India for protecting original databases. But protection of non-original databases is problematic in India. A database can be protected under the copyright law either as a compilation of works, collection of independent works or database as literary works. Databases are always updated and are protected for 15 years in EU. There can be evergreening of copyright protection for databases. Hence, when adopting sui generis protection it may not be suitable to developing countries, originality to be kept as the core principle of protection.

Strict application of the "sweat of the brow" doctrine per se also may not be suitable to India as the copyright law is confined to originality of works. Non-creative non-original works may not be protected in India as it will lead to over protection and it will undermine the access to information to public at large. There must be correct balance between owner's rights and access to information to public.

It is better to adopt the principles held in *Feist* decision by the US Supreme Court that "selected, coordinated, or arranged in such a way that the resulting work as a whole constitutes an original work of authorship". The originality criteria along

[56] Schneider 1998.

[57] Powell 1996.

with the "sweat of the brow" principle and "substantial investment" criteria can be adopted in the Indian database law.

"Skill, labour and creativity" can be the basic principle on which the database protection can be provided in India as held by Indian courts. Copyrighted and digitally stored databases are going to increase in India. India should come with appropriate protection for databases which is a need of the hour as lot of foreign companies are outsourcing their work in India and databases has to be protected in an appropriate form in conformity with international agreements.

References

Copyright and Databases. http://www.esa.int/About_Us/Law_at_ESA/Intellectual_Property_Rights/Copyright_and_databases. Accessed 20 Feb 2016

Database Legal Protection. http://www.bitlaw.com/copyright/database.html. Accessed 22 Feb 2016

Existing National and Regional Legislation Concerning Intellectual Property in Databases, WIPO. http://www.wipo.int/meetings/en/doc_details.jsp?doc_id=687. Accessed 25 Feb 2016

Gupta A (2007) Protection of databases in India: copyright termination Sui generis conception. J Intellect Property Rights 12: 422–427

HSBC case. http://www.moneycontrol.com/news-topic/hsbc-data-theft-case/. Accessed 09 Mar 2016

Manap NA et al (May 2012) Is database protected under copyright? A legal analysis Int J Inf Electron Eng 2(3): 414–417

Nelson (1999) Recent development: seeking refuge from a technology storm: the current status of database protection legislation after the sinking of the collection of information anti-piracy act and the second circuit Affirmation of Matthew V. West Publishing 6. J Intellect Property Law 453–455

Powel M (1996) The European Union's database directive: an international antidote to the side effects of feist. Fortham Int Law J 20(4): 1215–1250

Report on Legal Protection for Databases, US Copyright Office. http://www.copyright.gov/reports/db4.pdf. Accessed 20 Feb 2016

Schneider M (1998) The EU database directive. Berkeley Tech Law J 13(1): 551–564

Study on Copyright Piracy in India, Ministry of Human Resource Development Government of India. http://copyright.gov.in/Documents/STUDY%20ON%20COPYRIGHT%20PIRACY%20IN%20INDIA.pdf. Accessed 2 Feb 2016

The EU Single Market. http://ec.europa.eu/internal_market/copyright/prot-databases/index_en.htm . Accessed 25 Feb 2016

The Future of Database Protection in US Copyright Law, 2001 Duke Law and Technol Rev, 22 May 2001

Copyright and the Digital Media: Perspective and Challenges in the New Legal Regime in India

C.P. Dayananda Murthy

Abstract The intellectual property rights have undergone a major transformation in the fast paced economic, social, cultural and technological development. The technological development has increased the contours of intellectual creation and innovation. We are living in the knowledge economy which has enhanced the focus on intellectual creation. This has lead to the debate on whether the intellectual property requires greater protection. Whether there is a requirement of change in the existing law or they are sufficient to protect the intellectual property in this technological world. The technology has digitalized the form of creation and innovation. This has affected all form of intellectual properties i.e. patent, trademarks, copyright, trade secrets, etc. The author will explore issues and challenges and the changes in the copyright law due to the technological development. Copyright law protects the author or creator who by skill, capital and labour creates an original work. Copyright protects the author by providing exclusive rights to create and reproduce the work. However, technology allows flawless, inexpensive and instantaneous copying, reproducing and distributing the work. There is an enormous growth not only in the creation of works but also the illicit consumption. The protection of copyright work in the digital world is the greatest challenge faced by the copyright law. The copyright and its infringements have no territorial boundaries. The International Conventions including the WIPO Copyright Treaty, 1996 and the WIPO Performances and Phonograms Treaty, 1996 oblige countries to provide adequate legal protection and remedies against the circumvention and also imposes obligations concerning Digital Rights Management. India amended its Copyright law in 2012 to be in consonance with these developments. The chapter looks into the key issues, challenges and implications to the copyright and the judicial response to the changes.

C.P. Dayananda Murthy (✉)
Damodaram Sanjivayya National Law University, Visakhapatnam, Andhra Pradesh, India
e-mail: dmurthy70@gmail.com

M.K. Sinha and V. Mahalwar (eds.), *Copyright Law in the Digital World*,
DOI 10.1007/978-981-10-3984-3_11

1 Introduction

Computer and internet Technology have led to the major transformation of economic, social, cultural issues with reference to the Intellectual Property Rights (IPR). The technological development has increased the contours of intellectual creation and innovation. In this knowledge economy, the debate was whether the IP requires greater protection, which also focused on, whether existing legal regime would suffice for protection of digitalized form of creation and innovation or new laws would be essential. The change in law had become imperative. The existing law needs to undergo the change as the technological innovations happening need a newer protection to all form of IP, i.e. patent, trademarks, copyright, trade secrets, etc. and in particular have heralded considerable effect on copyright protection. This chapter explores the issues and challenges to the copyright material in the digital media and the effect of Copyright (Amendment) Act, 2012.

The digital media has opened a new vista of dealing with copyright and related issues. The new legal regime in India and its implications on copyright have to be understood on the basis of the amendments to the Copyright Act, 1957 (The Act). The Copyright law protects the author or creator of an original work. The creation of work shall be encouraged and rewarded which has a necessity for the progress of the society. The primary function of copyright law is to protect the fruits of a man's work, labour, skill, capital and judgment.[1] Copyright law as known is to reward the owner/creator of a work in economic terms.[2]

Copyright provides the exclusive right to create and reproduce the work. Hence, the objective of copyright law is virtually to protect and promote new creative works based on the idea of their own or with the existing information or work.[3] Creation of copyright works is a cumulative process where one work builds upon its

[1] *Sulamangalam R Jayalakshmi* v. *Meta Musicals,* AIR 2000 Mad. 454. (the plaintiffs claim for temporary injunction granted in respect of musical work and literary works).

[2] "The copyright, protection finds its justification in fair play. When a person produces something with his skill and labour, it normally belongs to him and the other person would not be permitted to make a profit of the skill and labour of the original author and it is for this reason the Act, gives to the authors certain exclusive rights in relation to certain work referred in the Act. The object of the Act is to protect the author of the copyright work from an unlawful reproduction or exploitation of his work by others. Copyright is a right to stop others from exploiting the work without the consent or assent of the owner of the copyright. A copyright law presents a balance between the interests and rights of the author and that of the public in protecting the public domain, or to claim the copyright and protect it under the copyright statute." Quoted in *Eastern Book Company* v. *D.B. Modak,* (2008) 1 SCC 1.

[3] *Ibid., Sony Corp.* v. *Universal City Studios, Inc.* 464 U.S. 417(1984)*; Fiest Publication Inc.* v. *Rural Telephone Service,* 499 U.S. 340 (1991).

predecessor and vitally depending on access to works in the public domain[4] and at the same time, it serves the public interest by making available any creative works to the public. Therefore, on one hand it protects the authors with an incentive to create new and original works and on the other hand balancing it, by limiting the protection in order that no person monopolises the creativity of any work.[5] Copyright is a property worthy of protection with certain limitation and exceptions keeping in mind the public interest.[6]

The Act had to undergo changes from time to time, due to technological developments. Number of questions arise as to when and what kind of protection can be provided to the works available in the digital media. The works including computer programmes or software have been protected under the copyright law in almost all the countries. In few countries particularly the United States it is also protected under the Patent law. This chapter attempts to understand the key issues, challenges and implications to the copyright law and the judicial response to the changes.

The WWW and the Internet has made the law makers to think of broadening the scope of copyright protection in the digital media. All kinds of works including e-books, musical works, artistic works, films and sound recording including performances are now made available over internet. Technology allows flawless, inexpensive and instantaneous copying, including the reproduction and distribution of the work. There is enormous growth in the creation of works and also in its illicit or illegal consumption. The protection of copyright work in the digital media poses the greatest challenge for the legal systems. The piracy of copyright work not only affects the owners but, also hampers the economic development and loss to the state exchequer.

Copyright and its infringements have no territorial boundaries. The WIPO Copyright Treaty, 1996 (WCT) and the WIPO Performances and Phonograms Treaty, 1996 (WPPT) obliges countries to provide adequate legal protection, remedies against the circumvention and also imposes obligations concerning Digital Rights Management. The WCT and WPPT oblige, the member states to make provisions for protection of technological measures and anti-circumvention devices. India though, not a member of the WCT or WPPT, but, by virtue of the Agreement on Trade Related Intellectual Property Rights (TRIPs), the law had to be amended in order to protect the computer programme and performers and phonogram rights.

[4] For e.g. "composers recombine sounds that they have heard; novelists draw on other plots; playwrights use other literary characters; multimedia artists combine many small pieces of existing works into new creations; software writers use logic and algorithms from other software; and cinematographers, actors, choreographers, architects and sculptors transform currently existing works." Chandra 2010.

[5] *Computer Associates International Inc* v. *Altai Inc.*, 982 F.2d 693 (2d Cir. 1992).

[6] Penguin *Books Ltd* v. *India Book distributors*, AIR 1985 Del 29.

India amended its Copyright law in 2012 to be on at par with the international scenario.[7] India being a member of the Berne Convention, 1886 and TRIPs Agreement, 1994, has complied with the international norms.

2 Nature and Scope of Copyright in the Digital Media

The IP is recognized as goods entailing intangible rights in all jurisdictions. Copyright may exist in the literary work, artistic works, musical work, cinematograph or sound recording and all related rights. The way any publication is made of such work, after the invention of computer and the internet has undergone a major change. Computer and software programmes have entered into the arena of IP, wherein new issues and challenges have emerged on the rights and obligation for a copyright owner. The theft of IP is occurring in large scale and beyond territorial boundaries. Piracy over internet or cyber space is widespread.

Copyright law protects creation of original work for a limited period with the right to enjoy an exclusive right to reproduce the work. The protection rests on the principle that, anyone who by skill, capital and labour creates an original work shall reap the benefits.[8] Digital piracy is about questions of ownership and the right of developers to benefit from their creations, including monetary benefits.[9] Piracy leads to loss of revenue to publishers (in terms of fewer sales), authors (non-payment of royalty) and the national exchequer (non-payment of income tax and other levies payable by publishers/authors).[10] The study listed the different forms of piracy in computer software.[11]

---

[7] The Act was amended from time to time to the changing circumstances and technological developments, the Act has been amended in 1983, 1984, 1992, 1994, 1999 and 2012.

[8] *Supra* note 2. See *Sony Corp.* v. *Universal City Studios, Inc.* 464 U.S. 417(1984); *Fiest Publication Inc. v Rural Telephone Service,* 499 U.S. 340 (1991). *MacMillan* v. *Cooper,* AIR 1924 PC 75.

[9] Atallah et al. 2008, Turner and Von Heusinger 2008.

[10] Study on Copyright Piracy in India, Ministry of Human Resource Development, Government of India, with the National Productivity Council, 1999, *available at:* http://copyright.gov.in/Documents/Study%20on%20copyright%20piracy%20in%20India.pdf. (last visited on Dec. 25, 2016).

[11] According to the study the software piracy takes place in the following circumstances

- Office copying—illegal copies being made from a licensed programme and get installed in many other computers
- Network Piracy—software programme is accessed by more than permitted
- Internet Piracy—programmes are downloaded or sent via electronic mails without licence
- Resellers—unauthorised retailers sell pirated software by copying software into floppy discs or CD ROMs and sell them
- Hardware Sellers—suppliers assembling components sell computers with pirated software already installed.
- Counterfeiting—sell duplicate software unknown to the users (user believes it to be legitimate).

Ranking	Top ten countries leading the online piracy	%
1.	China	91
2.	Columbia	90
3.	Russia	80
4.	Malaysia	75
5.	India	60
6.	Turkey	45
7.	Taiwan	44
8.	Brazil	35
9.	Saudi Arabia	35
10.	Italy	20
Sl. No.	Most pirated items on the web	%
1.	Pornography	35.8
2.	Movies	35.2
3.	TV Shows	14.2
4.	PC/Console Games	6.7
5.	Software	6.7
6.	Music	2.9
	E books	0.2

Source for the tables 34 Startling Internet Piracy Statistics, Nov 24, 2014. 34 Startling Internet Piracy Statistics.

The Hindu Business Line news reports that the piracy level in India remains at 60%. About $ 2.9 billion worth of unlicensed software were being installed in 2013 as per Business Software Alliance (BSA) survey. India was just behind China, in the Asia Pacific region in terms of commercial value of unlicensed software sold in 2013. However, India's piracy level reduced to 60% in 2013 from 63% in 2011.[12] Globally, 43% of software installations were unlicensed (value of $62.7 billion).[13] National Association of Software and Service Companies (NASSCOM), BSA/SPA estimated that 20–25% of the books sold were pirated. Further, the revenue losses of computer software worked out to be about Rs. 545 crores.[14] BSA identified the illegal software used, via various Web sites and P2P networks and issued "take-down" notices to the Internet Service Providers (ISPs) to remove or disable

[12] *Ibid.* About 60% of the software installed on personal computers in India in 2013 were not properly licensed. China piracy level was 74% in 2013.

[13] "Software piracy rate falls to 60%, but costs industry $2.9 bn" *The Hindu.*

[14] National Association of Software and Service Companies (NASSCOM), BSA/SPA estimate of 60% piracy rates during 1996, revenue loss to the software companies due to this works out to be around Rs. 545 crore (US $ 151.3 million). Based on the methodology adopted by BSA/SPA, it is estimated that total value of installed softwares (both legal and illegal) works out to be around Rs. 908 crore. Therefore, only Rs. 363 crore worth of legal software has been installed in India. This works out to be only around 21.7% of the total domestic software market which was Rs. 1670 crore during the year 1995–96.

access to the pirated software.[15] The extent of illicit use of copyright works in digital form, like music file sharing or movies distributed suggests that potential efficiency gains can be realised by applying advances in digital technology to legal markets for creative works.[16]

Copyright is a property right in different kinds of works, such as literary, dramatic, musical or artistic works, sound recording, and cinematograph films.[17] The owner of the copyright has exclusive rights to do certain acts in relation to the work like reproduction right, use in any other way including issuing the work to the public, renting or lending copies to the public, performing, showing or playing in public, communicating to the public. This right extends to broadcasting and making available to the public of the work by electronic transmission in such a way that member of the public may access it from a place and at a time individually chosen by them and adaptation of the work or doing any of the above in relation to the adaptation. Copyright may exist in any tangible medium of expression giving the holders the exclusive right to reproduce adapt, distribute, perform and display the work.[18] Hence, the author has the bundle of rights for limited period. The author is benefited by recouping and protecting his economic rights. The infringement of copyright occurs, when any person does any of the acts restricted by the Act without the licence of the owner or authorises another to do so. The law provides the owner with a right to prevent others from infringement of copyrights which may entail civil and criminal liability.

The current copyright regime faces the challenge of balancing the private incentives with social benefits. The copyright law does not provide monopoly and hence, facilitates also to advance public welfare by granting permission for free use and providing space for the development of non-protectable ideas and processes[19] without making it as an instrument of oppression and extortion.[20] As public interest is also paramount, certain acts do not amount to an infringement of copyright which provide for fair use of copyright work.

The digital media has provided a platform for the authors of copyright in making available the creative works in the electronic form. Any work like literary, music, sound recording, cinematograph and software can be in the digital form.[21] The authors in this digital age are literally controlling the utility of the work in the

---

[15] The Business Software Alliance (www.bsa.org) is the foremost organization dedicated to promoting a safe and legal digital world. International Data Corporation, (IDC), www.idc.com is the premier global provider of market intelligence, advisory services, and events for the information technology, telecommunications, and consumer technology markets.

[16] "A CBO Paper-Copyright in the Digital Media".

[17] The Copyright Act, 1957, s.14.

[18] *Black's Law Dictionary* 36 (Thomson West, St. Paul MN, 7th edn., 1999).

[19] *Computer Associates International Inc.* v. *Altai Inc.*, 982 F.2d 693 (2d Cir. 1992.).

[20] *Hanfstaengl* v. *Empire Palace,* (1894) 3 Ch. 109 at 128.

[21] eBook Web reports traffic of 500,000 page views per month and Palm Digital Media reported sales of 180,000 titles in 2001; The Museum Computer Network and Virtual Library Museums Pages list more than 1,000 museums and museum related sites globally that maintain digital collections online, Referred in Rodney D. Ryder.

digital form. Transformation of expressive works into digital electronic format facilitating the reproduction, transmission and re-transmission has been possible and is made simple and inexpensive. The greatest challenge is to identify and control the piracy in digital media. Peter S. Menell stated that, digital uprising is the third of the technological invention which heralded considerable affect on copyright protection referring "Digital Media" as the new mode of expressing the creative work. The computer programming and digital sampling empowers anyone with internet connection to flawlessly, inexpensively and instantaneously not only copy or reproduce but to distribute the work.[22] Any work may be accessed easily and carried without much difficulty in and from any jurisdiction.

3 Copyright in International Perspective and Relevance of Other Jurisdictions

International law prescribes that, states are free to define the scope of IP protection and the method of enforcement of copyrights. The International conventions impose certain broad parameters for protection of copyright. "Berne Convention for the Protection of Literary and Artistic Works" (Berne Convention), 1886 is governing the copyright issues which are now administered by World Intellectual Property Organisation (WIPO). The TRIPs under the World Trade Organisation (WTO) incorporates the governing law relating IP.

India is a member of the Berne Convention, Universal Copyright Convention (UCC) and the TRIPs Agreement. India by adopting the International Copyright Order, 1999 affords protection to the members of the Berne Convention, UCC or the WTO Countries. The TRIPs, particularly does not afford protection to ideas, procedures, methods of operation and mathematical concepts.[23] It can be machine readable or other form. It also provides that, copyright shall extend to expressions and not to ideas, processes, methods of operation or mathematical concepts as such.[24] The TRIPs protects computer programmes as literary works.[25] It protects the databases or other compilations, whose arrangement or selection make them

[22] The first was the printing press which brought in the methods of mechanically storing and reproducing works of authorship, such as photography, motion pictures and sound recordings. Secondly, it was the advent of broadcasting, where it enabled to perform the work of an author at different locations. Also read, Menell (2002).

[23] The Agreement on Trade-Related Aspects of Intellectual Property Rights (*hereinafter* TRIPs), Article 9.

[24] *Id.*, Article 9(2).

[25] *Id.*, Article 10. TRIPs opts for copyright and trade secret protection of computer programs and not patent protection. This is because TRIPs provisions do prohibit field-specific exclusions of patentable subject matter. However, suggesting that domestic patent laws must recognise some program related inventions if they meet other criteria of eligibility, including the non-obviousness standard. Thus, TRIPs "leaves both developed and developing countries free to determine the level of patent protection to be afforded program-related inventions within their domestic jurisdictions,

intellectual creations, even when individual elements are protected.[26] Hence, underlying innovative functional elements of a computer program, including the architecture, algorithms and data structures are not directly protected as part of the expression of a literary work under the TRIPs.[27] The TRIPs provides authors of computer programme and films, the right to authorize or prohibit commercial rental of their copyright works. In case of reproduction right, member states shall permit the reproduction in special cases, which positively fulfils the three step test.[28] This three step test is also incorporated into the TRIPs, WCT and WPPT.[29]

As internet began to exert greater protection under the copyright regime, the efforts led to the adoption of two additional treaties which are now known as supplements to the Berne Convention.[30] WIPO stepped into providing new rules to suit the online environment.[31] The WIPO with an intention of bringing in conformity with the technological development and a possible additional obligatory provisions relating to the Berne Convention including the law relating to performers

(Footnote 25 continued)

but not free to impose their… respective decisions on other member countries." See Reichman 1993.

[26] *Supra* note 24, Article 10(2).

[27] Jones 1999.

[28] *Supra* note 24, Article 9(2). Then the determination of the order of application of the other two conditions follows. If it is considered that reproduction conflicts with the normal exploitation of the work, reproduction is not permitted at all… if it is considered that reproduction does not conflict with the normal exploitation of the work, the next step would be to consider whether it does not unreasonably prejudice the legitimate interests of the author. Only if such is not the case would it be possible in certain special cases to introduce a compulsory licence, or to provide for use without payment. See Dr. Ficsor 2002.

[29] Berne Convention for the Protection of Literary and Artistic Works (*hereinafter* Berne Convention), Article 16, reads as: "(1) Infringing copies of a work shall be liable to seizure in any country of the Union where the work enjoys legal protection.

(2) The provisions of the preceding paragraph shall also apply to reproductions coming from a country where the work is not protected, or has ceased to be protected.

(3) The seizure shall take place in accordance with the legislation of each country."

It also implicitly provides for the reproduction right. It applies to reproductions coming from a country where the work is not protected, or has ceased to be protected.

[30] "The digital environment now allows users of electronic media to send and retrieve perfect reproductions of copyrighted material easily and nearly instantaneously, to or from locations around the world. With this evolution in technology, the law must adapt in order to make digital networks safe places to disseminate and exploit copyrighted works." See HR. Rep. No. 551 (Part I), 105th 2nd Sess 9 (22 May, 1998), referred in Dratler and McJohn 2000.

[31] WIPO actually considered the legal protection of computer program under the Union of the Protection of Industrial Property rather than the Berne Union. Then the WIPO Model Provision on the Protection of Computer Software was adopted in 1977. It provided for a sui generis protection mainly by copyright inspiration. However, these Model Provisions were not followed by any countries. Then, it was directly covered under the copyright law. The change of stance to protect under copyright law was due to a study conducted by Michael S Keplinger in 1985, "Legal Protection for Computer Programs: a Survey and Analysis of National Legislation and Case Law" which was at the request of WIPO and UNESCO.

and phonogram[32] producers came out with, two treaties, the WCT[33] and the WPPT (referred as "Internet Treaties.") were adopted in 1996. The WCT protects the computer programmes as literary works within the meaning of the Berne Convention.[34] According to WCT, the member countries shall provide adequate legal protection, remedies against the circumvention and imposing obligations concerning Digital Rights Management Information (DRM).[35] The WPPT affords to protect the performers and phonogram right to an author in the digital era. The WPPT protects the aural aspects of performances not audio-visual performances.[36] The laws in almost all countries provide for protection of performances.[37] Audio-visual performances are now made available over internet through music videos or cinematograph work requiring the possible extension of protection in the international scenario. It is necessary, as it is possible to manipulate and distort the performers images and voices in the digital technology, e.g. morphing where it transforms one image into another. Hence, protection of performers has to be addressed in the present internet context.[38]

Copyright law in the United States is governed by the United States Copyright Act, 1976 (USCA) and the Digital Millennium Copyright Act, 1998 (DMCA). The DMCA refers to "anti-circumvention" provision, protecting the works against infringement in the digital media. The DMCA affords legal protection and effective legal remedies against unlawful circumvention of technological measures. The DMCA imposes

---

[32] 'Phonograms' is commonly refers to protection of sound recordings.

[33] WIPO Copyright Treaty (*hereinafter* WCT) was adopted in Geneva on 20th December 1996. Preamble to WCT reads:

- To develop and maintain the protection of the rights of authors in effective and uniform way.
- To introduce new International rules and clarify the interpretation of certain existing rules in order to provide adequate solutions to the questions rose by new economic, social, cultural and technological development.
- To recognise the impact of Development and Convergent of Information and Communication Technology on the creation and use of literary and artistic works.
- To emphasise the outstanding significance of copyright protection as an incentive for literary and artistic creation.
- In total to balance the rights of authors and the larger public interest, particularly education, research and access to information, as reflected in the Berne Convention

[34] *Id.*, Article 4.

[35] Id., Article 12(1) reads as: "Contracting parties shall provide adequate and effective legal remedies against any person knowingly performing any of the following acts knowing or with respects to civil remedies having reasonable grounds to know, that it will induce, enable facilitate or conceal an infringement of any right covered by this Treaty of the Berne Convention:

(i) To remove or alter any electronic rights management information without authority;
(ii) To distribute, import for distribution, broadcast or communicate to the public, without authority, works or copies of works knowing that electronic rights management information has been removed or altered without authority."

[36] WIPO Performances and Phonograms Treaty (*hereinafter* WPPT), *Article 3.*

[37] The Copyright Act, 1957, s.38.

[38] See presentation of Jean Vincent, 2002.

liability not only on infringement of copyright but also the technologies that facilitate infringement. As circumventing the original work may occur even now, the right holders are haunted and left with insecurity in posting the work on the internet. Further, it imposes liability on the ISP for online infringement of copyright.

In the United Kingdom, the law is dealt within the Copyright, Design and Patent Act, 1988 (CDPA). European Council Information Directive 1991 confers certain rights on the owner of copyright in computer programme. The right includes the control of temporary reproduction, running of storage of the programme, translation or adaptation, distribution or rental of programmes. It also enlists certain liabilities for secondary infringement.

4 Copyright Issues and Challenges in the Digital Media: Indian Perspective

The major challenges in the digital media are to analyse the scope of copyright and exceptions, infringement, liabilities and implementation. The 'analog' methods of recording works referred as traditional, are either on paper, film or on magnetic tape. The work when digitalized, converts word, images, sounds, graphics and films into binary numbers of 1's or 0's. The digitally stored works, as bits grouped in bytes, disassociated from their physical form are then transferred over the networks to be finally reconstructed into recognisable art by a reference to their binary values. The source, assembly and object code get protection under the copyright law. [39] Copyright works in digitalised form reduce text, visual images and sound to computer-readable and grouped in bits and bytes which travel over networks and has enabled efficient transfer of copyright work to the Internet.[40] The internet connectivity has increased the trading in goods and services including IP material and copyright work is no exception.[41] Internet is characterised as a giant copying machine facilitating flawless, extensive reproduction and also difficult to detect the copyright infringement. The owners of copyright contended that, creative work would be taken or stolen easily or at least feared to provide the work in the digital form.[42] The encryption and watermarking technology have provided certain requisite protection to the owners in the digital environment. The Digital Right Management (DRM) though provides safeguard, the owners are still apprehensive about the extent of protection.[43] The owners are also of the view that, it would be

[39] *Ibcos Computers* v. Barclays Mercantile Highland Finance, 1994 FSR 275.

[40] *Ibid.*

[41] The digital media has become precursor of 'information age' revolutionizing in providing ready information on every conceivable area. See "Intellectual Property on the Internet: A survey of Issues", *2002*.

[42] Litman 2006.

[43] Nelson 2002. Also read, "Intellectual Property on the Internet: A survey of Issues", 2002.

better to educate and persuade the public to buy legitimate products than a pirated version. The reason for this may be that, it becomes difficult and expensive to keep a continuous check on infringements.

The subscription services provide a secure platform and monitoring the content use where downloading is permitted (See, for e.g. eMusic, MusicNet, Full Audio).[44] The unauthorised music sharing sites have been out of the market (See for e.g. Napster, KaZaA and Morpheus).[45] The 'Peer-to-peer' network enabled users to upload and share music and movie files through the digital media, infringing the copyright.[46] Napster for example was using centralised server to process the transfer which made it difficult to regulate, wherein the music industry had to suffer losses in this regard.[47] Pirated distribution technologies are capable of destroying the value of the copyright.[48] The MP3 (mpeg3) compression software enables music files to be stored in the digital form and easily made available for uploading and downloading freely from the Web or file transfer protocol sites. The music and film industries have been more vulnerable in the digital media as they are most suited for distribution.[49] The personal computers with CD burners are used to compress and store movies on discs which can be downloaded without losing the substantial quality. The increased bandwidth has made it possible that, a large data file which transmits video has been made easy to download. The technology provides with access by video-on-demand and pay per view, which was followed by film industry in providing movie on demand. The introduction of internet radio has increased the copyright material online with webcasting industry. It has taken the traditional customers, luring them to access, thousands of global radio broadcasts.[50] Webcasting, Digital cinematograph and television online are offered in the global market via internet.[51] The process does not allow creating a permanent copy to the end users computer hard drives. Though, few software are available, allowing users to convert streamed audio files into other formats, which can be then transferred via peer-to-peer systems. New legislations have come into place to regulate this method of communication.

---

[44] *Ibid.*

[45] See presentation of Gooch 2002.

[46] See "Kazaa Denies Copyright Infringement Claims; Developer Says P2P No Different Than HTTP", 2002.

[47] 950 million pirated music discs were sold in 2001, in a world pirate-music market valued at US $4.3 billion. See IFPI's "Music Piracy Report 2002".

[48] *A&M Records, Inc.* v. *Napster*, 239 F.3d 1004(9th Cir. 2001). Although recording industry failed to present evidence of such an impact.

[49] "Downloads Did Not Cause the Music Slump, But They Can Cure It," 2002.

[50] In the U.S., internet radio and webcasting are now regulated by the DMCA, wherein it provides that the webcasters have to pay royalties by acquiring compulsory licences taken from any recording company in the digital form. See "*Webcasters of Radio Broadcasts Not Exempt from Paying Royalties to Record Companies*," 2001. Since January 2001, the total audience time spent listening to monitored Web radio stations increased by 749%, Referred in Dr. Mihály Ficsor 2003.

[51] See Sople 2012.

The piracy has become so rampant that a pirated version of the movie may be available before its official release, which is a great cause of concern to the industry.[52] In the digital interactive television (iTV), new developments have taken place wherein, the use of personal or digital video recorders allow viewers to record shows by genre or actor and pause and rewind live TV; Video-on-demand (VOD) allows viewers to choose which programme to watch either by pay-per-view or by subscription; and the two-way-programming, enabling viewers to interact with other viewers which has entered into the competition.[53]

Another pertinent issue in the digital media is the hyperlinked or hypertext reference linked facilities within the sites permitting information sharing. The user can activate the link by clicking on linked element. The hyperlinks are indicated in a hypertext document through tags in mark-up languages such as SGML and HTML. These tags are generally not visible to the user, (also known as hot link, hypertext link or link).[54] User may search or link to another material content when he/she is using a work in question. If it is within the websites home page, it may not be a major concern as it will be within the link provided, where user only views content on the linked site and has knowledge that it is derived from a different website.[55] Though, the linked work is created in RAM of a computer but, the process does not create a copy. There exists no obligation to seek permission for linking, as it is presumed to be fair use and hence an implied licence is granted to view the content hyperlinked.[56] However, in the deep-linking, user directly getting connected to secondary material on another site, bypassing a current site's home page, may involve infringement in secondary material. "Embedded hyperlink" (in-line links) creates a reference to content from another website such that, the secondary material appears to be content originating from the first site. It may not require a copy to be created of material content linked but, may infringe the right to

---

[52] It is said that 4,00,000–6,00,000 films a day are downloaded over file sharing networks and pirate video-on-demand. Research by Viant, at http://www.viant.com, The Motion Picture Association of America (MPAA) shut down a pirated video-on-demand site, Film 88, based in Tehran, which showed full length movie for US$1 without authorization of the movie studios, referred in Rodney D. Ryder. A similar operation, Movie88.com was earlier shut down in Taiwan, Province of the People's Republic of China. Read also, Olsen 2002.

[53] Bond 2002.

[54] Garrote 2002.

[55] In some jurisdictions, such as the United States of America, copyright infringement has been found as a result of the simple act of linking, if such links facilitate copyright infringement or piracy; see *Intellectual Reserve Inc.* v. *Utah Lighthouse Ministry Inc.*, 75 F. Supp. 2d 1290. A similar reasoning was followed by the Belgian court in *IFPI, Belgiumv* v. *Beckers* ARK No. 99/594/C (Antwerp Court, 21 Dec. 1999) confirmed by Antwerp Court of Appeal 21 June 2001 RG 99/23830, 92, However, in Germany, this practice would seem not to give rise to legal liability, in accordance with §5(3) of the Teledienste-Gesetz, following court decisions in Pfälzer-Links (LG Frankenhalt, Urt. vom 11.28.2000) and Swabedoo (OLG Schleswig-Holstein Urt vom 12.19.2000), *Supra* note 55 at 184, 188, 190–191.

[56] *Supra* note 55 at 184, 187–188. Read also, O'Rourke 1998.

display or communicate the work to public.[57] 'Framing' is where, by using browser software content from another online source is possible. The user visualises the original website content framed by a different website having a different URL which may contain copyright protected content. A copy of content is made available in the user's computer memory and may involve copyright infringement. The copies are created over the RAM it may amount to reproduction of original work and attracts copyright liability.[58]

The ISP plays an important role who, participate in transmission and making available the copyright material. ISP's role, responsibilities and liabilities in the cyber space have received considerable attention and in particular copyright protection and infringements issues. The question of liabilities for infringed work in the cyber space is not only on the person illegally using the copyright material, but also on the ISP. The ISP's liability may arise, when a copyright work is reproduced or communicated to the public by them, without the owner's authorisation. The ISP may contribute or facilitate for the infringement of copyright work. The issue of ISP's liability involves greater implication within the countries. In India, the Information Technology Act, 2000, (IT Act) provides for the rights and liabilities of an ISP to some extent.[59]

5 Copyright Amendment Act 2012: Assessment on Copyright Issues in Digital Media

In the Indian scenario, the copyright issues have to face the challenges as mentioned above and facilitate in entitling the copyright protection to the owners. The Copyright (Amendment) Act 2012 has made its way towards such protection. The author presents the new legal regime and judicial response to the amendment.

The basic premise in India of copyright protection is to promote in furthering new creative works based on the idea and information of the existing work.[60] The primary function of copyright law is to protect the fruits of a man's work, labour, skill and judgment.[61] The Act seeks to reward the owner/creator of a work in

[57] Supra note 55 at 184, 194.

[58] *Supra* note 55 at 196.

[59] The Information Technology Act, 2000, s.79.

[60] *Eastern Book Company* v. *D.B. Modak,* (2008) 1 SCC 1*; Sony Corp.* v. *Universal City Studios, Inc.*, 464 U.S. 417 (1984)*; Fiest Publication Inc.* v. *Rural Telephone Service,* 499 U.S. 340 (1991) at 351–352.

[61] *Sulamangalam R Jayalakshmi* v. *Meta Musicals,* AIR 2000 Mad. 454.

economic terms[62] and at the same time, serves the public interest by making available any creative works to the public in certain circumstances (making provision for fair use or compulsory licensing). Hence, copyright is recognised as a property worthy of protection with certain limitation and exceptions to benefit the public.[63] Any infringement of copyright entitles the owner with both civil and criminal remedies. The owner shall be entitled to all such remedies by way of injunction, damages and accounts for profits. In addition, the owner may take proceedings for the recovery of possession of infringing copies.[64]

The Copyright (Amendment) Act, 2012 was enacted with an objective of proposing changes in the context of technological development including the Internet. The Amendment Act seeks to extend protection to the copyright and related rights in the digital era. The Amendment Act extends copyright material/content protection over digital networks in respect of literary, dramatic, musical, artistic works, cinematograph films, sound recordings, work of performers and producers of phonograms. This Amendment seeks to harmonise and bring the copyright law to be "Internet Treaties" i.e. the WCT and the WPPT compliant.[65] It ensures protection against circumvention of effective technological measures applied for purpose of protection of their rights and circumvention of rights management information (DRM).

[62]The copyright protection finds its justification in fair play. When a person produces something with his skill and labour, it normally belongs to him and the other person would not be permitted to make a profit of the skill and labour of the original author and it is for this reason the Act, gives to the authors certain exclusive rights in relation to certain work referred in the Act. The object of the Act is to protect the author of the copyright work from an unlawful reproduction or exploitation of his work by others. Copyright is a right to stop others from exploiting the work without the consent or assent of the owner of the copyright. A copyright law presents a balance between the interests and rights of the author and that of the public in protecting the public domain, or to claim the copyright and protect it under the copyright statute." *Quoted in Eastern Book Company* v. *D.B. Modak*, (2008) 1 SCC 1.

[63] *Penguin Books Ltd* v. *India Book distributors, AIR 1985 Del. 29 (DB);* See also *Computer Associates International Inc* v. *Altai In.*, 982 F.2d 693 (2d. Cir 1992). Thus, on one hand the Act protects the authors with an incentive to create works and on the other hand balances it by imposing limitation on the protection so that no person monopolizes the creativity of any works.

[64] The Copyright Act, 1957, s.62.

[65] The WCT deals with the protection for the authors of literary and artistic works such as writings, computer programmes; original databases; musical works; audiovisual works; works of fine art and photographs. The WPPT protects certain "related rights" which are the rights of the performers and producers of phonograms.

5.1 Protection of Computer Programme as Literary Work

The general principle that the copyright does not exist in idea, but in the expression is applicable even to the works in the digital form.[66] In *Bharat Matrimony Com. Pvt. Ltd v People Interactive (I) Pvt. Ltd*,[67] referring to *Whelan Associates* case held that, the law protects the manner in which the author expresses an idea or concept, but not the idea itself.[68] However, the court did not make any reference to the three step test of "Abstraction-Filtration-Comparison" applied in *Altai case* to identify the idea/expression dichotomy.[69] However, work must be of original thought not novel or inventive.[70] Furthermore, the fixation is a necessary element to claim copyright. The Act protects computer or software programme as a literary work.[71] The idea-expression dichotomy with reference to computer programmes gets complicated in the digital media.[72]

The Act defines "literary work" to include *computer programmes, tables and compilations including computer databases.*[73] Further, in relation to any literary, dramatic, musical or artistic work, *which is computer-generated*, the author is the person who causes the work to be created.[74] "*Computer*" for the purpose of law includes any electronic or similar device having information processing capabilities.[75] And, *"Computer programme"* means a set of instructions expressed in words, codes, *schemes or in any other form*, including a machine readable medium,

[66] *R.G. Anand* v. *Delux Films,* AIR 1978 SC 1613*; Burroughs Wellcome (India) Ltd.* v. *Uni-Sole Pvt. Ltd.*, (1999) 19 PTC 188 (Bom)*; Zee Telefilms Ltd. and Film* v. *Sundial Communications Pvt. Ltd,* 2003 (27) PTC 457 (Bom);. Read also, *Copinger and Skone James on Copyright,* 1994.

[67] AIR 2009 Mad 78; the Madras High Court held that copyright protection does not extend to any idea, procedure, process, system, method of operation, concept, principle, invention or discovery, regardless of the form in which it is described, illustrated or embodied. The system developed has been used by many industries including the banking sector. If such work is allowed to be protected it would monopolize a common system and there would not be any invention in the future computer programmes. Also read, *Zee Entertainment Enterprises Ltd.* v. *Gajendra Singh; (*2007) 109 BOM LR 2072; *Barbara Taylor Bradford* v. Sahara Media Entertainment Ltd, 2004 (28) PTC 474 (Cal).

[68] *Whelan Associates Inc.* v. *Jaslow Dental Laboratory Inc. and others,* 479 U.S. 1031 (1987).

[69] *See Computer Associates Int'l Inc* v. *Altai Inc.* 982 F.2d 693 (2d Cir. 1992); See also *Pepsi Co. Inc.* v. *Hindustan Coca Cola and others,* 94 (2001) DLT 30.

[70] *Eastern Book Company and others* v. *D.B. Modak,* (2008) 1 SCC 1*; CCH Canadian Ltd.* v. *Law Society of Upper Canada,* (2004) 1 SCR 339*; Feist Publications, Inc.* v. *Rural Telephone Service Company, (1991) 499 US 340; Key Publications, Inc.* v. *Chinatown Today Publishing Enterprises, Inc,* 945 F 2d 509(2d Cir 1991).

[71] The Copyright Act, 1957, s.14.

[72] *Computer Associates Int'l Inc.* v. *Altai Inc.*, 982 F.2d 693 (2d Cir. 1992).

[73] *Supra* note 72, s.2(o). Read also, J.A.L. Sterling 2003.

[74] *Supra* note 72, s.2(d) reads as: "'author' means—in relation to any literary, dramatic, musical or artistic work, which is computer-generated, the person who causes the work to be created."

[75] *Supra* note 72, s. 2(ffb).

capable of causing a computer to perform a particular task or achieve a particular result.[76] Schemes or in any other form, refers to the source code and object code of the computer programme.[77] Thus, computer programme is a list of instructions or routines or actions set out in a logical order and designed to solve a particular problem. A series of such instructions may be combined together in order to solve a more complex or number of separate problems. Such series might equally be described as a single programme.[78]

The general principle of copyright law is that the works include all expressions in writing whether they have any literary merit or not.[79] The work is protected even though they have no appeal to the aesthetic sense. They are more apt to produce a feeling or revulsion than a sense of beauty.[80] The Act requires that the work should be in writing or in print.[81] Hence, a literary work must be expressed in some form of notation. In case of a computer programme, it would suggest that the fixation of such work stored in an electronic form or means would be sufficient to afford copyright protection. The right to reproduce includes "storing of the work in any medium by electronic means" and it finds a place in the Act in relation to literary, dramatic and musical works. The Amendment Act extends this to the artistic works, cinematograph films and sound recordings.

The test of originality, traditionally applied to the works may not be feasible in case of a computer programme, and if the amount of skill, labour and judgment is too trivial to consider the work as original, the author may not be able to claim copyright. For e.g. the multiplication tables, alphabets in a computer programme cannot get protection.[82] Computer programme manuals and papers, punched cards and magnetic tapes or discs can be considered to be literary works. Punched cards which contain information by way of notation are considered as literary work. Magnetic tapes and discs containing information by means of electronic impulses can be a literary work. Similarly, programmes devised for the working of computers are also literary work. The instructions through computer, capable of causing a computer to perform a particular task or achieve a particular result get protected as

---

[76] *Id.*, s.2(ffc).

[77] The Information Technology Act, 2000, explanation to s.65 reads as: "'computer source code' means the listing of programmes, computer commands, design and layout and programme analysis of computer resource in any form."

[78] *John Richardson Computer Ltd* v. *Flanders,* (1993) FSR 497 (Ch D).

[79] *Agarwala Publishing House, Khurja* v. *Board of High School and Intermediate Education, U.P.,* AIR 1967 All 91; *Misra Bandhu Karalaya* v. *Shivratanlal Koshal,* AIR 1970 MP 261 (arithmetic work is a literary work).

[80] *Ladbroke (Football) Ltd.* v. *William Hill (Football) Ltd,* (1964) 1 ALL ER 465 *(football coupons, income tax returns are literary works); Ghafur Bakhsh* v. *Jwala Prasad Singhal,* (1921) 43 All 412 *(a text of grammar).*

[81] *Eastern Book Company and others* v. *D.B. Modak,* (2008) 1 SCC 1.

[82] Rodney 2007.

copyright.[83] The data entry and its conversion, data processing, data analysis, data control and management are within the definition of "computer programme" under the Act.

The term "literary work" includes computer programmes, tables and compilations including computer databases. It may include any work written or printed in any language.[84] Hence, the computer programmes written in high level language are protected as literary work. The instructions encoded on silicon chips are protected.[85] Any programme devised for the working of the computers,[86] a computer programme recorded on any disc, tape or perforated media or information storage device are considered as literary work.[87] Hence, copyright protection extends, to the literal elements of computer programmes i.e., the source code and object code version of the programme,[88] depending on the originality requirement.[89] The subsistence and extent of copyright are not affected by the fact that, a programme may embody functional elements which may be achieved in one or a limited number of ways.[90] A computer programme may comprise of literal as well as non-literal aspects, that is, those aspects that are not reduced to a written code. Copyright protection in such case extends beyond a literary works which are strictly textual form to its non-literal components. Hence, when the fundamental essence or structure of one work is duplicated in another, it would amount copyright infringement. A programme's structure includes its non-literal components such as

---

[83] *Assistant CIT* v. *Amadeus India (P) Ltd*, (2001) 79I TD 407 (Delhi), the court was deciding whether the business of exporting computer software carried on by the assessee had clearly fulfilled the conditions mentioned in Copyright Act interpreting the term computer programme under the Income Tax Act. 1961. "Computer software" is defined in the Explanation (b) to Section 80HHE of the Act, which "means any computer programme recorded on any disc, tape, perforated media or other information storage device and includes any such programme which is transmitted from India to a place outside India by any means. The court interpreted broadly, liberally and consistently with other relevant legislations of Government to include export to "data processing software."

[84] *University of London Press Ltd* v. *University of Tutorial Press Ltd*, (1916) 2 Ch. D. 601; *Fateh Singh Mehta* v. *O.P. Singhal*, AIR 1990 Raj 8; *R.G. Anand* v. *Delux Films*, AIR 1978 SC 1613.

[85] *Atari Games Corp.* v. *Nintendo of America Inc.*, 975 F.2d 832 (Fed. Cir. 1992).

[86] *Apple Computer* v. *Formula International*, 725 F.2d 521 (9th Cir. 1984).

[87] *Rite Choice Technologies (Pvt) Ltd* v. *Circale Data Systems (P) Ltd*, 1996 SCC OnLine Mad 347.

[88] TRIPs, Article 10(1) provides that computer programs, whether in source code or object code, would be protected as literary works under the Berne Convention 1971; *Lotus Development Corporation* v. *Paperback Software International*, 740 F.Supp. 37 (1990); *Total Information processing Systems Ltd* v. *Daman Ltd*, (1992) FSR 171 (Ch D); *John Richardson Computer Ltd* v. *Flanders*, (1993) FSR 497 (Ch D); *Ibcos Computers* v. *Barclays Mercantile Highland Finance*, (1994) F.S.R 275; *Richardson Computer Ltd* v. *Flanders*, (1993) FSR 497 (Ch D).

[89] *Computer Associates International Inc* v. *Altai Inc.*, 982 F.2d 693(2d. Cir 1992); *Apple Computer* v. *Formula International*, 725 F.2d 521 (9th Cir. 1984)), *Williams Electronic Inc* v. *Artic International Inc*, 685 F.2d 870 (3d Cir. 1982); *Sega Enters Ltd* v. *Accolade Inc.*, 785 F. Supp. 1392 (N.D. Cal. 1992).

[90] *Ibcos Computers* v. *Barclays Mercantile Highland Finance*, (1994) F.S.R 275.

the general flow charts and more specific organisation of inter-modular relationships, parameter lists and macros. The academic debate is that, if the non-literal structures of literary works are protected by copyright, and computer programmes being literary works, the non-literal structures of computer programmes copyright gets protected.[91]

In *Syed Asifuddin v The State of AP*[92] considering Section 65 of the Information Technology Act, 2000, the court rejected the contention that, a telephone handset is neither a computer nor a computer system containing a computer programme.[93] The copyright exists in the source code developed by a programmer and any copying certainly violates the developer's right. A computer source code includes (a) list of programmes (b) computer commands; (c) design and layout and (d) programme analysis of computer resource in any form. The court concluded that, under Section 63 of the Act any infringement of the copyright in a computer programme or source code is punishable.[94] In *Burlington Home Shopping Pvt. Ltd. (BHS) v Rajnish Chibber*[95] it was held, that a computer database is a collection of information stored on computer media and protection to that extent is allowed.

The Supreme Court *in Eastern Book Company v D.B. Modak and another,*[96] held that, the head notes of the judgments in electronic form is a derivative literary work. It referred to few important decisions[97] and the principles adopted by foreign courts, including the "sweat of the brow" doctrine and concluded holding that, to secure a copyright for the judgments, it is necessary that the labour, skill and capital invested should be sufficient to communicate or impart, some quality or character which the original judgment does not possess and which differentiates the original judgment from the printed one. Accepting the principle in *CCH Canadian Ltd. v Law Society of Upper Canada case,*[98] wherein, the author's creation by exercise of his skill and judgment may not be creativity in the sense of it being novel or

---

[91] *Computer Associates International Inc* v. *Altai Inc.,* 982 F.2d 693 (2d Cir. 1992).

[92] 2005 Cri LJ 4314.

[93] The Information Technology Act, 2008, ss. 2 (1)(i), 2(1)(j).

[94] Held, unless FIR is shown to be illegal or would result in miscarriage of justice, ordinarily the criminal investigation cannot be quashed. The revision petition was dismissed.

[95] 61 (1995) DLT 6.

[96] (2008) 1 SCC 1; contention of EBC was that, the publication of SCC was their original literary work which includes computer programs as well, reproduction of the same by the DTS and SBS in a data-base programme is clearly an infringement of their copyright subsisting in their publications.

[97] *Macmillan and Company Limited* v. *K. and J. Cooper,* AIR 1924 PC 75*; Ladbroke (Football) Ltd.* v. *William Hill (Football) Ltd,* (1964) 1 ALL ER 465, (in UK the "sweat of the brow" doctrine is held to be valid); *Feist Publications, Inc.* v. *Rural Telephone Service Company,* (1991) 499 US 340 (mere facts are not protected); *Key Publications, Inc.* v. *Chinatown Today Publishing Enterprises, Inc.,* 945 F. 2d 509 (2d Cir. 1991) (US has rejected the "sweat of the brow" doctrine)*; CCH Canadian Ltd.* v. *Law Society of Upper Canada* (2004) SCC 13*; Matthew Bender & Co., Inc.* v. *West Publishing Co.,* 158 F.3d 674 (2nd Cir. 1933), *Feist Publications, Inc.* v. *Rural Telephone Service Company,* (1991 (499) US 340).

[98] (2004) SCC 13.

non-obvious, but at the same time it should not be a work of merely labour and capital. Any derivative work must thus, have some distinguishable features and flavour to raw text of the judgments.[99] The court has considered in *Chancellor Masters and Scholars of the University of Oxford v Narendera Publishing House*,[100] a paradigm shift of the originality test from the "sweat of the brow" doctrine in *University of London Press Ltd v University of Tutorial Press Ltd.*[101] to the "modicum of creativity" standard in *Fiest Publication Inc. v Rural Telephone Service.*[102] The court rejected the sweat of the brow doctrine, which conferred copyright on works merely because time, energy, skill and labour was expended. The court held that the work must be original "in the sense that by virtue of selection, coordination or arrangement of pre-existing data contained in the work, a work somewhat different in character is produced by the author." Hence, court preferred a higher threshold than the doctrine of "sweat of the brow" but not as high as "modicum of creativity." The ruling also holds that, not every effort or industry, or expending of skill results in copyright work but, only those works, which create somewhat different character, involve some intellectual effort, and involve a certain degree of creativity.

5.2 Right of Reproduction

The owner of computer programme has the similar rights as the owner of copyright in a literary work.[103] The owner will have the exclusive right to reproduce his works and thereby may exclude others from reproducing the work. In *Autodesk, Inc. & Microsoft v Prashant Deshmukh & others*[104] the court held that, the exclusive rights of the author are infringed when a reproduction of computer software is copied without the authorization. By using and installing the software of Autodesk and Microsoft in defendant's computers the pirated copies or versions

---

[99] *In Mattel, Inc.* v. *Jayant Agarwalla,* 2008(38) PTC 416(Del); Delhi High Court considering the doctrine of merger, refused to protect the expression of an idea, which can be expressed only in a very limited manner, because doing so would confer monopoly on the ideas itself.

[100] 2008 (38) PTC 385 (Del).

[101] (1916) 2 Ch. D. 601.

[102] (1991) 199 US 340; *Eastern Book Company* v. *D.B Modak,* (2008) 1 SCC 1.

[103] The Copyright Act, 1957, s.14 (b) (i) provides that in the case of a computer programme: right to reproduce; right to issue the copies to the public; to perform the work in public, or communicate it to the public; to make any cinematograph film or sound recording in respect of the work; to make any translation of the work; to make any adaptation of the work; to do, in relation to a translation or an adaptation of the work, any of the acts specified in relation to the work in sub-clauses (i)–(vi) to sell or give on commercial rental or offer for sale or for commercial rental any copy of the computer programme. Provided that such commercial rental does not apply in respect of computer programmes where the programme itself is not the essential object of the rental.

[104] 2011(122) DRJ 606.

have infringed the copyright.[105] Hence, any reproduction of the source code and object code of computer programme is protected under the Act.

5.3 *Distribution Rights*

The distribution right is the exclusive right of the owner to sell, lease or otherwise transfer copies of the work to the public.[106] The distribution rights are not "any distribution" but only those which "are made to the public". Computer software industry in majority of cases is not providing an outright sale but rather offering only a licence to use. This may be one of the reasons which has resulted in widespread piracy of copyright material. Hence, computer programme is distinguishable with the books, music, films, etc. So, the 'fair use' which is allowed in publication or musical work may not be applicable in the same manner in computer programmes. The law protects as 'fair use' of a work, if such work is used for research, criticism or private use. However, question has been raised whether "fair use doctrine" would be eliminated in the context of computer programmes. The U.S., the U.K and the European Union have adopted "fair use" even to the computer programmes.

The sale, rental, or lease of a licensed computer programme without permission will constitute an infringement. A person who owned a book may retain a copy that is protected by "first sale doctrine." But, a person who owns a book in electronic form may not be permitted for distribution and reproduction of a copy through the internet.[107] However, the owner of a computer programmes is making provision for the defence of "First Sale" by fulfilling certain conditions. Hence, any person in possession of a particular copy of a computer programme shall not dispose of, or authorise the disposal by rental, lease, or lending, or by any other act or practice in the nature of rental, lease, or lending, unless authorised by owner. This applies to a person in possession of a phonorecord or a film. The distribution rights of the owner of the computer programme or phonorecords gets violated and may entail liability for infringement of "distribution rights" on any person not licensed to do so. *In A&M Records, Inc v Napster Inc.*,[108] wherein Napster's facilitation of transmission and retention of digital audio files by its users was held to be a *prima facie* case of direct infringement. The Napster was held liable for secondary liability for facilitating such infringement of copyright holder's exclusive rights of reproduction and

[105] The Copyright Act, 1957, ss.14, 51. Read also, *SAP AG* v. *Somaya Kanti Dutta,* 2008(36) PTC 598 (Del).

[106] *Black's Law Dictionary* (Thomson West, St. Paul MN, 7th edn., 1999).

[107] Ferrera et al. 2011.

[108] 239 F.3d 1004 (2001)*; Hotaling* v. *Church of Jesus Christ of Latter-day Saints,* 118 F.3d 199 (4th Cir. 1997).

distribution.[109] In *Metro-Goldwyn-Mayer Studios Inc v Grokster Ltd*, the person distributing any device having an objective of promoting its use in infringing copyright by any clear expressions and other affirmative steps in fostering infringement will be liable for secondary infringement.[110]

5.4 Issues Relating to Rental Rights

The copyright law in its earlier phase did not provide for rental or lending rights. The Berne Convention also did not provide any such right as rental or lending rights. However, they are now recognised by the TRIPs Agreement, the WCT (in computer programmes) and the WPPT (to performers and in phonograms). The Act provides that, the owner of a computer programme has an exclusive right, *to sell or give on commercial rental or offer for sale or for commercial rental any copy of the computer programme.*[111] Hence, rental of copies of the original work to the public is an exclusive right. "Rental" means making a copy of the work available for use, on terms that it will or may be returned, for direct or indirect economic or commercial advantage.[112] The rental is possible when the public have access to the work through a rental library or outlet. The Act, in the proviso states that, any commercial rental, *does not apply in respect of computer programmes where the programme itself is not the essential object of the rental.* Thus, when a person purchases a computer programme, any sale or commercial rental by him shall require a licence or authority because, "*Rental Right*" by itself is an exclusive right. The violation would be an infringement of distribution rights of the owner. On the other hand, lending of a copy of a computer programme by one individual to another is excluded.[113] In *Australian Video Retailers Association case*, it was held that, "DVD discs being computer programmes are limited to the instructions and do not extend to the audio, video or caption content of the discs. When renting the DVD disc, the video rental outlet enters into a commercial rental arrangement but, if the computer programme embodied in the disc was not the essential object of the hiring, there would be no exercise of the commercial rental right conferred on

---

[109] *Rejected the test applied in Sony Corp.* v. *Universal City Studios, Inc.* 464 U.S. 417 (1984); *Recording Industries Assn of America* v. *Diamond Multimedia Sys Inc,;* 180 F.3d 1072, 1079 (9th Cir. 1999); see also *Re Aimster Litigation,* 334 F.3d 643.

[110] *Metro-Goldwyn-Mayer Studios Inc.*, Et Al v. *Grokster, Ltd.* et al., 545 U.S. 913 (2005*); Perfect 10, Inc* v. *Amazon.com, Inc.*, 508 F.3d 1146 (9th Cir. 2007).

[111] The Copyright Act, 1957, s. 14(b)(ii) (added by Copyright Amendment Act, 1999 with effect from January 15 2000).

[112] TRIPs Agreement, WCT and WPPT also recognize the rental rights. *Black's Law Dictionary* (Thomson West, St. Paul MN, 7th edn., 1999).

[113] This is in compliance with TRIPs Agreement.

computer programmes."[114] This principle may by utilised in interpretation of rental in Indian context.

The *Amendment Act* has defined "commercial rental" with a negative connotation that does not include rental, lease or lending of a lawfully acquired copy of a computer programme, sound recording, visual recording or cinematograph film for non-profit purposes by a non-profit library or non-profit educational institution.[115] An exception is, when a non-profit library or non-profit educational institution rents, leases or lends a lawful copy of a computer programme, sound recording, visual recording or film and will not be considered to be a commercial rental. Similar exclusive rights are provided in case of film or sound recording,[116] where the owner shall have a right to sell or right to rental.[117] Hence, when a copy of the film or sound recording has been acquired (purchased) by a person, any further sale or hire of such film or sound recording requires authorisation or licence of the owner.

The *Amendment Act* made certain changes in respect to the rental rights in case of films and sound recordings. Section 14(d)(ii) and 14(e)(ii) for cinematograph film and sound recording which provide *"to sell or give on commercial rental or offer for sale or for such rental, any copy of the "film" or "sound recording*" as the case may be, a visible change replacing the word "rental" to "commercial rental." However, exemption is provided where any rental is for non-profit use by a non-profit library or non-profit educational institution wherein they have the rental right.

5.5 *Broadcasting Rights*

In the case of broadcasting organisation, involving special rights known as broadcasting reproduction rights includes the *right to make* any sound recording or visual recording of the broadcast or *make any reproduction* of such sound recording or visual recording and sells or gives on commercial rental or offer for sale or for such rental, any such sound recording or visual recording referred to in clause (c) or

---

[114] *Australian Video Retailers Association Ltd.* v. *Warner Home Video Pty Ltd.*, (2001) FCA 1719, (copyright protection of computer programs is limited to the program instructions. It does not extend to the audio, video, and caption content of the DVDs.).

[115] The Copyright Act, 1957, s.2 (fa).

[116] The term "sound recording" is used as "phonogram" in the WPPT and in many countries.

[117] The Copyright Act, 1957, s.14 (e) (ii) provides in the case of a sound recording for the right to sell or give on hire, or offer for sale or hire, any copy of the sound recording regardless of whether such copy has been sold or given on hire on earlier occasions; s.14 (d) (ii) provides in the case of a cinematograph film for the right to sell or give on hire or offer for sale or hire, any copy of the film, regardless of whether such copy has been sold or given on hire on earlier occasions.

clause (d) (inserted by Amendment Act, clause (e)).[118] The *Amendment Act* replaces the clause with the words: "…gives on commercial rental"… "such rental", any such sound recording or visual recording…" Thus, as said earlier, if it is for non-profit use by certain organizations or institutions it gets exempted on fulfilling certain conditions.

Section 38 of the Act provides protection of performer's rights.[119] But, the Act did not provide for exclusive rights to the performer. It also did not provide for any such "right of rental" to the performer. However, the Amendment Act creates a new section in compliance of the WPPT with reference to performer's rights.[120] The Amendment Act provides the exclusive rights to performers. This will include *selling or giving it on commercial rental or offer for sale or for commercial rental any copy of the recording.* Hence, a performer shall have a rental right of his performances.

5.6 Issues Relating to Adaptation Rights

"Copyright can be claimed in derivative work. A derivative work consists of a contribution of original material to a pre-existing work so as to recast, transform or adapt the pre-existing work. In relation to the computer programme, adaptation

[118] The Copyright Act, 1957, s.37 (3).

[119] *Id.*,s. 2(qq) reads as: "performer includes an actor, singer, musician, dancer, acrobat, juggler, conjurer, snake charmer, a person delivering a lecture or any other person who makes a performance".

[120] *Id.*, s. 38A. reads as: "(1) Without prejudice to the rights conferred on authors, the performer's right which is an exclusive right subject to the provisions of this Act to do or authorise for doing any of the following acts in respect of the performance or any substantial part thereof, namely:

(a) to make a sound recording or a visual recording of the performance, including—

(i) Reproduction of it in any material form including the storing of it in any medium by electronic or any other means;
(ii) Issuance of copies of it to the public not being copies already in circulation;
(iii) communication of it to the public;
(iv) selling or giving it on commercial rental or offer for sale or for commercial rental any copy of the recording;

(b) to broadcast or communicate the performance to the public except where the performance is already broadcast.

(2) Once a performer bas, by written agreement, consented to the incorporation of his performance in a cinematograph film he shall not, in the absence of any contract to the contrary, object to the enjoyment by the producer of the film of the performer's right in the same film.

Provided that, notwithstanding anything contained in this sub-section, the performer shall be entitled for royalties in case of making of the performances for commercial use."

means an arrangement or altered version of it or a translation of it.[121] Translation with reference to any computer programme refers to the conversion of a source code to an object code or vice versa. This includes the acts of compiling, disassembling or decompiling of the computer programme. Similarly, any translation of a computer programme from one language is converted into another language also attracts the copyright provisions.

5.7 Communication to the Public or Public Performance

Communication to the public means when a work is made available for being seen or heard or otherwise enjoyed by the public.[122] In the internet scenario, the dramatic and musical works are made available in the digital form, and the mode of communication of a work has gained importance. Similarly, the role and challenges for the ISP's has gained significance. An ISP can be made responsible and liable for providing a place for infringement of copyright work. The Amendment Act defines "communication to the public" which covers performance within its meaning. Instead of using the words "issue of copies to the public" the change is to use the words "issuing physical copies of it. This is necessitated because the digital copies are now made available on-line, normally referred as "*On Demand Availability Right*," which is added into this section by using the words "at places and times chosen individually."[123] The Amendment Act thereby complies with the WCT, which provides for "...making available to the public of their works *in such a way that members of the public may access these works from a place and at a time individually chosen by them.*"[124]

[121] *Id.*, s.2(a) reads as: "(a) adaptation means,—

(i) in relation to a dramatic work, the conversion of the work into a non-dramatic work;
(ii) in relation to a literary work or an artistic work, the conversion of the work into a dramatic work by way of performance in public or otherwise;
(iii) in relation to a literary or dramatic work, any abridgement of the work or any version of the work in which the story or action is conveyed wholly or mainly by means of pictures in a form suitable for reproduction in a book, or in a newspaper, magazine or similar periodical;
(iv) in relation to a musical work, any arrangement or transcription of the work; and
(v) in relation to any work, any use of such work involving its re-arrangement or alteration".

[122] *Id.*, s.2(ff).

[123] *Id.*, s.2(ff) reads as: "communication to the public means making any work or performance available for being seen or heard or otherwise enjoyed by the public directly or by any means of display or diffusion other than by issuing physical copies of it, whether simultaneously or at places and times chosen individually, regardless of whether any member of the public actually sees, hears or otherwise enjoys the work or performance so made available."

[124] WCT, Article 8 reads as: "authors of literary and artistic works shall enjoy the exclusive right of authorizing any communication to the public of their works, by wire or wireless means, including the making available to the public of their works in such a way that members of the public may access these works from a place and at a time individually chosen by them."

6 Importance of Protection of Performer's Right

In view of the development of law with reference to the Performer's rights under the TRIPs Agreement and the WPPT, the scope has widened by providing certain special rights to the performers. The apprehension expressed by the Supreme Court of India seems to have been answered by providing for a change in law for the performer's rights.[125] The protection of performances existed by providing with certain special rights to the performer.[126] Performance in connection to the performer's right, means any visual or acoustic presentation made live by one or more performers.[127] The performer shall have certain exclusive rights:[128]

(a) to make a sound recording or visual recording of the performance
(b) to reproduce a sound recording or visual recording of the performance
(c) to broadcast the performance
(d) to communicate the performance to the public otherwise than by a broadcast.

And if any person does any said acts without the consent of the performer would be liable for infringement of performer's rights.

The Act also provides exceptions, wherein it would not be an infringement of copyright under following situations:

(a) the making of any sound recording or visual recording for the private use of the person making such recording, or solely for purposes of *bona fide* teaching or research; or
(b) the use, consistent with fair dealing of excerpts of a performance or of a broadcast in the reporting of current events or for bona fide review, teaching or research or
(c) such other acts which do not constitute infringement of copyright under Section 52.[129]

---

[125] *Indian Performing Rights Society* v. *Eastern India Motion Pictures Association*, AIR 1977 SC 1443.

[126] The Copyright (Amendment) Act, 1994.

[127] The Copyright Act, 1957, s.2 (q) reads as: "Performer includes an actor, singer, musician, dancer, acrobat, juggler, conjurer, snake charmer, a person delivering a lecture or any other person who makes a performance" The 2012 Act amended this definition by appending a Proviso to the section, which reads as: "Provided that in a cinematograph film a person whose performance is casual or incidental in nature and, in the normal course of the practice of the industry, is not acknowledged anywhere including in the credits of the film shall not be treated as a performer except for the purpose of clause (b) of Section 38B".

[128] *Id.*, s. 38.

[129] *Id.*, s.39; reproduction in a judicial proceedings (s. 52(1)(c)); use of sound recording or visual recording of the performance in the course of the activities of an educational institution if the audience are limited to the students, parents and guardians of the students and persons directly connected with the activities of the institution (s. 52(1)(i)); See also s. 39A applicability of other provisions like, assignment, licences, importation of infringing copies, civil remedies, etc. to performer's.

The Amendment Act incorporates two new sections which are in compliance with WPPT. The exclusive rights granted to the performers are as follows:

1. To make a sound recording or a visual recording of the performance, including—
   i. *reproduction of it in any material form including the storing of it in any medium by electronic or any other means;*
   ii. *issuance of copies of it to the public not being copies already in circulation;*
   iii. *communication of it to the public;*
   iv. *selling or giving it on commercial rental or offer for sale or for commercial rental any copy of the recording;*
2. To broadcast or communicate the performance to the public except where the performance is already broadcast.[130]

Further, performer's "moral rights" are first time recognised by the Amendment Act. The performer has a right to claim to be identified as the performer and to restrain or claim damages in respect of any distortion, mutilation or other modification of his performance that would be prejudicial to his reputation.[131] This right shall be independent and exists even after assignment. However, it may be observed that the word "reputation" only is proposed, which is verbatim taken from the WPPT, without referring to the word "honour" offered to other works under Section 57 of the Act. The Amendment Act thus, provides a respectful right to the performers.

7 Violation or Infringement and Its Consequences

The infringements of copyright in computer programmes, unlike literary works, which are capable of side-by-side comparison, are difficult to identify in certain cases. Software by magnetic or electrical means make the hardware do certain thing together which is recorded on various tapes and discs. By this, the letters, signs and numbers of the programme may be made to appear on a screen or on a print out which makes the familiar process of comparison possible. However, when

---

[130] *Id*, s.38 A.

[131] *Id.*, s.38 B reads as: "The performer of a performance shall, independently of his right after assignment, either wholly or partially of his right, have the right:

(a) to claim to be identified as the performer of his performance except where omission is dictated by the manner of the of the performance; and
(b) to restrain or claim damages in respect of any distortion, mutilation or other modification of his performance that would be prejudicial to his reputation.

Explanation.-For the purposes of this clause, it is hereby clarified that mere removal of any portion of a performance for the purpose of editing, or to fit the recording within a limited duration, or any other modification required for purely technical reasons shall not be deemed to be prejudicial to the performer's reputation."

copyright in the programme itself is claimed, the results produced by operating the programme must not be confused with the programme in which copyright is claimed. Many different processes may produce the same answer and yet remain different, having not been copied from another. For a computer, the comparison must be between, the thing said to have been copied and the thing said to be an infringing copy. If the infringing copy and the programme said to have been copied are invisible, then normally they must be reproduced in visible form or in a form that in some way is perceptible, before it can be determined whether one infringes upon the other. In some cases, it may be possible to demonstrate in any other way that, one is a copy of the other. Normally, what is needed, is a print out or other documentary evidence of the programme alleged to have been copied and of the alleged infringing programme or sufficient parts of each. The programmes must be looked in a sense, not merely at what they do or can do but also what they are. The print out of computer programmes conveys little or no meaning to any, save the experts. However, it may provide a means, whereby anybody can detect similarities and dissimilarities when compared with the print out of another programme.[132] In such cases the courts may take the help of expert evidence while deciding whether any piracy is involved or not. If the expert evidence leads to circumstances of copying, the court may hold the person copying liable for infringement.[133]

8 Role, Responsibilities and Liabilities of the Internet Service Provider

The Amendment Act introduced Section 52 (b) providing a "fair use" in case of the transient or incidental storage of a work or performance purely in the technical process of electronic transmission or communication to the public. Section 52(c) provides safe harbor provision for an ISP.[134] The DMCA in United States provides for the same, referred as "notice and take down procedure." An ISP after receiving a complaint from the owner of the copyright, that the transient or incidental storage is

---

[132] *John Richardson Computer Ltd* v. *Flanders*, (1993) FSR 497 (Ch D); *Thrust Code Ltd* v. *WW Computing Ltd.*, (1983) FSR 502.

[133] *Government of West Bengal* v. *Nitya Gopal Basak*, 1985 CriLJ 202.

[134] *Id.*, s.52(1)(c) reads as: " the transient or incidental storage of a work or performance for the purpose of providing electronic links, access or integration, where such links, access or integration has not been expressly prohibited by the right holder, unless the person responsible is aware or has reasonable grounds for believing that such storage is of an infringing copy. Provided that if the person responsible for the storage of the copy has received a written complaint from the owner of copyright in the work, complaining that such transient or incidental storage is an infringement, such person responsible for the storage shall refrain from facilitating such access for a period of 21 days or till he receives an order from the competent court refraining from facilitating access and in case no such order is received before the expiry of such period of 21 days, he may continue to provide the facility of such access."

an infringement has an obligation to refrain from facilitating access. Such restraint shall be for 21 days or till it receives an order from the competent court.

The Amendment Act has literally followed the provision of the WCT and the WPPT. The Amendment Act introduces the "Rights Management Information" and the Digital Rights Management (DRM) i.e. making provision for protection of technological measures. The Right Management Information means:

(1) the title or other information identifying the work or performance;
(2) the name of the author or performer;
(3) the name and address of the owner of rights;
(4) terms and conditions regarding the use of the rights; and
(5) any number or code that represents the information referred to in sub-clauses (a)–(d), but does not include any device or procedure intended to identify the user.[135]

The new section, intends to provide protection to the owner of the copyright by technological measures. It provides an anti-circumvention measures by the owner. Hence, any person who circumvents an effective technological measure for the purpose of protecting any of the rights shall be made punishable under the Act.[136] The Amended section also provides for the following exceptions:

(1) doing anything referred to therein for a purpose not expressly prohibited by this Act
(2) doing encryption research using a lawfully obtained encrypted copy
(3) for conducting any lawful investigation
(4) testing the security of a computer system or a computer network with the authorisation of its owner or operator
(5) for identification or surveillance of a user
(6) for national security.

Further, a new section is inserted for protection of the DRM.[137] Any person who knowingly does the following acts is liable for punishment. They are:

(1) Removes or alters any rights management information without authority or
(2) Distributes, imports for distribution, broadcasts or communicates to the public, without authority, copies of any work, or performance knowing that electronic rights management information has been removed or altered without authority.
(3) If the rights management information has been tampered with in any work, the owner of copyright in such work may also avail civil remedies.

This section has adopted the DMCA model by providing the exceptions to circumvention of technological measures. First exception will provide, "doing anything referred to therein for a purpose not expressly prohibited by this Act." The

---

[135] The Copyright Act, 1957, s.2 (xa).

[136] *Id.*, s. 65A.

[137] WCT, Articles 11, 12; WPPT, Articles 18, 19; The Copyright Act, 1957, s.65B.

specific exceptions for computer programmes are referred under the "fair use" in the subsequent paragraph. The Act only lists, the broad heads of certain acts not to be considered as infringement of copyright. The Act provides for fair use of a literary, musical or artistic work not being a computer programme for private use, including research or criticism or review, whether of that work or of any other work.[138] The private use, reporting news, teaching and research, educational purposes also stand as a valid defence of fair use in the case of computer programmes.[139] The Act provides a separate list of non-infringing acts for computer programme. The 'fair use' with reference to a computer programme is as follows:

1. The making of copies or adaptation of a computer programme by the lawful possessor of a copy of such computer programme, from such copy:[140]
   (a) In order to utilise the computer programme for the purpose for which it was supplied
   (b) To make back-up copies purely as a temporary protection against loss, destruction or damage
2. Necessary to obtain information essential for operating inter-operability of an independently created computer programme with other programmes by a lawful possessor of a computer programme.[141]
3. The observation, study or test of functioning of the computer programme.[142]
4. The making of copies or adaptation of the computer programme from a personally legally obtained copy for non-commercial personal use.[143]

The intention of providing these exceptions is to allow persons in lawful possession of copies of a computer programme to use without any threat of copyright infringement actions. e.g. if copyright law prevents users from making hard drive copies, they would not be able to use the computer programme, without apprehending infringement liability. Even in this case, any such copying is permitted only for personal use. If copying is made for commercial purpose "fair use" defence cannot be claimed. Even if the terms of agreement prevent any permitted acts, the court may treat those conditions as void.

Further, the Act provides any act done by way of reverse engineering shall be a fair use. The fair use for reverse engineering will be permitted under following circumstances:

(a) The decompilation is to obtain the information necessary to create an independent programme;
(b) the user is a lawful possessor of computer programme;

[138] The Copyright Act, 1957, s.52.
[139] Verma and Mittal 2004.
[140] The Copyright Act, 1957, s.52 (1)(aa).
[141] Id., s. 52(1)(ab).
[142] Id., s. 52(1)(ac).
[143] Id., s. 52(1)(ad).

(c) such information is not otherwise readily available;
(d) the information is used strictly within the permitted use.

The reverse engineering wherein extracting of unprotected ideas to improve upon the existing computer programme may be lawful to an extent. In reverse engineering, as there exists no meaning in taking only part of a work the possibility of complete reproduction may become necessary. However, fair use does not justify extensive efforts to make profit from replicating the protected expression of a work.[144] The reproduction of the work must not exceed, what is necessary to understand the unprotected elements of a work.[145] This limited exception is however, not an invitation to misappropriate any expression having copyright. Therefore, if a person does not confine decompilation to the acts, which were permitted acts but, uses such information and creates a substantially similar computer programme by way of copying there exist no protection. The DMCA provides for this exception. However, the copyright owners are now resorting to the DRM wherein, the fair use doctrine is said be getting blurred. The courts have widely interpreted fair use doctrine even after DRM has been introduced by the owner's of copyright.

Furthermore, an act will not be an infringement, if the computer programme is

(a) Used for any observation, study or test of functioning of the computer programme;
(b) It should be in order to determine the ideas and principles which underline any elements of the programme;
(c) Necessary for the functions for which, the computer programme was supplied.

Any encryption research is permitted for identifying flaws and vulnerabilities of the technology. The encryption research is conducted in advancing the state of knowledge in the field of encryption technology or to assist in the development of encryption products.[146] Hence, it may form a part of exception to infringement.

In addition, a person having a lawful copy of a computer programme making copies or adaptation shall not be liable for an infringement. However, such use should be for personal and not for commercial use. The Act does not define the term adaptation with reference to a computer programme. Adaptation in relation to a

---

[144] *Sony Corp.* v. *Universal City Studios, Inc*, 464 U.S. 417 (1984).

[145] *Atari Games Corp* v. *Nintendo of America Inc.*, 975 F.2d 832 (Fed Cir. 1992). (in this case Atari was in possession of the work without authorisation, the copying or derivative copying of source code was held not to qualify as fair use); *Sega Enterprises Ltd* v. *Accolade Inc.*, 977 F.2d 1510 (9th Cir. 1992) (The court considering the four factors under the US law held that, if reverse engineering is done for studying or examining the unprotected aspects of a computer programme would be a fair use); *Sony Computer Entertainment Inc.* v. *Connectix Corp*, 203 F.3d 596 (2000) (it has to be noted that, the fair use defence extends to disassembly only. If the third person markets an ultimate product embodying copyright owner's protected expression, an infringement action exists. Following *Sega case*, the court found in favour of Connectix for fair use).

[146] 17 United States Code, s. 1201 (g); *Universal City Studios Inc. and ors* v. *Reimerdes and ors*, 111 F.Supp.2d 294; *Universal City Studios Inc* v. *Corley*, 273 F 3d 429 (2nd Cir. 2001).

computer programme means an arrangement or altered version of the programme or a translation of it.[147] Translation in relation to a computer programme includes a version of the programme wherein, it is converted into or out of a computer language or code or into a different computer language or code, otherwise than incidentally in the course of running the programme.[148] However, the U.K law provides that, any such copying or adaptation may be for correcting errors in a programme or for any other purpose. The contract may provide that, any such copy with errors may be sent back to the manufacturer or supplier for debugging and other maintenance.[149]

These exceptions are generally in line with the common licensing practices of the computer programmes and the fair use clauses of copyright. Though, the licensing agreement "may provide any restrictions, the user shall have the rights to

(a) Make copies for archival purposes
(b) Reproduce the copyright work if such use is for purposes of operating the programme
(c) Decompilation for the purpose of creating compatibility with hardware or operating system."[150]

Finally, the issue of what constitutes a copyright violation would require an analysis on a case-by-case basis with considerations of fair use and on whether the unauthorised copying of a limited portion of the content would be held non-infringing.[151]

9 Conclusion

The owners of copyright always had apprehensions about their work being protected. This has always been a challenge which has become more difficult in the digital context. As observed, the work which can be replicated with ease and made available instantaneously without reducing the quality of such work by generating perfect copies are some of the reasons. Reproduction in the digital form has enabled to reduce the time for copying without reducing the quality and also can instantaneously reproduce quantities as desired. The online transmission of books, music, movies, computer programme or software has made possible the work to be used by public at a time and without limitation of geographical boundaries. Any texts,

---

[147] Copyright, Designs and Patent Act, 1988, (*hereinafter* CDPA), s.21 (3) (ab).

[148] *Id.*, s. 21 (3).

[149] *Software Directive Article 5(1) and 9(1);* Cornish and Llewelyn 2003.

[150] *Supra* note at 140.

[151] *Burlington Home Shopping Pvt. Ltd.* v. *Rajnish Chibber,* 1995 (35) DRJ 335 (the court considering National Commission on New Technological Uses of Copyrighted Works (CONTU) in U.S.).

images, sounds, animation, and photograph can be transformed, manipulated or mixed in such a way that it could be treated as completely a new work. The task of the owner of copyright has become more difficult in controlling the reproduction of the work and also restricting the unauthorised use of such work. The courts while dealing with these cases have to exercise caution and protect the owners and simultaneously balance it with the public interest.

References

"A CBO Paper-Copyright in the Digital Media". The Congress of the United States, A Congressional Budget Office, August 2004. https://www.cbo.gov/sites/default/files/108th-congress-2003-2004/reports/08-09-copyright.pdf. Accessed 30 Dec 2016

Atallah M, O'Rourke M, Mason M, Wade J (2008) Steal this article: battening down the digital hatches. Risk management, pp 26–35

Bond P (2002) Weapon of choice. The Hollywood Reporter, pp 8–11

Chandra R (2010) Knowledge as property: issues in the moral grounding of intellectual property rights, 1st edn. Oxford University Press India, New Delhi, pp 123–124

Copinger and Skone James on Copyright, 13th edn. Sweet & Maxwell, London, p 720, 24 Nov 1994

Cornish and Llewelyn (2003) Intellectual property: patents, copyright, trade marks and allied rights, 5th edn. Thomson Sweet and Maxwell, p 772

"Downloads Did Not Cause the Music Slump, But They Can Cure It," Forrester Research Report, Cambridge, MA, August 13, 2002, referred in Dan Bricklin, The Recording Industry is Killing the Goose that lays the Golden Egg". http://www.bricklin.com/recordsales.htm. Accessed 30 Dec 2016

Dratler J, McJohn SM (2000) Cyberlaw intellectual property in the digital millennium, Akron School of Law, Law Journal Press. http://www.lawjournalpress.com/player/eBook_131_Cyberlaw__Intellectual_Property_in_the_Digital_Millennium.html. Accessed 30 Dec 2016

Ferrera GR, Lichtenstein SD et al (2011) Cyber law: text and cases, 3rd edn. Thomson Learning, Cincinnati: OH, p 82

Ficsor M Dr (2002) Collective management of copyright and related rights, WIPO, 2002. https://books.google.co.in/books?id=PCjHYqsnUEoC&printsec=frontcover#v=onepage&q=reproduction%20conflicts%20with%20the%20normal%20exploitation%20&f=false. Accessed 30 Dec 2016

Garrote IJ (2002) Linking and framing: a comparative law approach. Eur Intell Property Rev 24:184–198

Gooch R (2016) Senior Technology Adviser, International Federation of Phonographic Industry (IFPI), London, at WIPO Seminar on the WCT and WPPT: Opportunities and Challenges, Geneva, May 16, 2002. http://www.wipo.int/edocs/mdocs/copyright/en/wct_wppt_ge_02/wct_wppt_ge_02_inf_1.html. Accessed 30 Dec 2016

IFPI's Music Piracy Report 2002. http://www.ifpi.org. Accessed 30 Dec 2016

Intellectual Property on the Internet: A survey of Issues. World Intellectual Property Organisation (2002). https://books.google.co.in/books/about/Intellectual_Property_on_the_Internet.html?id=104YeGJVsG4C&redir_esc=y. Accessed 30 Dec 2016

Jones A (1999) The protection of computer programs under TRIPS: the subject matter. J L Inf Sci 7(10). http://www.austlii.edu.au/au/journals/JlLawInfoSci/1999/2.html. Accessed 30 Dec 2016

"Kazaa Denies Copyright Infringement Claims; Developer Says P2P No Different Than HTTP", 7 (5) Electronic Commerce and Law Report 99 (Jan 2002), cited in, Stanislava Nikolaeva Staykova, Sound Record Producers' Rights and the Problem of Sound Recording Piracy, D.S.,

Sofia University & J.D., Sofia University, 2004. http://doczz.net/doc/2106214/sound-record-producers–rights-and-the-problem-of-sound. Accessed 30 Dec 2016
Litman J (2006) Digital copyright, 2nd edn. Prometheus Books, Amherst, New York
Menell P (2002) Envisioning Copyright Law's digital future. N Y L Sch L Rev (46):63
Nelson C (2016) "Springsteen Protects His New CD's Online in an Old-Fashioned Way". The New York Times, July 15, 2002. http://www.nytimes.com/2002/07/15/business/springsteen-protects-his-new-cd-s-online-in-an-old-fashioned-way.html. Accessed 6 April 2016
Olsen S (2002) $1 Movie site finds shelter in Iran. ZDNet News, June 5, 2002. http://www.zdnet.com/article/1-movie-site-finds-shelter-in-iran/. Accessed 30 Dec 2016
O'Rourke MA (1998) Fencing Cyberspace: drawing borders in a virtual world. Minn L Rev 82:609
"Protection of Copyright and Related Rights in the Digital Context: The WIPO "Internet Treaties". Lecture prepared by Dr. Mihály Ficsor, Director, Center for Information Technology and Intellectual Property (CITIP), Budapest, Wipo-Escwa Arab Regional Conference on Recent Developments in the Field of Intellectual Property Organized by the World Intellectual Property Organization (WIPO) and the United Nations Economic and Social Commission for Western Asia (ESCWA) in Cooperation with the Ministry of Economy and Trade, Beirut, 2003, WIPO-ESCWA/IP/BEY/03/06. Accessed 30 Dec 2016
Reichman JH (1993) The TRIPS Component of the GATT's Uruguay Round: competitive prospects for intellectual property owners in an integrated world market. Fordham Intell Prop Media Ent L J 4(171), 173–78, 254–266
Rodney RD (2007) Guide to Cyber Laws (Information Technology Act, 2000, E-Commerce, Data Protection and the Internet), 3rd edn. Lexis Nexis, Butterworths Wadhwa Nagpur, p 267
Ryder RD Copyright, technology and digital rights management. http://www.nalsarpro.org/CL/Articles/Copyright_DRM.pdf. Accessed 30 Dec 2016
See presentation of Jean Vincent, General Secretary of the International Federation of Musicians (FIM) (2016) Opportunities and Challenges: Performers in the Digital Environment. Seminar on the WCT and WPPT: Opportunities and Challenges, May 16, 2002. https://www.fim-musicians.org/wp-content/uploads/jean-vincent-wipo-2002.pdf. Accessed 30 Dec 2016
"Software piracy rate falls to 60%, but costs industry $2.9 bn". The Hindu, June 24, 2014. http://www.thehindubusinessline.com/info-tech/software-piracy-rate-falls-to-60-but-costs-industry-29-bn/article6145366.ece. Accessed 3 April 2016
Startling Internet Piracy Statistics, Nov 24 (2014), http://brandongaille.com/34-startling-internet-piracy-statistics/. Accessed 3 April 2016
Sople VV (2012) Managing intellectual property: the strategic imperative, 5th edn. PHI Learning Pvt. Ltd., referring the Recording Industry Association of America (RIAA)'s Webcasting FAQ. http://www.riaa.com/licensing-licen-3a.cfm. Accessed 30 Dec 2016
Sterling JAL (2003) World Copyright Law, 2nd edn. Sweet & Maxwell, London, p 994
Turner K, Von Heusinger K (eds) (2008) Strategic direction. In floating or drowning in a sea of piracy—how do you take on the hacker?, vol 25. Emerald Group Publishing Limited.
Verma SK, Mittal R (eds) (2004) Legal dimensions of cyberspace, 1st edn. Indian Law Institute, New Delhi, p 177
"Webcasters of Radio Broadcasts Not Exempt from Paying Royalties to Record Companies," 6(31) Electronic Commerce and Law Report 839 (August 8, 2001)

First Sale Doctrine in the Digital Era

Amit Jyoti S. Gomber

Abstract This chapter describes the origin and existence of the principle of exhaustion, generally and specifically for copyright laws, by referring to the first sale doctrine or doctrine of parallel imports. Internationally, Paris and Berne convention do not take any stand on the validity or invalidity of international exhaustion. The TRIPs agreement in Article 6 leaves it to each country to adopt any regime for exhaustion of intellectual property rights. Taking from the failure of TRIPs to address exhaustion, the chapter will analyze the controversy surrounding the provisions in the Copyright Act, 1957 and proposed amendments. The chapter would further elaborate on the recent shift in exhaustion regime followed in the United States as held by the US Supreme Court in Kirtsaeng v. John Wiley & Sons, Inc. case. Finally, the chapter would examine the most suitable approach for India in the digital age.

Intellectual property is an umbrella term that protects the creations of intellect in the form of copyrights, trademarks, geographical indications, industrial designs, patents, layout designs of integrated circuits, and trade secrets. Each category of intellectual property creates a bundle of rights for the creator upon fulfilment of the minimum standards prescribed according to the nature of intellectual property in the laws of a country. The nature of such minimum requirements varies according to the category and scope of the intellectual property protection. Protection through the discipline of intellectual property is an endeavor to strike a balance between the private interest of the creator to obtain financial rewards for her creations and the public interest in accessing those intellectual creations.

Copyright is an exclusive protection granted for the creation of an original work when fixed in a tangible medium. The scope of copyright protection is limited to the subject matter identified as '*work*' under the national laws. Generally, the works that attract copyright protection on being original are literary, dramatic, musical and

A.J.S. Gomber (✉)
Centre for Intellectual Property and Technology Law, Jindal Global Law School,
O.P. Jindal Global University, Haryana, India
e-mail: ajsandhu@jgu.edu.in

M.K. Sinha and V. Mahalwar (eds.), *Copyright Law in the Digital World*,
DOI 10.1007/978-981-10-3984-3_12

artistic works, cinematographic films, sound recordings and computer programmes.[1] Copyright owners hold an exclusive right to use or authorize others to reproduce, distribute, publically perform, adapt and translate the work. These exclusive rights aren't however unbridled. The limitations act as a tool to balance the interests of the right holders and the public at large. One such limitation to control copyright owner's exclusive right to distribute the copy of the work once lawfully sold by her is the first sale doctrine, also known as the exhaustion principle. The rationale behind the recognition of this doctrine is that the creator has once benefitted financially by the first sale of the copy of her work.

The first sale doctrine, often also referred to as the principle of exhaustion, had its origin in common law and is claimed to have "*an impeccable historic pedigree*."[2] Justice Breyer, while delivering the judgment of the U.S. Supreme Court in *Kirtsaeng* v. *John Wiley & Sons*[3] referred to a 17th century treatise by Lord Coke where he explained how a seller of a chattel would not be allowed to control its alienation by the buyer as such restraint would be "against Trade and Traffi[c], and bargaining and contracting betwee[n] man and man."[4] Here, Lord Coke emphasized on the liberty of the buyer to decide whether to resell the property or to dispose it through any other means available. In the United States, the first sale doctrine evolved in the *Bobbs-Merrill Co.* v. *Strauss*[5] where the Supreme Court expounded on whether the meaning of "the sole right of vending the same?" as provided in the statute, is that the copyright owner can restrict the subsequent alienation of the subject matter because of a notice in the book that a sale at a different price will be treated as an infringement.[6] Deciding against the copyright owner, the Court stated that the copyright statutes do not allow the owner of the copyright to impose, by notice, any limitation on the future sale of such copy by a lawful purchaser. Also, such interpretation of the statute, does not conflict with the copyright holder's right to multiply and sell his work.

Therefore, the exhaustion doctrine was created and is still recognized to achieve the essential stabilization of the monopolistic exercise of rights by the copyright holder with the public interest to use or dispose of the lawfully procured copy, unhindered. Exhaustion defines the territorial scope of the exclusive rights of the copyright holder after the first sale of her work. Scholars have recognized four categories of benefits of first sale: access, preservation, privacy, and transactional clarity to which Professors Aaron Perzanowski and Jason Schultz have suggested two more in the form of increased innovation and platform competition.[7] First sale promotes affordability and accessibility of the copyrighted works by supporting a

---

[1] The Copyright Act, 1957 (Act 14 of 1957), s. 2(y).

[2] 568 U. S.____(2013), at 17, citing Coke, (1628).

[3] 568 U. S.____(2013).

[4] *Supra* note 2 at 17, *citing* Coke, (1628).

[5] 210 U.S. 339 (1908).

[6] *Id.* at 350.

[7] Perzanowski and Schultz 2011.

secondary market business model.[8] Secondly, first sale allows preservation of the works that may no longer be available from the copyright owner.[9] Thirdly, by the operation of first sale doctrine, a consumer's privy is also maintained and she can transfer the work to anyone without notifying the copyright holder.[10] Fourthly, first sale promotes transactional clarity and market efficiency as it reduces information and transaction costs to be borne by the buyer at the time of purchase.[11] Fifthly, exhaustion promotes innovation by the copyright holders, secondary market providers and users where each stakeholder shall work to improve her position than the other.[12] Lastly, first sale promotes platform competition by reducing consumer lock-in.[13]

A few factors that generally govern application of the doctrine of exhaustion are:

(a) Exhaustion is applicable if the first sale is lawful i.e. made with the consent of the copyright holder or her authorized agent;
(b) Exhaustion is applicable only to that copy of the work on which the first sale right has been exercised;
(c) Exhaustion does not affect the other rights of the copyright holder, like reproduction, public performance etc., but only her right to distribute that copy subsequently.[14]

It is pertinent to note here that exhaustion concerns rights in the physical product that is sold and not the intangible copyrights embodied in that product. Further, the application of exhaustion doctrine may vary depending upon the geographical scope of the doctrine adopted by a country. Also, rules of exhaustion may differ within copyright law depending on the nature of copyrightable work involved.[15] Conditional on where the first sale is made and the country to which such lawfully sold copies are being imported, exhaustion can be classified into three regimes:

(a) *National Exhaustion*: Under the national exhaustion regime, once the copyright holder has exercised her distribution rights on a copy of a work in a domestic market, she cannot control the subsequent sales of the work within the territory of first sale. National exhaustion allows the copyright holder to further block the importation of 'infringing' copies sold in other territories to the domestic market.

For instance, assume that 'A' is a multinational publishing house and copyright owner in a few books in country 'P', 'Q' and 'R'. If country 'P' follows a national

---

[8] *Id.* at 894.
[9] *Id.* at 895.
[10] *Id.* at 896.
[11] *Ibid.*
[12] *Id.* at 897–900.
[13] *Id.* at 900.
[14] Basheer 2012 *citing US* v. *Moore*, 604 F.2d 1228.
[15] *Supra* note 14 at 337.

exhaustion of rights, then sale of a copy of the book by 'A' to a third party in country 'P' would result in the exhaustion of distribution rights by 'A' in territory 'P' only. 'A' can prevent the importation of the copies of its work from other countries into country 'A'.

Those arguing in favor of national exhaustion believe that it allows the creators to recoup their investments and reinvest it further for the benefit of the consumers.[16] Further, allowing parallel importation promotes undue exploitation of the investments of the copyright holder in the form of marketing, publicity etc.

(b) *International Exhaustion*: Under the international exhaustion regime, upon the first lawful sale of the copy of a work, copyright holder relinquishes her exclusive distribution rights all over the world, allowing parallel imports. That lawfully sold copy can now freely move anywhere in the worldwide market.[17]

For instance, assume that 'A' is a multinational publishing house and copyright owner in a few books in country 'P', 'Q' and 'R'. If country 'P' follows an international exhaustion of rights, then sale of a copy of the book by 'A' to a third party in country 'P' would result in the exhaustion of distribution rights by 'A' internationally. 'A' cannot further control the importation the lawfully purchased copies of the book from anywhere in the world to country 'A'.

Proponents of international exhaustion regime emphasize that parallel imports increase competition in the international markets which serves the interests of the consumers, particularly in the developing countries.[18] This would improve the accessibility and availability of the work for the public.

(c) *Regional Exhaustion*: Regional exhaustion is a hybrid approach developed to regulate parallel imports recognizing the benefits of a single, barrier free common market.[19] In this regime of exhaustion, a few countries in a region can agree to treat the first sale of a work in either of their markets by the copyright holder exhaustion of her distribution rights in the region. Copyright owner cannot restrain the subsequent sale of the work in the region but its importation from countries outside the region.[20] The regional exhaustion regime has been adopted in the European Economic Area (EEA) by the signatories to the Treaty

---

[16] Bonadio 2011.

[17] *For instance*, Australia and New Zealand permit parallel importation for copyrighted works. Australian legislation legislation in regard to parallel importation of copyrighted works differs in regard to the type of work. Abbott 1998.

[18] Abbott, 607 1998.

[19] Conley 2007.

[20] *Id.* at 190.

of Rome (the EEC Treaty) to harmonize the intellectual property laws within the European community.[21]

For instance, assume that 'A' is a multinational publishing house and copyright owner in a few books in country 'P', 'Q' 'R' and 'S'. Countries 'P', 'Q' and 'R' have adopted regional exhaustion regime. Therefore, sale of a copy of the book by 'A' to a third party in country 'P' would result in the exhaustion of distribution rights by 'A' in countries 'Q' and 'R', as well. Any third person upon the purchase of copies from country 'P' can import or resell it in countries 'Q' and 'R' without any permission of the copyright holder. But importation of these copies in country 'S' may be considered infringing.

An obvious consequence of exhaustion, specifically international and to an extent regional, are parallel imports. It may be noted that parallel imports are not pirated or counterfeit works but legally acquired copies of the work from a foreign jurisdiction. Such products are also referred to by the term grey market goods, which is in contrast to the term black market goods. While former concerns genuine products, latter is related to pirated or counterfeit goods. These goods are referred to as 'grey' due to the unauthorized distribution channels by which these lawfully acquired goods make their way to the importing country.[22] The most common method of parallel importation is passive imports whereby the work is purchased by the third parties in a foreign market and then resold in the domestic market.[23] On the other hand, active parallel importation occurs where a foreign licensee exploits the work within the territory of her license and then enters the domestic market in direct competition with the copyright holder and other official domestic licensees. Any kind of parallel importation, active or passive, creates havoc for the copyright holder in a market as these goods are sold by the third party at a significantly lower price than the copyright owner or authorized sellers. The choice of an exhaustion regime does strongly impacts the international trade of goods.[24] Following the national exhaustion regime or for that matter even the regional exhaustion regime, allows the copyright holder to segregate the markets and enforce price discrimination whereas international exhaustion creates an opportunity for the buyer to arbitrage the price

[21] DIRECTIVE 2001/29/EC OF THE EUROPEAN PARLIAMENT AND OF THE COUNCIL of 22 May 2001 on the harmonisation of certain aspects of copyright and related rights in the information society, Article 28 says, "Copyright protection under this Directive includes the exclusive right to control distribution of the work incorporated in a tangible article. The first sale in the Community of the original of a work or copies thereof by the rightholder or with his consent exhausts the right to control resale of that object in the Community. This right should not be exhausted in respect of the original or of copies thereof sold by the rightholder or with his consent outside the Community". Council Directive of May 14, 1991 on the Legal Protection of Computer Programs (91/250/EEC) states, "The first sale in the Community of a copy of a program by the rightholder or with his consent shall exhaust the distribution right within the Community of that copy, with the exception of the right to control further rental of the program or a copy thereof."

[22] Christopher Heath, "Parallel Imports and International Trade".

[23] *Supra* note 16.

[24] *Supra* note 16.

differences. Price differentiation occurs where different prices are charged to different consumers for the same good. Market differentiation and price discrimination strategies adopted by the copyright holder may stem from various reasons like difference in production or distribution costs, ability of the consumers to pay for the product, difference in marketing investments and national differences in government price controls.

The popular assumption is that developed economies follow national exhaustion for they are the net creators of intellectual property.[25] A possible explanation for developed economies to adopt national exhaustion is based on the relationship between domestic and foreign prices for IP-related goods.[26] When the domestic prices are lower than foreign jurisdictions, national exhaustion protects income transfers to national IPR holders in "foreign" premium markers by protecting them against exports from the lower cost domestic market.[27] Developing economies on the other hand are the consumers of intellectual property and would support international exhaustion to eliminate the barriers in accessibility. However, as would be clear from the discussion below this assumption may not stand true in all cases. U.S. Supreme Court in *Kirtsaeng*[28] upheld the international exhaustion regime for copyright law in the United States (a developed country) and the Indian copyright law seems to follow the principle of national exhaustion, to an extent, for the territory of India (a developing country).

1 International Conventions on First Sale and Parallel Imports

The development of a consistent policy on exhaustion has globally continued to be a grey area of intellectual property law. Countries around the world have been given liberty to choose and establish their own exhaustion regime pursuant to national interests and priorities. Consequently, the lack of uniformity in policy has made exhaustion and parallel imports controversial.

The Paris Convention for the Protection of Industrial Property, 1883[29] and the Berne Convention for the Protection of Literary and Artistic Works, 1886,[30] also referred to as the "Great Conventions" do not address the principle of exhaustion.[31] Though, it is argued that Berne Convention impliedly follows national exhaustion as the rights are territorial in nature and the acts held to be lawful in a country do

[25] Chiappetta 2000.

[26] *Id.* at 352.

[27] *Id.* at n99.

[28] *Kirtsaeng* v. *John Wiley & Sons, Inc.*, 568 U. S. ____ (2013).

[29] Hereinafter Paris Convention.

[30] Hereinafter Berne Convention.

[31] Jerome H. Reichman, Ruth L. Okedijı*et.*

not *ipso facto* become lawful in another country.[32] Thereby, allowing copyright owners to segment the markets and practice price discrimination and permitting countries to seize goods lawfully made in other countries under the principle of territoriality. Though it is widely contested that international exhaustion regime is more consistent with the free-trade paradigm purported in the General Agreement on Tariffs and Trade (GATT) (1994) and the General Agreement on Trade in Services (GATTS).[33] These differential national and regional positions couldn't even be resolved during the Uruguay Round of Multilateral Trade Negotiations in 1990s that lead to the establishment of World Trade Organization (WTO) and adoption of Agreement on Trade-Related Aspects of Intellectual Property Rights (TRIPs).[34] Accordingly, Article 6 of the TRIPs Agreement avoids addressing the issue of parallel imports in the following words:

> For the purposes of dispute settlement under this Agreement, subject to the provisions of Articles 3 and 4 nothing in this Agreement shall be used to address the issue of the exhaustion of intellectual property rights.[35]

While Article 6 takes a neutral stand on exhaustion, it cautions the member nations to abide by both the national treatment [Article 3] and most favored nation (MFN) [Article 4] principles while adopting any exhaustion regime (national, international or regional). Application of national treatment to the exhaustion regime would mean that a member State should treat the works of the foreign nationals at par with its own nationals. If it accords national exhaustion to the works of its own nationals then it cannot practice international exhaustion on foreign copyright holders. Similarly, under MFN principle a member state cannot apply different exhaustion rules to nationals of different members. It can be argued here that the regional exhaustion regime followed by the European Union is inconsistent with the MFN principle for it adopts a differential treatment for the goods imported from other countries within the region than to the countries from outside the region.[36] It also clarifies that irrespective of the regime chosen; there would be immunity from legal actions before WTO's dispute settlement body.[37] This provision has been suggested to amount to "an agreement to disagree."[38]

---

[32] *Id.* at 3, n15.

[33] *Supra* note 16.

[34] *Supra* note 25 at 345.

[35] Available at https://www.wto.org/english/docs_e/legal_e/27-trips_03_e.htm. (Last accessed on April 3, 2016).

[36] Exhaustion of Rights, available at http://www.iprsonline.org/unctadictsd/docs/RB_Part1_Nov_1.4_update.pdf. (Last accessed on April 12, 2016).

[37] The Brussels draft of the Agreement did not provide for limitation on the dispute settlement on the subject of exhaustion. However, later DSB's power was precluded due to inability of the members to reach a consensus on the exhaustion issue. Available at http://www.iprsonline.org/unctadictsd/docs/RB_Part1_Nov_1.4_update.pdf. (Last accessed on April 12, 2016).

[38] *Supra* note 16.

Further, Doha Ministerial Declaration on TRIPs Agreement and Public Health, 2001 in paragraph 5(d) provides as follows:

> The effect of the provisions in the TRIPs Agreement that are relevant to the exhaustion of intellectual property rights is to leave each member free to establish its own regime for such exhaustion without challenge, subject to the MFN and national treatment provisions of Articles 3 and 4.[39]

The two recent copyright treaties under WIPO, WIPO Copyright Treaty, 1996[40] and the WIPO Performances and Phonograms Treaty, 1996[41] follow the silence of Article 6 of the TRIPs agreement and reiterate the lack of consensus amongst the members in adopting a harmonized approach for exhaustion of rights.[42]

Therefore, none of these provisions in the intellectual property conventions could provide an authoritative resolution to the controversies concerning the legality of international exhaustion. This may frustrate the interests of the copyright holder in a market place where she cannot prevent the parallel importation into a 'high-priced' market due to international exhaustion but may instead file infringement action in the 'low-priced' national exhaustion market.[43]

Professor Abbott, as the Special Rapporteur for TRIPs in the Second Report (Final) to the Committee on International Trade Law of the International Law Association on the Subject of the Exhaustion of Intellectual Property Rights and Parallel Importation upon assessing the arguments of the proponents and opponents of exhaustion, suggests incorporation of a general rule of international exhaustion for all kinds of intellectual property rights and additionally creating exceptions accommodating the needs of developing countries.[44] Speaking for copyright law, he recommends adoption of different approaches to parallel imports of different forms of expression of the work.[45]

---

[39] Available at https://www.wto.org/english/thewto_e/minist_e/min01_e/mindecl_trips_e.htm. The Doha Declaration on the TRIPs Agreement and Public Health was adopted on November 14, 2001 by the WTO Ministerial Conference. It has been argued that Paragraph 5 is only applicable to the public health sector as it is part of a declaration dealing exclusively with the protection of public health.

[40] World Intellectual Property Organization: Copyright Treaty [adopted in Geneva, Dec. 20, 1996].

[41] World Intellectual Property Organization: Performances and Phonograms Treaty [adopted in Geneva, Dec. 20, 1996].

[42] WIPO WCT, Article 6(2) states, "*Nothing in this Treaty shall affect the freedom of Contracting Parties to determine the conditions, if any, under which the exhaustion of the right in paragraph (1) applies after the first sale or other transfer of ownership of the original or a copy of the work with the authorization of the author.*" WPPT, Article 8(2) states, "*Nothing in this Treaty shall affect the freedom of Contracting Parties to determine the conditions, if any, under which the exhaustion of the right in paragraph (1) applies after the first sale or other transfer of ownership of the original or a copy of the fixed performance with the authorization of the performer.*"

[43] *Supra* note 25 at 356.

[44] *Supra* note 18.

[45] *Ibid*. Different forms here means works in tangible forms like printed books and intangible works like e-books.

Many countries have utilized the exemption provided under Article 1(1) of the TRIPs agreement whereby WTO members are free to introduce a stronger intellectual property protection, beyond the minimum standards of protection prescribed therein.[46] The NAFTA[47] and the MERCOSUR[48] are two such regional free-trade agreements whereby the member states have adopted TRIPs-plus provisions to strengthen the regional intellectual property rights and remove trade barriers. However, these agreements also leave the international exhaustion as a question for national law.[49] United States free trade agreement with Jordan and Morocco,[50] respectively, supports national exhaustion for copyright laws thereby allowing copyright holders to block parallel importation.[51]

2 Indian Copyright Law on First Sale and Parallel Imports

The extent of application of the exhaustion principle on the works protected under the Indian Copyright Act, 1957[52] has been a vexing question. The definition for '*infringing copy*' under Section 2(m) is not only limited to unlawful reproduction of the work but also its importation to the territory of India.[53]

---

[46] Article 1(1) states, "Members shall give effect to the provisions of this Agreement. Members may, but shall not be obliged to, implement in their law more extensive protection than is required by this Agreement, provided that such protection does not contravene the provisions of this Agreement."

[47] North American Free Trade Agreement, 1994 between Canada, Mexico and the United States of America.

[48] The MERCOSUR is an agreement between Argentina, Brazil, Paraguay and Uruguay.

[49] *Supra* note 18.

[50] Jordan (2001) and Morocco (2004).

[51] Tightening TRIPs: The Intellectual Property Provisions of Recent US Free Trade Agreements. Available at http://www.cptech.org/ip/health/trade/worldbank02072005.pdf. (Last accessed on April 12, 2016).

[52] Here in after referred to as the Act.

[53] The Copyright Act, 1957 (Act 14 of 1957), Section 2(m) "infringing copy" means,–

(i) in relation to a literary, dramatic, musical or artistic work, a reproduction thereof otherwise than in the form of a cinematographic film;
(ii) in relation to a cinematographic film, a copy of the film made on any medium by any means;
(iii) in relation to a sound recording, any other recording embodying the same sound recording, made by any means;
(iv) in relation to a programme or performance in which such a broadcast reproduction right or a performer's right subsists under the provisions of this Act, the sound recording or a cinematographic film of such programme or performance, if such reproduction, copy or sound recording is made or imported in contravention of the provisions of this Act;

According to Sections 14(1)(a)(ii), (b)(i), and (c)(iii), it is the exclusive right of the copyright owner of a literary, dramatic, musical and artistic work, respectively, to issue copies of the work to the public not being copies already in circulation. Further, explanation in Section 14 provides that for the purposes of Section 14 a copy which has been sold once shall be deemed to be a copy already in circulation. These sub-clauses under Section 14 appear to support the exhaustion of a copyright owner's right to control the subsequent distribution of the work after its first lawful sale. It could be claimed with certainty that Section 14 endorses national exhaustion but whether it supports international exhaustion is questionable.[54] Question here is if "*copies already in circulation*" and "*a copy once sold*" refers to such circulation and sale, respectively, anywhere in the world or only in the territory of India? It may be assumed to apply only to the copies lawfully sold in the territory of India as the Government and the Parliamentary standing Committee had sought to amend Section 2(m) with the Copyright Amendment Bill, 2010 and applying the doctrine of international exhaustion.[55] This strengthens the interpretation of the current provision as limited to national exhaustion.[56] However, so far as rights of a copyright owner in a computer programme, cinematographic film and sound recording are concerned, Section 14(1) (b), (d) and (e), respectively do not adapt the phrase "*not being copies already in circulation*", implying non-applicability of the exhaustion principle. For cinematographic works and sound recordings, the copyright holder can exercise an exclusive right to "*sell or give on hire, or offer for sale or hire, any copy of the*" film or sound recording "*regardless of whether such copy has been sold or given on hire on earlier occasions.*"[57]Aside, Section 53 of the Act empowers the Commissioner of Customs to act on the notice of the copyright owner in prohibiting the importation of infringing copies of the work to the territory of India.

In *Penguin Books Ltd. vs. M/s India Book Distributors and Ors*,[58] India Book Distributors imported, distributed and offered for sale 13 titles for which Penguin Books was the exclusive licensee in the territory of India. It was held by the Division bench of the Delhi High Court that copyrights are territorial in nature. Lawful sale of books in the United States cannot abrogate the protection of the laws of the territory in which they are imported.[59] Citing Section 14(1)(a)(i) and (ii) along with Section 51, the Court found India Book Distributor liable for infringement for importing "infringing copies of the work".[60] Persuaded by the

---

[54] *Supra*note 14 at 338.

[55] *Ibid*.

[56] *Ibid*.

[57] The Copyright Act, 1957 (Act 14 of 1957), ss. 14(1)(d)(ii) and (e)(ii) of the Act.

[58] ILR (1985) I Delhi 35.

[59] *Id*. at 40 para 10.

[60] *Id*. at 44 para 22 and 23.

Delhi High Court's decision in *Penguin Books*, Justice S.C. Dharmadhikari for the Bombay High Court in *Eurokids International Pvt. Ltd. vs. India Book Distributors Egmont Books Ltd.*[61] reiterated the national exhaustion regime of the Copyright Act, 1957 whereby importation and distribution of the titles lawfully procured from outside India amounts to infringement in the territory of India.

In *Warner Bros Entertainment Inc. vs. Santosh V.G.*,[62] Delhi High Court again had the opportunity to refer to the exhaustion principle but this time it was in relation to cinematographic films. In this case, the defendant ran a video rental service by the name "Cinema Paradiso" where he was renting out DVDs/CDs that were lawfully sold in the United States. The plaintiff, a leading film production company in the USA and copyright owner in many of the cinematographic works being rented out by the defendants, filed a copyright infringement suit against the defendant. The plaintiff argued that CDs and DVDs procured by the defendant were only meant for sale in Zone 1 i.e. USA and Canada. Such sale or rental in Zone 5 countries like India amounts to infringement under Section 14(d)(ii) read with Section 51 of the Act. The defendant tried to argue his case on the basis of the first sale doctrine claiming that since the plaintiff has exhausted its rights upon the first legally authorized sale, it cannot control or restrict the terms of sale or rental thereon. To support its case for national exhaustion, the plaintiff refers to Section 51 (b)(iv) proviso of the Act contending that if there was no restriction on the import of genuinely made cinematographic films outside India then there wouldn't be a need to incorporate any such proviso.[63]

The Delhi High Court considered various authoritative sources dealing with the exhaustion principle and held that the extent of applicability of this principle would be determined by the national law as there was no universally applicable rule. The court carefully classified the applicability of national and international exhaustion to the varied works under the Act. It stated that in the case of literary, dramatic or musical work the copyright owner's right is confined to issuance of copies of the work to the public when such copies were "not already in circulation" whereas for cinematographic film the copyright owner has the exclusive right to sell or give on hire or offer for sale or hire, any copy of the film, regardless of whether such copy has been sold or given on hire on earlier occasion.[64] Thus, found the defendants liable for infringement.

In *John Wiley & Sons vs. Prabhat Chander Kumar Jain*,[65] while deciding the alleged copyright infringement against the defendant for export of low priced editions from India to Western countries, the Delhi High Court extended copyright

---

[61] (2005) 6 Bom CR 198.

[62] 2009 SCC OnLine Del 835.

[63] The Copyright Act, 1957 (14 of 1957), Section 51 (b)(iv) proviso: Provided that nothing in sub-clause (iv) shall apply to the import of one copy of any work for the private and domestic use of the importer.

[64] *Supra* note 62 at para 63 and 64.

[65] 2010 (44) PTC 675 (Del).

protection to the realm of exports. In this case, plaintiffs are the leading publishers and copyright holders in various books circulated worldwide. They have exclusively licensed some other plaintiffs based in the territory of India to publish and distribute the lower priced editions of their books only in the territories of India, Bangladesh, Nepal, Pakistan, Sri Lanka, Indonesia, Myanmar, Philippines and Vietnam. It came to the notice of the plaintiffs that the defendants are exporting these low cost editions from India to the USA, UK and other countries for which books aren't meant.

The Delhi High stated that in absence of an express provision on international exhaustion in India law, it would be appropriate to support national exhaustion.[66] However, in the given case the question of exhaustion did not arise at all. The Court granted injunction in favor of the plaintiffs stating that the copyright owner would have the worldwide right to issue copies of its work as the rights under the Act are not circumscribed by any territorial limitation. The correctness of this judgment as often been questioned in absence of any express provision in the Act granting exclusive rights to the copyright holder to prevent export of any lawfully procured titles.[67] Also, by extending protection to Indian editions outside the territory of India the Court has given an extra-territorial effect to the Act.[68]

In 2010, the Government proposed to comprehensively reform the Act vide Copyright Amendment Bill, 2010. The Amendment Bill, in its first version, had the following proviso to Section 2(m) that sought to legalize parallel importation propounding the principle of international exhaustion:

> provided that a copy of a work published in any country outside India with the permission of the author of the work and imported from that country shall not be deemed to be an infringing copy.

When the bill was reviewed by the Parliamentary Standing Committee, it strongly supported the introduction of international exhaustion of copyrights by stating it to be "a step in the right direction, specially in the prevailing situation at the ground level … Nobody can deny the fact that the interests of students will be best protected if they have access to latest editions of the books … The Committee would, however, like to put a note of caution to Government to ensure that the purpose for which the amendment is proposed i.e. to protect the interest of the students is not lost sight of."[69] The introduction of this proviso led to varied reactions from various stakeholders. Thomas Abraham, MD of Hachette India, described the amendment as "*The Death of Books*."[70] He asserted that India is

[66] *Id.* at para 104.

[67] *Supra* note 14 at 343.

[68] Padmanabhan 2012.

[69] 227th Report on Copyright (Amendment) Bill, 2010, Department—Related Parliamentary Standing Committee on Human Resource Development, p. 68, http://www.prsindia.org/uploads/media/Copyright%20Act/SCR%20Copyright%20Bill%202010.pdf. (Last accessed on April 12, 2016).

[70] Abraham 2011.

already amongst the lowest priced markets in the world and introduction of exhaustion principle would reduce India into a 'remainder bin' where surplus stocks from around the world would be imported to India and would wipe off local editions and the Indian publishing industry.[71] Thomas Abraham argued that there weren't any accessibility and affordability issues for the Indian students.[72] In fact he suggested that prices of some text books go as low as one tenth of their cost in the USA.[73]

Promoting Public Interest Lawyering (P-PIL), an organization for public interest issues, conducted an empirical study to test the claims of accessibility and affordability for students and libraries.[74] The report demonstrated the paucity of availability of low priced Indian editions of foreign titles. Most of the foreign titles were found to be procured at an equivalent or higher cost than in the West.

However, due to strong opposition and persistent lobbying by the publishers guild, amendment to Section 2(m) was given a miss by the Government in the final version of the Bill. The Government further referred the issue of inclusion of the proviso for examination to the National Council of Applied Economic Research (NCAER). NCAER, in 2014, released its report on '*The Impact of Parallel Imports of Books, Films/Music and Software on the Indian Economy with Special Reference to Students*'. Considering the opposing interests of the consumers and the producers, the report recommends to amicably search for an optimal solution based on cogent evidence. Given the difficulty in achieving harmonious results, the report suggests to make the amendment to Section 2(m) with requisite safety valves.[75]

Thus, concluding the position of the Act along with the interpretation provided by the courts we may say that copyright exhaustion in India is limited to the principle of national exhaustion.

3 United States of America's Position on First Sale and Parallel Imports in Copyright Law

U.S. adopts a different approach to exhaustion of copyrights, trademarks and patents. As discussed in the beginning, exhaustion of distribution right in a copyrighted work was recognized by the U.S. Supreme Court in 1908 in *Bobbs-Merrill*

---

[71] *Ibid.*

[72] *Ibid.*

[73] Thomas Abraham's rebuttal to 'Why Parallel Importation of Books Should Be', 2016.

[74] Basheer 2011.

[75] National Council of Applied Economic Research report on The Impact of Parallel Imports of Books, Films/Music and Software on the Indian Economy with Special Reference to Students, (Ministry of Human Resource Development, Copyright Division, Department of High Education, Government of India) pp. 108, http://copyright.gov.in/documents/parallel_imports_report.pdf. (Last accessed on April 3, 2016).

v. *Strauss*.[76] The doctrine was codified in the Copyright Act of 1909 and re-codified in Section 109(a) of the Copyright Act of 1976, which states: "*Notwithstanding the provisions of* Section *106(3) the owner of a particular copy or phonorecord lawfully made under this title, or any person authorized by such owner, is entitled, without the authority of the copyright owner, to sell or otherwise dispose of the possession of that copy or phonorecord.*" This section acts as a limitation on the exclusive right of the copyright owner to "*distribute copies or phono-records of the copyrighted work to the public bysale or other transfer of ownership, or by rental, lease, or lending*."[77] However, the exception in Section 109(a) is not applicable to the exercise of exclusive right "*for rental, lease, or lending*" by the copyright owner since the privilege can only be exercised by the "*owner*" as opposed to the "*possessor*" of a copy or phonorecord in this situation.[78] Other provisions of Section 109 provide the application of the exhaustion principle for specific categories of works: for copyrighted software and phonorecords, the copyright owner shall retain the rental rights even after a first sale[79]; purchaser of a PGS work can display the work without copyright owner's permission[80]; owner of a copy of electronic audiovisual game can publicly perform or display that game in coin-operated equipment.[81] The development of debate over international exhaustion in the US can be understood through the trinity of cases discussed below.

In *Quality King Distributors, Inc. vs. L'anza Research International, Inc.*[82] instead of a trade mark infringement, Quality King was sued for copyright infringement (for violation of the distribution right). Quality King was importing hair care products with labels printed in the US and protected under the copyright law by L'anza. The infringing products involved in this case in fact originated in the US, were then exported from the US to other countries and after several transactions overseas, were being imported back to the US by Quality King. Quality King asserted the first sale doctrine defense. Interpreting the exclusive importation right of the copyright owner under Section 602(a) along with Section 109(a) that acts as a limitation on Section 106(3), the Court stated that because the first sale rule is an exception to the exclusive distribution right, it must also be an exception to the exclusive importation right. It was held that the first sale rule permits the importation of copies lawfully made in the US even if the copyright owner intended them exclusively for the foreign market. The Court, however, did not decide whether same rule would apply to foreign made copies imported to the US. This allowed the copyright owners to assert their distribution rights on importation of copies made outside the US. Section 602(a).

---

[76] 210 U.S. 339 (1908).

[77] 17 U.S.C. § 106(3).

[78] Ghosh 2014.

[79] 17 U.S.C. § 109(b).

[80] PGS stands for Pictorial, graphic or sculptural work. 17 U.S.C. § 109(c).

[81] 17 U.S.C. § 109(e).

[82] *523 U.S. 135 (1998)*.

In *Costco Wholesale Corp. vs. Omega, S.A.*,[83] Costco was found importing and selling in the US watches made and sold overseas by Omega. Omega did not sue for trademark infringement as the products were genuine and not materially different. It filed a copyright infringement case on the basis of engraved omega globe design on the back of the watches. The Ninth Circuit analyzed the interplay among Section 106, 109(a) and 602(a)(1) of the Copyright Act to decide for Omega.[84] Costco's petition in the Supreme Court could not reach a decision as the Court was evenly split on exhaustion question.[85] Yet, again the question was left in murky waters.

Finally, the question of exhaustion was settled by the US Supreme Court in *Kirtsaeng vs. John Wiley & Sons, Inc.*,[86] Inc. case where the majority favored international exhaustion. This case involved a Thai student in the US, SupapKirtsaeng who bought low priced text books from Thailand and resold them at a higher price in the US market. John Wiley Publishers contended violation of the importation and distribution rights in the copyrighted textbooks to which Wiley asserted the first sale doctrine. The Court held that according to the statute there is no geographic limitation on the first sale doctrine. The doctrine is applicable to all copies lawfully made, irrespective of their place of origin. Adopting the principle of international exhaustion, the Court interpreted the words "*lawfully made under this title*" to mean by the legal authority of the copyright holder. Thus, unauthorized importation of the copies lawfully sold outside the US was allowed by the Court.

However, three judges (Justices Ginsburg, Scalia and Kennedy) expressed their dissent stating the implications of adopting international exhaustion. They supported national exhaustion to regulate the import of pirated or counterfeit products in the US market by unscrupulous importers.

Together, these decisions of the Supreme Court have defeated the long practice of trade association to divide their domestic and foreign market maintaining high prices of the products in the US.

4 European Union's Position on First Sale and Parallel Imports in Copyright Law

The European Union (EU) is an economic and political union of 28 countries: Austria, Belgium, Bulgaria, Croatia, Republic of Cyprus, Czech Republic, Denmark, Estonia, Finland, France, Germany, Greece, Hungary, Ireland, Italy, Latvia, Lithuania, Luxembourg, Malta, Netherlands, Poland, Portugal, Romania, Slovakia, Slovenia, Spain, Sweden and the UK. The EU operates an internal

[83] *Omega S.A.* v. *Costco Wholesale Corp.*, 541 F.3d 982 (9th Cir. 2008).

[84] *Ibid.*

[85] *Costco Wholesale Corp. vs. Omega*, 562 U.S.___ (2010). Although there are nine justices in the Court, Justice Kagan was not allowed to decide as she was involved in the case as Solicitor General.

[86] 568 U. S.____(2013).

uniform market facilitating free trade between the member states.[87] Iceland, Liechtenstein and Norway are also included in the European Economic Area (EEA) allowing these countries to be part of EU's single market.[88] Switzerland, neither an EU nor an EEA member, is also part of the single market.[89] With its complex governance structure for commerce, each member state is allowed to exercise its sovereign powers in formulating substantive laws subject to Directives from the European Council, Commission and Parliament, decisions from the European Court of Justice, and treaties such as the EU Treaty and the Treaty on the Functioning of the European Union (TFEU).[90]

EU's copyright legislation comprises of ten directives, which aim to harmonize the essential segments of copyright law amongst all the member states.[91] Within copyright, the community has adopted a principle of regional exhaustion to consistently promote the free movement of goods as provided under Article 34 of the TFEU and its limitation under Article 36.[92] Thus, when a copyright owner has extinguished her right to distribution over a copyrighted work in any country of the EU, she cannot prevent the subsequent importation of the work into any other country of the Union. In *Warner Brothers* v. *Christiansen,*[93] the European Court held that exhaustion does not apply to the rental right, which is different from the right to distribute. It has been observed that in a few situations national difference in the copyright laws of member states can override the principle of regional exhaustion.[94] There exist a few issues on regional exhaustion of distribution right given varied works and consequent challenges of distribution in this age of technology.[95] It has been proposed that to effectively achieve a single market for goods and services the problem of territoriality in copyright must be confronted by the introduction of a unified European Copyright Law.[96]

---

[87] https://www.gov.uk/eu-eea. (Last accessed on April 13, 2016).

[88] *Ibid.*

[89] *Ibid.*

[90] *Supra* note 78 at 56.

[91] https://ec.europa.eu/digital-single-market/en/eu-copyright-legislation. (Last accessed on April 2, 2016).

[92] Article 34, Quantitative restrictions on imports and all measures having equivalent effect shall be prohibited between Member States. Article 36, The provisions of Articles 34 and 35 shall not preclude prohibitions or restrictions on imports, exports or goods in transit justified on grounds of public morality, public policy or public security; the protection of health and life of humans, animals or plants; the protection of national treasures possessing artistic, historic or archaeological value; or the protection of industrial and commercial property. Such prohibitions or restrictions shall not, however, constitute a means of arbitrary discrimination or a disguised restriction on trade between Member States.

[93] *[1988] ECR 2605.*

[94] *Supra* note 78 at 56. *Citing EMI Electrola* v. *Patricia*, [1989] ECR 79 where Denmark did not allow the importation of videotapes of a copyrighted film from United Kingdom where such importation was allowed.

[95] *Id.*

[96] BerntHugenholtz 2012.

5 Exhaustion & Parallel Importation in the Digital Era

Copyright continues to be the dynamic field of law as the corpus of protected works keeps expanding to accommodate new technological developments. New rights have been added to accommodate the variety of ways that the work could be exploited in the marketplace. However as the mediums of expression of the work by the creator continue to evolve with technology; its further exploitation by unauthorized users has taken new forms. As it has been observed that Amazon sells more e-books than traditional tangible books, sale of music is more through online downloads than CDs.[97] Therefore, digital marketplace has increasingly marginalized the first sale doctrine and dramatically increased the need of a uniform policy on exhaustion of rights and parallel importation.

As noted Professor Abbott in Second Report (Final) to the Committee on International Trade Law of the International Law Association on the Subject of the Exhaustion of Intellectual Property Rights and Parallel Importation,[98] digital electronic commerce involves some of the following issues:

(a) Use of digital networks to advertise and promote sales: This may not raise exhaustion issues as the question whether distribution rights will get exhausted when a copy of a work is placed by the copyright holder on a digital network would continue to be regulated the law in the country of importation.
(b) Distribution of a digital work over electronic media: This remains an emerging and significant issue. Transactions through the electronic medium would be different from the physical sale of the work as electronic technology provides the ease to the end user to copy and re-transmit the work. Electronic distribution of works is anyway an inexpensive affair. To control such infringement becomes difficult given the barrier free nature of the virtual world. Thus, unless regulated, international exhaustion may govern the transmissions in the digital environment.

Aside, transmission of a work on internet creates an 'ephemeral' or temporary copy of the work on the system. Whether this reproduction constitutes copyright infringement? Would the copyright holder be deemed to have exhausted her rights over such transient reproduction? Is this exhaustion national or international? Courts around the world are attempting to answer these questions posed by the new digital age. Some of the solutions require the expansion of the application of the first sale doctrine beyond the exclusive right to distribute.

There also exists a contrary view on the effect of technology on the exclusive rights of the copyright owner. Proponents of this view believe that purchase of the digital copy of a work does not allow the owner to exploit it in a similar fashion to a non-digital content. Rather technology has created new opportunities for the copyright holders to practice market discrimination. If I purchase J.K. Rowling's

---

[97] *Supra* note 7 at 890, n2 and n3.

[98] *Supra* note 18.

Harry Potter from a book store, by operation of the first sale doctrine I can gift it to a friend, sell it to another upon reading it, and get it hardbound to preserve it better. On the other hand, if I buy an e-book on Kindle, I would have to part with the device itself to give the e-book to someone else for the book is stored for use only on that device, similar would be a situation if I wish to sell it to another after reading. Apart from the lock-in issues, I cannot re-sell or transfer any of this digital content to another as in most the transactions I only became a licensee of the content not the owner.[99] Thus, there's no question of applicability of the first sale doctrine to such a 'licensing' transaction and consequently, the copyright owner can regulate the parallel imports.[100] Digital era to an extent has allowed copyright owners to circumvent the exhaustion of rights through first sale. This eventually affects the existence of secondary marketplace which is not completely in the interest of the consumers.

Another limitation on the application of the first sale doctrine was stated in the *Capitol Records, LLC* v. *ReDigi Inc.*,[101] whereby the Court held that customers cannot resell their pre-owned digital musical files as the exhaustion by first sale does not apply to digital transfers of copyrighted works because the transferred file is not identical to the original file. It is, in fact, a copy of the original file amounting to unauthorized reproduction. Such interpretation threatens the existence of the first sale doctrine in the digital era.

6 Digital Exhaustion in India & US

The current NDA government has launched the Digital India programme that aims to improve the digital infrastructure and e-governance services and digitally empower the citizens of India.[102] This programme is of particular importance to our discussion here as it would have implications on the exclusive rights of the copyright holders and accessibility of information for the consumers.

Through the Copyright (Amendment) Act, 2012 India harmonized its law with the two WIPO treaties—WCT and WPPT—to extend adequate protection for copyrighted works in digital India and recognized solutions to the questions raised by technological developments.[103] Section 65A and 65B provide for protection of technological measure and right management information, respectively and

---

[99] For instance, Kindle Store Terms of Use, available at https://www.amazon.in/gp/help/customer/display.html?nodeId=201014950. (Last accessed on April 14, 2016).

[100] Asay 2016.

[101] *Capitol Records, LLC* v. *ReDigi Inc.*, 934 F. Supp. 2d 640, 655 (S.D.N.Y. 2013).

[102] *See* Vision of Digital India at http://www.digitalindia.gov.in/content/vision-and-vision-areas. (Last accessed on April 14, 2016).

[103] As stated in the Preamble to WCT and WPPT, available at http://www.wipo.int/treaties/en/text.jsp?file_id=295166 and http://www.wipo.int/wipolex/en/treaties/text.jsp?file_id=295477. (Last accessed on April 13, 2016).

prescribe imprisonment and fine for infringement. However, Section 65A(2) provides for certain exceptions like—doing acts not prohibited under the Act, allowing third parties to facilitate circumvention, provided he maintains a complete record of the details of the person and the purpose for which circumvention was facilitated, circumvention of technological measures for the purpose of certain activities like encryption research, lawful investigation, security testing of a computer system or a computer network with the authorization of its owner or operator, protection of privacy, and measures necessary in the interest of national security.

US adopted the WIPO copyright treaties by implementing the Digital Millennium Copyright Act (DMCA) in 1998.[104] DMCA provides protection against anti-circumvention of the technological measures that protect copyrighted works in two forms: measures that prevent unauthorized access to a copyrighted work and measures that prevent unauthorized copying of a copyrighted work.[105] It provides for certain limitations including fair use, use by nonprofit library, archive and educational institution, encryption research, security testing etc.[106] At the time of DMCA's enforcement, some concerns were raised by the consumer protection groups about the effect on accessibility of the works due to technological measures.[107] Consequently, the Copyright Office and the Department of Commerce jointly evaluated the effect of Section 1201 on the first sale doctrine and related exhaustion rules.[108] The report advised against expanding the first sale doctrine to digital technologies as it believed that DRM-protected works were largely distributed on physical media such as DVDs and CDs, which could be freely transferred.[109] It noted several distinctions in online transfer and transfer of tangible goods as problematic in extending the first sale doctrine to digital content.[110] This report was written 16 years ago and since then technology has progressed manifolds.

7 Conclusion

From the above discussion, we may say that the relationship between the exclusive rights of the copyright holder and limitation of first sale is complex due to the conflicting interests of the stakeholders: copyright owner, consumer, secondary market, libraries, etc. This relationship becomes strained in the absence of uniform minimum standards globally governing the non-digital and digital exhaustion of

[104] 17 U.S.C. §§ 1201–1205 (2000).
[105] See 17 U.S.C. § 1201.
[106] *Ibid.*
[107] *Supra* note 7 at 903.
[108] *Ibid.*
[109] *Ibid.*
[110] Reis 2014.

rights. In its present state, first sale doctrine may become a history in absence of clear uniform laws specifying the nature of transactions online and the extent to which the buyer can use the work. WIPO Copyright treaties and their subsequent implementation in the laws of India and the US show that they are insufficient to strike an apt balance between accessibility for the consumers and economic interests of the copyright owners. Adoption of anti-circumvention measures are more or less IP maximalist as they have ensured that distribution of works in the digital economy does not lead to any infringements but there are no clear guidelines on mode of transactions by the copyright owners for the buyers in the digital world. The standard click-wrap-agreements and browse-wrap-agreements enforced at the time of online transactions are not the sale-purchase agreements but standard licensing agreements. Consumer gets an impression that she is a buyer when in fact she is a non-exclusive licensee of the copyright owner. Thus, it allows copyright owners to exercise their monopolistic rights on the copy of the work even after reaping financial gains from it. This requires adjustments of the first sale doctrine in the digital context by adoption of clear universal standards for digital-first-sale doctrine.[111] Digital-first-sale doctrine would enable instantaneously transfer of digital content at the buyer's discretion and copyright owner's interest can be preserved by imposing a resale royalty.

It must be noted that General principles of the GATT/TRIPs agreement support removal of trade barriers and free movement of goods while ensuring mutual advantage of the producers and the social and economic welfare.[112] Recital 1 in the TRIPs Agreement provide to *"reduce distortions and impediments to international trade, and taking into account the need to promote effective and adequate protection of intellectual property rights ...*"[113] It reiterates the need for a generalized and compulsory system of international exhaustion for a better commercial and economic integration that fosters competition and benefits consumers. The policy makers should now recognize the need to tailor exhaustion rules according to the copyrightable works in the digital age to enforce a technologically sustainable approach that continues to incentivize the creators and promote affordability and accessibility for the consumers.

---

[111] *Supra* note 100. It is contended that adoption of digital-first-sale-doctrine would decrease piracy.

[112] TRIPs Agreement, Article 7: Objectives—The protection and enforcement of intellectual property rights should contribute to the promotion of technological innovation and to the transfer and dissemination of technology, to the mutual advantage of producers and users of technological knowledge and in a manner conducive to social and economic welfare, and to a balance of rights and obligations.

[113] TRIPs Agreement, Preamble, available at https://www.wto.org/english/tratop_e/trips_e/t_agm1_e.htm. (Last accessed on April 14, 2016).

References

Abbott FM (1998) First report (Final) to the committee on international trade law of the international law association on the subject of parallel importation. JIEL 1: 607

Ananth Padmanabhan (2012) Intellectual property rights—infringement and remedies 407 (LexisNexis Butterworths Wadhwa, Nagpur, 1st edn 2012)

Asay CD (2016) Kirtsaeng and the first-sale doctrine's digital problem. Stan L Rev, 1 Online 17, http://www.stanfordlawreview.org/online/kirtsaeng-and-first-sale-doctrines-digital-problem Accessed on 14 April 2016

Basheer S (2011) Parallel imports: The unexpected dumping of Section 2(m) 4 September 2011, http://spicyip.com/2011/09/parallel-imports-unexpected-dumping-of.html Accessed on 3 April 2016

Basheer S et.al. (2012) International exhaustion, parallel imports, and the conflict between the patent and copyright laws of the United States. J Intellec Property Rights 17 (7): 335, 336–337

BerntHugenholtz P (2012) Harmonization or unification of european copyright law, 2012 http://www.austlii.edu.au/au/journals/MonashULawRw/2012/2.pdf Accessed on 3 April 2016

Bonadio E (2011) Parallel imports in a global market: should a generalized international exhaustion be the next step? Euro Intellect Property Rev, 33(3), pp 153–161, http://openaccess.city.ac.uk/4106/ Accessed on 4 April 2016

Chiappetta V (2000) The desirability of agreeing to disagree: the WTO, TRIPs, International IPR exhaustion and a few other things. Mich J Int'l. 21: 333, 351

Coke (1628) Institutes of the Laws of England §360, p 223

Conley CB (2007) Parallel imports: The tired debate of the exhaustion of intellectual property rights and why the WTO should harmonize the Haphazard laws of the international community Tul J Int'l & Comp. L 16: 189

Ghosh S (2014) The Implementation of Exhaustion Policies: Lessons from National Experiences, Legal Studies Research Paper Series Paper No 1248, pp 31 http://papers.ssrn.com/sol3/papers.cfm?abstract_id=2390232 Accessed on 2 April 2016

Heath C (2016) Parallel imports and international trade http://www.wipo.int/edocs/mdocs/sme/en/atrip_gva_99/atrip_gva_99_6.pdf Accessed on 6 April 2016

Perzanowski A, Schultz J (2011) Digital Exhaustion. UCLA Law Rev 889, 58: 894–901

Reichman JH, Okediji RL et al., (2016) The WTO compatibility of a differentiated international exhaustion regime proposed by the eurasian economic community—a consultancy report http://www.eurasiancommission.org/ru/act/finpol/dobd/intelsobs/Documents/WTO%20Compartibility%20of%20Exhaustion%20Regimes_EEC_SkHSEreport.pdf Accessed on 12 April 2016

Reis S (2014) Toward a "Digital Transfer Doctrine"? The first sale doctrine in the digital Era. Nw Univ L Rev 109: 173, 184

Thomas Abraham (2016) The Death of Books. In The Hindustan Times, 14 June 2011. http://www.hindustantimes.com/india/the-death-of-books/story-43h5QiSXDHL6tKwiaU5WhM.html Accessed on 3 April 2016

Thomas Abraham's rebuttal to 'Why Parallel Importation of Books Should Be Allowed'—2 (2 m and copyright law) (2016) http://withinthepurview.blogspot.in/2011/02/thomas-abrahams-rebuttal-to-why.html Accessed 3 April 2016

Hosting Service Providers' Liability for Third Party Content: A Malaysian Perspective

Cheng Peng Sik and Pek San Tay

Abstract The Copyright Act 1987 of Malaysia was last amended in 2012. The introduction of an entirely new part, Part VIB entitled 'Limitation of liabilities of the service provider', was among the substantive amendments brought by the Copyright (Amendment) Act 2012. Part VIB provides for the limitation of liabilities of certain categories of online service providers, including hosting service providers which provide storage of content at the users' direction. Notably, Part VIB introduced a notice and takedown procedure with which hosting service providers are required to comply. The design and provisions of Part VIB, as a whole, bear significant impact on the balance of interests of the relevant stakeholders, namely, copyright owners, online service providers and the public. Hence, the object of this chapter is to examine the provisions of Part VIB relating to hosting service providers, with the concern in mind whether the provisions strike a balance of interests between the said stakeholders. The chapter begins with an introduction on Part VIB of the Copyright Act 1987, particularly Section 43E which provides for hosting service providers. This is followed by a more in-depth analysis of the problems which may arise in relation to the requirements that hosting service providers must satisfy in order to enjoy the limitation of liabilities under Part VIB. Thereafter, the chapter focuses on the notice and takedown procedure implemented under Part VIB, specifically analysing whether the procedure adequately caters to or strikes a balance between the interests of the concerned stakeholders. The chapter concludes with some thoughts and suggestions on how the relevant provisions may be improved to achieve a balance of interests between the relevant parties.

S. Cheng Peng (✉) · P.S. Tay
Faculty of Law, University of Malaya, Kuala Lumpur, Malaysia
e-mail: sikcp@um.edu.my

P.S. Tay
e-mail: tayps@um.edu.my

M.K. Sinha and V. Mahalwar (eds.), *Copyright Law in the Digital World*,
DOI 10.1007/978-981-10-3984-3_13

1 Introduction

Connecting to the internet and browsing the Web would be impossible without internet service providers[1] who provide services relating to connections for the access, transmission or routing of data. At the same time, the internet would be a less resourceful world without the online service providers[2] offering various types of services and facilities, such as storage of content. However, copyright owners are legitimately concerned about protection of their copyright works in the online environment in view of the extreme ease in reproducing and distributing digital copies over the internet. Hence, safe harbour provisions were introduced into the US copyright law in 1998.[3] The safe harbour provisions compel cooperation of both copyright owners and service providers[4] in combating online copyright infringement by placing the duty on copyright owners to keep service providers informed of any alleged infringement as well as sheltering service providers from liability if they meet the relevant requirements.

In 2012, the Malaysian Copyright Act 1987 ('the CA 1987') experienced substantive amendments.[5] The changes include the introduction of an entirely new part, namely, Part VIB titled 'Limitation of liabilities of the service provider'. Part VIB contains provisions which are similar, but by no means identical, to the US safe harbour provisions. Among the provisions under Part VIB, Section 43E provides the limitation of liabilities for hosting service providers who provide storage at the users' direction. Section 43E states that a service provider[6] shall not be held liable for copyright infringement where such infringement takes place 'by reason of the electronic copy of the work being stored at the direction of a user of its primary network'.[7] In view of the booming of user-generated content on mega websites such as YouTube, Facebook or Wikipedia, the provision of the limitation of liabilities for hosting service providers is clearly desirable.

To enjoy the limitation of liabilities under Section 43E, a hosting service provider shall satisfy several conditions. First, the service provider shall not have

---

[1] 'Internet service providers' herein refers to service providers who provide services for connecting to the internet.

[2] 'Online service providers' herein refers to service providers who provide facilities and information resources on the internet.

[3] The Online Copyright Infringement Liability Limitation Act, which is a part of the Digital Millennium Copyright Act (DMCA), inserted Section 512 into Title 17 of the US Code.

[4] 'Service providers' herein refers to both internet service providers and online service providers.

[5] The Copyright (Amendment) Act 2012 (Act A1420) came into force on February 9, 2012.

[6] Section 43B of the CA 1987 defines a 'service provider' other than a mere conduit service provider as 'a person who provides, or operate facilities for, online services or network access'.

[7] Section 43E(1)(a) of the CA 1987. Section 43B defines 'primary network' as 'a network controlled or operated by or for the service provider'.

knowledge, actual or constructive, of the infringement.[8] Second, the service provider does not enjoy any financial benefit directly attributable to the infringement.[9] Third, the service provider does not have the right and ability to control the infringing activity.[10] Fourth, the service provider removes or disables access to the alleged infringing material upon receipt of a notice served by the copyright owner under Section 43H.[11] Section 43E(3) of the CA 1987 states that a service provider shall not be held liable under the section if the copyright owner or his agent has not served any notice under Section 43H. This subsection appears to place the obligation to police copyright infringement on copyright owners. It follows that there is no general duty on service providers to monitor infringement which may occur on their networks.

2 Eligibility of a Hosting Service Provider for the Limitation of Liabilities

2.1 The Meaning of 'By Reason Of'

First and foremost, the limitation of liabilities for hosting service providers under Section 43E of the CA 1987 is only for copyright infringement which takes place *by reason of* the storage of the electronic copy of a work at the direction of a user of its primary network.[12] Section 43E closely resembles Section 512(c)(1) of Title 17 of the United States Code ('the 17 USC') which also contains the phrase '*by reason of*'. The meaning of the phrase '*by reason of*' was considered in *UMG Recordings, Inc. v Veoh Networks, Inc.*[13] In this case, the plaintiffs, as the copyright owners of sound recordings and musical compositions, sued the defendant who provided an internet-based service enabling users to share videos. The court held that the phrase '*by reason of*' means 'as a result of' or 'something that can be attributed to…'.[14] Applying such meaning of '*by reason of*', the court held that the display or distribution of copyright works on the defendant's website was *a result of* or *attributable to* the act of the defendant's users in uploading videos to the defendant's servers. The safe harbour does not shelter only infringing conduct in the form of

---

[8] Section 43E(1)(i) of the CA 1987 provides that the service provider '(A) does not have actual knowledge that the electronic copy of the work or activity is infringing; or (B) in the absence of such actual knowledge, is not aware of the facts or circumstances from which the infringing activity is apparent'.

[9] Section 43E(1)(ii) of the CA 1987. Section 43E(2) of the CA 1987 lists down the factors to be considered in determining whether a financial benefit is directly attributable to the infringement.

[10] Section 43E(1)(ii) of the CA 1987.

[11] Section 43E(1)(iii) of the CA 1987.

[12] Section 43E(1)(a) of the CA 1987.

[13] 620 F. Supp. 2d 1081 (C. D. Cal. 2008).

[14] *Id* at 1089.

providing storage itself. Instead, it covers infringing acts *by reason of* storage. Hence, a hosting service provider does not become ineligible for the safe harbour by providing facilities and service *in addition to* 'storage'. On appeal, this interpretation of '*by reason of*' was affirmed by the US Court of Appeals for the Ninth Circuit.[15] It was held that the phrase 'by reason of the storage' covers the access-facilitating processes which automatically take place when a user uploads a video to the defendant's website.[16]

The phrases 'by reason of' and 'at the direction of a user' specify the scope of the limitation of liabilities of hosting service providers under Section 43E of the CA 1987. The safe harbour should shelter only hosting service providers who provide the facilities for online storage of content without active participation in or supervision over the users' acts. In *CoStar Group, Inc v LoopNet, Inc.*,[17] the defendant's service allowed its subscribers to upload real estate pictures to a folder on its system. The defendant's employees briefly reviewed the pictures. Only pictures that showed real estate and were clearly not copyrighted by any third party were allowed to be posted on the defendant's website. It was held that the defendant satisfied the condition regarding storage '*at the users' direction*' because the pictures were uploaded at the will of the users. The review conducted by the defendant's employees did not amount to active participation but merely a 'gateway' function.

In *Io Group, Inc. v Veoh Networks, Inc.*[18] the defendant's system automatically converted the video files uploaded by users into Flash format and extracted still images from the files. The plaintiff argued that the Flash files were created and stored by the defendant's own acts and decisions and, thus, the defendant should not be entitled to the safe harbour. The court found that the defendant did not itself actively participate in or supervise the uploading of the files. It did not preview or choose the files before uploading since the process of uploading video files was started wholly at the volition of the users.[19]

The scope of the safe harbour for copyright infringement 'by reason of the storage at the direction of a user' was also contended in *Viacom International, Inc. v YouTube*.[20] In this case, the defendant, who operated a website on which users may upload video files[21] free of charge, applied for a summary judgment that they

[15] 718 F. 3d 1006 (9th Cir. 2013).

[16] *Id* at 1031.

[17] 164 F. Supp.2d 688 (D.Md. 2001).

[18] 586 F. Supp.2d 1132 (N.D. Cal. 2008). The plaintiff, the copyright owner of various adult entertainment works, applied for summary judgment on liability of copyright infringement against the defendant, which was an internet TV network providing software and a website on which the sharing of user-submitted video was facilitated.

[19] This case was followed in *Viacom International, Inc. v YouTube* 718 F. Supp. 2d 514 (SDNY, 2010).

[20] *Id.*

[21] The files uploaded by the users were copied and formatted by the defendant's computer systems and were then made available for viewing on its website.

were sheltered under Section 512(c) of the 17 USC. The plaintiff argued that the replication, transmittal and display of videos on the defendant's website fell outside Section 512(c) because the said activities were not 'by reason of the storage at the direction of a user'. However, the court disagreed with the plaintiff and held that 'such service, access, and operation of facilities' are sheltered because they 'flow from the material's placement on the provider's system or network.'[22]

In view of the similarities in the statutory language, the scope of Section 43E of the CA 1987 is likely to be construed in a way similar to the US approach. Section 43E should apply even if a hosting service provider furnishes services, in addition to storage, to facilitate or enable access to the content uploaded by its users. This may include the provision of access to a copy of a copyright work that is uploaded on the website, or conversion of files into a particular format, which automatically takes place when the copy is placed on the hosting service provider's network. To interpret it otherwise would render the scope of the safe harbour for hosting service providers too narrow. It would also be meaningless for service providers of user-generated content platforms such as YouTube, in respect of which access thereto by the public is essential and the key factor for the flourishing of those websites.

2.2 *No Knowledge of Infringement*

In order to enjoy the safe harbor under Section 43E of the CA 1987, a hosting service provider shall have no knowledge of copyright infringement taking place on its network.[23] Knowledge may be actual or constructive. Actual knowledge of infringement on the part of a hosting service provider may be established if the copyright owner has served on the hosting service provider a notice complaining of infringement on the latter's network. However, a copyright owner's notice is only one of the means to establish actual knowledge on the part of hosting service providers. Constructive knowledge, on the other hand, may be imputed to the hosting service provider where the service provider is aware of the facts or circumstances from which the infringement is apparent to any reasonable person.

The provision on a service provider's constructive knowledge under Section 43E of the CA 1987 is similar to that found in Section 512(c)(1)(A)(ii) of the 17 USC, which is also known as the 'red flags' test. The US court in *Viacom*

[22] *Supra* n 19 at 527–28.

[23] Section 43E(1)(i) of the CA 1987 states that the service provider '(A) does not have actual knowledge that the electronic copy of the work or activity is infringing; or (B) in the absence of such actual knowledge, is not aware of the facts or circumstances from which the infringing activity is apparent.' In *Perfect 10, Inc. v CCBill LLC* 488 F.3d 1102 (9th Cir. 2007), the court held that a service provider may lose the safe harbour 'if it fails to take action with regard to infringing material when it is aware of facts or circumstances from which infringing activity is apparent' (at 1114).

International, Inc. v YouTube[24] held that the 'red flags' test involves subjective and objective components.[25] It is a subjective question to determine whether the service provider *is aware of* the facts or circumstances from which infringement is obvious, namely, the red flags.[26] On the other hand, an objective standard should be applied in deciding whether those facts or circumstances constitute 'red flags'.[27] In other words, it is an objective question as to whether the infringing activity would be obvious to any reasonable person in the same or similar circumstances.[28]

The application of such test was illustrated in *Io Group, Inc. v Veoh Networks, Inc.*[29] In this case, the plaintiff argued that its copyright registration notices constituted the defendant's constructive knowledge of infringement. The court found none of the video files in question contained the plaintiff's copyright notices. The court also rejected the plaintiff's argument that the professionally produced nature of the videos in itself amounted to a sufficient 'red flag' of infringement for the purpose of imputing the defendant with the necessary degree of knowledge or awareness.[30] The question as to whether a particular fact or circumstance constitutes a red flag was approached objectively, whereas the question whether or not the defendant was aware of the alleged red flags was determined subjectively. In sum, the question to be considered is whether the service provider 'deliberately proceeded in the face of blatant factors of which it was aware'.[31] Such apparent knowledge may be established if a service provider 'turned a blind eye to "red flags" of obvious infringement.'[32]

The question of what may constitute red flags was also contended in *Perfect 10, Inc. v CCBill LLC.*[33] In this case, the plaintiff claimed that the names of the websites to which the defendants provided web hosting and other services were sufficient to raise 'red flags'. The said websites were named 'illegal.net' and 'stolencelebritypics.com'. The US Court of Appeals for the Ninth Circuit did not find the names of the websites amounted to an admission that the photographs thereon were actually illegal or stolen.[34] The court refused to encumber the duty of scrutinizing whether photographs were actually illegal on a service provider.[35]

---

[24] *Supra* n 19.

[25] *Id* at 520.

[26] *Ibid.*

[27] *Id* at 520–521.

[28] *Ibid.*

[29] *Supra* n 18.

[30] *Id* at 1149.

[31] *Corbis Corp. v Amazon.com, Inc.* 351 F. Supp. 2d 1090 (W.D. Wash., 2004) at 1108 quoted: *Id* at 1148.

[32] *Ibid.*

[33] *Supra* n 23.

[34] *Id* at 1114. The court observed that 'When a website traffics in pictures that are titillating by nature, describing photographs as 'illegal' or 'stolen' may be an attempt to increase their salacious appeal, rather than an admission that the photographs are actually illegal or stolen' (at 1114).

[35] *Ibid.*

It follows that if an investigation of facts and circumstances is needed to determine whether the material is infringing, then these facts and circumstances are not 'red flags'.

The knowledge requirement on the part of hosting service providers may not be easily established in view of the vast amount of content usually stored by the service providers, such as Facebook, Photobucket, and YouTube. However, if there are facts or circumstances which constitute red flags but a hosting service provider deliberately ignores them, constructive knowledge should therefore be imputed to the service provider. In this way, the knowledge requirement imposes a reasonable and feasible duty on hosting service providers to take proper steps in response to rampant and obvious infringing activities taking place on their networks.

2.3 No Direct Financial Benefit from Infringement

Section 43E(1)(ii) of the CA 1987 requires a service provider not to receive a 'financial benefit directly attributable to the infringement'. The provision closely resembles that as found in Section 512(c)(1)(B) of the 17 USC. Section 43E(2) of the CA 1987 lists several factors that a court should take into account in deciding whether a financial benefit is directly attributable to the infringement. The factors are the industry practice as regards the charging of services by a service provider; whether the financial benefit was bigger than the benefit usually resulting from charging in line with accepted industry practices; and any other matter that the court considers relevant.

As explained in *Ellison v Robertson*,[36] whether a financial benefit is directly attributable to infringement depends on 'whether the infringing activity constitutes a draw for subscribers, not just an added benefit.'[37] In *Wolk v Kodak Imaging Network, Inc.*,[38] the US court expressed that in the absence of evidence that the service provider had 'attracted or retained subscriptions because of the infringement or lost subscriptions because of [its] eventual obstruction of the infringement',[39] it may not be concluded that the service provider received a direct financial benefit simply because it offered access to the infringing material.[40]

It is crucial to determine whether a service provider derives direct financial benefit from copyright infringement committed via their services or facilities. This requirement ensures that service providers who have infringing copies as their main attraction will not be sheltered under Section 43E of the CA 1987. At the same

[36] 357 F.3d 1072, 1076 (9th Cir. 2004).

[37] *Id* at 1079.

[38] 98 U.S.P.Q.2d (BNA) 1152 (SDNY, 2011).

[39] Reference was made to *Perfect 10, Inc. v CCBill LLC*, *supra* n 23 at 1117; and *Ellison v Robertson*, *supra* n 36 at 1079.

[40] *Supra* n 38 at 1157–1158.

time, by emphasizing on financial benefit '*directly*' resulting from infringement, Section 43E does not exclude service providers who may gain from infringement but whose survival does not depend on infringement. As such, the determination of the question as to whether a service provider gains direct financial benefit from copyright infringement is crucial to striking a balance of interests between hosting service providers and copyright owners under copyright law.

2.4 No Right and Ability to Control Infringement

Section 43E(1)(ii) of the CA 1987 also requires a service provider not to have 'the right and ability to control' the infringing activity in order to enjoy the safe harbour. This requirement is similar to that prescribed in Section 512(c)(1)(B) of the 17 USC. The degree of a hosting service provider's right and ability to control infringement is thus pertinent as it may disqualify the service provider from the safe harbour under Section 43E. This requirement ensures that hosting service providers are exempted from liability only for copyright infringement over which they have no rights and ability to control. If hosting service providers have such right and ability, they should therefore take proper actions to stop or prevent the infringing activities over their networks.

As the US court in *Io Group, Inc. v Veoh Networks, Inc.*[41] observed, the question to be considered is not whether a service provider has the right and ability to control its *system*, but rather whether it has the right and ability to control *the infringing activity*.[42] The court explained further that the service provider's right and ability to control infringement cannot simply mean the service provider's ability to block or remove access to materials posted on its website or stored on its system.[43] It was held that the defendant did not have the right and ability to control the alleged infringement due to the absence of evidence to show that the defendant could control on the content that the users decide to upload before it is uploaded.[44] The court found it unreasonable to expect the defendant to perform a comprehensive review of every file uploaded to its website. Even if such review is possible, there is

[41] *Supra* n 18.

[42] *Id* at 1151. Section 43E(1)(ii) of the CA 1987 also provides that the SP 'does not have the right and ability to control the infringing activity'.

[43] *Ibid.* See also *Corbis Corp. v Amazon.com, Inc., supra* n 31 at 1110; *Perfect 10, Inc. v CCBill LLC, supra* n 23 at 1098; *Hendrickson v Ebay, Inc.* 165 F. Supp. 2d 1082 (C.D. Cal. 2001), at 1093. In *Tur v YouTube, Inc.* No. CV064436, 2007 WL1893635 (C.D. Cal., 2007), it was held that the phrase 'right and ability to control' 'presupposes some antecedent ability to limit or filter copyrighted material.'

[44] *Supra* n 18 at 1153.

no guarantee that the defendant could have precisely identified the infringing content in question.[45]

In *Viacom International, Inc. v YouTube*,[46] the court was of the opinion that the service provider must first have knowledge of the alleged infringing activity before it could control that activity and the service provider was under no duty to monitor or seek out facts indicating such activity.[47] The service provider's right and ability to control infringement may exist in the form of pre-screening content, giving comprehensive help and advice to users about the content and editing the user-submitted content.

In general, hosting service providers have no control over the uploading of user-generated content which is entirely within the users' control. If a hosting service provider has actively participated in the determination over the content to be uploaded and stored on its network, it will then be ineligible for the safe harbour. It follows therefore that only passive hosting service providers who do not exercise editorial control are entitled to the safe harbour under Section 43E of the CA 1987.

3 Notice and Takedown Procedure

Apart from the requirements discussed in Section 2 above, a hosting service provider is also obliged to comply with the notice and takedown procedure in order to enjoy the safe harbor under Section 43E of the CA 1987. This requirement is provided in Section 43E(1)(iii) of the CA 1987 which states that upon receipt of a notice regarding any infringement under Section 43H, the service provider shall respond within the time specified to remove or disable access to the alleged infringing material.

3.1 No General Duty to Monitor Infringement on Service Providers

As explained by the US Court of Appeals for the Ninth Circuit in *Perfect 10, Inc. v CCBill LLC*,[48] the fundamental objective of the notice requirements is to 'place the

[45] *Ibid.* The court found no evidence of failure on the part of the defendant in policing its system to the fullest extent permitted by the architecture of its system. The case of *A & M Records, Inc. v Napster, Inc.* 239 F.3d 1004 (9th Cir. 2001) was distinguished on the basis that the sole purpose of the existence of Napster was to offer the site and facilities for copyright infringement and its control over its system was directly intertwined with its ability to control the infringing activity. However, the defendant in *Io Group, Inc. v Veoh Networks, Inc.*, *supra* n 18, did not aim to promote copyright infringement on its system.

[46] *Supra* n 19.

[47] *Id* at 527.

[48] *Supra* n 23.

burden of policing copyright infringement—identifying the potentially infringing material and adequately documenting infringement—squarely on the owners of the copyright'.[49] This was followed in *Wolk v Kodak Imaging Network, Inc.*[50] In this case, the plaintiff, a visual artist, served notices requesting some of her copyrighted images to be removed from the defendant's website, Photobucket, which hosted user-generated photographs for storage and sharing. The defendant complied with the plaintiff's statute-compliant notices and also removed certain photographs which were sufficiently identified by the plaintiff. The plaintiff argued that since the defendant was aware of infringement of her works on its website, the defendant must patrol its website to detect current infringement and prevent future infringement without the need of the plaintiff to give notices in every case. The plaintiff's argument was rejected by the court which held that such an argument attempted to place a burden on the defendant beyond what was demanded by the statute.[51]

It should be noted that Section 512(m)(1) of the 17 USC clearly refutes any attempt to place a duty on service providers to monitor their services or affirmatively seek facts showing infringing activity.[52] The CA 1987 does not contain a provision similar to that found in Section 512(m)(1) of the 17 USC. However, Section 43E(3) of the CA 1987 emphasizes that a service provider shall not be held liable under the section if a Section 43H notice has not been served on the service provider. This provision indicates that it is the copyright owners' duty to make use of, or initiate, the notice and takedown procedure.[53] It is submitted that Section 43E (3) has the effect of placing the burden squarely on copyright owners to alert service providers of any infringing activity taking place on their networks.

This argument may be supported further by considering the roles played by the relevant stakeholders in the notice and takedown procedure outlined under Part VIB of the CA 1987. Upon receipt of a notice from the copyright owner, a service provider shall remove or disable access to the copy complained of within 48 h from the receipt, as stated in Section 43H(2) of the CA 1987. Section 43F(2) of the CA 1987 requires the service provider to notify the user whose copy was removed or to which access has been disabled, as far as may be practicable, of such action and enclose it with a copy of the notice from the copyright owner. The user may serve a counter notice to the service provider requesting restoration of the copy or access to it, as provided in Section 43H(3). When this takes place, Section 43H(4)(a) requires the service provider to promptly provide a copy of the counter notice to the copyright owner informing the latter that the copy or access to it will be restored in

---

[49] *Id* at 1113.

[50] *Supra* n 38.

[51] *Id* at 1156.

[52] An exception to this is found in Section 512(m)(1) which states: '... except to the extent consistent with a standard technical measure complying with the provisions of subsection (i)...'

[53] See also Section 43F(4) of the CA 1987 which stresses that a service provider shall not be regarded as having authorized the doing of any infringement under the CA 1987 solely by reason of the service provider having provided a facility that was used by a person to carry out the infringing act.

ten business days. Unless the copyright owner has issued another notice to the service provider, which informs the service provider of the filing of an action seeking a court order to stop the relevant user from infringing his copyright, the copy or access to it shall then be restored within ten business days as stated in Section 43H(4)(b). Section 43F(3) provides that the service provider is also obliged to restore the copy or access to it when it receives a written notice from either party to do so as a result of a settlement between the copyright owner and the user; or when the user was adjudicated by a court or tribunal as the rightful copyright owner of the work.[54] It is obvious that service providers play the role of neutral intermediaries who merely act in response to the notices served on them in the notice and takedown procedure under the CA 1987.

In addition, either the copyright owner's notice or the user's counter notice shall include an undertaking by the issuer to compensate the service provider or any other person against any damages, loss or liability resulting from the compliance by the service provider of the notice.[55] Section 43F(1) states that a service provider who acts in compliance with Subsection 43H(1) and in accordance with Part VIB shall not be subject to any liability in respect of an action taken in good faith in removing or disabling access to an electronic copy of a work. It is thus clear that the sole responsibility placed on a service provider is to duly comply with the notice served by either the copyright owner or the user, without the burden to monitor or determine the nature of the relevant copy or activity, and without liability for any compensation in performing such actions.

3.2 The Details to Be Included in a Notice

Section 43H(1) of the CA 1987 provides that a copyright owner may serve on the service provider a notice 'in the manner as determined by the Minister' but to date there have been no rules or regulations made on this matter.[56] By way of comparison, it is noted that Section 512(c)(3)(A) of the 17 USC expressly details the requirements that a copyright owner's notice shall substantially comply with,[57]

---

[54] The proviso to Section b43F(3) of the CA 1987 explains further that in such circumstances the service provider shall be furnished with the proper documentation about the settlement or the judgment or decision of the court or tribunal.

[55] See proviso to subsections (1) and (3) of Section 43H of the CA 1987 respectively.

[56] Section 43H(5) of the CA 1987 prescribes the information that shall be included in a counter notice served by users. Oddly, there is no corresponding provision with regard to a notification from copyright owners.

[57] Section 512(c)(3)(A) of the 17 USC provides, 'To be effective under this subsection, a notification of claimed infringement must be a written communication provided to the designated agent of a service provider that includes substantially the following: (i) A physical or electronic signature of a person authorized to act on behalf of the owner of an exclusive right that is allegedly infringed. (ii) Identification of the copyrighted work claimed to have been infringed, or, if multiple copyrighted works at a single online site are covered by a single notification, a representative list of

while Section 512(c)(3)(B)(i) provides that a defective notification shall not be taken into account in deciding whether a service provider has actual or apparent knowledge of the alleged infringement.[58]

Under the 17 USC, a copyright owner's notice shall include the details including 'identification of the material that is claimed to be infringing or to be the subject of infringing activity and that is to be removed or access to which is to be disabled, and *information reasonably sufficient* to permit the service provider to locate the material.' An example of such sufficient information could be a copy or description of the alleged infringing material and the 'uniform resource locator' (URL) which is alleged to contain the said material. The question of whether a notification complies substantially with the requirements is a crucial factor in determining the knowledge on the part of a service provider. For instance, in *Viacom International, Inc. v YouTube*,[59] the plaintiff complained that the defendant removed only the specific video clips identified in the notices but not the other clips which infringed the same works. The court noted that the statute allowed a notice to describe the works representatively but it should identify the infringing material with 'information reasonably sufficient to permit the service provider to locate the material.'[60] Thus, the deficient notice was not taken into account in determining the service provider's knowledge about the alleged infringement as stated in Section 512(c)(3)(B)(i) of the 17 USC.[61]

The purpose of serving a notice is to keep the relevant service provider informed of the alleged infringing material so that the service provider could remove or disable access to the said material. Accordingly, a notice served on a service provider should effectively identify and locate the alleged infringing material. However, the Malaysian CA 1987 does not prescribe the details to be included in a notice. It is uncertain as to when a notice may be regarded as defective, and thus, whether it should be considered in determining the service provider's knowledge of copyright infringement.

(Footnote 57 continued)

such works at that site. (iii) Identification of the material that is claimed to be infringing or to be the subject of infringing activity and that is to be removed or access to which is to be disabled, and information reasonably sufficient to permit the service provider to locate the material. (iv) Information reasonably sufficient to permit the service provider to contact the complaining party, such as an address, telephone number, and, if available, an electronic mail address at which the complaining party may be contacted. (v) A statement that the complaining party has a good faith belief that use of the material in the manner complained of is not authorized by the copyright owner, its agent, or the law. (vi) A statement that the information in the notification is accurate, and under penalty of perjury, that the complaining party is authorized to act on behalf of the owner of an exclusive right that is allegedly infringed.

[58] See *UMG Recordings, Inc. v Veoh Networks, Inc.*, *supra* n 13.

[59] *Supra* n 19.

[60] Section 512(c)(3)(A)(iii) of the 17 USC.

[61] Section 512(c)(3)(B)(i) of the 17 USC provides that a notification from a copyright owner or his agent that fails to comply substantially with Section 512(c)(3)(A) shall not be considered in determining whether a service provider has actual or apparent knowledge about infringement.

3.3 Removal upon Copyright Owner's Notice

It is noted that in the notice and takedown procedure under the CA 1987, a service provider shall remove or disable access to infringing content on its network within 48 h from the receipt of a notice from the copyright owner.[62] The service provider is required to inform as far as may be practicable the person who uploaded the content, and enclose a copy of the copyright owner's notice upon removal or disabling of access to the alleged infringing copy.[63] The latter may then, if he or she wishes to, serve a counter notice on the service provider requesting to restore the content or access to it.[64] When such a counter notice is issued, the service provider shall promptly provide the copyright owner a copy of it and inform the latter that the content or access to it will be restored in ten business days.[65] The service provider shall restore the content or access to it within ten business days unless the copyright owner issues a notice informing that an action has been filed seeking a court order to restrain the user, that is, the person who uploaded the content at issue, from engaging in any infringing activity.[66]

There are a few points about the notice and takedown procedure under the CA 1987 which are noteworthy. First, the service provider is required to remove the content upon receipt of a complaint from the copyright owner within 48 h, which is a relatively short period as compared to the period of ten business days within which the service provider is required to restore the content or access to it if a counter notification is received from the user. This means the content in question will be removed or access to it disabled in a quicker manner than its restoration.

Furthermore, the service provider is required to inform the user only 'upon removing or disabling access to' the content in dispute.[67] In comparison, the service provider who has been served with a counter notice from the user shall inform the copyright owner that the content or access to it 'will be restored' in ten business days.[68] It is clear that the service provider is expected to keep users informed of the removal of or disabling of access to the content which *has already been undertaken*, while the service provider is obliged to inform the copyright owner about the restoration of the content or access to it that *will take place*. This supports further the proposition that the notice and takedown procedure under the CA 1987 favours prompt removal of content upon copyright owners' request.

[62] Section 43H(2) of the CA 1987.
[63] Section 43F(2) of the CA 1987.
[64] Section 43H(3) of the CA 1987.
[65] Section 43H(4)(a) of the CA 1987.
[66] Section 43H(4)(b) of the CA 1987.
[67] Section 43F(2) of the CA 1987.
[68] Section 43H(4)(a) of the CA 1987.

In addition, the CA 1987 does not stipulate clearly the period within which the service provider is required to inform the user of the removal of or disabling of access to the content in dispute. Section 43F(2) provides that the service provider has to notify the user about the removal of or disabling of access to the content 'as far as may be practicable' upon removing or disabling access to it. The phrase 'as far as may be practicable' carries the meaning to the extent that it is feasible for the service provider to notify the user, which depends on the capability of the service provider to do so.[69] This appears to give service provider leeway in informing users about the removal or disabling of access. On the other hand, Section 43H(4)(a) requires the service provider to inform the copyright owner about the imminent restoration 'promptly', which means that the service provider has to inform the copyright owner without delay.[70] Furthermore, when read together with Section 43H(4)(b) which requires the service provider to restore the material or access to it within ten business days *following the receipt of the counter notification*, the service provider must inform the copyright owner before the end of the 10-day period. In this sense, it is submitted that there is a certain degree of urgency for the service provider to inform the copyright owner, which is lacking in the corresponding duty to inform the user.

More significantly, as mentioned earlier, the service provider shall remove or disable access to the content complained of upon the copyright owner's notice. If the user wishes to object to the removal or disabling of access, it is for the user to serve a counter notice after the removal or disabling of access. In other words, by default, the content will be removed, or access to it will be disabled, within 48 h from the receipt of the notice. This could create a situation where copyright owners may issue such notices unduly and excessively, causing the service provider to be obliged under the CA 1987 to comply. At the same time, the fear of litigation and considerations of financial costs may discourage the user from contending for the content at issue or access thereto be restored even in circumstances where the user has a very strong case of entitlement to any exception to copyright infringement.[71]

As a whole, it may be concluded that the notice and takedown procedure under the CA 1987 appears to favour copyright owners over users. More specifically, it is submitted that the procedure finds favour with, if not encourages, prompt removal of or disabling of access to the content uploaded by users, without giving an opportunity to users to object before the said removal or disabling access. This may not be desired as it may have negative impact on public interest. As the US court

[69] 'Practicable' is defined in the Oxford English Dictionary as 'Able to be done or put into practice successfully; feasible; able to be used; useful, practical, effective.'

[70] 'Promptly' is defined in the Oxford English Dictionary as 'In a prompt manner; readily, quickly; at once, without delay; directly, forthwith, there and then.'

[71] The exceptions to copyright infringement are provided under Section 13(2) of the CA 1987.

commented in *Lenz v Universal Music Corp.*,[72] 'the unnecessary removal of non-infringing material causes significant injury to the public where time-sensitive or controversial subjects are involved and the counter-notification remedy does not sufficiently address these harms.'[73]

3.4 Good Faith Belief Statement

The purely 'notification-compliant' nature of the duty placed on a service provider is strengthened by the good faith belief statement which is required to be included in the counter notice served by a user on the service provider. Section 43H(5)(c) of the CA 1987 requires the counter notice to contain 'a statement under penalty of perjury that the issuer has a good faith belief that the material was removed or disabled as a result of mistake or misidentification of the material to be removed or disabled'. This is *in pari materia* with Section 512(g)(3)(C) of the 17 USC.

By requiring such a good faith belief statement from the user, it is submitted that the law shifts the duty from a service provider to the user in ensuring that the notice and takedown procedure is not abused. Strangely, a similar good faith belief statement is not expressly required to be contained in the copyright owner's notice in Section 43H. Section 512(c)(3)(A)(v) of the 17 USC, on the other hand, expressly requires a good faith belief statement from the copyright owner that the 'use of the material in the manner complained of is not authorized by the copyright owner, its agent, or the law'. It was held in *Hendrickson v eBay, Inc.*[74] that the copyright owner's good faith belief statement was an essential requirement of a takedown notice and its absence rendered the notice deficient. It is submitted that the same good faith belief statement should be included in the copyright owner's notice as well in order to distribute the burden equally between the user and copyright owner in the notice and takedown procedure.

The significance of a good faith belief statement is illustrated in *Lenz v Universal Music Corp.*[75] where the question whether a copyright owner is obliged by Section 512(c)(3)(A)(v) of the 17 USC to evaluate a fair use in formulating a good faith belief of copyright infringement before sending out takedown notices was raised. Section 512(c)(3)(A)(v) of the 17 USC requires a notice to include a statement that the complainant has a '*good faith belief*' that use of the material in dispute 'is not authorized by the copyright owner, its agent, or the law'. In this case, the plaintiff uploaded to YouTube.com a video file of her toddler son dancing to a

[72] 572 F. Supp. 2d 1150 (N.D. Cal., 2008).

[73] *Id* at 1156.

[74] *Supra* n 43 at 1089–1090.

[75] *Supra* n 72.

song of which the copyright was owned by the defendant.[76] The plaintiff alleged that the takedown notice sent by the defendant was not based on any good faith belief that the video actually infringed copyright. The defendant filed the motion to dismiss the case. The court held that the obvious meaning of 'authorized by law' in Section 512(c)(3)(A)(v) of the 17 USC is clear,[77] that is, 'an activity or behaviour "authorized by law" is one permitted by law or not contrary to law.'[78] Even though the fair use doctrine was not expressly mentioned in the Digital Millennium Copyright Act ('the DMCA') which introduced the safe harbours, the court noted that Section 107 of the 17 USC explicitly provides that fair use of a copyright work is not an infringement of copyright.[79] As such, a copyright owner must evaluate whether the material makes fair use of the copyright work before he may proceed with a 'good faith belief' that the material is infringing.[80] The court expressed its view that such an interpretation is in accordance with the objectives of the DMCA and copyright law generally. As noted by the US Congress in legislating the DMCA, the provisions of the Act 'balance the need for rapid response to potential infringement with the end-users [sic] legitimate interests in not having material removed without recourse.'[81]

In *Lenz*, in response to the defendant's claim that the need to evaluate fair use before issuing takedown notices may cause the copyright owners to lose the ability to respond rapidly to any potential infringement,[82] the court felt that the actual impact was exaggerated as 'there are likely to be few in which a copyright owner's determination that a particular use is not fair use will meet the requisite standard of subjective bad faith required to prevail in an action for misrepresentation' under

---

[76] The song was 'Let's Go Crazy' by the artist 'Prince'. The video was 29 s in length while the song was audible for about 20 s. The sound quality of the video was poor and, thus, the song can be heard with difficulty. The defendant sent a takedown notice pursuant to Section 512(c) of the 17 USC demanding YouTube to remove the said video alleging copyright infringement. YouTube complied with the notice and informed the plaintiff via an e-mail of the removal. The plaintiff served a counter notice on YouTube under Section 512(g) of the 17 USC requesting the reinstatement of her video on the ground that it was fair use of the song and, thus, did not infringe the defendant's copyright. YouTube complied with the counter notice.

[77] Section 512(c)(3)(A)(v) of the 17 USC provides that a notification should include, 'A statement that the complaining party has a good faith belief that use of the material in the manner complained of is not authorized by the copyright owner, its agent, or the law.'

[78] *Supra* n 72 at 1154.

[79] The court was of the view that even if fair use only excuses infringement, it remains a lawful use of a copyright: see *Sony Corp. of America v Universal City Studios, Inc.* 464 U.S. 417 (1984) at 433: '[a]nyone ... who makes a fair use of the work is not an infringer of the copyright with respect to such use.'

[80] Without such a 'good faith belief', a copyright owner who has issued a takedown notice may be subject to a misrepresentation claim under Section 512(f) of the 17 USC.

[81] US Sen. Rep. No. 105–190 at 21 (1998).

[82] The defendant also highlighted that the determination of fair use is a 'fact-intensive inquiry' and that it is hard for copyright owners to foresee whether a court may ultimately rule in their favour. *Supra* n 72 at 1155.

Section 512(f) of the 17 USC.[83] The court reasoned that the compulsory evaluation of fair use by copyright owners will help to guarantee that 'the efficiency of the Internet will continue to improve and that the variety and quality of services on the Internet will expand' without compromising creative copyright works.[84]

Unfortunately, the Malaysian CA 1987 does not expressly require such a good faith belief statement to be contained in the copyright owner's notice while expecting the same in the counter notice issued by the user. In this way, the notice and takedown procedure under the CA 1987 appears to favour copyright owners more as compared to users in general. It is noted that Section 43I(1) of the CA 1987 provides for an offence when any notice maker makes a false statement, 'which he knows to be false or does not believe to be true and relates to a material point to the object of the notice'.[85] In view of the requirement on 'knowingly' making such a false statement, Section 43I provides for a narrow cause of action as it requires a degree of knowledge which differs from that in relation to a good faith belief statement.

Similar to Section 43I of the CA 1987, Section 512(f) of the 17 USC provides that a person is liable for any damages resulting from him knowingly making a material misrepresentation that an activity or material is infringing; or that a material was removed or an activity was disabled by mistake or misidentification.[86] As observed by the US Court of Appeals for the Ninth Circuit in *Rossi v MPAA*,[87] Section 512(f) of the 17 USC provides for an 'expressly limited cause of action' for only improper notifications which constitute knowing misrepresentations. It is not a knowing misrepresentation if the copyright owner makes an unknowing mistake, even an unreasonable one. Actual knowledge about the untrue statements on the part of the copyright owner must be established. The court, in comparing the 'good faith' provision with the 'knowing misrepresentation' provision, found 'an apparent statutory structure that predicated the imposition of liability upon copyright owners

---

[83] *Ibid.*

[84] *Id* at 1156.

[85] Section 43I(1)(b) provides for the punishment for the offence as a fine of maximum RM 100,000 or imprisonment for a term of maximum 5 years or both. In addition, he shall also be liable to compensate any person for any loss or damage resulting from the making of the notification as stated in Section 43I(1)(b). Section 43I(2) further explains that the same applies to a statement made outside Malaysia and the person doing so will be dealt with under Section 43I(1)(a) as if the offence was committed in Malaysia. The offence in Section 43I may be established in circumstances where a false statement is made in either a notification issued by a copyright owner or a counter notification issued by the user whose copy is the subject matter in dispute.

[86] Section 512(f)(1) & (2) of the 17 USC. As stated in Section 512(f), the damages could be those incurred by the claimed infringer, copyright owner or copyright owner's authorized licensee, or by a service provider; which is due to the service provider's reliance on such misrepresentation in removing or disabling access to the claimed infringing material or activity, or in restoring the removed material to ceasing to disable access to it.

[87] 391 F.3d 1000 (9th Cir. 2004).

only for knowing misrepresentations regarding allegedly infringing websites', which is not satisfied by a lesser 'objective reasonableness standard'.[88]

The above position which places emphasis on the subjective mental state of knowledge about a material misrepresentation was followed in *Lenz v Universal Music Publishing Group*[89] where, consequent to the defendant's takedown notice with regard to the plaintiff's video and the counter notice by the plaintiff requesting the reinstatement of the video, the plaintiff commenced an action seeking redress for the alleged misuse of the takedown process by the defendant. In particular, the plaintiff applied for summary judgment based on the alleged misrepresentation by the defendant under Section 512(f) of the 17 USC. The court held that the plaintiff had failed to show facts from which a knowing misrepresentation by the defendant could be inferred. Additionally, the plaintiff had also failed to demonstrate that her use of the song was a 'self-evident' fair use.

The district court's decision in *Lenz* was affirmed by the US Court of Appeals for the Ninth Circuit in *Lenz v Universal Music Corp.*[90] The court made it clear that a copyright owner who ignores or neglects the requirement of considering fair use before serving a takedown notice is liable for damages under Section 512(f) of the 17 USC. A copyright owner who pays lip service to the consideration of fair use is also liable under Section 512(f) of the 17 USC. For instance, when a copyright owner sends a takedown notice when there is sufficient evidence that he intentionally requests removal of a material he knows he has no right to remove, he could be liable under Section 512(f) of the 17 USC. However, in circumstances where a copyright owner forms a *subjective* good faith belief that a material does not constitute fair use, the court would not dispute his belief even if the court holds the opposite belief.

An example of a 'knowing' and 'material' misrepresentation may be seen in *Online Policy Group v Diebold*[91] in which the content at issue was internal emails among the employees of the defendant which produced voting machines. The emails showed the knowledge of some employees that the machines were unreliable and were published by college students in several websites including an online newspaper. The defendant demanded the internet service providers of the college students and the online newspaper to remove access to the emails or face liability for copyright infringement. The college students and the internet service provider of the online newspaper filed a suit against the defendant alleging its copyright infringement claims were misrepresentations under Section 512(f) of the 17 USC.

The court held that the defendant's misrepresentation was made 'knowingly' as the use of the emails to expose the problems relating to the voting machines to the public was clearly a fair use. It was explained that 'knowingly means that a party actually knows, should have known if it acted with reasonable care or diligence, or

[88] *Id* at 1004–1005.

[89] 2008 U.S. Dist. LEXIS 44549; Copy L. Rep. (CCH) P29, 540.

[90] 801 F. 3d 1126 (9th Cir. 2015).

[91] 337 F.Supp. 2d 1195 (N.D. Cal. 2004).

would have had no substantial doubt had it been acting in good faith, that it was making misrepresentations.'[92] Besides, the misrepresentation was 'material' by virtue of the fact that it actually resulted in the removal of the said emails. The court described a misrepresentation as 'material' if it affected the service provider's response to the notice.[93] The court concluded that the defendant sought to use the safe harbour provisions as 'a sword to suppress publication of embarrassing content rather than as a shield to protect its intellectual property'.[94] The defendant was therefore liable for misrepresentation under Section 512(f) of the 17 USC.

It is not an easy task to prove the required 'subjective mental state of actual knowledge' that one is making a material misrepresentation. A user is required to show that the copyright owner's takedown notice is made in 'subjective bad faith'.[95] It was evident in *Lenz v Universal Music Publishing Group*[96] that the defendant was not liable under Section 512(f) of the 17 USC even where the court may hold the opposite belief, as compared to the defendant's, as to whether the material in dispute was fair use. The 'objective reasonableness standard', which applies to determine whether a copyright owner has a good faith belief about the alleged infringement, is a lesser standard than the subjective mental state of actual knowledge required to establish knowing misrepresentation. The absence of the requirement for a good faith belief statement to be included in the copyright owner's notice under the Malaysian CA 1987 therefore results in a weaker machinery to counter abuse of the notice and takedown procedure by copyright owners. Section 43I is considered the only means to reduce the said abuse under the CA 1987. Unfortunately, it would not be easy to establish an offence under Section 43I because the subjective knowledge of the maker of a false notice has to be demonstrated.

3.5 Is the Service Provider Obliged to Take Action upon Acquiring Knowledge of Infringement in the Absence of a Notice?

Section 43E of the CA 1987 states that a service provider 'shall not be held liable under this section if the copyright owner or his agent has not given any notification under Section 43H'. This means service providers under Section 43E would not lose the limitation of liabilities if the copyright owner has not served any notice. It is questionable as to whether service providers are obliged to remove or disable access to infringing materials if they know about the infringement, despite the fact that

[92] *Id* at 1204.

[93] *Id* at 1204–1205.

[94] *Ibid.*

[95] *Rossi v MPAA*, *supra* n 87.

[96] *Supra* n 90.

they receive no notice under Section 43H and, thus, their entitlement to the limitation of liabilities is not at risk.

The meaning of Section 43E(3), when read together with the conditions in Section 43E(1)(b)(i)[97] and (iii),[98] may raise some questions. It is uncertain as to whether the absence of a notice under Section 43H will have the effect of dispensing with the need to impute knowledge of the alleged infringement on the part of the service provider under Section 43E(1)(b)(i). This interpretation would contradict the statutory language of Section 43E(1)(b)(i) in which a service provider may be disqualified for the limitation of liabilities if the service provider has actual or apparent knowledge about infringement. It is submitted that if Section 43E(3) is interpreted as such it would have the effect of condoning a service provider being indifferent or turning a blind eye to the obvious or apparent infringing activity taking place over its network simply because no statutory notice has been issued. It would tilt greatly in favour of the service provider whose entitlement to the limitation of liabilities in Section 43E is not undermined regardless of its knowledge of the infringement as long as it has not received any notice under Section 43H. This will render the knowledge requirement in Section 43E(1)(i) superfluous and meaningless, in particular with regard to the apparent knowledge of red flags.[99]

Another question that may arise with respect to Section (3) is whether a service provider, upon acquiring actual or apparent knowledge of the infringement, is obliged to remove or disable access to the alleged infringing material in the absence of a notice under Section 43H. Section 43E(1)(b)(iii), as mentioned earlier, requires a service provider to remove or disable access to the alleged infringing material 'upon receipt of a notification of any infringement under Section 43H'. This requirement, when read together with Section 43E(3), appears to suggest that a service provider is not obliged to remove or disable access to the alleged infringing material if it has not received a notice despite the fact that it does know about the infringement. It follows that a service provider on whom no notification has been served is not obliged to remove or disable access to the infringing material but may nonetheless lose the limitation of liabilities in Section 43E if it has knowledge about the infringement.

By comparison, Section 512(c)(1)(A)(iii) of the 17 USC expressly requires a service provider infringement to remove or disable access to the relevant material expeditiously upon obtaining actual knowledge or apparent awareness of infringement. It is submitted that a similar provision which expressly imposes a duty to remove or disable access to the infringing material upon acquiring actual or constructive knowledge on the part of the service provider should be included in Section 43E of the CA 1987 to get rid of any doubt as regards this matter. More importantly, it is submitted that the duty to remove or disable access should be

---

[97] Section 43E(1)(b)(i) of the CA 1987 provides for the requirement on a SP's knowledge of the alleged infringing material or activity.

[98] Section 43E(1)(b)(iii) of the CA 1987 requires a SP to take the necessary action upon being served with a notice under Section 43H. Failure to do so will disqualify the SP from the liability limitation.

[99] See Section 2.2.

imposed on a service provider who has knowledge about the infringement in order to ensure a more efficient protection of copyright, irrespective of whether or not a Section 43H notice has been served on the service provider.

4 Conclusion

The scope of the limitation of liabilities for hosting service providers under Section 43E of the CA 1987 clearly hinges on whether the infringing activities occur 'by reason of' the storage of content by the service providers. Section 43E does not shelter hosting service providers only for copyright infringement which lies in 'storage' itself. Hosting service providers do not lose the safe harbour merely for the provision of access or processes that take place automatically when the users upload content to their networks.[100]

Section 43E of the CA 1987 ensures that hosing service providers may enjoy the limitation of liabilities only if they have no knowledge of infringement as well as no right and ability to control infringement. In addition, hosting service providers shall not derive financial benefit directly attributable to copyright infringement.[101] The imposition of the requirements helps to ensure that hosting service providers who knowingly participate in or contribute to the users' infringing activities, as well as those whose survival relies on copyright infringement, will and rightly so, be held liable.

However, as the earlier discussion reveals, the notice and takedown procedure to which hosting service providers are subject does not maintain a balance of interests between copyright owners and the users. The provisions governing the notice and takedown of content under the CA 1987, as a whole, do not burden hosting service providers with a duty to monitor or actively prevent copyright infringement. However, an express provision to that effect is desirable so as to clear any doubts regarding hosting service providers' duty in relation to copyright infringement in the online environment.[102] The lack of express and clear regulations on the content of a copyright owner's notice, in particular, a good faith belief statement, is regrettable.[103] The notice and takedown procedure, as a whole, favours prompt removal of content and, thus, does not aptly provide for the users' interests.[104] At the same time, the confusing provisions in respect of the duty on service providers who know about the infringing activities taking place on their network in the

[100] See Section 2.1.

[101] See Sections 2.2–2.4.

[102] See Section 3.1.

[103] See Sections 3.2 & 3.4.

[104] See Section 3.3.

absence of copyright owners' notices, are highly ill-suited to ensure a balance of interests between copyright owners and hosting service providers.[105]

In sum, the provisions on the limitation of liabilities for hosting service providers under the CA 1987 demonstrates inadequacy in several aspects. Until and unless the deficiencies are rectified and reformed, the CA 1987 does not provide a balance of interests between copyright owners, hosting service providers, and the public.

[105] See Section 3.5.

Criminalization of Copyrights Infringements in the Digital Era with Special Reference to India

C.P. Nandini

Abstract The beginning of the Internet since 1970s and the commercialization of its use in 1990s has been a challenging era for the Law makers and the Intellectual Property Right holders/owners. The copyright protection in the digitalized technology has witnessed an economic setback to the copyright holder and its quick and simple accessibility; a boon to the violators. Digitalization has also enabled information to be easily stored, reproduced and transmitted through internet as the web 2.0 era has made information storage, sharing and collaboration easier. The digitalisation has made the cyberspace an interwoven virtual community. While the digitalization of copyright material has made the information access easy and available, it has rather posed complications, technical and non-technical hitches to the holders/owners in a multi-faced ways. Combating piracy i.e. mass piracy, counterfeiting, circumventing methods etc., have all challenged the existing laws. The international pressure of the copyright holders has pressured the states to pass various laws and under the ambit of the WIPO that brought WCT and WPPT, most of the states are proposing their laws to be at par with the international changes in the copyright law. The copyright protection had problems and challenges during all the phases of digital technology. The major changes that took place with serious concerns are in the two major phases' that are well known as Low-Tech and High-Tech Era. The further classification of the Digital Era can be basically divided into the Analog Phase and Digital phase which have further intensified the infringements with greater challenges to the law makers. However, it is found that states are slowly sliding from the civil remedy approach to that of criminalisation of the copyright law, aiming to fulfil the demands and rationale anguish of the copyright holders'. This change is seen rather in almost all the countries, as the copyright holders are keen for criminal law to prevail at least in few circumstances. In the US both these phases have seen various laws passed by the congress to criminalise copyright like the ACPA, RICO, NET, DMCA, Pro-IP Act etc. The European Union has also brought in changes in order to criminalise the copyright

C.P. Nandini (✉)
Damodaram Sanjivayya National Law University, Visakhapatnam, Andhra Pradesh, India
e-mail: nandinicp@gmail.com

M.K. Sinha and V. Mahalwar (eds.), *Copyright Law in the Digital World*,
DOI 10.1007/978-981-10-3984-3_14

infringements with the Directive on the harmonisation of certain aspects of copyright and related rights in the information society and Directive on Enforcement of Intellectual Property Rights along the lines of WIPO and TRIPs. India though is not a signatory to the WCT and WPPT; it amended the Copyright Law in the year 2012 and added section 65A, that criminalises the copyright infringement in the electronic/digital forms especially relating anti-circumvention and Rights Management Information. The criminalisation of copyright violation is shaping up in a new direction since the advancement of technology. The criminal liability is present either with the civil remedy or in addition to the civil remedy. The digital era has three fold violators i.e. the mass violators who violate copyright law for the commercial purpose, the user (individual users) and the new member is the Online Service Provider (OSP) who may have knowledge of copyright violations while providing services. Overall it can be observed that there is an overthrow of laws since Napsters (P2P) and in addition with the online hosting. As they pose newer challenges that are expected to have deadly effects on the copyright. In this paper the author would look into the changes in copyright law and its inclination towards criminalisation and its impact.

1 Introduction

The beginning of the Internet era has given a collective test to the Intellectual Property Right (IPR) holders/owners as well as the States in protecting the IPR of these right holders. Among the most common violation is the copyright. Especially after the digitalisation, the number of copyright violations has drastically increased. Even with various steps taken by government and industry in their private capacity, there is set back to copyright protection. The digitalization was an instant hit for the copyright holders, as it made their creation reach any interested user to buy it from any part of the world, just at a click. When the users are benefitted to buy copyright material (online), the violators or wrong doer are also benefitted; as digitalization has enabled them also to easily store, reproduce and transmit these copyright material. The development of World Wide Web to 2.0 eras has made information storage, sharing and collaboration for good and bad easier. The digitalisation has made the cyberspace[1] a right place for the people to interact and make the information available in abundance with easy access with online buying tools that are interwoven in the virtual community of buyers and sellers. Though, the copyright holders are greatly excited in getting a larger market for their copyright material, it has also posed difficulties for the owners in a numerous ways. These threats of copyright violations are rampant with offences like piracy,

[1] The online world of computer networks and the Internet (Merriam-Webster 2016).

counterfeiting, circumventing etc. It has in toto challenged the existing laws and protection tools are being defaced immensely. This circumstance has been created because of its easier and effectiveness in infringement techniques. Now the question to be answered is who is this new culprit in the digital world? Are the violators only those who are violating copyrights for commercial use or it also includes the individual user who uses or downloads the copyright material for his own use or is the Internet/online service provider (ISP/OSP) also equally liable for these infringements? The ISP is the new player in this arena who is either directly or indirectly an intermediatory to set on or help the violators (innocently or knowingly. The file hosting services or the P2P,[2] Bit torrent[3] or the cyber lockers[4] have all played havoc on the copyright owner's protection. There is a war between the owners and the infringers, as the user's needs have forced the State to make various laws in an attempt to expand legislative actions against the violations in the digital era.

Generally, a copyright being an intangible property and if any person knowingly takes or uses it without permission of the owner/holder, it is an offence. Once we tend to consider such taking or using as a crime, certainly it creates a doubt, as to whether, can we bring it at par with a theft attracting the criminal law provisions or does it need a different treatment altogether from the stringent control of criminal law. However, it can easily be understood that the common meaning of theft under criminal law cannot mean the same for copyrights, as the objective of copyright is quite different. The basic feature is the transfer of information, knowledge, and ideas (that can be protected under copyright) that are part of copyright law.[5] This meaning is given by those authors who have recommended freedom and access to knowledge to be used for free, made through internet. Whereas the basic Criminal Law Theory suggests that it is appropriate to punish conduct that imposes community harm or breaches a moral standard. In contrast to this theory, the practice that is taken for the understanding of the meaning of theft is, if such infringements are caused by the competitors or for commercial and the new generation (or new category) of violators, who can be called as the self-enriching e.g. the file sharing facilitators or the free downloader's. These new generation users (violators are

---

[2] Peer-to-peer (P2P) is a decentralized communications model in which each party has the same capabilities and either party can initiate a communication session (searchnetworking.techtarget.com/definition/peer-to-peer).

[3] BitTorrent is a leading software company with the fastest torrent client and sync and share software for Mac, Windows, Linux, iOS and Android, *available at:* www.bittorrent.com (last visited March 12, 2016).

[4] An on-line internet site for storage of personal digital files. Cyber lockers are also known as cloud storage or file storage services, enable users to keep files, or back them up, on the internet. Users can access files from these virtual storage lockers, which operate on remote servers, from any computer with an internet connection, often more quickly than on personal computers. Many of these sites offer limited free storage, and users can pay for more capacity through subscriptions, *available at:* http://in.reuters.com/article/newzealand-dotcom-cyberlockers-idINDEE90I03320130119 (Last Visited March 12, 2016).

[5] Geraldine Szott Moohr.

justifying their act as a Fair Use), argue that such acts of use may not wholly be treated as infringement. The moral consensus that would condemn personal use is far from being strong and basis for a rationale for the equivocal criminalization of copyright material. Moreover, the results of criminalizing personal use of copyright material are inconsistent with the underlying policy of copyright law. In the pre-digitalization era, the courts have not treated the copyright violation seriously especially for criminal liability and most of the cases are taken to civil courts for damages and injunction including other remedies.

In this chapter, the author would attempt to highlight the development of copyright laws in the digital era and the criminal liabilities. The first part of the chapter would be to understand who and how the perpetrators of copyright infringements are and what punishments are provided for the same. Later part of the chapter aims to provide an understanding whether these laws are over powering user rights or the criminality are imposed, following correct steps towards making copyright violation stringent, just to satisfy its correctness and protect the copyright owners' rights. The last part of the chapter is an attempt to understand, if these laws are successful in order to control and curb copyright violation through criminalisation. This chapter attempts to understand the interpretation of the provision i.e. Section 65A and 65B and other relevant sections of Indian copyright amendment laws of 2012 and also make a comparative study in this connection with the US to a large extent and a brief note on the EU Laws, which imposes criminal liability only for subsequent violations rather than the first.

The new Section 65A protects the Technological Protection Measures (TPM) used by copyright owners against circumvention. TPM is used by a copyright owner to protect his rights over the work. In case a person circumvents it with the intention of infringing such rights, then that person would be punishable with imprisonment up to 2 years and shall also be liable for fine. Further with the insertion of Section 65B, the Act intents to make removal of Right Management Information without authority and distribution thereafter to be a criminal offence. Information Rights Management (IRM) is a term that applies to a technology which protects sensitive information from unauthorised access. So, any unauthorised and intentional removal or alteration of any rights management information is a criminal offence punishable with imprisonment. The introduction of Sections 65A and 65B is expected to help the film, music and publishing industry in fighting piracy.[6] This change of imposing criminal liability has been criticised for indirectly barring the right of the owner to claim damages that might be going against the interest of the owner. In the process of understanding Section 65 A, the exceptions that bar liability and provide safe harbour to the ISP especially in the cyberspace will be of great interest to understand as to how criminal liability will retort the violators as against the interest of the copyright owners. In the process of harmonising the law, the author in this chapter attempts to know, if India went little too far and a step further than its counterparts like the US and the EU by imposing criminal liability

[6] Swaraj Paul Barooah.

on the infringers through its Copyright Amendment Act, 2012. Whether criminalisation of the copyright law is successful in making the violators conscious about being violators is still an analysis to be successfully proved. But the question is whether the copyright law by imposing a criminal liability without providing a concurrent civil liability is stepping towards too much of control for the genuine or the innocent user. In comparison to its counterpart's like the US and EU, is Indian law treating these users, who may need just an admonition to correct their behaviour pattern, as grave offenders.

2 Digital Piracy, Piracy Online and Broadcast Piracy

The increased availability of Internet with the broadband connections has, increasingly made easy accessibility, with sophisticated Smartphone and the growth of ICT inclusive of mobile technology is generating significant benefits ranging from economic activity with e-commerce and other information (including large number of copyright material made available to netizens). It has also challenged the owners and the State with extremely efficient vehicle for disseminating infringing content, and in superseding legitimate opportunities for copyright holders and providing access through the online platforms that deliver licensed content. It is estimated that Internet piracy costs US businesses as much as $250 billion a year. It now seems, however, that the era of blatant copyright infringement of music and other content through file-sharing technologies is on the decline, as recently demonstrated by Kazaa's (Sharman Network Ltd.) payment of $115 million dollars to the recording industry in the *MGM v Grokster case*[7] on remand by the US Supreme Court.[8] Even though digital piracy affects the economy, it can be difficult to determine the precise impact it has on each individual industry. Estimates range from $446 million to $20.5 billion per year. It is argued that theft of intellectual property not only stifles innovation, but harms job creation in all areas of the economy. In 2011, the global piracy rate for computer software reached 42% with the United States accounting for 19% of the global software piracy rate. In 2011, the market value of the pirated software industry reached a record of $63.4 billion.[9]

The U.S. Government's 2014 Notorious Markets List[10] includes examples of online marketplaces reportedly engaging in commercial-scale IPR counterfeiting

[7] 545 U.S. 913(2005). Here the defendant distributed free software that allowed private individuals to share copyrighted electronic files without authorization. Some files were movies and songs that were copyrights of MGM. The issue was whether the distributor of a product is capable of lawful and unlawful use is liable for infringement as per the copyright law by a third party, when the distributor takes affirmative steps to foster infringement through the use of its product, or will the distributor liable for that infringement conducted by 3rd parties.

[8] Brown 2006.

[9] Shadow Market 2012.

[10] *Ibid.*

and piracy, including sites hosted in, or operated by, parties located in Brazil, Canada, China, Russia, Switzerland, Ukraine, and elsewhere. These infringements are in addition to the optical disc piracy that continues to be sold in many countries like China, India, Paraguay, and Vietnam. Piracy over the Internet has been treated as a priority for copyright infringement and a major enforcement issues in the world market and a concern to the trading partner. Apart from books, recorded music and video cassettes of films and TV programmes reproduced, distributed and sold on a massive scale in many parts of the world without any remuneration to the authors, artists, publishers and producers is an added concern. The emergence of new techniques of recordings, fixation and reproduction of audio programmes, combined with the advent of video technology has greatly helped the pirates. It is estimated that the losses to the film producers and other owners of copyright amount to several crores of rupees. The loss to Government in terms of tax evasion also amounts to crores of rupees.[11] In the list of copyright holders suffering losses, the major industry that loses to the maximum extent is the music and movie industry. Hollywood, Bollywood and other regional cinema industries, including the e-commerce are insisting for changes in law by bringing in various reports and research studies to highlight their problems. In addition to these violations the trademarks and unauthorized retransmission of live sports programming over the Internet has invaded the television operator's rights and continues to grow in a large number of countries and regions, particularly in China, Latin America, the Middle East, and the Caribbean region. Though piracy is in existence since ages, the digitalised world through its websites link to infringing content is intensifying the problem day by day. In addition, pirate servers or "grey shards" that allow the users to play unauthorized versions of cloud-based entertainment software, and the development and online distribution of devices that allow for the circumvention[12] of TPMs, including "game copiers" and mod chips, are allowing users to play pirated games on physical consoles and they are also presenting unique enforcement challenges for rights holders.[13] "Camcorded" copies (i.e., unauthorized recordings made in movie theatres) of first-run motion pictures that are distributed worldwide via the Internet result in economic harm not only in the market where the film was originally shown, but in other markets as well. The availability of, and recourse by rights holders to, enforcement procedures and remedies is a critical component of the online ecosystem. However, government and judiciary including the industry in themselves have played a vital role in dealing with online piracy, which unite multiple jurisdictions. Governments should avoid creating a domestic environment that offers a safe haven for piracy on the Internet.[14]

---

[11] *Girish Gandhi and* etc. v. *Union Of India (UOI) And Anr.* AIR199Raj78.

[12] To avoid being stopped by (something, such as a law or rule): to get around (something) in a clever and sometimes dishonest way. *Merriam-Webster* 2016.

[13] DMCA prohibits circumventing ace control measures as per the 17 U.S.C §1201 (a) (1). DMCA makes it unlawful to bypass this ACM. These control systems are in e books also. But some copyright holder merge access control and copyright control measures in the same DRM system.

[14] Moohr 2003.

3 Changing Scenario of Copyright Violation

The birth of criminalisation of copyright has been there since 1897. The progression can be easily divided into two separate phases. First phase that took place till the end of the 19th century i.e., the low phase and the second phase known as the High-tech phase that is further divided into Analog Phase till 1970s and the High-Tech Phase since 1990s. The onslaught of the digital phase is continuous with progress of technical changes and with the high rate of violations, has gradually displeased the copyright holders; as the methods of copyright violations have rapidly augmented. The first of its kind that has immensely affected the copyright violation in the digital era is the P2P files sharing. It is estimated to cost Hollywood billions of dollars annually, yet very few creators or distributors of these applications have been held liable. Neither the traditional doctrines of secondary liability for copyright infringement nor the inducement theory that was recently adopted by the Supreme Court of the US has changed the dynamic methods of infringements. Additionally, the staple article of 'Commerce Doctrine' articulated by the Supreme Court as a defence against contributory copyright infringement is inadequate to protect the rights of copyright holders in a digital world. This unhelpful point in the P2P applications enabled individuals to make unauthorized duplication of copyright work and subsequently distribute thousands of copies worldwide.[15] The secondary liability for copyright infringement of modem P2P applications and then the uses of Bit Torrent for justifying a revision of the "staple article of commerce doctrine"[16] was first articulated in *Sony Corp. of America* v *Universal City Studios, Inc*[17] where the court held that the sale of the video cassette recorders (VTR's) to the general public does not constitute contributory infringement of respondents' copyrights. The primary holding was, if a device is sold for a legitimate purpose and has a substantial non-infringing use; its manufacturer will not be liable under copyright law for potential infringement by its users.[18] The Sony doctrine provides a defence for contributory copyright infringement where a staple article of commerce (the Betamax VTR) is "capable of commercially significant non-infringing uses." This decision has credited Sony in allowing the development of VCR's, Digital Video Recorders, and other devices capable of duplicating copyright work.[19] The traditional doctrines of secondary liability for copyright infringement, describes the rules as held in *Sony* and *Metro Goldwyn-Mayer Studios Inc. v Grokster, Ltd,*[20] where the court while referring to a question on distributors liability and consideration on what

[15] Helton 2007.

[16] (The staple article of commerce test and the inducement test, respectively), and provides a deeper analysis of the staple article of commerce doctrine under patent and copyright law.

[17] 464 U.S. 417 (1984).

[18] *Ibid.*

[19] *Supra* note 16.

[20] 545 U.S. 913 (2005).

circumstances should the distributor of a product (either lawfully or unlawfully using) can be liable for acts of copyright infringement by third parties. The court held that "one, who distributes a device with the object of promoting its use to infringe copyright, as shown by clear expression or other affirmative steps taken to foster infringement, is liable for the resulting acts of infringement by third parties".[21] Copyright protection provides its owners with the following exclusive rights: reproduction, adaptation (the right to create derivative works), distribution, performance, and display. When a person violates any of these exclusive rights without the permission of the author, that person has infringed upon the author's copyrights. The author may then bring a claim against the infringer. A cause of action can be brought for both direct infringements, where an individual violates an exclusive right without the permission of the copyright owner, and for secondary liability. Secondary liability is a common law judicial doctrine that recognizes vicarious liability and contributory infringement for direct acts of infringement committed by others.[22] In analyzing the contributory infringement issue, the Supreme Court imported the patent law doctrine of staple articles of commerce into copyright law[23] for contributory infringement[24] (the Betamax videotape recorder) and is "capable of commercially significant non-infringing uses". The Supreme Court concluded that the Betamax recorder satisfied the standard and Sony was not liable. The Court was also able to reach to this conclusion because most Betamax duplication of copyright material was either authorized or unauthorised, but is considered non-infringing because unauthorized time shifting constitutes it as fair.[25] In the 1990s developed the

[21] "Grokster's eponymous software employs what is known as FastTrack technology, a protocol developed by others and licensed to Grokster. StreamCast distributes a very similar product except that its software, called Morpheus, relies on what is known as Gnutella technology".

[22] *Kelly* v. *Arriba Soft Corp.*, 280 F.3d 934 (9th Cir. 2002); *Nunez* v. *Caribbean Int'l News Corp.*, 235 F.3d 18 (1st Cir. 2000); *Castle Rock Entertainment, Inc.* v. *Carol Publishing Group, Inc.*, 150 F.3d 132 (2d Cir. 1998); See Elisa Vitanza, Castle Rock Entertainment, Inc. v. Carol Publishing Group, Inc., 14 Berkeley Tech. L.J. 43 (1999).

[23] *Sony Corp. of Am.* v. *Universal City Studios, Inc.*, 464 U.S. 417, 442 (1984) (noting the "historic kinship between patent law and copyright law.") Notably, courts have not imported this patent law doctrine into the analysis of vicarious copyright infringement. See *A&M Records* v. *Napster, Inc.*, 239 F.3d 1004 (9th Cir. 2001) (noting that "Sony's 'staple article of commerce' analysis has no application to Napster's potential liability for vicarious copyright infringement.").

[24] Staple Article of Commerce under Patent Law—The legal treatise Patent Law Fundamentals explains that, "[w]ith respect to patents, the applicability of the doctrine of contributory infringement is limited by statute to a component (or a combination of components) which has no substantial non-infringing use and which therefore must be almost uniquely suited for use as a component of the patented invention." This principle has been codified into patent law as the "staple article of commerce doctrine," which recognizes that the distribution of a component of a patented device will not violate the patent if it is suitable for other, non-infringing uses. Justice Blackmun, dissenting in Sony, noted that "[t]he 'staple article of commerce' doctrine protects those who manufacture products incorporated into or used with patented inventions—for example, the paper and ink used with patented printing machines, or the dry ice used with patented refrigeration systems.

[25] Helton 2007.

computer age, and the twist was towards violations in the Computer software, that poses difficulty of categorising them as a product, service, or interactive network, but some software, like Microsoft Word (a digital typewriter) or video capture software (a digital videotape recorder), can be more easily classified within the standard conception of a staple article of commerce. Thereby, software such as P2P applications arguably fall outside this classification like that of non-traditional products that are capable of global copyright infringement and the same was not anticipated in the Sony era.[26] In July 2000, a district court enjoined Napster, ordering its service to shut down. Subsequent appeals failed, and, in July 2001, Napster agreed to remove copyright content from its network, filed for bankruptcy, and shut down its service. New waves of P2P applications like BitTorrent developed and succeeded Napster. BitTorrent[27] practically is distinct from its earlier P2P applications, because the application does not require a centralized server and therefore complicates the imposition of secondary liability for copyright infringement. In addition, to open source software distribution, BitTorrent and similar applications are legally used to distribute numerous large-scale media such as Revelation, the Star Wars, Peter Jackson's video production diaries for King Kong, Rock Bands, Television and Radio etc. BitTorrent certainly has a wide range of non- infringing uses, because it was specifically designed to facilitate transfers of large data files, it has also become the tool of choice for software, music, and films distribution leading to copyright infringements. According to industry executives, this infringement costs the industries billions of dollars annually.[28] The global broadband Internet access is inevitable and bandwidth costs continue to plummet, the reality may be that efficient file transfer programs and architectures like BitTorrent are the necessary components of the evolution of the Internet. Based upon the current jurisprudence surrounding the staple article of commerce test, BitTorrent, Inc and the like would be shielded from liability under the Sony Doctrine because, like the Sony Betamax videotape recorder, the BitTorrent file-sharing device is capable of substantial non-infringing uses. The Supreme Court was able to provide specific examples of Grokster's intent:

> Three features of this evidence of intent are particularly notable. *First*, each company showed itself to be aiming to satisfy a known source of demand for copyright infringement, the market comprising former Napster users…. *Second*, the evidence of unlawful objective gave an added significance by MGM's showing that neither company attempted to develop filtering tools or other mechanisms to diminish the infringing activity using their software…. *Third*, a further complement to the direct evidence of unlawful objective is also available.

---

[26] In *Re Aimster Copyright Litigation*, 252 F. Supp. 2d 634 (N.D. 111. 2002).

[27] The BitTorrent homepage describes BitTorrent as a "free speech tool," giving individuals the freedom to publish that was previously enjoyed by only a select few with the right equipment and requisite finances.

[28] Om Malik to GigaOM, gigaom.com/2005/08/10/p2p-is-bere-tostay-deal-witb-it (last visited on December 26th, 2016) (noting that the transfer of video files, which are typically large in size; now accounts for 61.44% of file sharing activity on the P2P networks, while audio is only 11.24%).

The liability to be understood, here will be useful, if a recall can be taken on both StreamCast and Grokster that provided copyright content with advertising space for making profit and directing ads to the screens of computers employing their software. Liability in such cases likely would not lie under the Grokster inducement theory, as well. In Grokster, inducement was obvious: Grokster not only advertised itself as an alternative to Napster, but also published newsletters containing links to articles promoting the software's ability to access popular copyright music. Additionally, the Supreme Court found it relevant that the Grokster name was an apparent derivative of Napster, as evidence of an attempt to capture the market of former Napster users. However, BitTorrent, Inc. entered as a different species of company: it never advertised BitTorrent as a vehicle for copyright infringement and have a name that invokes the image of a vehicle for infringement, rather and in fact it can be used for legitimate, unobjectionable purposes. Unlike Grokster, which the Supreme Court found operated and advertised in such a way, so as to intentionally induce its users to commit copyright infringement; BitTorrent advertises itself as a free speech tool. Programmes, developers, and distributors of software applications, specifically P2P applications, such as Bit Torrent, now would fail to qualify under the new definition of staple articles of commerce and would face liability for contributory infringement. This new standard will advance the cause of responsible innovation, while promoting the development of technologies that do not contribute to copyright infringement and pose a threat to entire industry. As technology advances, copyright law must also respond to the changes. Narrowing the applicability to Sony in the manner proposed above that results in a more effective balance of technological development and advancement against the exclusive rights of copyright holders. These developments forced the Congress to enact the Digital Millennium Copyright Act, 1998 (DMCA)[29] and its subsequent interpretation by the courts in copyright infringement lawsuits brought by the entertainment industry against the (P2P) networks like Napster, Aimster, and Grokster.[30] In furtherance of this, it is found that YouTube also seeks shelter from copyright infringement liability under the safe harbor provisions of the DMCA. If the ISP's liability has to be understood, as per the provisions of DMCA, an ISP is not liable for monetary, injunctive, or other equitable relief relating to material online so long as the service provider does not adopt an "ostrich-like" approach (the meaning—was evidence in understanding as to why they did not want to provide the details as to how many

[29] The DMCA is a federal law that increases penalties for online copyright infringement. The DMCA criminalizes circumventing DRM software designed to prevent file sharing. The creation and sharing of technology or software that is designed to defeat copyright protections is also criminalized. There are both civil and criminal penalties for violations of the DMCA. Intentional violations of the DMCA can result in monetary damages as well as imprisonment.

[30] Civil Penalties: The DMCA allows registered copyright owners to file a lawsuit in a federal district court. The federal court has the power to grant injunctions against the defendant to prevent future infringements. The defendant may have to pay actual damages up to $2,500 per violation, or statutory damages up to $25,000. The plaintiff may also recover any profits the defendant made from the infringement. Repeat offenders may face triple damages if they violate the DMCA within three years of a judgment.

violations of copyrights were taking place) to copyright infringement, as the court criticized in Aimster, and follows the notice and take-down provisions of the DMCA.[31]

> Section 1204 creates criminal penalties for persons who violate §§ 1201 or 1202 "wilfully and for purposes of commercial advantage or private financial gain." These penalties go up to a $500,000 fine and or up to a 5-year prison sentence for a first offense and can be as high as a $1,000,000 fine and or a 10-year prison sentence for subsequent offenses.[32] Non-profit libraries, archives and educational institutions are exempt from criminal penalties[33] for violations of §§ 1201 or 1202. The other remedies provided in DMCA are destruction of goods[34] and false claims.[35]

The remedy stated above keeps the violators at bay[36] but creates a safe harbour to limit ISP's liability for information stored on a computer system or network when that information is at the direction of users. In general, ISP's are not subject to monetary or equitable relief for infringing works that are stored on their computer systems or networks if they can fulfil the following essentials[37]:

(1) that the ISP lacks "actual knowledge that the material" is infringing, is unaware of "facts or circumstances from which infringing activity is apparent," or expeditiously acts "to remove, or disable access to, the material,"
(2) It does not directly benefit financially from the infringing activity, and
(3) It expeditiously acts "to remove, or disable access to, the material that is claimed to be infringing."

The *first* safe harbor, "Transitory Digital Network Communications," applies when the ISP would be liable for providing a connection to transmit infringing material through its system or network. The *second* safe harbor, "System Caching," limits copyright infringement liability for intermediate and temporary storage (or caching) of copyright material on the ISP's system. The *third* safe harbor, for "Information Residing on Systems or Networks at the Direction of Users," shelters

---

[31] Supra Note 30.

[32] Juille 1998–1999.

[33] *Ibid.*

[34] The federal court can impound property that it believes was used to violate the DMCA. If the defendant is found to have violated the DMCA, the court can order the destruction of the defendant's property; the court can also order the destruction of goods produced by those tools. Any technology a defendant used to circumvent copyright protections or violate the plaintiff's copyrights, such as CD and DVD burners, computers and software disks can be seized or destroyed. A court can order the destruction of tools used to violate the law.

[35] Copyright owners may send a "take down" notice to an ISP demanding that copyright material be removed from a website. The ISP must act quickly to remove or block access to content described in the notice. The person who uploaded the content may respond with a counter notice to restore the content. A person who sends takedowns or counter notices without proof or files frivolous notices faces fines and attorney fees. There is also the possibility of criminal sanctions because DMCA notices are signed under penalty of perjury.

[36] H. Maria Perry.

[37] *Ibid.*

the ISP from liability so long as it does not know, or have reason to know, about infringing activity or material on its network and "does not receive a financial benefit directly attributable to the infringing activity, in a case in which the ISP has the right and ability to control such activity. It also contains the so-called notice and take-down provisions of the DMCA. The provisions also require the ISP:

(1) To designate an agent to receive notifications of claimed infringement,
(2) To identify that agent to the Copyright Office, and
(3) To "respond expeditiously to remove, or disable access to, the material that is claimed to be infringing."

The *fourth* safe harbor, providers of "Information Location Tools," protects ISP's that refer or link users to infringing material or infringing activity.[38]

In varied efforts taken to combat infringement of copyright protected digital content, the manufacturers of digital content are embedded to control access with the use of technologies within digital products. These access control technologies are often referred to as "Digital Rights Management" (DRM).[39] To further aid copyright owners in preventing infringing uses of copyright material, the World Intellectual Property Organization Copyright Treaty, 1996 (WCT) was created to provide "writers, artists, and other creators of copyright material global protection from piracy in the digital age." The DMCA was amended (Title 17) to impose civil and criminal penalties for the circumvention of DRM technologies for protecting copyright works. The DMCA is treated as US Governments vital attempt to protect copyright owners from digital piracy by balancing the interests of both copyright owners and consumers. However, the DMCA tends to subject consumers to more violations in attempting to protect copyright owners. Though, these changes expected to facilitate copyright holders but the frustrated consumers circumvent DRM technologies to customize legally purchased digital devices and violate copyright law.[40] The law makes even manufacture, import, or sell of a product that is primarily to be used in circumventing DRM technologies an offence to protect the copyright owner. In an attempt to achieve the intended balance of rights between copyright owners and consumers, the law makers have a task to analyse the DRM being utilized to protect copyright works and to determine whether such DRM technology adversely affect the public by limiting lawful consumer uses of copyright materials.[41] Section 1201(a) (2) prohibits ISP and devices primarily used to

[38] *Supra* note 9.

[39] "Digital Rights Management (DRM) & Libraries", American Library Association.

[40] Norwood 2014.

[41] "During the triennial process, consideration is given to the availability of the copyrighted work, which includes its use for non-profit preservation efforts and educational purposes. The effects a prohibition on circumventing DRM technologies would impose upon "criticism, comment, news reporting, teaching, scholarship, or research," is also considered. Further consideration is given to the copyrighted work's market value. Cellular service providers agreed and would have supported a specific exception to permit individual consumers of wireless carriers to unlock phones for the purpose of switching networks. Such a carefully drafted exception arguably would have

circumvent access control technologies within copyright works. Although not aimed at devices capable of significant non-infringing use, Section 1201(a)(2) is focused on the prohibition of devices intended to aide consumers in bypassing protective measures in order to gain access to a protected work. Similarly, Section 1201(b)(1) prohibits services and devices primarily used to circumvent the protection of a copyright owner's rights that are provided by technological measures. Therefore, it is not only a violation for a consumer to bypass technological protections used by copyright owners; but a violation to provide services or devices that would aide consumers in bypassing the technology.[42] Content industry trade associations, such as the Motion Picture Association of America and the Recording Industry Association of America, have strongly opposed such proposals for fear of experiencing further harm due to digital piracy. The Digital Media Consumers' Rights Act, (DMCRA) (2003 & 2005) was introduced to benefit the Authors without Limiting Advancement or Net Consumer Expectations (BALANCE) Act, 2003, and the Freedom and Innovation Revitalizing U.S. Entrepreneurship (FAIR USE) Act, 2007 was enacted to provide and extend the relief to the consumers. All of which proposed stronger protection of consumer fair use[43] principle. Norwood has studied and analyzed both consumer behaviour and consumer attitude toward the lawful and unlawful use of copyright material on the Internet. Copyright types that are grouped by him are six (content wise) that include music, films, television programming, computer software, books and video games.[44]

In a study by Ofcom, the result has seemingly supported a finding that copyright owners could in reality gain more profit by abandoning such access control technologies. The reason for the same is that majority of all copyright infringers consistently agreed that illegal content violation was more attractive. Focusing on innovative ways to offer consumers quick, easy, and convenient access to legal digital content may make circumvention of DRM technologies a less attractive option. But practically abandoning such technology would leave copyright owners' with unprotected and to a large extend unenforceable rights. Thereby Norwood suggests that a more balanced proposal to amend the DMCA would provide protections for consumer fair use along with protections for copyright owners against digital piracy. It is expected that by implementing laws intended to protect the interests of both copyright owners and consumers are enforceable through an administrative process, the US copyright law may move to a better position in order to keep pace with the increasingly rapid advancements in technology. By bringing about new modes of expression (such as computer programming and digital

(Footnote 41 continued)

maintained a balance between copyright owner rights and consumer rights without stifling competition and innovation. Rather than narrowly tailoring the exemption to allow consumers to unlock cell phones in order to obtain service from another provider, the Librarian of Congress simply eliminated the cell phone exemption completely".

[42] *Ibid.*

[43] *Ibid.*

[44] Media 2012.

sampling of music) and empowering anyone with a computer and an Internet connection to flawlessly, inexpensively, and instantaneously reproduce and distribute works of authorship on a wide scale, digital technology helps the violators and in a minimal way represents possibly the most profound challenge to copyright law. For a better understanding the analysis of digital technology is divided into two categories: "(1) squeezing computer software within copyright's non-functionally oriented protection regime and (2) developing new rules and governance institutions to address the ease of reproduction and porosity of the digital platform".[45]

4 Development of Criminal Jurisprudence

The methods of commission of copyright infringements in the five decade old cyberspace have increased enormously and sophisticated and hi-tech techniques are used by the perpetrators with new forms of offences. Personal use and economic or financial gain is the main reasons for these violations.[46]

The copyright law in India until 2012 did not make any serious attempt to make necessary laws relating to copyright infringement in cyberspace or through internet. The Copyright Act, 1957 did not have the imagination of the 21st century requirement. Although there were two amendments in 1983 and 1984 it was not until 1994, that 'computer program' was included explaining the rights of copyright holder, position on rentals of software, the rights of the user to make backup copies etc. The 1994 amendment imposes fines and punishes for infringements of copyright of software. It also makes it illegal to make or distribute copies of copyright software without proper or specific authorization.[47] This amendment included Computer and Computer Program within the definition of 'Literary work'. In addition to the Copyright Amendments in 1994 and 2012 (Major Amendment to

[45] Menell 2002–2003.

[46] Amrendra N. Tripathi.

[47] *SAP Aktiengesellschaft and another* v. *Appsone Consulting India Private Limited and another* (27th July, 2015) 2015 Indlaw DEL 3523, here it was a case of the plaintiffs, that the plaintiff No. 2 through its Agents EIPR India Limited, immediately on becoming aware of the defendants' activities lodged a criminal complaint with the Police in Navi Mumbai, on 1st October, 2008. The Police Team, accompanied by representatives of the plaintiff No. 2, carried out investigations at the Navi Mumbai premises of the defendant No. 1. During the search operations, the Police team was able to recover hard disks, servers, containing pirated software SAP R.3 Release 4.6B of the plaintiffs, SAP Brochures, SAP Study materials, record book of SAP certificates issued to the students, 12 nos. of SAP loaded CDs, which were being used for providing training on SAP software. The Police team thereafter seized these servers. Thereafter, FIR No. 119/08 dated 1st October, 2008 was registered in this regard for offences committed under the provisions of Sections 51, 52, and 63 of the Act and also under Section 420 IPC. It is alleged that the defendants are not spending any amount for the research work of softwares and the defendants are merely doing illegal activity without any investment therefore the profit margin of the defendants is very high.

impose criminal liability), Information Technology Act, 2000 (IT Act) has also given an added advantage to punish for Tampering the Computer Source Documents, Hacking of Computer System Piracy, unauthorised access/alternation etc. Section 79 of the IT Act provides for safe harbour to the intermediaries[48] and Section 81[49] of IT Act, has an overriding effect. The provisions under the Copyright Law that deal with the criminal liability are mainly provided in the chapter Offences and Penalties. Ss. 63,[50] 63A, 63B,[51] 64,[52] 65,[53] 65A (Protection of

---

[48] Intermediaries are given immunity under The Information Technology Act, 2000, s.79. However, they can still be held liable under Section 72A for disclosure of personal information of any person where such disclosures are without consent and with intent to cause wrongful loss or wrongful gain or in breach of a lawful contract. Proviso to Section 81 of the Information Technology (Amendment) Act, 2008 states that nothing contained in the Act shall restrain any person from exercising any right conferred under the Copyright Act 1957 and the Patents Act 1970. Though experts state that, this provision has created a lot of confusion as to the extent of liability provided under Section 79. The Information Technology (Amendment) Act 2008 makes a genuine effort to provide immunity to the intermediaries but needs to plug in some gaps so as to enable the intermediaries to operate without fear and inhibitions. Also read, India: Intermediaries Under The Information Technology (Amendment) Act 2008, *available at:* http://www.mondaq.com/india/x/225328/Telecommunications+Mobile+Cable+Communications/Intermediaries+Under+The+Information+Technology+Amendment+Act+2008 (last visited April 1, 2016).

[49] The Information Technology Act, 2000, s. 81. reads: "The provisions of this Act shall have effect notwithstanding anything inconsistent therewith contained in any other law for the time being in force."

[50] The Copyright Act, 1957, s.63 reads: "Any person who knowingly infringes or abets the infringement of—

(a) the copyright in a work, or

(b) any other right conferred by this Act, shall be punishable with imprisonment which may extend to 1 year, or with fine, or with both.

Explanation—Construction of a building or other structure which infringes or which, if completed, would infringe the copyright in some other work shall not be an offence under this section"

[51] *Dhiraj Dharamdas Dewani* v. *Sonal Info Systems Private Limited and other,* 2012 SCC OnLine Bom 351. The court has stated as to how both civil and criminal remedies are alternative remedies. Penal provisions of ss. 63, 63-B and 64 of the Copyright Act clearly show that a person knowingly making use of a computer by infringing copy of a computer programme shall be criminally liable. It is well settled that provisions relating to penal provisions are required to be interpreted strictly.

[52] The Copyright Act, 1957, s.64 reads: "(1) Where a magistrate has taken cognizance of any offence under Section 63 in respect of the infringement of copyright in any work, it shall be lawful for any police officer, not below the rank of sub-inspector, to seize without any warrant from the magistrate, all copies of the work wherever found, which appear to him to be infringing copies of the work and all copies so seized shall, as soon as practicable, be produced before the magistrate.

(2) Any person having an interest in any copies of a work seized under sub-Section (1) may, within 15 days of such seizure, make an application to the magistrate for such copies being restored to him and the magistrate, after hearing the applicant and the complainant and making such further inquiry as may be necessary, shall make such order on the application as he may deed fit"

[53] *Id.*, s.65 reads: "Any person who knowingly makes, or has in his possession, any plate for the purpose of making infringing copies of any work in which copyright subsists shall be punishable with imprisonment which may extend to one year, or with fine, or with both."

technological measures) & 65B (Protection of Rights Management Information),[54] 66,[55] etc. Section 63–70 of the Copyrights Act, 1957 amended by the Act of 2012 has provided for new provisions to impose criminal liability. Sections 63–70 of the Act, provides wide range of criminal penalties for infringing copyrights that are punishable with terms of imprisonment that may be extended up to 3 years along with a fine. First and repeated commission has been treated with enhanced punishment. These offences are taken cognizance of and tried at the court of the Metropolitan Magistrate or Judicial Magistrate of the First Class under Section 70 of the Code of Criminal Procedure, 1973. Section 64 empowers the police officers of the rank of a sub-inspector and above, to seize without warrant all infringing copies of works if the officer is satisfied that an offence of infringement under Section 63 has being or is likely to be committed. The Act further lays down various kinds of offences such as the knowingly making use of infringing copy of computer program (Section 63 B), possession of plates for purpose of making infringing copies of any copyright work (Section 65), unauthorized violation of technological protection measures (Section 65A), violation of Rights Management Information (Section 65B), making or causing to be made a false entry in the Register of Copyrights kept under this Act, or tendering or causing to be tendered as evidence any such entry or writing (Section 67), making false statements for the purpose of deceiving or influencing any authority or officer (Section 68), offences by company (Section 69). Section 66 provides that the court trying any offence may, whether the alleged offender is convicted or not, order that all copies of the work or all plates in the possession of the alleged offender, which appear to it to be infringing copies, or plates be delivered to the owner of the copyright. In *Girish Gandhi & Ors.* v. *Union of India,*[56] the petitioner had challenged the constitutional validity of Section 64 of the Copyright Act, as he was apprehensive that he would suffer harassment and unnecessary litigation, if the provisions of Section 64 of the Act are allowed to remain intact and not declared *ultra vires*. In the writ petition, the petitioner had also challenged Section 19, Section 52A and Section 64, but the arguments have been confined to the challenge of Section 64 only and no arguments are addressed on other Sections. The petitioner apprehends that provisions of Section 64 itself give arbitrary and naked powers without any guidelines to the

[54] *Id.*, s.65B reads: "Any person, who knowingly,—(i) removes or alters any rights management information without authority, or (ii) distributes, imports for distribution, broadcasts or communicates to the public. without authority, copies of any work, or performance knowingly that electronic rights management information has been removed or altered without authority, shall be punishable with imprisonment which may extend to two years and shall also be liable to fine: Provided that if the rights management information has been tampered with in any work, the owner of copyright in such work may also avail of civil remedies provided under Chapter XII against life persons indulging in such acts."

[55] *Id.*, s.66 reads: "The court trying any offence under this Act may, whether the alleged offender is convicted or not, order that all copies of the work or all plates in the possession of the alleged offender, which appear to it to be infringing copies, or plates for the purpose of making infringing copies, be delivered up to the owner of the copyright."

[56] AIR 1997 Raj 78.

police officer to seize any material from the shop and thus, drag the video owners to the litigation. He has given instances in the petition that police officer usually demands for video cassettes to be given to them free of charge for viewing it at their homes and in case, on any reason either the video cassette is not available or it is not given free of charge, there is likelihood that police officer shall misuse his powers and try to seize material for prosecution under the various provisions of the Act, therefore prayed that Section 64 of the Act may be declared *ultra vires.*[57] However, the court dismissed the petition as there was no harm caused to the petitioner and it also observed that the section has enough safeguard under section 64(2) relating to the power of search and seizer by the police officer. However, the section makes it mandatory to prove the knowledge[58] or *mens rea* of the accused as an essential ingredient. Proof of *bonafide* belief on part of the accused in the existence of a copyright is sufficient proof of knowledge of infringement.[59] The accused must have knowingly infringed the copyright. Knowledge of infringement by the accused may be proved by the production of infringing copies.[60] In *Cheria P. Joseph* v *K. Prabhakaran Nair,*[61] the court ruled that the burden as usual is on the prosecution to prove all the ingredients. For other remedies, the owner has to file a civil suit as criminal court cannot grant injunction. The burden of proving subsistence of copyright infringement or abetment of infringement, as the case may be, and guilty intention on part of the accused is on the prosecution. The standard of proof is similar to the other criminal prosecution. The burden of proving jurisdiction is also on the prosecution. Where the accused has given explanation of his action, pleaded by defence available under Section 52(1), the onus of proving that the explanation is not true or that the action of the accused does not come within the scope of the statutory exceptions to infringement is on the prosecution. The intention of the accused has to be inferred from the facts and circumstances of each case.[62] The basic elements of criminal copyright infringement as per the US law for prosecuting the infringer is as follows and the Government has the burden of proving these four elements:

(1) Infringement[63] of a copyright;

---

[57] *Ibid.*

[58] Knowledge of an accused is an essential ingredient to constitute the offence of infringement for criminal prosecution. Neglect to ascertain the facts relating to copyright will not be tantamount to knowledge. Clear and cogent proof of knowledge is necessary to establish the offence.

[59] *Sheo Ratan Upadhya* v. *Gopal ChandraNepali and Anr.*, AIR 1965 All 274.

[60] **Ghurey Lal And Ors. v. State Through Ram Narain Pathak 1965 CriLJ 530**.

[61] AIR 1967 Kar 234.

[62] Narayan 2007.

[63] *Infringement.* Although the statutory definition of infringement is ambiguous, the basic requirement in both civil and criminal cases is that the defendant unlawfully copied a work protected by a valid copyright. Copying can be established by direct evidence, but this is rarely available. As a result, the government will generally prove copying indirectly-by establishing the circumstances surrounding the defendant's access to the copyright owner's work and the substantial similarity between the defendant's work and the copyright work.

(2) That the work has not been the subject of a first sale;
(3) That the violation was performed willfully; and
(4) That it was for profit.[64]

In most of the laws, it is seen that intention is an ingredient to make a perpetrator liable. None of the country had laws for imposing criminal liability without culpability. However, the owners are pressuring for a strict liability, rather than for seeking criminal liability as an alternative remedy.

5 Strict Liability

The law has seen a rapid change since 1980s and the same is evident as industry is in continuous attempt to influence the law makers to enforce copyright infringements with criminal liability. The criminal liability is gaining momentum due to the influence of the industry. Though criminal liability is an alternative remedy with the civil liability, there is a sea change, from just being one of alternative remedies to become the only remedy, especially when we refer to the new sections inserted by the Copyright (Amendment) Act, 2012 in India, though appreciatively it has not rooted for strict liability.

These changes are not only reflected in the changes brought in India, but these changes are highlighted (Dane S. Ciolino and Erin A. Donelon—2002) and elaborated to highlight the development of strict liability with the case of late George Harrison who innocently incorporated the 1962 Chiffons' hit "He's So Fine" into his own "My Sweet Lord"[65] during a recording session some eight years after the original songs released, but was held liable.[66] The author also uses another example that is in contrast; to consider a rogue clothing manufacturer who reaps enormous profits by impudently reproducing copyright cartoon characters and company logos on cheap t-shirts and violating the copyright law despite the levels of moral culpability of these infringers. Historically, it can be noticed that American copyright law has changed since 1909 and may now hold both the above infringers to be strictly liable irrespective of absence of culpability in the Harrisons' Case. Courts and commentators have consistently adhered to this strict liability framework for decades with little debate.[67] The 21st century times have changed the types and aim of fixing liability for infringements. The recent development of ICT and proliferation of internet i.e., "information superhighway" has endeavoured to make strict liability impend on the ISP along with other types of budding high-tech infringers

[64] Soffer 1986–1987.

[65] *Bright Tunes Music Corp. v. Harrisongs Music Ltd.*, 420 F. Supp. 177, 179-81 (S.D.N.Y. 1976).

[66] Ciolino and Donelon 2001–2002.

[67] *Fitzgerald Publ'g Co.* v. *Baylor Publ'g Co.*, 807 F.2d 1110, 1113 (2d Cir. 1986). ("[R] eliance-justified or otherwise-is irrelevant in determining whether [the defendant] infringed [the plaintiffs] copyrights. Even an innocent infringer is liable for infringement."); FN 5 Ibid.

including the innocent infringers. The policy of holding innocent infringers strictly liable has in the earlier time been described as a policy by Judge Learned Hand as "harsh" and worthy of "hesitat[ion]".[68] Bringing in strict liability law for such infringers has been the subject of vigorous debate and scholarly criticism. Though strict liability law is present both in British and American law since ages, the same has been questioned time and again. However, when a close examination of both laws is observed (by various authors and studies with statistical methods and results) it does not reveal the existence of strict liability laws never existed in the beginning of copyright laws that date backs to more than 300 years. On the contrary, it is always been taken care that the culpability of the infringer is an important ingredient for assessing liability. The law relating to criminal liability has seen a coarse development and slowly forced the law makers to bring more laws towards imposing criminal liability. Though, criminal law needs the ingredient of culpability (the infringer's culpability plays a critical role ever since the first Western copyright legislation i.e., even in the Statute of Anne),[69] copyright owners insists on strict liability laws to be enacted. Many studies conducted are not in support for strict liability, as the same has not even proved to be economically viable for being costly and inefficient. Though few scholars have suggested that strict liability is necessary; because an infringer is best able to be controlled to "avoid the loss" through infringement and thereby; strict liability somehow fosters administrative efficiency. Both of these rationales are unsubstantiated as there is lack of research with statistical proof of deterrence even with strict liability laws. Innocent infringers are often unaware of the specific definitions of copyrights and the sources from where they are receiving such copyright material and also lack the understanding. Likewise, no evidence supports the contention that strict liability promotes administrative efficiency in copyright infringement litigation. On the contrary, the inevitable result of strict liability is showing a marked increase in the overall number of infringement cases, with each case unbearably taking lengthened litigation time with over complex, fact-specific issues.[70] In order to understand the strict liability dilemma, it is required for us to understand whether the strict liability policy is in the tort claim or for the criminal copyright infringement. The meaning of the word "wilfulness" for the purpose of assessing actual damages is generally different from its meaning to be proved for statutory damages and in criminal copyright infringement. Here, it needs to be understood that strict liability rule under tort law shall not be adopted to criminal law, as it may have reverse effect and be harmful to the infringer[71] as the purposes of both these laws are in their entirety

[68] *Ibid.* Also read, *Barry* v. *Hughes*, 103 F.2d 427, 427 (2d Cir. 1939).

[69] 1710, Enacted by the parliament, available at: http://www.copyrighthistory.com/anne.html (last visited December 26th 2016).

[70] *Supra* note 71.

[71] *See* NIMMER, *see also Kamar Int'l* v. *Russ Berrie & Co.*, 752 F.2d 1326, 1331 (9th Cir. 1984). Samuelson and Wheatland 2009

different. In one of the well known cases[72] the United States court (Morans Case) has reiterated the meaning of this word as (17 U.S.C. §506(a)[73]) while finding the perpetrator Not Guilty[74]:

> [W]illfully" means that in order to be criminal the infringement must have been a "voluntary, intentional violation of a known legal duty." I am so persuaded because I believe that in using the word "willful" Congress intended to soften the impact of the common-law presumption that ignorance of the law or mistake of the law is no defense to a criminal prosecution by making specific intent to violate the law an element of federal criminal copyright offenses.

The above decision and other judgments by the US courts have highlighted that criminal liability for copyright infringement can be imposed only when the required degree of culpability on the part of the infringer is proved. The offence should have been committed for the purpose of any kind of commercial advantage or private financial gain when done 'willfully'. The standard for determining willfulness for purposes of criminal copyright infringement has long been the subject of debate among courts and commentators[75] as copyright exists to create a "thriving culture" that produces "as many original works available as possible".[76] The reason for

---

[72] *United States* v. *Moran,* 757 F. Supp. 1046 (D. Neb. 1991).

[73] In pertinent part 17 U.S.C. §506(a) punishes as a criminal any "person who infringes a copyright willfully and for purposes of commercial advantage or private financial gain." Pursuant to 17 U.S. C. §106(3), the owner of a copyright has the exclusive right to "distribute copies . . . of the copyrighted work to the public by sale or other transfer of ownership, or by rental, lease, or lending." The "exclusive right" of the owner of a copyright is subject to a variety of exceptions. See 17 U.S.C., §§107–118.

[74] In summary the judge stated "When Moran's actions were viewed from the totality of the circumstances, the government failed to convince beyond a reasonable doubt that Moran acted willfully. Moran is a long-time street cop who was fully cooperative with law enforcement authorities. He is obviously not sophisticated and, at least from the record, his business operation of renting movies to the public was not large or sophisticated. Rather, Moran's business appears to have been of the "mom-and pop" variety. Moran's practice of "insuring," while obviously shifting the risk of loss from Moran to the copyright holder, was conducted in such a way as not to maximize profits, which one assumes would have been his purpose if he had acted willfully. For example, Moran purchased multiple authorized copies of the same movie, but he made only one unauthorized copy for each authorized Version purchased. This suggests that Moran truly believed that what he was doing was in fact legal. I therefore find Moran not guilty". http://cyber.law.harvard.edu/people/tfisher/IP/1991%20Moran%20Abridged.pdf (last visited 27th March, 2016).

[75] Arguing that "a defendant should be guilty of willfully infringing a copyright only if the government can prove an intentional violation of a known legal duty"); also read, Samuelson and Wheatland (2009).

(proposing a two-prong test for willful infringement consisting of actual knowledge and a violation of an affirmative duty to investigate to determine whether the activity will infringe upon those rights). *Compare Fitzgerald Publ'g Co.* v. *Baylor Publ'g Co.*, 807 F.2d 1110, 1115 (2d Cir. 1986) (finding willful infringement based on defendant's knowledge and experience), *with Original Appalachian Artworks, Inc. v. J.F. Reichert, Inc.*, 658 F. Supp. 458, 464 (E.D. Pa. 1987) (requiring knowledge plus outrageous conduct-reckless disregard-for willful infringement). See *supra* note 70

[76] *Ibid.*

criticism of imposing criminal liability with strict liability is that; it affirmatively harms the copyright utilitarian goals. The other main reason is that the accounting for the innocence of infringers would matter by assuring that innocent singer-songwriters (like George Harrison), or the misled magazine editors (like those at *Cosmopolitan),* and faultless ISP's do not meet the same fate as brazen and malicious t-shirt pirates as done against the Napsters.[77]

Now it is sure that criminal copyrights infringement are on rise and are taken seriously, it becomes relevant to understand whether it is more of a white collar crime.[78] Hardy (2003) states that, technical and sophisticated methods are used in understanding such crimes and the challenges in dealing with them will have a paradigm shift in the justice system. In the past, there are hardly any criminal actions for copyright infringements and thereby, it being measured a white collar crime was far from thought. Most of the copyright infringement cases have been dominated by civil actions by copyright owners and even in India it can be observed in various cases that punitive damages are awarded in order to make such suits to have a deterrent effect, whereas very less number of criminal actions are taken.

As it is expected from various studies that, copyright infringements in the internet age are going to see a sharp rise, it is assumed economically that unsympathetic treatment to the violators may theoretically be underpinning for that prediction.[79] The increase in the use of computers and internet are sophisticated resources that often are available at home, workplace, Smartphone's, etc., making the frequency of infringement higher and easy.[80] The basic characteristic of harm as in a blue collar crime is absent i.e., physical violence, but fraud or deceit for financial gain (at least wrongful gain even if it is temporary in nature) is present in most of the cases.[81] So, whether these violators fit into the sophisticated white collar criminal needs to be studied and is a major issue? It has been a sophisticated crime since the Analog age and has continued to be infringed in more easy and faster way in the highly sophisticated digital age. Not only the copyright violations, but even the category of copyright violators is increasing due to these technological developments. In the past, the copyright infringements have tended to fall into two different categories, the "good" and the "bad." These two categories still continue to exist. Here, the author's (Tardy-2003) explanation is retained for the impact it can have, to understand the criminal liability. The "bad" infringers are those who

---

[77] *Ibid.*

[78] The Department of Justice, for example, defines white-collar crime by listing several elements, including deceit.' The Department's definition also refers to the status of the defendant and the defendant's special skills or training, but as one thoughtful commentator has noted, many wrongful acts like mail fraud are thought of as "white-collar" crimes, even though they do not involve a special skill or status of the defendant. The same commentator also has shown that the United States Chamber of Commerce, for instance, identifies "deceit" as the salient characteristic of such crimes.

[79] Hardy 2002–2003.

[80] *Ibid.*

[81] *Ibid.*

deliberately enter the business of infringing for profit—audio tape bootleggers selling from the trunk of a car, for instance. The "good" infringers are those who, at worst, act inadvertently, and at best, act in a kind of naive good faith that they are promoting the public good—the university professor who assembles a course packet for students…". These definite characteristics have two opposites and it can be taken for our understanding that "bad" infringements are for financial gains and thereby they are committed in large scale. However, when it comes to "Good" infringements; they do not aim at immediate financial and even if they intent, it will be minimal in numbers, and warning of a sanction may be capable of deterrence. Bad infringements aim harming the copyright owner for financial gain and need a thorough adaption of law. But the concern is about the new entrant as a third category of infringer i.e., individuals who are in between the good and the bad, while infringing each category has different objectives, but the new entrant/middle category do not have intention to gain financially for themselves (but they intent to utilize the services free of cost), it causes large scale losses to the copyright owner. Though, this category has no intention for financial gain, they make use of the services with an intention of gaining or using the facility for themselves, their family and friends. These users are on a high and cause huge losses to the copyright owners. These individuals may use the facility through internet and avail it and even share it with their subscriber like Napsters.[82] These file copying and sharing services are one example of this new category of infringer. These infringers are described by one court as "heedlessly irresponsible, and at worst … nihilistic, self-indulgent, and lacking in any fundamental sense of values." Though these new entrants challenge the other two categories in the infringers' activities.[83] Technically speaking these actors have no overt or immediate commercial motive,[84] but they operate on a large scale and cause huge loss for the owners. Congruence is absent: there is harm to the copyright owner, though there is no obvious matching gain to the infringer.[85] Legally dealing with this class of infringers has been one of the main aims of the Digital Copyrights laws in the 21st century and a challenge by itself.

The WIPO and its initiative aimed to expand the protections of the copyrights through "obligations concerning the technological measures and has shown the path requiring all the contracting parties to afford "adequate legal protection and

[82] The creator of the Napster software, Shawn Fanning, apparently did not have a profitable business in mind when he wrote the Napster program. Other relatives joined in and clearly were thinking of the file sharing system as a major business opportunity. But to end no profit motive appeared, as all downloads were free. Supra FN 83.

[83] Examples these days are legion: the teenagers who make a sport of finding and publicizing ways to defeat copy-protection technologies; or the computer scientists who believe that the research ethic requires them to publish their findings of vulnerabilities in a commercial encryption technology; or the college students who accumulate a collection of MP3 music files for their own enjoyment.

[84] Hardy 2002–2003.

[85] *United States* v. *LaMacchia*, 871 F. Supp. 535, *545* (D. Mass. 1994).

effective legal remedies against various kinds of violations. The WCT and WPPT (WIPO Performances and Phonograms Treaty, 1996) have extended the laws for the protection of copyright law in the digital era. The US enacted DMCA[86] and Sonny Bono Copyright Term Extension Act, NET,[87] etc. which have criminalisation policies for copyright violations.[88] The protection is extended to circumvention and "copyright management information" against removal or alteration that facilitates infringements.

The European Commission has also made laws in the protection of manufacture and distribution of devices and other related rights. In 2001, the European Union adopted the Copyright Directive.[89] Though, India is a non-signatory to the internet conventions, understanding the WIPO Internet treatise, it harmonized its law with the WCT and WPPT. Compared to civil remedies, criminal copyright prosecutions are relatively infrequent and are usually reserved for the most egregious violations only.[90] In prosecutions for criminal copyright infringement, the Government bears the burden of proving *three elements*: infringement of a copyright, that the infringement was willful, and that the infringer was motivated by profit. Additionally, persons who knowingly and willfully aid or abet copyright infringement, so as to be subject to criminal prosecution.[91]

The recent changes in India, through the Copyright (Amendment) Act 2012 have been to enact the laws on par with International Conventions, but it is noticed that there are still varied challenges in copyright protection to the owners.[92] This

86 The Digital Millennium Copyright Act, 1998.

87 No Electronic Theft Act, 1997.

88 *LaMacchia* case by adopting the "No Electronic Theft Act" (the "N.E.T" Act) in 1997 By the mid-1990s, the "new breed" of copyright infringers, whom we might characterize as falling between the "good" and "bad" ones, had clearly appeared on the scene. University student Brian LaMacchia heralded their arrival. LaMacchia started an online computer service with commonly available file uploading and downloading facilities. Not so commonly, however, he encouraged his users to upload commercial software packages for the privilege of being able to download still other commercial software packages that other users had uploaded. He did not, however, charge any fee or receive monetary compensation for this entirely unauthorized service. The lack of any purpose of "commercial advantage or private financial gain" meant that LaMacchia, although responsible for the production of perhaps thousands of infringing copies of commercial software, could not be charged with criminal copyright infringement. The government charged him instead with what must have looked to be the closest applicable criminal offense—wire fraud. The trial court found that the government could not establish the elements of that offense, however, and so the trial court exonerated him. In reaching that conclusion, the court essentially invited Congress to correct the problem of the inapplicability of criminal copyright infringement statutes to activities like those undertaken by LaMacchia.

89 Directive on the harmonisation of certain aspects of copyright and related rights in the information society (2001/29/EC), *available at:* http://eur-lex.europa.eu/homepage.html (last visited April 8, 2016).

90 *United States* v. *Wise*, 550 F.2d 1180, 1188 (9th Cir. 1977).

91 *United States* v. *Schmidt,* 15 F. Supp. 804, 807 (M.D. Pa. 1936).

92 Krishnakumar and Saha 2012.

amendment introduces criminal and monetary sanctions for the circumvention of DRM.[93] Many provisions relating to facilitation of special formats for the disabled and the recognition of rights of contributors to films (such as composers and lyricists), were appreciated as a progressive step for reform. While few provisions were lauded, the provisions relating to DRM[94] techniques fell short and were criticised. DRM techniques though grant right of fair use and full enjoyment as a right of consumer for works purchased by him, are considered to be excessive, as they have a chilling effect on free speech as comment and discussion (In recent days it can be observed with what is happening with Apple I-Phones[95]). The act of introducing DRM protection is justified (by Government) as a necessary to bring India's copyright law with WCT and WPPT treaties. This justification of the government is alleged to be made as a colourable intention, knowing that India had not ratified, much less signed, either of these treaties. Above all, the TRIPs makes no mention of an obligation on signatories to protect DRM measures. In the amended statute, the DRM-linked changes are introduced by the amendment feature in three parts of the amended Act. The consumer interest groups state that these changes were brought due to international lobbying by the interest groups of the copyright owners.

Among the changes brought to the Copyright Law is *firstly* by insertion of Section 2(xa)—Rights Management Information (RMI),[96] *Secondly*, the introduction of Section 65A that introduces TPM (Technological protection Measures) into Indian copyright law. Here the section criminalizes the circumvention of an effective TPM for protection of rights conferred by the Act and the offender shall be punishable with imprisonment for up to 2 years and fines (Section 65A(1)). As a general exception, Section 65(2)(a) states that anything that is not expressly prohibited by the Act. The proviso to this sub-clause conditions the operation of the general exception to the maintenance of complete records and particulars, of the person performing the circumvention, by anyone facilitating such circumvention. Other sub-clauses (b) to (g) provide specific exceptions to criminal liability for

---

[93] *Ibid.*

[94] "As is commonly understood, DRM relates to the techniques and methods used to limit access or control over protected intellectual property after the initial sale by the right holder. Common examples include encryption or 'scrambling' of copyright music CDs and DVDs to prevent copying (or 'ripping'), the locking of smart phones to particular service providers and the imposition of restrictive licensing agreements".

[95] Panzarino 2016 FBI filed an order compelling Apple to unlock iPhone used by the attacker in San Bernardino and apple planned to fight back the battle for protection of consumer interest.

[96] The Copyright Act, 1957, s. 2(xa) reads as: " 'Rights Management Information' means—

(i) the title or other information identifying the work or performance;

(ii) the name of the author or performer;

(iii) the name and address of the owner of rights;

(iv) terms and conditions regarding the use of the rights; and

(v) any number or code that represents the above information; but does not include any device or procedure intended to identify the user."

circumvention including those relating to encryption research and the same has been listed.[97] Other provisions are related to lawful investigations (Section 65 A (2) (c)), authorized cyber-security testing (Section 65A (2) (d) and (e)), user identification or surveillance (Section 65 A(2)(f)) and in interests of national security (Section 65A(2)(g)). *Thirdly*, the new Section 65B provides for the protection of RMI. The Section is two-pronged with the (i) knowing unauthorized removal of any RMI (Section 65B (i) and the (ii) knowing distribution, broadcasting or communication to the public of any work or performance with the knowledge that the RMI has been removed or altered without authority (Section 65 B (ii)) being made offences punishable with imprisonment for up to 2 years and fine. The proviso to this section also enables the copyright owner whose interests have been affected by the removal of RMI to seek civil remedies under Chapter XII of the Act. By introducing these changes, the Act has given recognition to DRM protection in India, both for TPMs and RMI.

Section 65 aims at the prevention of unauthorized copying, broadcasting, communication and the like, 65A envisages mental element as a crucial ingredient for imposition of criminal sanctions. Thereby, as per this provision mere circumvention is insufficient without the intention to infringe the rights. While this requirement is likely to increase the burden when prosecuting the alleged offenders, it has the potential to shield 'innocent' or unintended acts of circumvention from criminal liability. The amended law in India Criminalises the RMI & TPM, whereas DMCA criminalises even facilitation of circumvention. The question of imposing liability is unanswered if the records are not maintained. Section 65B deals with protection for RMI and makes it an offence if the offender removes the originality or alters RMI embedded. The second clause provides that anyone who, in an unauthorized manner, distributes, broadcasts, communicates to the public or otherwise markets copies of the work with the knowledge that RMI has been removed or altered is made equally culpable as the person who removed it in the first place. RMI can also collect information about users from their devices without their explicit consent and Section 65 B read with 2(xa), prohibits these forms of RMI. This might be to ensure the consumer privacy. Now the question to be answered is whether criminal sanctions are warranted for RMI violations.

Since making of codified laws, it is well known and understood in the Indian context that effective laws were never lacking in India. But, the challenges have been in relation to efficient working of the criminal justice system as a whole. The reactive police rather than a proactive policing system are ill-equipped and overworked and the same hamper efforts to enforce DRM protection on a large scale. Lack of interest in investigation and rewards for copyright violation cases over the murder or rape cases are certainly going to hinder the required actions in high-tech offences and especially in the digital era. The insertions of these new offences are

---

[97] The Copyright Act, 1957, s. 65A(2)(b).

certainly heading towards flooding of criminal cases leading to consumer rights against the criminal cases even for the new entrant (third category) innocent infringer.

6 Remedies for Copyright Infringement

The author lastly revolves the study towards the remedies available under copyright law. The domestic law provides the modes of granting remedies. The Berne Convention for the Protection of Literary and Artistic Works, 1886 (Berne Convention) also provides that, member countries shall make provision for the remedies in copyright infringement cases. The following Table 1 represents the remedies available to the copyright owner for infringement of copyright available in India, the U.S and the U.K:

The Copyright Act provides right holders dual legal machinery for enforcing their rights. The enforcement is possible through the Copyright Board and the Courts. The owner of copyright has various remedies provided under the Act for any infringement. The infringer shall be made liable for all his acts of infringement. The owners continue to have civil remedies or criminal remedies.

7 India's Efforts to Reduce Copyrights Violation

India is one country that remains on the Priority Watch List in 2015 of the US based on the study conducted Out-of-Cycle Reviews (OCR) of India in the autumn of 2014 to evaluate U.S.—India bilateral engagement on IPR. India through its administration is taking steps to review its laws on key IPR issues. One such step is India's establishment of a domestic IPR-focused experts group, commitment to technical engagement on specific issues of concern, and the issuance of encouraging domestic policy pronouncements, including establishment the High Level Working Group on Intellectual Property. The U.S. is continuously encouraging for judicial efficiency and for reducing backlogs of cases on IPR through electronic case management. It has also initiated efforts in criminal investigations and launches raids at counterfeit goods markets; combat the manufacture, sale, and distribution of counterfeit medicines; initiate investigations and judicial actions against Internet-based piracy; and seek deterrent sentences against persons or entities engaging in copyright piracy and trademark counterfeiting. It intends to help India in "IPR regime to "nurture the IP culture and address all facets of the IP system including legal, administrative and enforcement infrastructure, human resources, institutional support system and international dimensions." The draft policy has aimed at working with "Indian policymakers: transparency and stakeholder consultation; coordination among national and state authorities; public awareness; legal

Table 1 Remedies available in India, the U.S and the U.K. for copyright infringement

Indian Copyright Act, 1957	USCA, 1976	U.K CDPA, 1988
Civil remedies for infringement of copyright **Injunction** **Damages** **Accounts for Profit** **(S. 55)**	Remedies for infringement: Injunctions Damages (actual/statutory) Profits (17 USC SS 502 & 504) For circumventing Technology under the DMCA Injunctions; order the impounding; award damages recovery of costs; award reasonable attorney's fees (S. 1203)	Infringement actionable by copyright owner- **Injunction** **Damages** Accounts for Profit (S. 96) If no knowledge- such profits as may have accrued (S. 97) Injunctions against service providers- ISP have actual knowledge of another person using their service to infringe copyright. (S. 97A)
Seize infringing copies and all plates used for the purpose of making infringing copies (S. 64)	Order the impounding Order the destruction or Other reasonable disposition Forfeiture, Destruction (SS 503 & 506)	Seize infringing copies and detained Notice to local police station. Enter premises with conditions (S. 100) Search warrants and forfeiture (S. 296ZC)
Disposal of infringing copies or plates for purpose of making infringing copies- to be delivered up to the owner of the copyright. (S. 66)	Restitution (S. 506)	Order that the infringing copy or article be delivered up (S. 99)
Costs of all parties in any proceedings (S. 55)	Costs and attorney's fees (SS. 505 & 1203))	costs of all parties in any proceedings
Remedy in the case of groundless threat of legal proceedings **Obtain an injunction against the continuance of such threats** **Recover such damages, if any, as he has sustained by reason of such threats (S 60)**	Fraudulent Copyright Notice Fraudulent Removal of Copyright Notice False Representation (S. 506)	
Who knowingly infringes or Abets the infringement *Imprisonment-* shall not be less than six months—may extend to 3 years and *Fine-* which shall not be less than Rs. 50,000 & may extended to Rs. 2,00,000; If it is not for gain may impose lesser punishment. (S. 63) **Enhanced penalty on second and subsequent convictions**	Criminal offenses wilfully infringes a copyright Imprisoned not more than 5 years shall be imprisoned not more than 10 years for second or subsequent offence (S. 506)	Criminal liability for making or dealing with infringing articles Summary conviction to imprisonment for a term not exceeding six months or a fine not exceeding the statutory maximum On conviction on indictment to a fine or imprisonment for a term not exceeding 10 years, or both. (S. 107)

(continued)

Table 1 (continued)

Indian Copyright Act, 1957	USCA, 1976	U.K CDPA, 1988
With imprisonment- not less than 1 year may extend to 3 years. *Fine*- Not less than Rs. 1,00,000 may extend Rs. 2,00,000 (S. 63A) ***Knowingly makes*, has in his possession, any plate for the purpose of making infringing copies- punishable with imprisonment extending to 2 years and fine (S. 65)**		

Courtesy Dr. Dayananda Murthy C P

and legislative reforms; administration; commercialization; and enforcement".[98] The Indian vibrant market needs a check as the US urges India to: "enact anti-camcording legislation; model its statutory license provisions relating to copyright works on the standards of the Berne Convention; ensure that collecting societies are licensed promptly and able to operate effectively; and provide additional protections against signal theft, circumvention of technological protection measures, and online copyright piracy". With "Make in India" and "Digital India" campaigns these measures are vital to be head on head in IPR protection. With internet usage going to be about 370 million and to be second largest in the world, there is apprehension that piracy will grow as a negative corollary. The U.S. has been helping in adopting best measures, including appropriate notice-and-takedown procedures and other efficient mechanisms for rights holders to seek removal of infringing content from websites, consistent with international best practices. A study (Motion Pictures Distributors Association of India (MPDA-2013) has found that incidents of highest rate of video piracy are half of all such incidents in the Asia-Pacific region. The high incidence of camcording in India underscores the importance of developing an effective legal framework to address this problem. In this process various states (Tamil Nadu, Andhra Pradesh, and Maharashtra) have made video piracy a legal offence and there is also a positive step in bringing national anti-cam-cording legislation through (Cinematography Bill-2013).[99]

[98] National IPR Policy (First Draft), December 19, 2014, *available at:* http://dipp.nic.in/English/Schemes/Intellectual_Property_Rights/IPR_Policy_24December2014.pdf (last visited March 12, 2016).

[99] See 2015 Special 301 Report, April 2015, *available at:* https://ustr.gov/sites/default/files/2015-Special-301-Report-FINAL.pdf (Last visited March 12, 2016).

8 Conclusion

There is a change in the approach of the law makers to criminalise copyright violation. It may be a happy note for the copyright owners, but it may also add to the bane of criminal administration especially in the Indian system. Beyond this, India in its 2012 amendment has imposed criminal liability for RMI and TPI without just making it as an alternative remedy. Even though India to a large extend is following its U.S. counterpart while making these changes, it took an extra step of precaution by making it an offence. The criminal liability is imposed since 300 years, but sparingly used. If the criminal liability is imposed on "bad" infringers it may not affect the society at large, but if the same is used for "good" or the "innocent" infringers, it make hinder the growth of information sharing as expected by the internet users. A relook into these provisions would suffice by providing civil and criminal actions, which may be more appropriate for the Indian market, which is a price conscious market and those consumers especially the (innocent infringers) who would be using, distributing, transmitting, music, movies, copyright material and software's for free downloads and also distribute among friends and family would be pulled to criminal courts for not really directly gaining but certainly making loss to the copyright holder loss. So the provisions need to have relook and provide for a civil liability as an alternative to criminal liability in its newly inserted provisions.

References

Brown JC (2006) Copyright infringement liability for video sharing networks: grokster redux or breaking new ground under the digital millennium copyright act. 23 The Computer & Internet Lawyer 10

Ciolino DS, Donelon EA (2001–2002) Questioning strict liability in copyright. 54 Rutgers L Rev 351

Digital Rights Management (DRM) & Libraries American Library Association. http://www.ala.org/advocacy/copyright/digitalrights (last visited December 26th 2016)

Grokster was capable of noninfringing uses. Posting of Om Malik to GigaOM

Helton M (2007) Secondary liability for copyright infringement: bittorrent as a vehicle for establishing a new copyright definition for staple articles of commerce. 40 Colum JL & Soc Probs 3

Hardy T (2002–2003) Criminal copyright infringement. 11 Wm & Mary Bill Rts J 305

Juille C (1998–1999) The digital millennium copyright act: taming the wild web. 4 Ent & Sports Law 135

Krishnakumar T, Saha K (2012) India's new copyright law: the good, the bad and the DRM. 8 JIPLP 15 (Dec. 2012). http://jiplp.blogspot.in/2012/12/indias-new-copyright-law-good-bad-and.html (last visited March 12, 2016)

Merriam-Webster.com. Merriam-Webster, n.d. Web. 26 Dec 2016. (last visited March 12, 2016)

Moohr GS (2003) The crime of copyright infringement: an inquiry based on morality, harm, and criminal theory. 83 BU L Rev 731 (2003)

Media K (2012) OCI Tracker Benchmark Study 'Deep Dive' Analysis Report, OFCOM 6. http://stakeholders.ofcom.org.uk/binaries/research/telecoms-research/online-copyright/deep-dive.pdf. (last visited on December 26th, 2016)

Menell PS (2002–2003) Envisioning copyright law's digital future. 46 NYL Sch L Rev 63

Narayan P (2007) Law of copyright and industrial design 345-46, 4th edn. Eastern Law House, New delhi

Norwood PE (2014) Consumer v. copyright: balance in an era of digital rights management. 83 UMKC L Rev 257

NIMMER, § 14.04[B][3], at 14–55 n.81.6

Panzarino M (2016) Why apple is fighting not to unlock iPhones for the government. https://techcrunch.com/2016/02/17/why-apple-is-fighting-not-to-unlock-iphones-for-the-government/. Posted 17 Feb 2016 by Matthew Panzarino (last visited December 26th, 2016)

Samuelson P, Wheatland T (2009) Statutory damages in copyright law: a remedy in need of reform. 51 Wm & Mary L Rev 439. http://scholarship.law.berkeley.edu/facpubs/1151

Shadow Market: 2011 BSA global software piracy study, 9th edn. (2012) http://globalstudy.bsa.org/2011/downloads/study_pdf/2011_BSA_Piracy_Study-InBrief.pdf. (last visited December 26th 2016)

Soffer SB (1986–1987) Criminal copyright infringement. 24 Am Crim L Rev 491

The manufacturer's authorised representative in the EU is Springer Nature Customer Service Centre GmbH, Europaplatz 3, 69115 Heidelberg, Germany. If you have any concerns regarding our products, please contact ProductSafety@springernature.com

Printed and bound by CPI Group (UK) Ltd, Croydon, CR0 4YY
25/09/2026
02222898-0013